Politics 1972

WADSWORTH CONTINUING EDUCATION SERIES
Leonard Freedman, General Editor

ARMAMENT AND DISARMAMENT: THE CONTINUING DISPUTE
edited by Walter R. Fisher, University of Southern California
and Richard D. Burns, California State College, Los Angeles

CONTEMPORARY LABOR ISSUES
edited by Walter R. Fogel and Archie Kleingartner
University of California, Los Angeles

CONTEMPORARY MORAL ISSUES, SECOND EDITION
edited by Harry K. Girvetz
University of California, Santa Barbara

CONTEMPORARY RELIGIOUS ISSUES
edited by Donald E. Hartsock
University of California, Los Angeles

ISSUES OF THE SEVENTIES
edited by Leonard Freedman
University Extension, University of California, Los Angeles

METROPOLIS: VALUES IN CONFLICT
edited by C. E. Elias, Jr., University of Southern California
James Gillies, York University, Toronto, Ontario
and Svend Riemer, University of California, Los Angeles

THE NEW TECHNOLOGY AND HUMAN VALUES, SECOND EDITION
edited by John G. Burke
University of California, Los Angeles

POLITICS 1972
edited by Francis M. Carney and H. Frank Way
University of California, Riverside

POVERTY: AMERICAN STYLE
edited by Herman P. Miller
U. S. Bureau of the Census

PROBLEMS AND PROSPECTS OF THE NEGRO MOVEMENT
edited by Raymond J. Murphy
University of Rochester
and Howard Elinson
University of California, Los Angeles

TENSION AREAS IN WORLD AFFAIRS
edited by Arthur C. Turner
University of California, Riverside
and Leonard Freedman
University Extension, University of California, Los Angeles

TWENTIETH CENTURY: THE GREAT ISSUES
edited by William R. Hitchcock
University of California, Santa Cruz

Politics 1972

Edited by

Francis M. Carney
H. Frank Way, Jr.
University of California, Riverside

Wadsworth Publishing Company, Inc.
Belmont, California

ISBN-0-534-00146-7

L. C. Cat. Card No.: 78-180236

Printed in the United States of America

1 2 3 4 5 6 7 8 9 10—76 75 74 73 72 71

Preface

Thomas Carlyle was surely wrong when, in his rage against the bleak orthodox economics of his day, he labeled it "the dismal science." It is the "respectable professors" of politics who are the real practitioners of the dismal science. ". . . How we live is so far removed from how we ought to live," said Machiavelli, "that he who abandons what is done for what ought to be done, will rather learn to bring about his own ruin than his preservation." Max Weber not only characterized power and violence as the means specific to politics, but went on to insist that to have the "calling for politics" is to live with the fact that one's soul may be lost. For Thomas Paine, government was a "badge of lost innocence," and John Madison called it the greatest of all reflections on man's nature.

One need not subscribe to some sweeping theory of an ineradicably sinful, corrupt, or bestial human nature to understand that one task of the political theorist is to explain or make an accommodation for the fact that men can behave and often do behave wickedly or foolishly. One needn't think of politics as devoid of ethical content to understand that from time to time the responsible politician must not shrink from using odious means. One knows that, if he is to adopt the political frame of reference, he must seem to be muttering a sour and crabbed negative to some of the loftiest, most generous aspirations of man. One enters politics as the gentle teacher and leaves as the strident martinet, if not as the hangman. Men in politics dream of justice, liberty, community, peace, truth, and the good life. But they find themselves in a world of power, struggle, interest, calculation, and obduracy. At best, politics is, as Weber said, a "strong and slow boring of hard boards."

It is no wonder, then, that men have almost always sought some substitute for politics, some rule or formula for ordering the myriad, messy affairs of men and societies. Wisdom, scripture, the teachings of Jesus, natural law, the absolute sovereign, the general will, unregulated competition, no competition, class struggle, scientific planning, direct democracy, unlimited instinct gratification, universal love, and the eroticization of every relationship have all been offered as The One True Way, which, if followed, would eliminate the need for politics.

Why should it be so? What is the "dismal" element of politics? We think there are two conditions essential to politics, and that these conditions singly or in combination have the potential for estranging people from politics. In the first place, to be in politics is to be inextricably enmeshed in rule, power, authority, and conflict. The very words can be harsh and threatening, especially to men of humane and generous impulses. Rule, or authority, and the power behind it are external to their objects, alien to them, and implicitly coercive. No amount of flummery about the Real Will, the Rational Self, or the Social Compact can wholly obscure the alien and coercive character of authority. Yesterday's unquiet flower children offer us but the most recent and flamboyant expression of the sense that politics and love have an antipodal relationship. The old men who comprise the intellectual paternity of the flower children—Herbert Marcuse, Erich Fromm, N. O. Brown are among the more notable—have brilliantly and seductively juxtaposed Eros Vanquished and Politics Triumphant. The crucial metaphors of politics also indicate the antithesis of politics and love; politics is almost unimaginable without contest, conflict, power, struggle, campaign, opposition, force, pressure, victory, and defeat. Under such metaphors, Eros cannot reign. Rue and melancholy will be the sometime companions of the thoughtful man in politics.

Here we would simply note that to be for politics is not to oppose Eros. If man were merely *Homo homine lupus,* politics would not be possible. But so long as man has the potential to be wolfish, politics is necessary.

A second "dismal" element of politics is its moral ambiguity. We have just acknowledged that politics is not love; if men could always love one another, politics would not be necessary. But if men only hated—if they never loved one another—politics would not be possible. To speak of the moral ambiguity of politics is to pile paradox upon paradox. To think of politics as no more than means, as no more than a vehicle for resolving disputes, as no more than a somewhat mechanical calculation of material interests, as subsumable under the rubric of Realpolitik, is to vulgarize the thought of those who, like Weber, have stressed the elements of prudence, civility, restraint, and responsibility in politics. For politics is surely invested by our passionate attachment to our values. If politics is unimaginable without conflict and calculation, it is also unimaginable without man's attachment to liberty, equality, justice, and fraternity. The paradox lies in the fact that, despite its inherent moral element, politics functions most effectively when it serves to reduce or transform its own ethical components. This is, of course, unsatisfying to the pure moralist. It is frustrating to one who views politics solely as the vehicle of expression or realization of a profound ethical commitment.

It is just this sense of politics—as serving to reduce moral tension—that such writers as Walter Lippmann and Hans J. Morgenthau have in mind when they urge the use of diplomacy as an alternative to using naked power or drawing sharp moral distinctions in international affairs. We would illustrate the point further by suggesting that our own Civil War was a consequence of the failure of our political system to reduce the sectional tension over the moral issue of human slavery. To say this, however, is not to make the crude error of thinking of politics as "the art of compromise." Politics involves compromise, of course, but it also involves the deepest commitment to moral ends. To politicize a moral end is not to abandon it, but to express it in another context; one must frame it in a way that not only makes it a feasible object of public policy, but also draws the support of those who are indifferent to the end and those who had not hitherto envisioned it in terms of public policy.

To speak of politics in this way seems appropriate in 1972. The great issues of the 1972 election evoke deep and contrasting moral feelings. The crisis of the cities and the rebellion of youth inevitably evoke lingering attitudes about such matters as race, the poor, and drugs—attitudes that are often associated with strong moral positions. Similarly, it is usually difficult to discuss the quality of our environment without first encountering those who prefer to moralize about the rape of our land and the monstrous pollution of our water and air.

Finally, in the current debate over the nature and extent of American commitments abroad there is always a danger that the public policy debate will never move beyond the great moral questions inherent in the relationships of a powerful and wealthy nation toward the underdeveloped and less privileged nations of the world. We are convinced that none of these issues can be comprehended, let alone resolved, if viewed solely as moral issues. We have tried to design the readings in this book to assist in the politicization of the issues of 1972.

Politics 1972 presents the major economic, social, and international issues confronting both the nation and the voter in a presidential election year. This collection from the writings of the leading statesmen and political analysts in recent and current American politics has been prepared for the use of those concerned with the national and international politics that will play such a decisive part in choosing the next President of the United States. Even more than in recent presidential elections, the 1972 Republican and Democratic candidates, as well as the public, must be aware of their increasing responsibilities. The voter cannot analyze a candidate's awareness of his responsibilities without knowing what is going to be demanded of the next President. It has, therefore, been our objective to present various views of these responsibilities for the information and guidance of the voter.

Part One, "The Processes," presents a many-faceted analysis of our political system, especially as it operates in a presidential year and as it will influence and persuade the voter. Accordingly, the articles in this part focus on political parties and the electorate; the presidency is examined with particular emphasis on the question of the realities of presidential power, the democratic and constitutional accountability of the office, and finally the process by which the parties and the people select a president. The emphasis changes in Part Two, "The Issues," to present conflicting views about some of today's most important public and governmental issues. Regardless of which party the next President represents, he must have made his position on these vital issues sufficiently clear to have won the confidence of the majority of the American voters. Certainly, other important issues will confront the voter in 1972. Undoubtedly the economy and the issue of unemployment will be profoundly significant issues in the 1972 presidential election, as they were in the 1970 congressional elections. We feel that the issues we present are major ones; whether they are debated in the campaign on a partisan basis or not, they are part of the political climate of our time and thus deserve thoughtful consideration.

Since many of the selections included in this collection have been excerpted, we have taken the liberty of giving some of them titles to indicate the nature of their content as presented in this book. We have transcribed the articles as faithfully as possible—correcting only obvious misprints, eliminating footnotes where feasible, and renumbering footnotes that remain.

We wish to extend our appreciation to the numerous individuals and organizations that have contributed to this publication. In particular, we thank the various authors whose articles appear here. We would also like to express our special gratitude to Leonard Freedman, Dean of University Extension, University of California, Los Angeles for his thoughtful comments and assistance.

Francis M. Carney
H. Frank Way, Jr.

Contents

Part Two   The Issues

Part One

The Processes

1

Profile of the Electorate

It is ironic that in this nation which virtually created the idea of true universal suffrage, so few people have ever had much good to say about voters as individuals or as an electorate. The irony continues when we consider that we have just extended the vote to youth—that very segment of our population that seems to evoke from us emotions ranging from fear through rage, disgust, perplexity, or fawning sentimentality.

But this is nothing new in our history. The authors and apologists for the Constitution of 1787, while paying tribute to and making due reliance on the "Republican (majority) principle," nevertheless rigged a scheme of government explicitly designed to save the voters from the consequences of their own anticipated folly and excess. Their opponents, the Antifederalists, on the other hand, feared that in the new union the voters would be swiftly flattered and tricked out of their liberties and their money by packs of conniving "federal politicians." And so it has gone with rare exceptions in our national dialogue.

A few early Jacksonians openly expressed confidence in the wisdom and political virtue of the ordinary people. It was sometimes hoped that the extension of the vote to women would elevate the moral tone of political life. The Progressive reformers of the late nineteenth and early twentieth centuries produced measures that sought devolution of decision-making power to the voters, but they were animated mainly by distrust of parties, bosses, lobbyists, and legislators—all of whom, in the Progressive vision, were skilled in duping and plucking that very voter to whom the Progressives wished to decentralize power.

In the political theory of the multigroup society—which has been the dominant American political theory from 1787 to the present—the most expected of the American voter has been that he know his own interests and vote accordingly. But in that theory there is remarkably little expression of confidence in voting and participation in governance as, in it-

3

self, uplifting or ennobling. Few have seen the vote as a major agency of character formation or of turning an individual with interests into a citizen who cares about the public good.

In the middle of the twentieth century, as the study of elections metamorphosed into the near-science of psephology (*pseph* is derived from the Greek word for the small, granite-like pebbles that the ancient Athenians used as voting counters; psephology, hence, is the study of voting), the full authority of social science put its seal on the view that the American voter was, after all, a pretty dismal fellow. If multigroup society theory expected and asked little more of the voter than that he know and express his own interests, the newer social science propositions told us that he often did not really know what his real interests were, and that even when he did know, he seemed to have difficulty translating that knowledge into a meaningful vote. Let us look more closely at a consensus version of the American voter.

For one thing, it was widely noted that from one-third to one-half of us did not bother to vote even in presidential elections. These apathetic ones were largely the poor, the black, the migrant, the Spanish-speaking, and those between the ages of 21 and 29. Those who did vote did not carry much conviction that one's individual vote would materially affect the outcome or that the collective vote would seriously alter or affect public policy. An electorate with such feeble conviction of its own capacity and effectiveness would be unlikely to generate much concern over the election campaigns, unlikely to pay close attention to the candidates, the parties, and the media reporting campaign events. Thus the American voter, in their view, was both unconcerned and poorly informed. And, according to the dominant American political theory, he was not, and was not supposed to be, animated by principle or a generalized concern for the common interest. According to the voting-behavior scholars, such a relationship presumably obtains today.

On what basis, then, did the American voter vote? Again, according to the consensus among scholars, he voted out of habit or because he had a sense of duty to vote. Why did he decide to vote in a certain direction, for a certain candidate? Primarily because his conception of himself as citizen and as voter was somewhat dominated by his perception of party affiliation. The majority of American voters, in other words, and despite avowals to the contrary, voted for the party and not the man. To put it more precisely, for most voters the view of the candidates and of the issues was most strongly colored by party affiliation. Party affiliation, it turns out, was itself powerfully determined by a set of prior factors bearing upon the individual rather than rationally chosen by him from election to election: if we knew enough about the income, occupation, geographic location, religion, and ethnic origin of a voter we could with some certainty predict his party predilection just as his party predilection fixed the direction of his vote. While research showed that all of this was not true for each voter, it appeared to be a fair characterization of the dynamics of electoral choice for a majority and thus seriously impaired any claim to rationality in the electorate.

So, apathy, a feeling that the vote itself is ineffective, and an absence of rationality in individual choice were the major complaints developed in scholarly surveys of the voters. But there was more. Typically, the American voter displayed little programmatic or ideological consistency save as his party choice provided it for him. The scholarly surveys also showed us that varying but always substantial proportions of the electorate were poorly informed on the specifics of even major political issues and confused about the stands of contending candidates on those very issues. In the 1950s and 1960s, a prolific literature developed which sought to explain how so defective a human material could collectively serve to produce and maintain a political system so successful as the American system then appeared to be.

Now, after the torments and convulsions of the late 1960s, a new contempt for the voter has developed. We seem to have become a nation of backlashers and militants, of honkies and hardhats and bigots, of radiclibs and violence-prone dupes and crazies and permissivists, of welfare chiselers, merciless reactionaries, and law-and-order freaks, and, finally, in a term that is both ambiguous and condescending, a silent majority. It is as though the expert and the sophisticate had imposed their ruthlessly rational categories on the hundred million of us who make up the electorate. It is as though if one feared violence or crime or hated the Vietnam War, then fear and hatred must color all his preceptions.

We have deliberately chosen, then, for this profile of the electorate a set of essays that collectively add up to a more generous view of the voters. None of our writers is mawkish or sentimental about the voter. There is no tendency to romanticize the common man. Richard M. Scammon and Ben J. Wattenberg, in a selection from their celebrated book, stand close to a traditional view of the voter as politically oriented by his class, ethnic, and job interests. V. O. Key, Jr., perhaps the most revered of American political scientists, gives us a vintage example of his style, that of the man of science whose work is informed and inspired by a sturdy faith in the people. Key is not untroubled by the survey data, but he clearly suggests that blaming the voter for his occasional displays of apathy, ignorance, or irrationality may be a little like blaming a crime on the victim. Amitai Etzioni suggests that voters need not be polarized into radical and reactionary positions, that it need not be irrational for a voter to be attracted, say, to both George Wallace and Eugene McCarthy.

**Richard M. Scammon and
Ben J. Wattenberg:
Demography Is Destiny**

If young, poor, and black are what most voters aren't, let us consider the electorate for what it largely is: white; median family income of $8,622; median age of about forty-seven. In short: middle-aged, middle-class whites.

This middle constituency can also be described as middle-educated. Typically, the middleman in America is a high school graduate, no more, no less:

Voters, by Years of School Completed, 1968

Years of School Completed	% of Electorate
Elementary School or less	22%
High School:	
1–3 years	16%
4 years	36%
College:	
1–3 years	13%
4 years or more	13%

Source: U.S. Census Bureau.

In other words:

—Almost three in four voters have never set foot in a college classroom (74%).

—Only one in eight voters has been graduated from college—any college—with major fields of study including animal husbandry and physical education (13%).

Looking into the future, these figures will change, because larger proportions of young Americans are now going on to college. Yet because most of the electorate is middle-aged, the percentage of once-went-to-college among the electorate in the 1970's will not rise sharply. In 1968 about a quarter, 26%, had *some* college education. By 1972 this will have climbed to about 29%, and in 1976 to 31%. This will mean, still, that the greatest number of the electorate will have, at most, only the "middle" high school diploma. Accordingly, if we are to add to our categories of unyoung, unpoor, and unblack, we may say that the typical voter is, and will be through the seventies, "uncollege."

The typical voter is no "intellectual," if we assume that an intellectual has at least a college degree, but that not all college graduates are necessarily intellectual. If we move up the qualification a bit and apply the term only to those with *advanced* college degrees (MA, PhD, and the like) the weight of the oft-discussed "intellectual vote" is ridiculously minuscule.

But if the electorate is not "intellectual," it is mostly certainly not composed of ignoramuses. For a candidate to treat the voters largely as jerks (62% are at least high school graduates) would be as disastrous as considering them largely as intellectuals. Indeed, it might be impressionistically noted here that it is the authors' opinion that the inherent wisdom of the American voter is substantial. . . .

Middle-income, middle-aged, middle-educated, and white, the voters in the middle can also be viewed vocationally as men and women primarily "at work with their hands, and not exclusively their minds."

Voters by Occupational Status, 1968

	% of Total Electorate
High Level White Collar Workers*	19
Manual, Service, Clerical & Sales Workers	42
Farm Workers	3
Unemployed	1
Not in Labor Force	
Women (mostly housewives)	28
Men over 65 (mostly retired)	5
Other men	2

* Professional, technical, managerial, officials and proprietors.
Source: U.S. Census Bureau.

Some of the numbers need further explanations:

The number of high-level white-collar workers is climbing. In the 1964 election the percentage was 16% compared to the 19% in 1968. If one allocates a proportionate share of the "housewives" and considers them as the spouses of these high-level white-collar workers, we might estimate that about 27% of the voters are in the *families* of those white-collar workers.

Of course, that leaves about 73% who are *not* in such families, still the vast majority; all *those* voters are in families where the earners are working with their hands. When one realizes that fact, the rhetoric of George Wallace can be fully savored, at least for its demographic accuracy:

> Now what are the real issues that exist today in these United States? It is the trend of pseudo-intellectual government, where a select, elite group have written guidelines in bureaus and court decisions, have spoken from some pulpits, some college campuses, some newspaper offices, looking down their noses at the average man on the street, *the glassworker, the steelworker, the autoworker, and the textile worker, the farmer, the policeman, the beautician and the barber, and the little businessman,* saying to him that you do not know how to get up in the morning or go to bed at night unless we write you a guideline. . . .

Furthermore, consider for a moment that "policeman" falls into the "work with hands" category. When the "cops" clashed with the "kids" at the 1968 Democratic Convention in Chicago, the journalists and many liberal politicians (high-level white-collars both), picked up the cry, "They're beating up our children." This was accurate: Most of the "kids" came from high-level white-collar homes. On the other hand, the other 73% of the voters could say, "Those student punks are beating up *our* children, or *our* husbands, or *our* fathers." That, too, would be accurate if one considers the policeman as a respected part of the nonelite.

After the convention, the opinion pollsters asked the public what they thought about the Chicago confrontation, and about two of every three Americans said they thought the police acted correctly, which coincides rather well with the occupational categorizations above. The old political axiom applies: "It depends on whose ox is being gored," or, in other words, "It depends on who is the clobberer and who the clobberee."

The confrontation at Chicago probably etched the lines of social class as sharply as they have ever been drawn in America. The fight in the streets was not between hawks and doves. For many it was perceived as between "elitists" and "plain people." There are more plain people than elitists in America.

Finally, and paradoxically, how do these "high-level" families vote? Despite all the recent comment about elitist Democratic intellectuals, the cold fact remains that the elite in America has a Republican majority. They are the doctors, bankers, and businessmen, with a good proportion of the lawyers and scientists as well. Only the vocal minority of the high-level voters are generally Democratic leaners. In the 1968 election the "professional and business" group went 56–34% for Nixon over Humphrey. The Democrats, despite the Agnew hoopla about the Democratic elitist establishmentarians, are those "plain people who work with their hands." Manual workers went 50–35% for Humphrey over Nixon.

That the Democrats have held the allegiance of most of the "plain people" has been the critical fact in American Presidential politics for more than a third of a century. That is why Democrats have won so often. Now, upon the shoals of the Social Issue, there seems to be the possibility of a rupture in that pattern. If it happens, it will be bad news for Democrats. If it can be prevented from happening, if it can be reversed, it will be happy days again for Democrats.

Next, don't forget the farmer. Although, numerically, there are many more voting blacks than voting farmers, this is somewhat misleading. While the numbers of farmers has decreased strikingly in recent years,* there remains a substantial part of the population whose work is directly related to farming. A rural town in the Midwest may have few "farmers," but the townsfolk sell and repair tractors and reapers, store grain, work as agricultural extension agents, publish weekly newspapers for farmers, and give loans to farmers or all the people whose work is related to farming. The analogy might be to a "mining town." Perhaps no more than 20 to 30% of the population work as "miners," but close down the mine, and you've rather effectively closed down the town. In short, the "farm vote," in its broad sense, is still with us, particularly in the states of the Midwest and South.

Next item: More than half the voters are women—51.9% to be precise. They show up in the preceding table not only as housewives, but as substantial parts of both the large employed groups: clerks, secretaries, teachers, etc. In America today, 43% of the women are working.

Since the advent of woman suffrage, no candidate for President has been solidly identified as a "woman's candidate." Women vote pretty much as their men do, or vice versa. In the last five Presidential elections, the largest margin of variance between men and women voters was 6% in the 1956 election—with women more likely to vote for General Eisenhower than Adlai Stevenson. Curiously, despite the legend building that has gone on about John Kennedy's "appeal to women voters," he would have lost the 1960 election had only women voted. In 1960, men voted 52–48% for

---

* Compared to the 3% farmers in 1968, in the election of 1900 the percentage of farmers in the population was 38.

JFK; women voted 51–49% for Nixon. As solace to Mr. Nixon, had only women voted in 1968, Hubert Humphrey would have won the popular vote, but the differentials aren't great in either case.

Middle-income, middle-aged, middle-educated, white, and what else? Protestant, mostly:

Voters, by Religion

Protestant	68%
Catholic	25
Jewish	4

Catholics in America are substantially more likely than Protestants to be first- and second-generation Americans (Italians, Poles, Mexicans, Puerto Ricans) and are more likely to be residents of big cities. Residents of big cities and so-called ethnic Americans have traditionally been more likely to vote Democratic. Accordingly, Catholics are somewhat more likely to vote Democratic than are Protestants, but with the single exception of 1960, when Catholicism itself became an issue, there is little recent evidence that Catholics vote heavily *as* Catholics. Catholics will usually vote a few extra points for a Catholic candidate, but not always:

McCarthy vs. Humphrey, July, 1968

	McCarthy	Humphrey
National	48%	40%
Catholics	47	41
Protestants	49	39

Source: Gallup Poll.

It is interesting to note how fast an issue can be laid to rest in American politics. Such results—Protestants outvoting Catholics for a Catholic candidate—would have been wholly inconceivable in the years between the defeat of Al Smith in 1928 and the victory of John F. Kennedy in 1960. In November, 1928, a Midwestern newspaper reported the defeat of Al Smith, a Catholic, under the banner headline THANK GOD, AMERICA IS SAVED. Today Catholicism seems thoroughly dead as a political issue. An interesting parlor game to demonstrate this is to ask: "Is Spiro Agnew a Catholic?" (He is Episcopalian.)

Two of every three voters are Protestant. Less likely to be big-city urban, less likely to be first- or second-generation Americans, Protestants are somewhat more likely than Catholics to vote Republican in Presidential races. But with the apparent disappearance of Catholicism as an issue, no national candidate has been able to figure out a way to be the Protestant candidate.

Will religion be an issue if a Jew runs for President in the 1970's? Perhaps less so than we might imagine. A Gallup Poll in 1969 showed that only 8% would not vote for a candidate *because* he was Jewish. Gallup data from 1937 showed 46% would not vote for a candidate because he was Jewish. Of course, Barry Goldwater was born of a Jewish father, but as Harry Golden said ruefully: "I always knew the first Jewish President would be an Episcopalian."

With the exceptions of blacks and Latin Americans, the Jews in the United States are the most solidly liberal-Democratic bloc in the entire electorate. Thus, in 1968, Jews voted 81% for Humphrey. During the years of Franklin Roosevelt the proportion was even higher, according to the studies of Lawrence H. Fuchs in *The Political Behavior of American Jews*. Jewish voting patterns are generally unique in that the vote is usually a liberal and Democratic one even among the wealthy and well educated. Among the non-Jewish well-to-do the trend among the wealthy and well educated goes the other way: Republican.

The so-called ethnic vote is hard to calculate. For how many generations does an Italian-American family remain under the influence of the first half of the hyphenation? How does one classify the children of a Polish father and an Italian mother who moved recently from an in-city "Little Italy" to a suburban neighborhood called Piney Grove? Or, as the late Joseph P. Kennedy, Sr., said, "How long do I have to live here to be an American?"

Yet the ethnics exist, or at least there are many precincts where 70% or 80% of the voters are of Italian, or Slavic, or Mexican origin. For the most part, ethnics have tended to vote Democratic:

Ethnic Groups, Vote for President, 1968

	Humphrey	Nixon	Wallace
Latin Americans			
East (mostly Puerto Ricans)	81%	16%	3%
South (mostly Mexican Americans)	92	7	1
West (mostly Mexican Americans)	81	17	2
Slavic	65	24	11
Italian	51	39	10

Source: NBC data.

The "solid" Democratic-liberal group is clearly the "Latin-American" one.

Of more than passing psephological interest is the fact that ethnics are dying out in America and becoming a smaller percentage of the total population. In 1940, Americans of foreign stock (*i.e.*, first- or second-generation) constituted 26% of the population. Twenty years later, in 1960, the foreign stock constituted 18% of the population. An estimate for 1970 shows the foreign stock at 15%, and in ethnic neighborhoods all over America the remark one hears is the same: "All the kids are moving out to the suburbs."

On the surface of it, at least, these data would tend to say that as the masses of immigrants and their children breed and die out, then it may be said that ethnicism in American political life may be dying out also. A first-generation Polish stevedore from Brooklyn via Krakow may feel "Polish." His grandson, the electrician who lives in Hempstead, Long Island, may feel more like an "electrician from Hempstead" than like a "Pole." But even this is too simple. As Nathan Glazer and Daniel Moynihan have pointed out in *Beyond the Melting Pot,* the ethnic feelings may last for far longer than the point when, after two generations, the Census stops classifying people as "foreign stock." Surely, tens of millions of Americans still feel deep ties and ethnic, racial, or religious allegiance as Poles, Hungarians, Jews, blacks, Italians, Mexicans—as well as "just plain Americans." And frequently they still vote along these ethnic lines, and politicians can still attempt all the ethnic appeals with some success. In certain areas, a politician can do worse than to be found with his mouth full of blintzes and knishes, or kielbasa, or soul food.

A middle-aged, middle-income, high-school-educated, white Protestant, who works with his hands, decreasingly ethnic—our portrait of the Middle Voter is beginning to emerge. What else? Generally metropolitan, and increasingly suburban, following the pattern of the American postwar hegira: from farms to cities, from cities to suburbs.

U.S. Population Distribution

	1950	1960	1968	Gain in Population, 1950–68
Central cities	35%	32%	29%	6 million
Suburb	24	31	35	32 million (!)
Small cities, towns and rural	41	37	36	9 million

Those are population figures; the *voting* figures are about the same, but give the suburbanite a one-point bonus for a higher participation rate:

Voters by Place of Residence, 1968

Central cities	29.6%
Suburbs	35.6
Small cities, towns and farms	34.8

Among many of the biggest, and oldest, metropolitan areas the voting figures etch in sharp relief this demographic movement from city to suburb. Comparing the 1948 election to the 1968 election, one finds that New York City *lost* more than half a million voters, while the suburbs around New York City (Westchester, Nassau, and Suffolk counties) gained 750,000 voters. The city of Chicago *lost* 400,000 voters; the Chicago suburbs *gained* 500,000. The city of Minneapolis: down 40,000; the Minneapolis suburbs: up 160,000. The term "central cities" refers to cities with populations of 50,000 or more. Accordingly, 2 of every 3 American voters live in or near (suburb) a large city. About an additional 15% live in cities of between 10,000 and 50,000. Accordingly, it is fair to view most of the American electorate as metropolitan or, alternately, as urban.

And where are these metropolitan areas? On the next page is a map that shows where Americans live.

Because, at least through 1968, the state has been the basic unit of Presidential politics, it is very important to note in which *states* these metropolitan areas lie. And unless a national popular vote replaces the electoral college,* then the *state* will remain of vital importance to political strategists.

There has been much talk of a Southern Strategy, a Border State Strategy, a Sun State Strategy, each supposedly designed to corral enough states to win an election for Republicans. Those are excellent strategies to convince your opponents to use. As for the authors, our geographic strategy is an elementary one called Quadcali. It is the essence of simplicity. If one draws a *quad*rangle from Massachusetts to Washington, D.C., to Illinois, to Wisconsin, and then adds in *Cali*fornia, it includes a majority of Americans. Where Americans live, they vote. Where a majority of them live and vote is where Presidents are elected.

In all, 266 electoral votes are needed to win. It is estimated that Quadcali will comprise about 300 electoral votes after the 1970 census.

---

* Which is doubtful for 1972, possible for 1976.

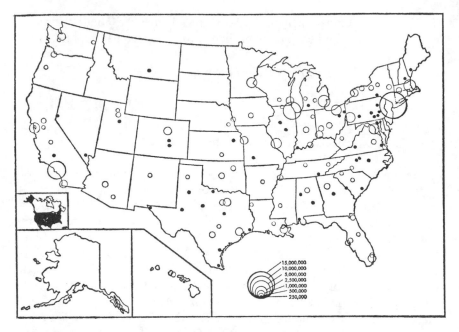

Population Distribution: 1960

Of the sixteen states in Quadcali, all but one (Indiana*) are either Democratic or close—the Republican margin of victory being no higher than 4.5% and usually slimmer than that. In a tidal year, all those close states can drop like a row of falling dominoes—a familiar image. Carry Quadcali—win the election. Lose Quadcali—lose the election. Split Quadcali close—and it will be a close election that no book can tell you about in advance.

So there you have it: Middle Voter. A metropolitan Quadcalian, middle-aged, middle-income, middle-educated, Protestant,† in a family whose working members work more likely with hands than abstractly with head.

Think about that picture when you consider the American power structure. Middle Voter is a forty-seven-year-old housewife from the outskirts of Dayton, Ohio, whose husband is a machinist. She very likely has a somewhat different view of life and politics from that of a twenty-four-year-old instructor of political science at Yale. Now the young man from Yale may feel that he *knows* more about politics than the machinist's wife from suburban Dayton, and of course, in one sense he does. But he does not know much about politics, or psephology, unless he understands what

---

* Which is more than balanced by Minnesota, Maine, Hawaii, Texas, and the state of Washington, all non-Quadcalian states that voted Democratic.

† Quadcalians would tend to be more Catholic than the rest of the country, but still predominantly Protestant.

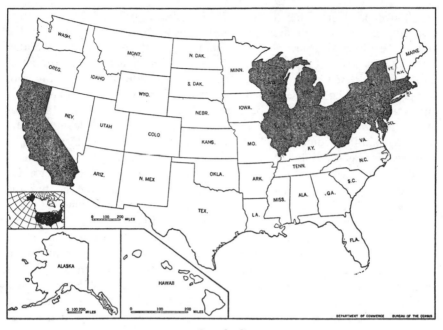

Quadcali

is bothering that lady in Dayton and unless he understands that her circumstances in large measure dictate her concerns.

To know that the lady in Dayton is afraid to walk the streets alone at night, to know that she has a mixed view about blacks and civil rights because before moving to the suburbs she lived in a neighborhood that became all black, to know that her brother-in-law is a policeman, to know that she does not have the money to move if her new neighborhood deteriorates, to know that she is deeply distressed that her son is going to a community junior college where LSD was found on the campus—to know all this is the beginning of contemporary political wisdom.

**V. O. Key, Jr.: The Voice of the
People: An Echo**

In his reflective moments even the most experienced politician senses a nagging curiosity about why people vote as they do. His power and his

---

Reprinted by permission of the publishers from *The Responsible Electorate: Rationality in Presidential Voting, 1936–1960*, by V. O. Key, Jr. Cambridge, Mass.: The Belknap Press of Harvard University Press. Copyright © 1966 by the President and Fellows of Harvard College. The late Professor Key was Professor of Government at Harvard University.

position depend upon the outcome of the mysterious rites we perform as opposing candidates harangue the multitudes who finally march to the polls to prolong the rule of their champion, to thrust him, ungratefully, back into the void of private life, or to raise to eminence a new tribune of the people. What kind of appeals enable a candidate to win the favor of the great god, The People? What circumstances move voters to shift their preferences in this direction or that? What clever propaganda tactic or slogan led to this result? What mannerism of oratory or style of rhetoric produced another outcome? What band of electors rallied to this candidate to save the day for him? What policy of state attracted the devotion of another bloc of voters? What action repelled a third sector of the electorate?

The victorious candidate may claim with assurance that he has the answers to all such questions. He may regard his success as vindication of his beliefs about why voters vote as they do. And he may regard the swing of the vote to him as indubitably a response to the campaign positions he took, as an indication of the acuteness of his intuitive estimates of the mood of the people, and as a ringing manifestation of the esteem in which he is held by a discriminating public. This narcissism assumes its most repulsive form among election winners who have championed intolerance, who have stirred the passions and hatreds of people, or who have advocated causes known by decent men to be outrageous or dangerous in their long-run consequences. No functionary is more repugnant or more arrogant than the unjust man who asserts, with a color of truth, that he speaks from a pedestal of popular approbation.

It thus can be a mischievous error to assume, because a candidate wins, that a majority of the electorate shares his views on public questions, approves his past actions, or has specific expectations about his future conduct. Nor does victory establish that the candidate's campaign strategy, his image, his television style, or his fearless stand against cancer and polio turned the trick. The election returns establish only that the winner attracted a majority of the votes—assuming the existence of a modicum of rectitude in election administration. They tell us precious little about why the plurality was his.

For a glaringly obvious reason, electoral victory cannot be regarded as necessarily a popular ratification of a candidate's outlook. The voice of the people is but an echo. The output of an echo chamber bears an inevitable and invariable relation to the input. As candidates and parties clamor for attention and vie for popular support, the people's verdict can be no more than a selective reflection from among the alternatives and outlooks presented to them. Even the most discriminating popular judgment can reflect only ambiguity, uncertainty, or even foolishness if those are the qualities of the input into the echo chamber. A candidate may win despite his tactics and appeals rather than because of them. If the people can choose only from among rascals, they are certain to choose a rascal.

Scholars, though they have less at stake than do politicians, also have an abiding curiosity about why voters act as they do. In the past quarter of a century they have vastly enlarged their capacity to check the hunches born of their curiosities. The invention of the sample survey—the most widely known example of which is the Gallup poll—enabled them to make fairly trustworthy estimates of the characteristics and behaviors of large human populations. This method of mass observation revolutionized the study of politics—as well as the management of political campaigns. The new technique permitted large-scale tests to check the validity of old psychological and sociological theories of human behavior. These tests led to new hunches and new theories about voting behavior, which could, in turn, be checked and which thereby contributed to the extraordinary ferment in the social sciences during recent decades.

The studies of electoral behavior by survey methods cumulate into an imposing body of knowledge which conveys a vivid impression of the variety and subtlety of factors that enter into individual voting decisions. In their first stages in the 1930's the new electoral studies chiefly lent precision and verification to the working maxims of practicing politicians and to some of the crude theories of political speculators. Thus, sample surveys established that people did, indeed, appear to vote their pocket-books. Yet the demonstration created its embarrassments because it also established that exceptions to the rule were numerous. Not all factory workers, for example, voted alike. How was the behavior of the deviants from "group interest" to be explained? Refinement after refinement of theory and analysis added complexity to the original simple explanation. By introducing a bit of psychological theory it could be demonstrated that factory workers with optimistic expectations tended less to be governed by pocketbook considerations than did those whose outlook was gloomy. When a little social psychology was stirred into the analysis, it could be established that identifications formed early in life, such as attachments to political parties, also reinforced or resisted the pull of the interest of the moment. A sociologist, bringing to play the conceptual tools of his trade, then could show that those factory workers who associate intimately with like-minded persons on the average vote with greater solidarity than do social isolates. Inquiries conducted with great ingenuity along many such lines have enormously broadened our knowledge of the factors associated with the responses of people to the stimuli presented to them by political campaigns.

Yet, by and large, the picture of the voter that emerges from a combination of the folklore of practical politics and the findings of the new electoral studies is not a pretty one. It is not a portrait of citizens moving to considered decision as they play their solemn role of making and unmaking governments. The older tradition from practical politics may regard the voter as an erratic and irrational fellow susceptible to manipulation by skilled humbugs. One need not live through many campaigns to observe politicians, even successful politicians, who act as though they regarded the people as manageable fools. Nor does a heroic conception of the voter emerge from the new analyses of electoral behavior. They can be added up to a conception of voting not as a civic decision but as an almost purely deterministic act. Given knowledge of certain characteristics of a voter—his occupation, his residence, his religion, his national origin, and perhaps certain of his attitudes—one can predict with a high probability the direction of his vote. The actions of persons are made to appear to be only predictable and automatic responses to campaign stimuli.

Most findings of the analysts of voting never travel beyond the circle of the technicians; the popularizers, though, give wide currency to the most bizarre—and most dubious—theories of electoral behavior. Public-relations experts share in the process of dissemination as they sell their services to politicians (and succeed in establishing that politicians are sometimes as gullible as businessmen). Reporters pick up the latest psychological secret from campaign managers and spread it through a larger public. Thus, at one time a goodly proportion of the literate population must have placed some store in the theory that the electorate was a pushover for a candidate who projected an appropriate "father image." At another stage, the "sincere" candidate supposedly had an overwhelming advantage. And even so kindly a gentleman as General Eisenhower was said to have an especial attractiveness to those of authoritarian personality within the electorate.

Conceptions and theories of the way voters behave do not raise solely arcane problems to be disputed among the democratic and antidemocratic theorists or questions to be settled by the elegant techniques of the analysts of electoral behavior. Rather, they touch upon profound issues at the heart of the problem of the nature and workability of systems of popular government. Obviously the perceptions of the behavior of the electorate held by political leaders, agitators, and activists condition, if they do not fix, the types of appeals politicians employ as they seek popular support. These perceptions—or theories—affect the nature of the input to the echo chamber, if we may revert to our earlier figure, and thereby control its output. They may govern, too, the kinds of actions that governments take as they look forward to the next election. If politicians perceive the electorate as responsive to father images, they will give it father images. If they see voters as most certainly responsive to nonsense, they will give them nonsense. If they see voters as susceptible to delusion, they will delude them. If they see an electorate receptive to the cold, hard realities, they will give it the cold, hard realities.

In short, theories of how voters behave acquire importance not because of their effects on voters, who may proceed blithely unaware of them. They gain significance because of their effects, both potentially and in reality, on candidates and other political leaders. If leaders believe the route to victory is by projection of images and cultivation of styles rather than by advocacy of policies to cope with the problems of the country, they will project images and cultivate styles to the neglect of the substance of politics. They will abdicate their prime function in a democratic system, which amounts, in essence, to the assumption of the risk of trying to persuade us to lift ourselves by our bootstraps.

Among the literary experts on politics there are those who contend that, because of the development of tricks for the manipulation of the masses, practices of political leadership in the management of voters have moved far toward the conversion of election campaigns into obscene parodies of the models set up by democratic idealists. They point to the good old days when politicians were deep thinkers, eloquent orators, and farsighted statesmen. Such estimates of the course of change in social institutions must be regarded with reserve. They may be only manifestations of the inverted optimism of aged and melancholy men who, estopped from hope for the future, see in the past a satisfaction of their yearning for greatness in our political life.

Whatever the trends may have been, the perceptions that leadership elements of democracies hold of the modes of response of the electorate must always be a matter of fundamental significance. Those perceptions determine the nature of the voice of the people, for they determine the character of the input into the echo chamber. While the output may be governed by the nature of the input, over the longer run the properties of the echo chamber may themselves be altered. Fed a steady diet of buncombe, the people may come to expect and to respond with highest predictability to buncombe. And those leaders most skilled in the propagation of buncombe may gain lasting advantage in the recurring struggles for popular favor.

The perverse and unorthodox argument of this little book is that voters are not fools. To be sure, many individual voters act in odd ways indeed; yet in the large the electorate behaves about as rationally and responsibly as we should expect, given the clarity of the alternatives presented to it and the character of the information available to it. In American presidential campaigns of recent decades the portrait of the American electorate that develops from the data is not one of an electorate strait-jacketed by social determinants or moved by subconscious urges triggered by devilishly skillful propagandists. It is rather one of an electorate moved by concern about central and relevant questions of public policy, of governmental performance, and of executive personality. Propositions so uncompromisingly stated inevitably represent overstatements. Yet to the extent that they can be shown to resemble the reality, they are propositions of basic importance for both the theory and the practice of democracy.

To check the validity of this broad interpretation of the behavior of voters, attention will center on the movements of voters across party lines as they reacted to the issues, events, and candidates of presidential campaigns between 1936 and 1960. Some Democratic voters of one election turned Republican at the next; others stood pat. Some Republicans of one presidential season voted Democratic four years later; others remained loyal Republicans. What motivated these shifts, sometimes large and sometimes small, in voter affection? How did the standpatters differ from the switchers? What led them to stand firmly by their party preference of four years earlier? Were these actions governed by images, moods, and other irrelevancies; or were they expressions of judgments about the sorts of questions that, hopefully, voters will weigh as they responsibly cast their ballots? On these matters evidence is available that is impressive in volume, if not always so complete or so precisely relevant as hindsight would wish. If one perseveres through the analysis of this extensive body of information, the proposition that the voter is not so irrational a fellow after all may become credible.

Amitai Etzioni: A Swing to the Right?

I live in a district of middle-class professionals that elected a liberal, William F. Ryan, to Congress; and, while I know no one personally who has lost a son in the war, I do have five neighbors who have recently been mugged and beaten, or their apartments have been burglarized. They are all angry as hell. Their experience, shared by many, has had a deep emotional effect on their families and friends as well. While they read about Vietnam, even see the war in color on television, student stoning and as-

From *Trans*-action, September 1971. Copyright © September, 1971 by *Trans*-action, Inc., New Brunswick, New Jersey. Reprinted by permission of the publisher. Mr. Etzioni is Professor of Sociology at Columbia University.

saults are part of their own personal experience. Columbia University is just two blocks away. "The University should give each of us a camera with infrared lenses, to take pictures of these bastards at night," said a professor of engineering, adding, "As far as I am concerned, they could put the lenses at the top of a gun." Shooting persons who loot shops in ghetto riots, a Richard Daley prescription, is a treatment many in mid-Manhattan would approve of. If this is where many members of the middle-class, professional, educated, hereto liberal groups are, isn't it indeed true that the city and the nation are endorsing a conservative stand and its promise that law and order shall be maintained?

"Everyone agrees that the country is swinging right: that the American people are more conservative in 1968 than they were in 1964 and that they will be more conservative still in 1972," replies Archibald MacLeish, the poet, expressing the heart of what passes for the collective wisdom on the condition and direction of American politics. He appears also to speak for the consensus of commentators. The press, in its survey of the sixties, takes historical note that the combined conservative vote in the 1968 presidential election was 57 percent (defined somewhat carelessly as all votes for Richard M. Nixon and George C. Wallace), that conservative candidates in New York City garnered 58 percent of the total vote and that mayoral offices in Los Angeles and Minneapolis were filled by law-and-order candidates. Clearly, one may conclude, a formidable trend is gathering momentum. Furthermore, the press tells us that Nixon's "southern strategy," applied at the expense of the minorities to the country's most conservative element—the backlashing whites—has been successful. And so the press describes a vast, ghostly image hovering conservatively over the American landscape, an image President Nixon conjured up in late 1969: the Silent Majority. Even as perceptive and usually cautious an observer as Richard H. Rovere writes bluntly that "the Silent Majority has been heard from, and it favors the Nixon Way." Haynes Johnson, writing for the *Washington Post,* suspects that "the Age of Agnew may be nearing."

To the Right, March

To explain the massive turn to the Right, a seemingly plausible sociopolitical theory is repeatedly applied: the Kennedy and Johnson administrations, it is said, were preoccupied on the domestic front with the needs of the blacks and the poor, neglecting problems of the white middle- and working-class majority, who now demand attention. The erosion of traditional foundations—the dollar, respect for authority, laws and morality—

frightens these mainstream Americans. Many in the cities feel directly challenged in competition for jobs, housing and attention given to public
schools. Even where crime is infrequent, as in the streets of Helena, Mon-
tana, or where minorities are few, as in Lincoln, Nebraska, members of
this majority are still gripped by fear. If "those others" get away with
rioting and promiscuity and the general order breaks down, the theory
says, the conservative personality is afraid the superego will not be strong
enough to contain the turmoil and violence within the self: restraining the
kids, the blacks, the poor keeps the lid on one's own instincts. Therefore,
candidates for public office who favor stability over change will, it is
argued, continue to receive the most support.

　　While there are obviously some grains of truth in these straws of analysis, I am of the opinion that the conclusion is nothing to make national
election bets on. But there is no reason to wait for another national election to learn whether or not the country is careening to the Right. Public
opinion polls taken over the past few years, comparisons of these polls with
older ones, interviews with members of the middle classes and reexamina-
tion of local election results all suggest that:

> The United States has never had a liberal majority—not, at least,
> since polling was begun some 40-odd years ago;
> The recent shift to the Right is rather moderate in proportions;
> The shift is unlikely to extend itself significantly—a reversal of the
> trend may well set in within three to five years;
> Even before any reversal takes place, the "Silent Majority" is not at
> this moment a conservative monolith but a conglomerate of various pub-
> lics, quite divergent, the majority of which—we shall demonstrate—
> favor most liberal programs, from the extension of Social Security to
> the expansion of Medicare, from increased help to the unemployed to
> reduction of defense expenditures.

　　In short, the swing to the Right, we shall see, is rather limited in scope;
only about 6 percent of the public seem to have changed sides. And the
tide is rather shallow: many people who have cast votes for conservative
candidates in recent elections are committed to a liberal viewpoint on a
number of key issues that happen to be temporarily dormant.

Rhetoric versus Deeds

　　One major reason the country appears to have turned sharply to the
Right is that there has been a surprisingly swift change in the political
tenor of the national leadership. In the early sixties, the oratory of social
justice issued from all lips. In 1970 we find that with the Nixon adminis-

tration the tone has altered drastically. Law and order is the keynote; the administration's primary targets, after inflation, are crime and pornography —not racism and poverty. Attorney General John Mitchell provides the keynote Robert Kennedy or Ramsey Clark once gave; where until recently former ADAer Hubert Humphrey was heard, Spiro Agnew now speaks.

In the tradition of American politics, each side tries, when it is helpful, to make the other side accountable for its statements, as if words reflected deeds. Actually, we must realize that while the rhetoric of the two previous administrations was much more emphatic in respect to social justice, little was achieved in terms of school desegregation, opening up of the building trades, low-cost housing or of practically any other concrete social program you carefully examine. Lots of laws were passed, but few were effectively applied. The Kerner Commission's rhetoric was resounding, but it did not provide a concrete plan for action. Despite the significantly altered tenor of the current administration, federally instituted domestic programs—thus far, anyway—have been changed rather little. There still is an Office of Economic Opportunity (OEO). Social Security benefits are being increased sharply (Congress boosted the benefits 15 percent; the administration itself asked for a 10 percent increase; Humphrey, if elected president, would, in all likelihood, not have asked for more). Nixon has requested a more expensive, federally funded welfare program based on what heretofore was considered a Left-liberal idea—negative income tax. Medicare expenditures are rising sharply, and federal aid to education is expected to expand despite the recent veto (the veto itself seems to be a gesture, part of the rhetoric, not the reality).

Very few of the numerous recommendations of either the antiviolence or the anticrime commissions are actually being implemented. While Congress and the public were very angry with the rioting students, none of the numerous bills requiring colleges to certify that they would penalize their rioters or lose federal support were ever enacted. (The Nixon administration, which first favored such a bill, soon came to oppose it!) And no enforcement mechanisms have been set up at this point for those riot penalty clauses attached to various appropriation bills. "Privatization" (the turning over of federal programs to the private sectors) remains almost exclusively a concept in Professor Peter Drucker's *The Age of Discontinuity* and in the mouths of a few of Nixon's aides. Decentralization, the turning over of federal programs to the states, a keystone in the conservative rhetoric, has been implemented only on a limited scale. Recently, a move to turn over control of OEO programs to the states was not actively supported by the White House, was opposed by Donald Rumsfeld, director of OEO, and defeated by Congress. To put it briefly, continuity has been very close between the Johnson and the Nixon administrative programs, but not between the speeches.

For years, the pollsters have been asking representative national samples of Americans, "What do you consider yourself in your political point of view—a conservative, a liberal, or a middle-of-the-roader?" As far back as there are data, which covers more than a generation, only a *minority* of Americans have answered that question by saying "liberal." At the end of 1968, 17 percent declared themselves liberals, the same proportion as at the end of 1967. The percentage of declared liberals was higher in 1964 —23 percent—but still less than a quarter of the country. When similar questions were asked on earlier occasions, in 1960 for instance, or even way back in 1938, the answers were very similar to those given in 1964, with the liberals gaining a few percentage points over the years.

Where Is the Center?

It is not that the remainder of our fellow citizens call themselves conservatives, although for decades more citizens have seen themselves so than as liberals, both before and after the drummed-up "backlash." At the end of 1968, 38 percent of a national sample of Americans defined themselves as "conservatives," a meager 3 percent more than the 35 percent who so declared themselves in 1967, and 1 percent less than the 39 percent of conservatives in 1964, before the backlash had even been mentioned.

A major part of the public, larger than the liberal camp and about the same size as the conservative one (but, we shall see, of much greater political importance) is made up of the middle-of-the-roaders (38 percent of the national sample in 1964, 32 percent in 1968). In the forties and fifties the American people were not asked the same question, but rather whether they wished the country to turn to the Left or to the Right. The majority preferred, on each of the ten occasions when the question was asked, for the nation not to turn either way: the size of the minority that favored a left turn ranged from 19 percent to 23 percent; from 17 percent to 24 percent chose a right turn.

In short, public opinion polls suggest only a small drift to the Right after 1964, with no majority on either the conservative or the liberal side— silent or otherwise. The majority went, and continues to go, to those candidates who can carry one of these political wings *plus* significant chunks of the pivotal middle-of-the-roaders.

Many commentators see a much sharper turn to the Right than polls indicate because they judge public attitudes according to election results. Voting in a presidential or mayoral election can be an atypical and unreliable expression of the underlying views of the public, because voting requires those citizens who hold conflicting views about various aspects of the nation's affairs and policies to cast one vote only. The voter must go through a kind of "averaging" process; he has feelings or articulated positions about quite a few issues, about the war in Vietnam, the racial situation, crime, federal aid to education, welfare programs, the space program and so on. (That is, about seven out of every ten citizens respond in some way to issues; the remaining three, surveys show, are rather uninterested and uninformed about most issues. Although they know about welfare, crime and so forth, they do not see these matters as political, as subject to policy or as dealt with in a way by which governments may be judged, but rather as "natural" occurrences, like freezing rain.)

Votes Do Not Show Basic Trends

Of the relatively informed and concerned citizens, a small minority maintains highly consistent views and hence can readily choose for whom to vote (or for whom not to vote). About 6 percent of the American public are die-hard liberals; they favor more welfare, more social justice, more federal aid to education; they regard the reports about rising crime rates as largely exaggerated and feel crime is best eliminated by providing more welfare services. These people easily vote for John Lindsay and against Richard Nixon. Similarly, there are about 6 percent "pure" conservatives who have relatively little difficulty in choosing, let us say, between Humphrey and Nixon. But the rest—about 20 percent moderate liberals, 24 percent moderate conservatives and, above all, the 34 percent who see themselves as middle-of-the-roaders between these two *moderate* positions—must find a way to combine conflicting positions in regard to various aspects of our social and political life into one vote. If these citizens favor increased welfare and more federal aid to education but also want more action against crime and price increases, and if they find one political candidate more likely than another to advance a certain program, they must decide which program is the most important and vote for its promulgator. Thus, in the process of selection, these citizens decide, in effect, to disregard some issues and to vote on the basis of others—*this* time around. However, these moderate and middle-of-the-road citizens who make up the actual majority are still committed to those programs they did not vote for this time. (If they had two votes each, they would have given only one to Nixon, while the consistent conservatives would have been inclined to give him both.) This majority would come out of their political computing in a similar way at the next election, only if they will continue to consider the same issues overridingly important, "bumping" off the other issues in their final decision for whom to cast their vote.

This weighing and averaging process is not explicit and conscious for many citizens; it frequently takes place subconsciously and emotionally. Nevertheless, a kind of averaging does occur, with some issues receiving extra weight, so that currently these citizens *feel* more strongly and react more to some issues than to others. For this reason, if you base your analysis of where the country is headed (or even where it is now) on election outcomes and voting patterns, as commentators and the press have been inclined to do, you will come up with an image of a country moving much more decisively to the Right (or to the Left) than the people really are. This image will reflect more accurately the key issues of the moment than it will long-term tendencies.

Public opinion studies tell us that many who voted conservatively in recent elections (in Minneapolis, for instance, Charles Stenvig, an obscure head of the Police Officers Federation, won the city's mayoralty by a margin of 74,748 to 46,739) actually did so only because they feel *at present* that two specific issues, law and order and inflation, are more salient than the others. Many liberal programs—expanded Medicare, improved welfare and so on—are favored by these conservatives, but their chief concern is focused elsewhere just now. To put it differently, the majority of the public, while neither liberal nor conservative, do *not* rest in the middle, in the sense of a moderate position somewhere between the liberal and conservative. The majority of voters are middle because they are *part* conservative, *part* liberal and shift, according to the issues that are foremost in their minds at a particular time, to support conservative or liberal political candidates. Therefore, even if the composition of the public or the list of issues does not change significantly, the election outcome can differ radically. This is a key reason why, with only a few more full-fledged, strongly committed conservatives than there were four years ago, there are many more middle-of-the-roaders who now support President Nixon or conservative mayors. It also explains why today's leading conservative candidates are far from secure in their offices. Governor Ronald Reagan, for instance, a much "purer" conservative than Nixon, should have—by the conservative-backlash theory—an easy ride back to his Sacramento post. Actually, he faces a tough challenge from his Democratic rival, Jesse Unruh, who emerged as a strong competitor in a recent poll (it showed him only 5 percent behind the governor in the voters' favor). Other pure conservative candidates have not fared well either. In California, Max Rafferty, the conservative educator, lost that 1968 race for Senate. In Cleveland, a liberal black mayor, Carl Stokes, was reelected.

The discrepancies between the results of an election and the much more complex positions most citizens hold can be determined in two ways: the position they take on domestic reforms (liberal issues) as opposed to their stand on law and order and inflation (conservative issues) and in the differences between their positions regarding specific programs and general political "philosophical" questions.

On Specific Issues

In 1969 Americans in a national sample were asked to comment on "priorities" for government spending. They were given a list of priorities and asked if they wished each particular category of programs to be cut, kept as it is or increased. Thus, according to a study of Middle America conducted by Gallup for *Newsweek* in late 1969, 56 percent of white, middle-class Americans favored more money allotted to job training for the unemployed, 47 percent favored medical care for the old and the needy, and 66 percent would cut the support of military aid to other nations such as South Vietnam. As in several other similar polls taken recently, law-and-order programs gain a high support (to 22 percent who would "keep or increase" for every 1 percent who would cut). However, a popular liberal program initiated by the Democratic administration gains an almost similar endorsement of 19 percent (keep or increase) to 1 percent (cut). Actually, six of the seven programs that rank highest in support are liberal ones. As other polls indicate, there is still a wide basis of sup-

National Priorities in Governmental Spending
Preferred by a Nationwide Sample,
February 1969

	Keep or Increase	Cut First
Anticrime, law enforcement programs	22%	1%
Aid to education	19	1
Antipoverty program	17	6
Medicaid	9	2
Antiair and antiwater pollution programs	8	2
Welfare and relief	8	10
Aid to cities	5	5
Subsidies to farmers	4	7
Financing Vietnam war	4	18
Highway construction	2	9
Space program	2	39
	100%	100%

Source: Harris, 18 February 1969.

port for various federally funded and directed domestic reforms: negative income tax (Nixon's welfare scheme); the food stamp program (a plan first advanced by Senator George McGovern); and of course, most popular of all, the fight against pollution.

Not only do many Americans partake of conservatism on a few specific issues and liberalism on others, they also subscribe to conservative principles, philosophies and clichés while seeking out programs derived from "liberal" principles. For instance, most citizens want to reduce the role of government in general and of the federal government in particular (on the general grounds that government, in the abstract, is bad); at the same time, however, they favor numerous new or expanded specific programs to be carried out by the government (for example, food stamps). In the most conclusive study on the subject, conducted by Professors Lloyd Free and Hadley Cantril, it was established that two-thirds (65 percent) of a national sample favored liberal programs; only an eighth (14 percent) took an opposing position, while 21 percent were middle-of-the-roaders. However, on the ideological front, the liberal philosophy won the support of only 16 percent, while the conservative polled 50 percent (with 34 percent falling in the middle).

Actually, there is only one kind of domestic program for which support *has* significantly declined over the last four to five years—and that is support for reforms favorable to the black people.

A Narrow Backlash

There is, according to polls, a backlash, but it is a sharply focused one, found primarily in attitudes toward the blacks and toward some of the youth. But these attitudes do *not* color significantly the "rest" of the domestic reform. To the question "Does the administration push racial integration too fast?" less than a third of those polled answered in the affirmative in 1964, but by October 1968 that proportion had grown to more than half (54 percent). In 1964 a third (34 percent) felt that integration had been pushed "too fast"; by 1968 their ranks had doubled, with two-thirds (67 percent) indicating they felt that Negroes were asking for more than they were ready to assume. Furthermore, about half of the sample felt that Negroes sought to live off handouts. The majority of Middle America now feels that Negroes already have the same or better opportunity than white Americans in getting jobs, education, housing and other advantages.

What these findings underscore is the selective reaction of the electorate to special programs. Among the domestic programs, those that are viewed by the public as catering to one group—farmers, users of highways, blacks or the poor—tend to be much less popular than those that are believed to benefit everyone, such as federal aid to education or Social Security. The only exceptions are those programs explicitly aimed at a group the majority considers deserving of charity—the needy, hungry or aged. In effect, there are two different politics at work—those of guilt (or altruism) and those of self-interest. The first allows support for a group other than your own; the second requires that your own group's interests merit priority. The politics of guilt are effective only as long as the amounts involved are not very large, times are prosperous and the recipients are or seem to be grateful; their gratitude is the major payoff to the donor groups, whose guilt is to be relieved. In recent years, the majority has come to think of blacks as ungrateful. By 1969, when asked over whom they feel guilty, 63 percent mentioned hungry people, 56 percent the aged, but only 35 percent listed Negroes. Support for depollution, Social Security and federal aid to education is based on self-interest, and these matters are much safer —even in a period when conservative issues have gained in saliency—than guilt issues.

The liberals tried too long to ignore the rather elementary fact that conservatives, too, have needs, some rather legitimate, and all needs which affect their votes. The liberals often proceeded as if it would suffice to motivate the public to support civil rights and anti-poverty legislation on the basis of altruism and guilt, and that the political payoff would be limited to relief from a bad conscience; however, this relief does not carry programs very far even for those liberals who do have a bad conscience. Many conservatives do not feel a special obligation to the poor or the minorities.

Appeal to self-interest offers an alternative to guilt politics if one wishes to rally conservatives to the support of social reforms—with Social Security and Medicare everyone gets a slice of the pie. But this appeal is rapidly diminishing. First, many such programs already exist, thus decreasing the saliency of additional health or education benefits; second, many of the other programs are not allocative but concern the quality of life, especially the quality of the environment; third, for the first time in several decades, conservatives, instead of chiefly opposing reforms, are actively promoting two programs: they wish to curb both crime and inflation and, beyond this, to restore respect for authority and morality.

Liberals are learning that crime and inflation are genuine issues. The rise in crime is a matter of concern to most citizens. This concern is not just a result of better reporting or of a change in statistical methods—facts long emphasized by liberals. Crime is a potent issue because of its saliency:

unlike taxes, which, after all, are just money, or debates about the deserving poor whom most taxpayers never see, or even the war, which until recently, was remote from the middle classes, crime hits close to home.

Rising prices do not pack the same emotional wallop, but nevertheless they are far from trivial, and they are encountered daily by everyone; they rob the aged of the value of their savings and pensions, and workers of their wage increases.

Now that these two issues, added to the underlying—and related—uneasiness about the erosion of morality and authority, have been mobilized into an active political demand, they must now be given the same kind of attention as the legitimate needs of the blacks and the poor. It is true, historically, that these disadvantaged groups have had to wait much longer before their needs were accorded attention and that they are still far behind, despite some progress between 1962 and 1967. But as of 1968 their time is up, and the needs and demands articulated by conservatives must now also be taken into consideration, one hopes without replacing the attention being given to those of the others, but in effect competing with them.

A Projection

The Talmud says that upon the destruction of the temple at Jerusalem, prophecy was given to "the deaf, fools, and minors." The record of social scientists who have tried their hands at prediction would support this ancient dictum. At most we dare point out that if the preceding analysis is correct and no new major forces will intrude themselves into the situation, the following predictions based on an investigation of the spectrum of feelings the majority has displayed *outside* the voting booths may not be too farfetched:

1. Just as it is a gross exaggeration to say that a major dramatic shift to the Right has occurred in the last two or three years, so it is a mistake to expect one in the future. Nixon may win the 1972 election (incumbents have the inside track), and the leaderless, splintered Democrats seem set on helping Nixon win by a wider margin than in 1968. But even so, we expect that at least 40 percent of the country will vote against him and that it is impossible for Wallace or someone like him to win the 1972 elections. Nor can we see Nixon implementing anything like the right-wing rhetoric his administration, specifically in the persons of Agnew and Mitchell, frequently expresses. Just as the extreme rhetoric of Rap Brown did not bring about a left-wing revolution, so will the inflammatory speeches of Agnew not bring about a right-wing repression. To put it less

cautiously, we expect the United States in 1975 to be very much as it was in 1968, with massive welfare systems, expanding Social Security, low unemployment rates and no significant increase in the abridgment of civil rights and civil liberties.

2. If the Nixon administration will successfully resolve salient issues by terminating the war and reducing crime, rebellion and inflation, then, most likely old and new demands for reforms (from improving public education to depollution) will increase in saliency and will either push the administration toward a more liberal program or, if it will not respond, elect a more liberal replacement. In this very way the Labor Party gained power in the United Kingdom in 1945, despite Winston Churchill's success, in part because this success was on a front (the international one) other than the one that had next to be faced (the domestic one).

However, if little is done, disappointment is likely to be unfavorable to the present administration. If the Nixon administration, after four years in office, fails to curb crime and inflation effectively and to end the war, then voters may well be much more disappointed than they are right now and turn their support to other possibilities: some will go to the far Right (Wallace), some will resign to apathy (by not voting), and some will turn to "more liberal" issues or new reforms, like the environmental ones.

Other factors will, of course, affect the situation, especially in the area of foreign policy (from Latin America to the Middle and Far East) and the extent to which the Democrats will be able to unite around a fresh person and a new program. But even if the present disarray of personalities, factions and programs continues, we expect the conservative trend to continue only slowly, extending itself, possibly, by a few percentage points in terms of electoral endorsement. And, as long as this disarray continues, few of the many domestic issues close to the hearts of the liberals, many conservatives and most of the pivotal middle-of-the-roaders will be effectively attended to. As of now, no one has a clear mandate, liberal or conservative.

2   Parties and Politics

So integral are parties to American politics that most political history tends to be an account of the ebb and flow of party fortunes from the founding of the Republic to the present. Democrats sometimes boast that theirs is the oldest continuously organized political party in the world—which, no doubt, it is. For nearly 120 years the Republicans have been contesting elections against the Democrats in their now almost formalized combat. Tens of millions of us make our first childish observations of politics through the screen of an inherited party allegiance. These same inherited party allegiances have a way of staying with us over time and through the most dramatic changes of circumstances in our lives. To put it simply, the Democratic and Republican parties are pervasive, persistent, even dominating features of our political landscape.

But what are the parties, really, and what do they do? Are they vital, generating forces in politics? Or are they passive receptors, empty vessels into which we put whatever content is generated by more vital forces? Do the parties create ideas, movements, policies? Or do they serve merely as customary and convenient vehicles for the expression of ideas, movements and policy demands that originate outside parties and relatively independently? The answers are not easy to come by, for the parties—despite their visibility—are elusive and even enigmatic. We speak of them in our everyday discourse as though they were great monoliths, each possessed of will and smoothly meshed power. We speak of them as though each had an enduring, conscious, and rational center. Yet, when one looks for enduring will and identity in them, he finds instead for all their formal structures of local, state, national, and parliamentary committees, the parties are actually loosely knit, almost amorphous, entities. This suggests that the parties are passive conductors of forces more than they are creative or generative forces themselves. This answer puts us close to the prevailing theory of the role of our parties in the national political life.

33

In a two-party system in the multigroup society, the parties are essentially engines of electoral victory. They are not companies of believers, not bands of brothers relentlessly dedicated to some principle beyond electoral victory itself. To achieve electoral victory, a party must attract a sufficiently broad variety of persons and groups to form a majority. As a party's appeal broadens, of course, it grows less coherent. A party's umbrella can be, and is, so broad that it sometimes covers antagonistic interests. The modern Democratic Party, for example, has been the party of Southern segregationists and simultaneously of the great majority of black voters. Two generations ago the Democrats could successfully appeal to both rural, dry-voting Southern Protestants and urban, wet-voting Roman Catholics in the North. Of course, if a party coalition becomes radically incoherent it becomes unstable. It is the genius of the party politician that he is able to play broker to the various interests or groups that comprise his coalition, inducing a modification or compromise of a group demand here, making an outright policy promise to another group there. Sometimes the coalition's incoherence cannot be plastered over by even the most skillful brokering, and electoral defeat results.

In our system, the party that wins the election also organizes the government. Its successful candidates comprise the majority in Congress and occupy the White House and staff the executive branch. Can an organization whose purpose is electoral victory in a diverse society also govern? The answer would appear to be negative. We have not had and do not have real party government in America. Our parties are electoral machines, not legislative machines. The victorious presidential candidate is not united with his fellow partisans in Congress upon a platform of either principle or ideology from which a coherent and clear set of public policies can be derived. The president, as leader of his party, cannot simply press a button or issue commands and get his party's platform promises enacted into law. Neither can the party leaders in Congress automatically bring their nominal majority into play. The electoral majority that produced the party victory often does not hold up even through the swearing in of the new government. Legislation in such circumstances requires the formation of new ad hoc coalitions, with all the bargaining, compromising, and reversing of prior positions that that may require.

Still, the parties are not simply empty vessels; they are not just superstructure. They have their respective character, traditions, and ideological and legislative tendencies. There is more than an accidental relationship between the electoral result and the style and movement of the government that is produced by that electoral result. The great modern electoral coalition was formed by the Democratic Party behind F. D. Roosevelt in 1932; it has maintained its essential composition until today. The New Deal and Fair Deal policy stances of Roosevelt and his successor, Harry S Truman, have been ratified over and over by the voters. Even when the national electorate has turned to Republican presidential nominees, as with Eisenhower and Nixon, they have returned Democratic majorities to Congress. As a result, Republican presidents have not tried to dismantle the policy structure developed under the Democrats. When a Republican nominee, Senator Barry Goldwater, seriously seemed to threaten in 1964 to reverse the direction of policy, he received the most decisive popular defeat in our history. President Nixon, as Republican nominee in 1968 and as president since, has clearly avoided Goldwater's error and has in fact sought to break important elements of the Roosevelt coalition away from the Democrats by explicitly embracing New Deal economic policies while simultaneously appealing to Southerners by his stance on racial desegregation.

A major question will be answered in 1972. Will a combination of adroit brokering by President Nixon and the emergence of different issues forcing different alignments at last destroy the old Roosevelt–Democratic coalition? The demise of that coalition has been freely predicted since Eisenhower's time, but it has held together with remarkable persistence for nearly 40 years. Most of the selections in this chapter explore in considerable depth the possibility of that old coalition eroding; most of the writers agree there is some promise for President Nixon as well as some peril, notably the threat to him of George Wallace's candidacy.

But questions deeper and more fateful than the puzzles about the future of the Democratic coalition are also explored in this chapter. Is the old party politics of brokering among groups now outmoded? Can the two-party system survive in its present form? Are we moving toward a politics of radical polarization rather than reconciliation and compromise? Can the parties as we know them adequately serve as vehicles for the expression and channeling of passions and demands as fierce and contradictory as those of today? These questions, too, must be faced in 1972.

James L. Sundquist: The Party Square Dance in America

The United States has had a two-party system continuously for 140 years. It is probably a safe prediction that a political system resilient enough to survive a Civil War, two world wars, the Industrial Revolution,

---

From "The Party Square Dance in America," by James L. Sundquist, *Interplay*, © October 1970, Vol. 3, No. 13. Reprinted by permission.

the urbanization of the country, the Great Depression and several lesser depressions will survive for the indefinite future, too.

But behind the stable facade of the two-party system great upheavals can occur. In the past, major realignments that altered the parties fundamentally—in their composition, their programs, and the basis of their competition—have occurred with pendulum regularity at intervals of almost exactly 40 years—in the 1850s, the 1890s, and the 1930s. On that basis, another one is just about upon us. The alignment established in the Roosevelt Revolution is just short of four decades old.

A realignment occurs when the electorate is subjected to an overriding new issue or set of issues—issues powerful enough to dominate political discussion and polarize large segments of the population for a sustained period of time. The voters who are attached, or driven, to each of the new "issue poles" necessarily find or fashion a political instrument to express their views. Either they capture one of the existing major parties or they form a new one. Eventually, if the new issue or set of issues maintains its force, the two-party system realigns to reflect the new polarity.

At the moment of realignment, the voter's attachment to his party is emotional, or even passionate. It is *his* party. It expresses his will on that burning issue of the day, whatever it may be, because it was formed or reformed for just that purpose. He is loyal to it because it is loyal to him.

As time passes, those feelings fade. But not quickly. In the case of realignments that arise from the most traumatic issues—a Civil War, say, or a Great Depression—a generation must pass and a new one must arise before the old attachments are seriously eroded. And that is why the 40-year periods that have defined our historic cycles seem more than accidental.

Let us examine the mathematics of voting generations. The median age of the country's voters is now 48. That means that 27 years must pass after a realignment before a majority of the voting public consists of persons who were too young to vote at the time of that realignment. But political awareness begins long before age 21. If we assume that teenagers are affected just as their parents are by the powerful issue or issues that realign the electorate, then about 35 years are required before persons whose political views were fixed during a period of realignment are supplanted as a majority of the voters by those who were too young to have been deeply influenced at that time.

There is no precision in these calculations, obviously. But there is no need to be precise. The main point is clear: as the realignment issues fade into history and a new generation comes of age, a rationale of party competition based upon the old issues has less and less meaning. The new voters are not stirred by the old political quarrels that still excite their elders. Traditional political rhetoric seems obsolete. More and more voters classify themselves as independents. And as the polarizing issues lose force, the parties come together in their political positions. It is easier, then, for voters to move back and forth between the parties from election to election. The cry, "There is no real difference between the parties" is increasingly heard—and more and more aptly.

At some point—probably before the end of the third decade but certainly by the fourth—the passage of time has set the stage for a new and more significant party alignment. All it takes is a new issue or set of issues that polarizes political opinion again. Then the weakened party ties are swept away as new ones form. The new attachments are emotional, and the cycle begins afresh.

In the 80 years before the 1930s, the pattern of party competition was primarily regional. That pattern took shape in the 1850s, when the Republican Party was formed as a regional anti-slavery party and quickly became dominant in the North. Inevitably the Democrats, as the opposition party, came to control the South. After the Civil War, economic discontent expressed itself in a series of third party movements, culminating in the Populist wildfire of the 1890s and the absorption of the Populists by the Democrats under William Jennings Bryan in 1896. But the net effect of that realignment was to reinforce the regional division of the parties. The Northeast became even more staunchly Republican; the solid Democratic South remained. And that was the basis of party competition until the Great Depression, when the current party alignment—what might be called the New Deal party system—was formed.

That system was at the outset one of sharp ideological conflict and deep hostility, with class overtones. The central issue was that of federal activism in coping with economic catastrophe—the role of the Federal government, the scope of its power and the size of its budget, and the scale of its intervention in the private economy to bring about recovery and reform. The Democrats were activist and identified with organized labor, the Republicans conservative and linked to the business and financial community. Explicit class parties on the European model were not formed, however, because the regional pattern of politics that had prevailed so long could not be quickly broken. Southern conservatives did not turn Republican in a body; they had too much to lose in local politics by doing that, so they remained Southern Democrats. By the same token, Republicans who backed Roosevelt did not all change parties; many simply called themselves Liberal (or Progressive) Republicans.

The Generations Shift

Yet it is in this kind of situation that the generational factor comes into play. Disaffected older voters, influenced by old loyalties, tend to retain their affiliation and split their tickets, but younger voters see less need for subterfuge. So the sons of Liberal Republicans in the North became Democrats, and the sons of conservative Southern Democrats became Republicans.

The shifting did not happen all at once. In the North, it took a decade or more in some states for the Democratic Party to reorganize under new leaders who could attract an eager young following and bring about effective two-party competition—not until the 1940s in Michigan with Mennen Williams and in Minnesota with Hubert Humphrey, not until the 1950s in Maine with Edmund Muskie and in Pennsylvania with Joseph Clark and George Leader, and not until the 1960s in Vermont with Philip Hoff.

The South has lagged about 20 years behind the North. Southern Republicanism had to await the Eisenhower crusade of 1952 before it could attract enough young and vigorous party workers to make it an effective competitive force. But after that the process of realignment was the same. One by one the state parties produced appealing leaders and candidates, most of them young, and the solid South was shattered in the 1960s as Republican governors and senators were chosen—John Tower in Texas, Winthrop Rockefeller in Arkansas, Claude Kirk and Edward Gurney in Florida, Howard Baker in Tennessee, Strom Thurmond in South Carolina, and Linwood Holton in Virginia—in every case the first Republican to occupy his office since Reconstruction. The number of Republican Congressmen elected from the 11 former Confederate states has risen year by year, from two in 1950 to 26 in 1968.

The Mellowing of the Parties

But even as the South is vigorously realigning to conform to the New Deal party system, with its activist–conservative cleavage over the role of government, that system itself is being rapidly eroded. That is why current political trends are so confused and contradictory, especially in the South.

The New Deal party system is obsolescent right on schedule, as it approaches 40 years of age. And there is every sign that the generational factors mentioned earlier provide a good part of the explanation. As time has passed, both parties have mellowed on the issues around which they polarized a generation ago. Democrats no longer talk the language of class struggle; Harry Truman was the last Democratic President to cuss out the Economic Royalists, and the party's current leadership is downright solicitous about their welfare.

Even more spectacular has been the mellowing of the Republican doctrine, perhaps because it came about so suddenly. The ideological anti–

New Deal rhetoric of the 1930s—the attacks on big government and its accompanying evils, like taxes and controls on business and "usurpation" of states' rights—survived all the way to 1960 with Dwight Eisenhower (who, after all, was 42 years old when the New Deal came into power) and reached something of a new crescendo with Barry Goldwater. But then it died. Richard Nixon does not spend his days denouncing the big government over which he presides, and trying vainly to dismantle it. Quite the contrary, he is pushing his own proposals for its further aggrandizement. He would, for example, expand the reach of welfare programs to cover the working poor, extend federal influence over state and local law enforcement, and introduce new programs in the field of education.

So the parties have drifted from their poles and are meeting somewhere in the middle, as the generational theory says they should. And the young are behaving as the theory says they should, too. The ardent reformers among them—and this generation of young people surely has as high a proportion of zealots as any since the 1930s—might be expected to find their political home in the activist party, the Democratic. But they don't. Only 27 percent of college students call themselves Democrats and 52 percent independents, according to Dr. Gallup. And the latter figure includes many who reject the party system altogether. The young activists were attracted in 1968 to Eugene McCarthy and to Robert Kennedy but Hubert Humphrey left them cold. As they see it, the Democratic Party has lost whatever zeal it may have had in New Deal days to achieve a genuine redistribution of wealth and opportunity; its foreign policy is a series of reflex actions reflecting a Cold War mentality frozen 20 years ago, and it has been so engrossed with the quantitative dimensions of the Gross National Product that it has hardly concerned itself with the qualitative side at all.

So party distinctions are vague. Party attachments are weak. Voters are independent. The young are disaffected. These are the standard symptoms of an electorate ripe for realignment.

But the passage of time and the coming of a new political generation only sets the stage. Still required is the realigning issue or set of issues— the questions powerful and emotion-laden and sustained enough to overshadow all the old issues, polarize the country, and reshuffle its political groupings.

Three issues in recent years have polarized a lot of people. One is Southeast Asia. The second is race. The third is a loosely-defined set of anxieties about the conduct of the young. A fourth issue—the environment —is now arousing attention and concern, symbolic of a broad concern with the quality of American life. And the state of the economy is an issue sometimes quiescent, but never dead. What is the potential of each of these as a realigning issue?

The Non-Issues

It is significant that at no time in the 140 years of continuous two-party politics has the party system been aligned or realigned on the basis of foreign policy. While domestic policy has cleaved the electorate, the big questions of foreign policy, involving peace and war, have been bipartisan. Politics have "stopped at the water's edge." The country has declined to second-guess the President and has fallen into step behind him. Up until recently, that is. The country refused to unify behind Truman in Korea. It denied its unified support to Johnson in Vietnam. And now it is denying it to Nixon in Vietnam, Cambodia and wherever else in Southeast Asia his policies may lead him.

It is possible to sketch out a scenario of realignment around the Southeast Asia issue: President Nixon finds he cannot extricate himself from Vietnam and announces his determination to fight until victory; anti-war demonstrations spread and provoke counter-demonstrations; the peace groups call their opponents war profiteers and murderers and in turn are labeled bugouts, appeasers and Communist sympathizers; as the quarrel goes on, more and more of the electorate is polarized; the Democrats, as the opposition party, are drawn inevitably into common cause with the peace advocates who are attacking the administration; the peace movement eventually captures the Democratic Party, whereupon Republicans in that movement become Democrats and pro-war Democrats become Republicans.

The odds are heavy, however, against any such eventuality. Nixon's Cambodia adventure seems to have taught him all over again what his predecessors learned: he has to yield to the objectors. No matter whether they are a majority or just a noisy minority—they are enough to divide the country, and without overwhelming support no President can fight a foreign war. This probably explains why the country has never polarized on foreign policy. In any case, it indicates that Nixon will be forced to pursue his announced course of continuing withdrawals, and that should keep the issue damped down.

Polarizing around Race?

A corresponding scenario could be written that leads to a country polarized around the race issue—on issues of school desegregation, open housing, fair employment practices, racial crime and violence, all leading to a polarization between the ghettoes and the "white nooses" that surround them. There have been times in the past dozen years when such a course seemed not beyond the bounds of possibility. But such times have not lasted long. Strong mediating forces in both communities have kept black–white conflict under control. The country could polarize on racial issues only if race conflict became so heightened and so sustained that those mediating forces were overwhelmed. If that were to happen, then one party, presumably the Democrats, might identify itself with the Negro cause and the other, presumably the Republicans, with the white backlash, and realignment would follow.

Such a course for the Democrats is not hard to visualize; blacks provide such a large bloc of Democratic votes that in a showdown they probably could not be denied. But for the Republicans to identify with the other side is harder to imagine. True, the GOP shows constant signs of being tempted. In terms of *realpolitik,* the party should—in Goldwater's deathless phrase—"go hunting where the ducks are." And the ducks for the Republicans are clearly not in the ghettoes, where their cause is close to hopeless, but in the white suburbs and the South. The Republicans even have a learned guide to *realpolitik,* Kevin Phillips' *The Emerging Republican Majority,* which offers enticing statistics to show that a majority will emerge when the Republicans undercut George Wallace and take away his following. And there is only one possible way they can do that.

Certainly within the administration the Phillips "Southern strategy" has had its advocates. Phillips himself was, for a while, an aide to the Attorney General. And, in recent months at least, they seem to have won more battles than they have lost. They were given two Supreme Court nominations, they obtained the ouster of Leon Panetta, and they are more than happy with the President's position on busing. Nevertheless, while the administration may be leaning, it has not fallen off the fence. And the probability is that it will not lean so far as to lose the support of its Northern integrationists and thus bring about a realignment.

Luckily for the republic, *realpolitik* is not easily pursued. Politicians cannot usually be so coldly calculating and statesmen, by definition, never are. It is difficult to visualize any Republican President (a Vice President, maybe, but not a President) reaching the deliberate conclusion that the Jacob Javitses and Clifford Cases and Hugh Scotts should be jettisoned in exchange for picking up the Wallaces and the Louise Day Hickses. It is much more in the nature of parties to straddle and avoid making such hard choices. As Republican Chairman Rogers Morton put it, the GOP will pursue a Southern strategy, but it will pursue a Northern strategy, too. In other words, it will limit its Southern strategy *to the South* and not embrace the anti-Negro backlash in the North. In that case, pressures toward polarization on this issue will be damped down, too.

Permissiveness

A large segment of the electorate is upset, clearly, at what is going on among the nation's youth. The hippie movement, the drug culture, the "new" sexual morality, the anti-draft and anti-Vietnam movements, the Black Panthers, and the general and random rebelliousness of college students were bound to become matters of political controversy once it was clear they were more than a passing eccentricity. When traditional values are under attack, it is the role—indeed, the duty—of political conservatives to rise to the defense of those values. And there is much political hay to be made, if they can succeed in attaching to their liberal opposition the blame for what is wrong.

The conservative defense and counter-attack are now vigorously under way. Liberals are being charged with responsibility for the breakdown of discipline in society. It is they who created the climate of permissiveness that leads to outrage, so the accusations run. They constituted a Supreme Court that "coddles" criminals. They dominate the big universities where the trouble centers, and there they appease the offenders and thus encourage erosion of the nation's basic values. And the hay is being harvested; one need only look at the evident invulnerability of Governor Ronald Reagan in California and the phenomenal rise in popularity of Vice President Agnew since he became the foremost spear-carrier in the counter-attack on the rambunctious young.

It will not be easy to polarize the country on this issue either, because the tendency will be for virtually all politicians to wind up on the same side. No one will run for office as the pro-drug or pro-hippie or pro-Panther candidate, and few will identify themselves with campus rioters. But the conservatives may find ways of forcing the issue, by pushing tougher and tougher measures of repression until the point is reached where the liberals have to say "No more." Then—assuming the young people continue their campus rampages and other offenses to traditional sensibility—a substantial segment of the electorate could conceivably polarize around the issue of permissiveness versus discipline, and party realignment would follow.

While none of the three issues of Southeast Asia, race and youthful conduct may be powerful enough separately to bring about a party realignment, they have come to be mutually reinforcing and in combination they possess far greater potency.

What seems to be the emerging conservative political course is exemplified by the Agnew speeches, and by the Lloyd Bentsen campaign in the Texas Democratic primary: a generalized attack on all of the alleged consequences of the liberal ascendancy, supported by illustrations from any of them that suits a particular audience or reflects a particular day's events. Unless the aggressive blacks and young people and anti-Vietnam marchers subside—which seems quite unlikely, for they consider their grievances to be real and redressable only through direct action—then the evident success of the Reagans and the Agnews and the Bentsens provides the model for the new generation of conservative politicians.

The Crisis over Morality

There is a real possibility, then, that it will be on this generalized moral issue—permissiveness versus discipline, or traditional values versus revised ones—that the realignment will take place. The new alignment would not be clear-cut; there would be enough dissimilarity among the constituent concrete issues to set up many conflicting cross-currents—a voter may be a dove on Vietnam and a hawk on campus disturbances, for example. But there would be a basic liberal-conservative cleavage around which the parties would reform themselves. That cleavage would reflect little of the economic conflicts of the New Deal era and the old quarrel about the role of the federal government. Indeed, the conservatives and liberals would have shifted sides on the old question of federal aggrandizement, for the conservatives would be for a stronger federal role to repress dissent and crack down on militant offenders while the liberals would be resisting the growing power of the state.

Asia, race and youthful discipline are not the only issues that have a realigning potential, however. Earth Day was a symbol of what may be in the offing. A broad range of related issues concerning the quality of American life has powerful appeal to a generation that is freed, for the first time, from a constant oppressive concern with just making a living. Air pollution, water pollution, the loss of open space and the decimation of wildlife, urban congestion and ugliness, traffic snarls, racial injustice, the continuance of poverty in a land of plenty, the hucksterism of the corporate economy and its disregard for the consumer and the community at large, the loss of individuality in an institutionalized society—these are all evils capable of arousing passionate opposition, and the newer generation of reformist politicians has begun to build campaigns around them. The new affluence appears to be laying the base for a new political altruism.

Back to the 1930s

If these prove to be issues of lasting appeal—and, by their nature, they appear unlikely to go away—political dynamics will tend to produce some degree of polarization. For as half measures to deal with pollution or poverty, for example, are tried and fail, the activists will be impelled to demand the bolder measures that may succeed. These will necessarily involve more federal spending and intensified use of federal police power—until at some point the conservatives inevitably cry halt.

If it is on these issues that public sentiment polarizes and parties take their postures, then the resultant pattern would resemble the one created in the 1930s. Political quarrels would center once again on questions of Big Government, of tax levels, of federal interference with free enterprise prerogatives.

It does not take a Great Depression to make unemployment a potent political issue. A severe recession, like that of 1957–58, is enough. That downturn, and the slowness of the subsequent recovery, contributed more than any other single factor to the election of John F. Kennedy in 1960. And no one knows that better than the man who was defeated in that election, and who is now in charge of the country's economic policy.

Since Eisenhower, the two parties have come together in a common pragmatism in dealing with economic matters—inflation as well as recession—and, to a large degree, a common set of policies. There will be minor differences at any given time, which politicians will seek to exploit, but not the sharp and sustained divergence that could precipitate a party realignment. The differences that do develop could, however, reinforce a realignment that was based upon the qualitative issues involving governmental activism discussed above.

Realignments of the past have come from single overriding issues, but presumably that does not have to be the case. If multiple issues excite the electorate, as at present, the question is whether they work at cross-purposes and retard polarization or reinforce one another and assist it. And there appears to be nothing incompatible among all of the issues discussed above that would prevent their working in combination.

A two-party system that would reflect that combination can be described. A new reformist program would evolve, centering on environmental and qualitative issues but with some carry-over of New Deal–type economic measures. Racial justice would be a top objective. So would be withdrawal from Southeast Asia. So would be the defense of dissent and, within limits, of behavioral nonconformity. The opposing conservative party would temper and delay, or oppose outright, the measures of reform. And it would counterattack the activists at their weakest points: to the conservatives the activist measures of withdrawal from Asia would be measures of surrender, the activist proposals for racial justice would be proposals for favoritism and hence injustice, and the activist defense of dissent and nonconformity would be defense of violence and crime and moral deviation.

The Likely Rise of Activism

It is easier to see the Democratic Party swinging to the activist pole in such a new alignment than it is to see the Republican Party arriving at the opposite position. There is little conservative resistance left in the Democratic Party, now that the Southern realignment is approaching its completion. Even on Southeast Asia, the party has come almost the whole way since 1968 toward accepting the position of the dissident youngsters who tried so hard to wreck it then. And weakened through loss of power, the Democratic organizations in many states and localities are ripe for take-over by a new activist group with ideas, energy, time and dedication. The body of standards for party organization laid down by the McGovern committee will make such take-overs even easier.

But if the polarizing forces gain momentum on all these issues in combination, the Republican Party will offer strong resistance. It has a powerful wing committed to activism on domestic issues and to the Negro cause, and in that wing are many also committed to disentanglement in Southeast Asia. The Republican Party would not move easily to the conservative pole of a realignment involving all those issues—even though, as of today, the lure of the "Southern strategy" may be pulling it ever so slowly in that direction.

The Ripon Society: The Lost Opportunity

The three men who faced the American electorate in fall 1968 found that among many major voting blocs there was an almost unprecedented lack of party loyalty and enthusiasm. For a large portion of the public, there was a genuine need for a new Roosevelt, a forceful and dynamic leader who could fuse old antagonists into a new and vigorous coalition, as the master of Hyde Park had done in 1932. And it did not have to be a Democrat this time who put the pieces together; 1968 could have seen the formation of a new Republican majority.

But by the time the shouting had died down and the votes had been cast, the old alignments stood pretty much intact. Hubert Humphrey had brought the bulk of the labor movement back into the Democratic Party, and George Wallace turned out to have less appeal than had been hoped or feared. As for Richard Nixon, his narrow victory was almost a replay of the 1960 election. In short, the Republican Party had lost, for four years longer, its chance to secure the allegiance of a majority of American voters.

The politics-as-usual nature of the 1968 election was reflected in the failure of any of the three candidates to bring great numbers of new voters to the polls. Despite the Gallup organization's prediction of a record 75 million ballots, and despite last-minute forecasts of a close election, only 73.2 million people bothered to vote—60 percent of the 122 million Americans of voting age. This represented a substantial decrease from the 69 percent who voted in 1960, and the 64 percent who cast ballots in 1964. Of the ten largest states, all but Texas and Florida had lower percentage turn-outs in 1968 than in 1960 or 1964, and the drop-off was especially noticeable in the largest cities. In fact, the absolute nationwide total might have been smaller than in 1964 if not for the big increases in the South resulting from Negro registration and the accompanying reaction of backlash white voters. Texas, Alabama, Mississippi, and Louisiana accounted collectively for more than 1 million new votes in 1968, but the increase for the entire nation was only about 1.6 million.

In recent years, according to the best available indicators, political parties as such have been losing their hold on the electorate. Since 1940, the Gallup pollsters have been asking voters to categorize themselves by party, and the proportion of self-styled independents has been rising steadily. As a matter of fact, independents have outnumbered Republicans for the last several years.

There is no precise way to determine the number of ticket-splitters in a given election but circumstantial evidence indicates that the number is rising. For example, the number of states simultaneously electing a governor from one party and a U.S. senator from the other has risen sharply since 1946. In that year, of the twenty-four states that held both gubernatorial and senatorial elections, only one elected a Democrat to one office and a Republican to the other. In 1964, 1966, and 1968, however, a majority of such states split their choices. In 1968, the figure was nine out of fifteen, and a month after the election, the Gallup poll reported that 54 percent of the voters had split their tickets.

Another sign of the instability of party allegiance was the Wallace movement of 1968. Political analysts, such as the late V. O. Key, Jr., and Samuel Lubell, have theorized that third parties represent an effort by members of the established parties to seek out new forms of political expression. In the North as well as the South, George Wallace built a substantial following on his contention that there was not "a dime's worth of difference" between the two major parties. (Like most minor candidates, however, his strength was greatest *before* election day.)

What explains these signs of atrophy in partisan loyalties? In general, parties lose their effectiveness when the issues around which they have been built become obsolete. The major parties as presently constituted were founded around economic issues in the years of the Depression. But by 1968, the great controversies raging in America were not primarily of an economic nature. The war in Vietnam was certainly a different kind of issue, and it split both parties down the middle. Although the problems of urban decay and discrimination have obvious economic relevance, they are not intrinsically economic; rather, they reflect moral and social concerns. Therefore, much of the debate on these issues is couched in noneconomic terms—"crime in the streets," "living off welfare," "Black Power," and so on. It is more like a clash between middle-class and lower-class *cultures* than one involving the familiar question of who gets what and how much.

With these new issues have come several new kinds of political cleavages—cutting across society in new ways, creating strange bedfellows and new hostilities. One of these cleavages might be termed the status cleavage, dividing the nation into three general groupings: those with power—labor unions, big business, farmers, the technocratic elite; those desiring new power relationships—the lower classes, blacks, the student left; and those whom power has left behind—small-town residents and ethnic groups who identify with traditional values. If the two latter groups are combined, they make up a coalition that is alienated from the dominant power structure of America, and especially from the policies of the federal government, leaving labor, farmers, big business, and the technocrats on the other side of this alienation cleavage. Another major cleavage is based on the question of what to do about various kinds of deviant social groups, such as criminals, black militants, campus protesters, hippies, and pornographers. Those who advocate a hard line in dealing with such nonconformists include businessmen, union members, farmers, small-town dwellers, and lower-class ethnics; those who are apt to be more tolerant include the disadvantaged, the student left, and the liberal elements of the intellectual and techno-cratic elites. None of these new cleavages is directly related to the economic divisions of the immediate post–New Deal period.

The old economic alignments still have meaning for people in poverty, who remain attached to the Democratic Party. Conversely, the very wealthy remain Republican. But the mass of Americans in between are no longer in economic need, and have shifted their concern to questions of status and power. They are shopping for new and lasting party affiliations.

The year 1968 was an excellent opportunity for the Republican Party to attain majority status with the American electorate. In control of neither elective branch of the federal government, it could not be blamed for troubles at home or abroad. In fact, as cited above, the GOP's rating with the public had risen to stunning heights compared with the unfathomed deeps to which it had sunk in 1964. The opportunity was so great that even the Republican professionals could scarcely comprehend it.

Some 10 million Americans went shopping on election day 1968 and bought Wallace. This massive dislocation of normal voting patterns—which could have been much larger if the major-party candidates had not altered their strategies and positions in response to the third-party chal-lenge—has been the subject of much speculation. Did Wallace take votes from the Democrats, votes that may return to the Democrats and oust Richard Nixon from the White House in 1972? Or did the Alabamian take votes from the Republicans, leaving the GOP the task of wooing them back in order to hold the line? Or did Wallace have an equal effect on both parties, and on balance not influence the outcome at all?

Because Wallace derived more than half his votes from the South, and because most Southerners consider themselves Democrats, it is easy to conclude that Wallace hurt Humphrey more than Nixon. But it is doubtful that the third-party voters, in the absence of Wallace, would have rushed headlong into the arms of Hubert Humphrey. More likely, Wallace's main support came from the far less predictable breed of Southern Democrat typified by the former governor himself; certainly many who voted for Wallace had voted for the Republican presidential nominee in 1964.

When the 1968 returns are studied closely, *Wallace does not seem to have influenced the final outcome at all.* This can be demonstrated by comparing the results of the 1968 election with those of 1960. The Re-publican candidate was the same in both cases, the political complexion of the Democratic ticket was similar—and the outcomes were similar enough to virtually discount the Wallace effect. For example, consider the states that Nixon took in 1960, and those he won in 1968.

For example, consider the relationship between the states that Nixon took in 1960 and those he won in 1968, as displayed in Table 1.

Note that 35 states (Nixon's 24 plus the 11 Humphrey states Nixon lost in 1960) went to the same party in 1968 as they had eight years earlier. Furthermore, the 8 states Nixon gained in 1968 were those he had narrowly missed taking in 1960. In other words, Richard Nixon's

Table 1

Nixon's Popular Vote, 1960	Nixon States, 1968	Humphrey States, 1968	Wallace States, 1968
50.0% or more	24	2	0
49.0–49.9%	5	2	0
47.5–48.9%	3	3	0
47.4% or less	0	6	5
Total	32	13	5

harvest of states in 1968 was exactly what he would have won in 1960 had he done slightly better—*despite George Wallace.*

The Wallace impact is also minimized when one looks at Nixon's share of the two-party vote in all sections of the nation in 1960 and 1968.

Table 2

	Nixon's Two-Party Percentage, 1960	Nixon's Two-Party Percentage, 1968
Northeast	47	46
South	48	53
Midwest	53	52
Far West	51	53
Nation	50	50

Except for the South, Nixon's proportion of the two-party vote in 1968 was almost exactly what it was in 1960—*despite George Wallace.*

Nixon's popular vote had the same geographic make-up in 1960 as in 1968.

Furthermore, the geographical breakdown of the Humphrey vote was nearly identical to Kennedy's in 1960.

That is to say, each party's 1968 electoral coalition was almost identical, on a geographic basis, to what it had assembled in 1960—*despite George Wallace.*

According to the Gallup poll, only nonwhites, the grade-school educated, farmers, and Catholics shifted their major-party preferences signifi-

Table 3

	1960	1968
Northeast	30.6	29.0
South	15.6	17.5
Midwest	36.8	34.2
Far West	17.0	19.3
Total	100.0	100.0

Table 4

	Kennedy, 1960	Humphrey, 1968
Northeast	34.1	34.2
South	16.6	16.0
Midwest	33.1	32.2
Far West	16.2	17.6
Total	100.0	100.0

cantly between 1960 and 1968. But most of the major demographic groupings—whites, both sexes, the college- and high-school educated, professionals and businessmen, white-collar and manual workers, all age groups, Protestants, Republicans, Democrats, and independents—came out about the same in both years—*despite George Wallace.*

For the most part, then, Nixon and Humphrey split the nation in 1968 much as Nixon and Kennedy had split it in 1960. This suggests that George Wallace took roughly the same number of voters from each party—although perhaps half those who supported him in the early autumn but deserted him by election day seem to have been Democrats.

This last observation tells a great deal about how the electorate behaved during the final months of the campaign. In mid-August—after the Republican convention, but before the Democratic meeting—Richard Nixon received a 45 percent rating in the Gallup poll, his highest since December 1967 (when he was paired against Lyndon Johnson, without Wallace). Even after the debacle in Chicago, however, Nixon slipped back to 43 percent, his high of the previous spring (against Humphrey and Wallace). From then until election day, he deviated no more than one percentage point from that rating. In the aggregate, all the action was between the Humphrey column, the Wallace column, and those who listed themselves as undecided. Though the Republican campaign may have been successful in its specific appeals to potential Wallace voters, it lost one vote to the Democrats for every one it picked up from Wallace. (This is not too surprising, considering what had to be done to attract Wallace's admirers.) Similarly, for every vote the GOP ticket won from the undecideds, it also lost one of its own to the Humphrey-Muskie team. And for every vote Richard Nixon won directly from Hubert Humphrey, Humphrey won one right back. (See Table 5.)

Table 5   Gallup Poll Figures for the Last Three Months of the Campaign

Date	Nixon	Humphrey	Wallace	Undecided
August 8–11	45	29	18	8
September 3–7	43	31	19	7
September 20–22	43	28	21	8
September 27–30	44	29	20	7
October 3–12	43	31	20	6
October 17–21	44	36	15	5
October 31– November 2	42	40	14	4
November 5 (actual)	43.4	42.7	13.5	

While the Nixon-Agnew ticket remained paralyzed at the 43 percent level, the Democrats chipped away at the American Independent Party's following, getting almost one third of this vote and all those who were undecided.* The old F.D.R. coalition had enough resiliency and tenacity after all to resist attacks by both Richard Nixon and George Wallace. As Richard M. Scammon, former head of the Bureau of the Census and now with the Governmental Affairs Institute, put it:

> The old Democratic coalition was not dead this year, except in the South. The Negroes, the Jews, the intellectuals, and much of labor remained loyal.

Scammon added, "But 1968 could be the coalition's last hurrah." During the 1968 campaign, however, neither Richard Nixon nor Hubert Humphrey had the nerve to roll the corpse into the grave and cover it up. The "old politics" of voting still prevailed in 1968 in the labor force, the suburbs, and even—despite Wallace's strong showing—the South.

---

* Again, this only represents what happened in the aggregate; the Gallup poll reported that "As many as 19 million voters (i.e., one quarter of the total) said they had at some point during the campaign intended to vote for a candidate other than the one they ended up voting for."

Organized labor is perhaps the most obvious example of a group once vitally concerned with economic issues, but now affluent enough to worry about such special questions as the race of the man next door and the deleterious effects of the welfare system on the nation's moral fiber. Therefore, this group was seen as the prime target for Wallace's appeals in the North—the celebrated backlash vote. Nixon assumed that by taking a relatively hard line on social issues, he could share these Democratic defectors with Wallace. What he forgot was the lesson of 1964—that a backlash appeal to the blue-collar vote will fail unless the candidate guarantees a continuation of the economic security that made this bloc susceptible to the backlash in the first place. And in 1968, as in most years, the Republicans fell short in this regard. Not always on merit, the Democrats succeeded in identifying themselves with such beneficial programs as Medicare and Social Security, and with a strong pro-labor philosophy.

According to Gallup, the Republicans have taken the following share of the union vote in recent presidential elections. (See Table 6.)

Table 6

1936–48	less than 30%
1952	39%
1956	43
1960	35
1964	27
1968	29

Nixon's 1968 share of the union vote dropped six percentage points from 1960, and (because Humphrey won 56 percent of this vote) he even netted less (34 percent) of the two-party union vote in 1968 than eight years before. And significantly, from early October to November 5, Humphrey (according to Gallup) picked up fifteen percentage points with the union vote.

In September 1968, the Gallup poll reported that Nixon and Humphrey were dividing manual laborers about evenly, each getting about one third, with Wallace getting one fourth and the rest undecided. On election day, however, one half of the manual labor vote went Democratic, and only a little more than one third stayed with Nixon. Indeed, Nixon's share of the two-party labor vote was up only one percentage point from 1960, despite the fact that George Wallace was supposed to draw many union members away from the Democratic column. Clearly, a magnificent opportunity to capture a major element of the Democratic coalition had been lost.

Much of the labor-backlash stereotype also includes the Roman Catholics, and a number of commentators have noted Nixon's sharp improvement over the Republican share of this vote in the past two elections. Of this there is no doubt, but when Nixon's 1968 showing is compared to Dwight D. Eisenhower's share of the Catholic vote, it is less impressive. (See Table 7.)

Table 7   GOP Share of Catholic Vote

1952	44%	
1956	49	
1960	22	
1964	24	
1968	33	(36% of two-party vote)

Nixon's percentage falls roughly halfway between the highs of the 1950's and the lows of the 1960's. It is highly misleading to suggest that the Catholic vote is going Republican to any significant extent, especially because the improvement may have been the result of the large numbers of Catholics who are joining the middle class. According to NBC's national precinct samples, even the Italians, the most Republican of all Catholic nationality groups, gave a majority of their vote to Humphrey.

Another economically liberated group with "swing" potential in 1968 was the suburbanites, who held the balance of power in several major states. Suburban voters supplied both Nelson Rockefeller and Eugene McCarthy with pre-convention support, and they were willing to cross party lines both ways for an appealing candidate.

By November 1968, these voters apparently realized that no such candidate remained in the race. Though *Time, Newsweek,* and *U.S. News and World Report* all noted a decline in the Republican share of the suburban two-party vote, it seems clear that the suburbs did not deviate very far from their 1960 performance. Take, for example, Nixon's showing in the counties surrounding New York City. (See Table 8.)

As with so many other groups, it was 1960 all over again for these suburbs.

The South has been a tempting target for Republican strategists for the last twenty years. Over this period, its electoral votes have been divided as shown in Table 9.

Generally, Republicans have sought to woo Southern voters with two approaches. One, the Eisenhower-Nixon strategy, was to aim at the more populous states of the so-called peripheral South (Florida, Kentucky, North Carolina, Tennessee, Texas, and Virginia), emphasizing a philosophical conservatism likely to appeal to the new business and professional

Table 8

	Nixon %, 1960	Nixon Two-Party %, 1968
Bergen, New Jersey	59	58
Essex, New Jersey	44	43
Fairfield, Connecticut	54	55
Hudson, New Jersey	39	41
Nassau, New York	55	54
Orange, New York	61	62
Rockland, New York	55	53
Suffolk, New York	59	64
Union, New Jersey	51	50
Westchester, New York	57	54

Table 9

	Democratic	Republican	Other
1948	99	0	39 (Thurmond)
1952	81	57	0
1956	60	77	1 (Jones)
1960	81	43	14 (Byrd)
1964	90	47	0
1968	25	66	46 (Wallace)

elite. The other approach, used by Barry Goldwater, was built on opposition to a strong federal civil-rights program and achieved its greatest success in the Deep South. As Goldwater discovered, the Deep South strategy is likely to cost the candidate the peripheral South (because of the rising black vote, overriding economic considerations, and a stubborn Democratic tradition), and the rest of the country as well.

This year, by following the first approach, the GOP candidate was able to increase his share of the major-party vote in the South over his 1960 showing, and his electoral votes as well. This was undoubtedly owing in large part to the absence of a Southerner on the Democratic ticket, and perhaps to Strom Thurmond's maneuverings in the Carolinas. But here again, Nixon gained few converts during the campaign, as shown by the Gallup figures for September and the final result. When the aggregate vote is considered, Humphrey appears to have picked up the bulk of the Wallace waverers and the undecided voters.

Republicans could view Nixon's performance in the South with complacency if it were not for his failure among two key groups within the region—blacks and Latin Americans. The NBC national-precinct sample indicated that Humphrey won more than 90 percent of both groups in the

Table 10

	Nixon	Humphrey	Wallace	Undecided
September	33	21	38	8
Election	35	31	33	

South (and more than 90 percent of *all* blacks in America). This is particularly significant because more and more members of these groups are being enrolled as voters each year; these groups are unquestionably responsible in large part for the fact that, although the percentage turnout of voters dropped during the 1960's in the nation as a whole, it rose in the South.

Table 11

	1960 Turnout	1964 Turnout	1968 Turnout
Alabama	31%	36%	51%
Arkansas	41	50	51
Florida	50	53	56
Georgia	30	43	44
Kentucky	59	53	51
Louisiana	45	47	54
Mississippi	25.5	33	50
North Carolina	53.5	52	54
South Carolina	30.5	38	46
Tennessee	50	51	53
Texas	42	44	49
Virginia	33	41	50

In the South, as in so many other parts of the nation, the Republicans failed to capture many voters who might have made a change. Furthermore, the GOP in 1968 seemed to lose contact with the newest groups in the electorate.

The Republican candidate in 1968 failed to take advantage of the numerous opportunities for party realignment that existed earlier in the year.

Though the GOP has been a minority party since the Depression, it seems unwilling or unable to take the steps necessary to broaden its appeal. And so it has left many disaffected members of the old Democratic coalition to wander, disappointed, back into the fold. A question remains, one that confronted the Republican presidential nominee this year and one that confronts all GOP candidates: What kinds of issues are likely to appeal to such diverse groups as union laborers, suburbanites, and Southerners (and which Southerners, black or white, urban or rural)?

At a minimum, it seems obvious that a Republican candidate must not:

1. **Appear too conservative on economic, bread-and-butter issues** He must not, in short, fit the usual Republican stereotype of being pro-big business, antilabor, antiminimum wage, and anti-Medicare. This should enable him to get his foot in the door with union labor.

2. **Appear too militant on foreign-policy issues** The swing vote in the suburbs is sensitive to these issues. With their high educational level, the suburbanites have been the key group to turn against the Vietnam war, and they comprise a highly internationalist segment of society. A return to cold-war clichés is likely to alienate them.

3. **Appear too unsympathetic to equal rights** The Southerners who voted Republican in 1956 and 1960 obviously remained in the party despite its moderately pro-civil-rights position (for the period). And if this group were combined with enough of the newly enfranchised black and Latin American voters, the Republicans could expect to carry the larger states of the South for many elections to come.

Before a candidate can hope to appeal for a specific bloc's votes, he must prove that he has its members' "gut" interests in mind. Republicans can use sophisticated, collateral approaches to seal the loyalty of a group ready to be persuaded, but if GOP candidates fail to demonstrate sympathy for a bloc's primary concerns, efforts at secondary appeals will not be accepted as having been made in good faith. Nixon's cries for law and order did not captivate union members, because he still looked too much like the candidate of big business—with his Wall Street letter suggesting a lenient approach to securities regulation, and his expressed willingness to keep the oil-depletion allowance (which even Wallace sporadically opposed). His sophisticated radio addresses on such subjects as the nature of the Presidency and new political alignments failed to win many intellectuals and suburbanites because he was coy about the war in Vietnam— to them the paramount issue. Nixon's proposals for black capitalism fell on deaf ears in the black community because he was Strom Thurmond's candidate and because the concept appealed more to worried whites than to poor blacks. Civil rights is one issue that unites all Negroes, but less was said on the subject in this election—by either major party—than in any presidential campaign of this decade.

Richard Nixon's strategy of noncommitment failed, according to practically all available data, to increase the Republican share of the two-party vote over 1960. (The only group with which Nixon did relatively well was the farmers. But they are declining in numbers, and have a notorious tendency to vote against the incumbent party. Orville Freeman probably delivered the farm bloc to Nixon in 1968; in 1972 Orville Freeman will not be around to help.)

But when all is said and done, the question of how to attract the wavering voters is probably not merely a question of issues. Political analysts were struck this year by a number of seemingly illogical phenomena: hawks voting for McCarthy; Robert Kennedy supporters winding up with Wallace; and similar developments. The reason seemed to be a respect for a man's style and courage rather than his position on specific issues.

Perhaps what the voters of 1968 were really seeking was a man of strong personal charisma—regardless of his stands on issues. Richard Nixon, dealing in platitudes, and Hubert Humphrey, beating the Administration's drums, simply did not fill the bill. Humphrey was finally able to lure the disenchanted by raising old specters, showing some spunk, and making a few gestures to the left. The bland campaign of Richard Nixon lured few new voters.

Samuel Lubell, who usually deprecates the importance of issues in American elections, commented in mid-October: "No candidate can hope to create the image of a leader who inspires trust and confidence unless he discusses the critical issues in specific detail." Continuing, Lubell wondered if "Nixon's 'play-it-safe' campaigning may not cause him to muff a historical opportunity . . . to develop and articulate a program of action around which the quiet, moderate majority in the country can rally."

And so it was in 1968, with the triumph of a lost opportunity to assemble a new American majority.

Gerald M. Pomper: Census '70:
Power to the Suburbs

Like a souvenir photograph, the national Census often captures a critical moment in the passage of time. Permanently recorded every 10 years, the Census can serve as an official testament to the trends of American history. In 1890, for example, the Census marked the authoritative end to the frontier, for there was no longer an unbroken line of new settlement

---

From "Census '70: Power to the Suburbs," by Gerald M. Pomper, *The Washington Monthly*, Vol. 2, Number 3, May 1970. Copyright © 1970 by The Washington Monthly Company. Reprinted by permission.

in the West. In 1920, the nation's transformation into an urban civilization was made clear by the population figures which showed, for the first time, that a majority of the population had deserted its rural roots.

The 1970 Census will record another major transformation of America. The nation is now suburban: the residents of split-level America are now the largest residential group in the population. The special importance of this Census is that, because of the series of court decisions on reapportionment, suburban numbers will be quickly translated into suburban voting power. Earlier Censuses, by contrast, were frequently ignored in the allocation of legislative seats. After the 1920 Census, for example, Congress denied the urban areas their voting majority by refusing to reallocate its seats. Similarly, the state legislatures were under no compulsion, until the one-man, one-vote decisions, to allocate their seats on the basis of population. Much reapportionment has, of course, already taken place, but it has been on the basis of the 1960 Census. Now the legislatures will have to be reshuffled on the basis of the 1970 figures, and the result will be suburban predominance in the House and in the legislatures of most of the important states.

Suburban Congressmen will be the largest geographical group in the House. In an analysis of Congressional districts based on the Census, Professor Richard Lehne of Rutgers University foresees 129 Members from the suburbs, and 62 more from mixed city-suburban districts. The central cities will have 100 Representatives, and the non-metropolitan areas, 37. Compared to the situation before the court decisions, the central cities will have lost half a dozen seats and the non-metropolitan areas 144. Ironically, the cities will lose voting power because of court decisions they actively sought. On the assumption that malapportionment was particularly detrimental to urban interests, city Representatives were active in bringing suits, in passing new districting legislation, and in resisting attempted rollbacks like the Dirksen Amendment. Having won their battle, the cities are now discovering they were fighting the wrong war. It was the suburbs not the cities that were underrepresented in the House, and it is the suburbs that have gained power, from rural areas and cities alike, as a result of the one-man, one-vote decisions.

Blacks are the one urban group that may gain political power through the new Census. The 1970 count will show blacks to be an increased portion of the nation—between 11 and 12 percent, compared to one-tenth in 1960. A majority of this black population will be found outside of the South, and principally in the big cities, which can provide a base of political power. Direct municipal control by blacks has been shown to be possible in Cleveland and Gary, and the importance of the non-white vote for white mayors was demonstrated in John Lindsay's reelection in New York. More blacks will also be elected to Congress from these areas. Total urban representation in Congress will shrink, making it more difficult to gerry-mander districts to preserve white majorities. The likely tendency will be to concentrate the ghetto areas within the same Congressional districts and concede the seats to the blacks.

This tendency has already been evident in recent redistricting. When new lines were drawn in New York, the black ghetto of Bedford-Stuyvesant in Brooklyn, previously splintered among the surrounding areas, was concentrated into a new district which elected Mrs. Shirley Chisholm, a black. The latest plan in that state also provides for a Puerto Rican seat constructed of parts of three counties. In St. Louis, previously split among three city-suburban constituencies, urban areas were combined to provide a district from which William Clay was elected as the first black Congressman from Missouri.

Throughout the nation, it is easy to forecast a substantial increase in the number of non-white Congressmen, although the number will remain far below the proportion of blacks in the population. According to the 1960 Census, the present nine black members of the House all come from districts with a majority of Negro residents. A number of other urban districts were then reported as having a 40 percent black population, and this number is likely to be substantially increased in the 1970 enumeration, providing a base for new black representation. A new Negro Representative is certain to be elected this year from Chicago, in addition to a replacement for retiring William Dawson. Others are quite likely soon from Baltimore, Detroit, Newark, New York, and Philadelphia. Altogether, there are 20 districts outside of the South with a black population over 30 percent, all of which are likely sources of new black Representatives in 1970.

Proportional representation for blacks in the Congress will not be achieved, however, until they win seats from the South. The barriers against such representation are stronger than in the Northern cities, but the considerable increase in black voting following the 1965 Voting Rights Act makes it possible. Three Southern districts, as drawn in 1960, had a black majority, and 30 others had at least a 30 percent black proportion in the total population.

Any urban gains by blacks will, however, appear only within the larger framework of an overall loss of power to the suburbs. If the suburbs call the tune, the music is not likely to sooth urban ears. Some preliminary notes have already been heard. In the reapportioned New Jersey legislature, Governor Richard J. Hughes tried to initiate special programs to aid Newark and other poor and riot-torn cities. By the time the suburban-dominated legislature got through with the Governor's program, the new aid benefited the affluent suburbs more than impoverished cities. In New York, the state legislature has refused to provide any significant amount of help for the New York City subways, which carry two million urban passengers a day, although it is willing to underwrite the losses of the Long Island Railroad, which brings 100,000 commuters to and from their suburban homes. In Michigan and California, relief for the property tax payer, usually suburban, is a popular cause; relief for the city-dwelling poor is not.

Suburban-controlled legislatures will spend money for purposes other than those favored by the cities. Education is the largest and most popular expenditure for suburbanites, and they will seek to increase their states' shares of this expense. While city residents need funds for education, they also desperately need aid for welfare, hospitals, housing, and law enforcement. In the clash of interests, spending for suburban education is likely to win over spending for urban welfare. Similarly, suburban programs for tax reform emphasize middle-class needs such as deductions for college tuition or user fees and tolls. Relief of low-income taxpayers is likely to be neglected. Furthermore, when urban aid is provided, suburban legislators can be relied upon to insure that these programs are not financed by their constituents—as through a tax on commuters—but by the urban residents themselves, through sales taxes, higher transit fares, and the like.

Similar results can be expected in Congress. The upcoming issues will be those with which suburban legislators can identify. Stress will be placed on education, inter-city transportation by road and rail, and environmental pollution. There is little reason to expect much pressure for public housing, a "Marshall Plan" for the ghettos, direct subsidy of city mass transit, or guaranteed employment for the poor and the black. Significantly, the Model Cities program has been broadened to make suburban areas eligible for assistance.

The main hope for the cities in a suburb-dominated political order lies in the fact that the suburbanites cannot, much as they might like to, entirely disown their poor urban relations. In some major issues of public policy, suburb and city are as indissolubly joined as Siamese twins. One twin contracts a disorder and, when it spreads to his brother, the second twin will have to help the first in order to help himself. Two current examples are air pollution and drug addiction. Air pollution is not new in cities; it has become politically significant because sulphurous breezes are now blowing over the green suburbs. Similarly, drug addiction has been prevalent in New York City for a quarter of a century, but it did not become a national issue until heroin invaded the sheltered schools of Westchester. In neither of these cases can the suburbs achieve their own goals without helping the cities. If they do not want their air to be poisoned, the suburbs will have to appropriate the money to control pollution at its urban source. And they will have to grapple with the fact that heroin cannot be kept out of the suburbs as long as their children can easily buy drugs on the streets of the cities.

Suburban power will influence the way both politics and government are conducted. In politics, the prospect is for a continuing decline in the strength of party organization. The organization is typically less disciplined and effective in middle-class areas which neither need nor want the traditional rewards of patronage. The suburban style is far more ideological and issue-oriented, as seen in both the Goldwater and McCarthy campaigns, which drew many suburban activists who had little loyalty to either party as such. More legislative districts will become competitive, with fewer safe Republican seats from the countryside and safe Democratic seats from the sidewalks. On the whole, the Republicans are likely to make a net gain, as Republican rural and Democratic urban districts are converted into suburban seats that more often than not vote Republican.

In Congress, the new suburban plurality will add muscle to movements for reform of the structure of the House. Congressmen from suburban districts are not likely to accept indefinitely a gerontocratic power structure based on safe city and rural seats (e.g., Speaker John McCormack and Democratic Majority Leader Carl Albert). Given the political style of their districts, suburban Representatives will feel less beholden to their weak party organizations than to the issues on which they were elected, and on which, in competitive districts, they can easily be defeated if they do not deliver. The seniority system has little appeal to a Congressman from a suburban district in contrast to the city or rural newcomer who sees his ultimate reward in lifetime loyalty to the organization that put him in office. These trends are already evident in the present House, where suburban districts supply a disproportionate number of the rebels in both parties: New York's Allard K. Lowenstein of Nassau County and Ogden Reid of Westchester are examples. The Congress which is elected in 1972 will undoubtedly have more such rebels, whichever party wins a majority. Ironically, the rebellion against seniority may be to the detriment of black Congressmen. Since blacks are typically elected from safe seats, they stand to gain from seniority: at one time two of the four black Congressmen, William Dawson of Chicago and Adam Clayton Powell of New York, were committee chairmen.

The shift in power toward the suburbs will help to meet some goals of the "good government" movements. Structural improvements and efficient administration are middle-class reforms likely to appeal to suburban legislators. Revised constitutions, increased civil-service coverage, and modern budgeting procedures are apt to be adopted in the redistricted legislatures. Reduction of rural political power will also probably lessen the imposition of rural morality on a state's citizens. The current movement toward liberalization of abortion and divorce laws, abolition of the death penalty, and easing of pornography statutes can be partially attributed to the more cosmopolitan disposition of the new suburban plurality.

Despite some such hopeful signs, the general effect of the Census is to give added power to people who have been unwilling to support major innovations in governmental policy. The continuing westward shift of population will benefit conservative politicians. More votes will be cast in Ronald Reagan's California, Lyndon Johnson's Texas, and Barry Goldwater's Arizona. The East, except for Florida, will lose votes and power. Sawing off the Eastern seaboard will be a more popular platform than when Goldwater first proposed it in 1964. All in all, those who will gain power from the Census do not seem to be people likely to be inspired by the onset of the third century of the American Revolution.

Richard N. Goodwin: The New Politics

The agency through which we can hope to formulate new policies is that strange American contraption, the political party. My own repository of hopes for change is the Democratic Party, for the Republicans seem unlikely to discard their historical role as defenders of things as they are. Since Nixon's victory, political men have begun to discuss the future of the Democratic Party. Such discussion must come to grips with one essential fact: There is no Democratic Party. There is the party of Daley in Illinois and the party of the county leaders in New York. There is the fragile alliance of liberals and leaders in California, and there is Kennedy in Massachusetts. In the South, there is almost nothing left at all. It is a truism to state that American political parties are not ideological in nature, since they embrace many diverse groups. Still, in the past most elements of the Democratic Party agreed on certain broad goals and assumptions. There was, with some dissent, general agreement on the economic goals of the New Deal. It was broadly assumed that the Democratic Party represented the disadvantaged and the poor against the great interests, and that it stood for alliance and tolerance in world affairs. There was, in other words, a base of generally accepted belief and emotional attitude. That this has largely dissolved becomes clear when we compare the parties of Daley, Meany, McCarthy, and Kennedy. The cause of the dissolution is

---

From "Sources of Public Unhappiness," by Richard N. Goodwin. *The New Yorker Magazine,* January 4, 1969. Copyright © 1969 by Richard N. Goodwin. Reprinted by permission of The Sterling Lord Agency, Inc.

that the issues of the past thirty years have lost their vitality. The consequence is that the Democratic Party is little more than an institutional
mechanism through which individuals hope to acquire public office. If the
Democratic Party has a future, it will come not by raising more money or
by hiring better advertising agencies but by developing a purpose and a
program. I have outlined some of the possible elements of purpose and
policy in support of which it might be possible to create a new, progressive
coalition to replace the alliance of minorities, labor, and the South which
has now fragmented and dissolved. The South has left; labor no longer
exists as a coherent electoral force, having divided into upper and lower
middle class; and the minorities are often at each other's throat. A new
coalition will have to be made up of the populations of the inner cities,
including some lower-income whites, and of the new suburbs inhabited by
those who work in offices, electronics factories, and so on. This is the
coalition that both Kennedy and McCarthy were trying to build, with Mc-
Carthy moving inward from the suburbs and Kennedy outward from the
inner city. Neither quite got across the bridge, but the fact that their
divergent constituencies responded to men who stood for enlightened and
progressive change is evidence that the possibilities of coalition are there.
However, the issues that will unite these groups are not only traditional
economic concerns—although there are specific economic problems that
must be met—but issues of the type I have set forth. For example, both in
the ghettos and in the suburbs there is a desire for increased control and
power over local affairs and public policy. If I am right in the belief that
such desires respond to deeply felt national needs, then failure to move in
this direction will leave public-spirited men with no alternative but to try
to form a new party to combat the forces of repression.

Finally, a few words of unsolicited advice to the next President. Since
we need fundamental changes in public policy, it would be a serious mistake to begin the work of the next Administration in the traditional way:
preparing budgets and policies for programs neatly tailored to old categories such as health, housing, and conservation. For the assumption of
fundamental change is that the old categories and ways of looking at
problems are no longer valid and that the structure of government itself
is the threshold barrier to new approaches and policies. The powers of
the Department of Housing and Urban Development, for example, are
fashioned and limited in such a way that the Department cannot hope to
deal with the problems of the city, however vigorous its leadership. The
first task of a new Administration should be to construct institutions with
authority and jurisdiction adapted to the policies they are to administer,
and to concern itself with reallocating responsibility within the federal
system. The secret of Roosevelt's success was his willingness to ignore or
dismantle existing structures and to set up new ones, shaped to his pur-

poses. Freud said that "anatomy is destiny." In government, structure is policy. If the existing structure of government is accepted, then serious change rapidly becomes impossible as bureaucracies, administrators, and ongoing programs begin to generate their inevitable and almost irresistible drive for survival. It is important to make structural changes early, and not only because a President is far more likely to have the necessary power at the beginning of his administration. The appointment of Cabinet officers, administrators, and even task forces immediately creates powerful vested interests. When a man becomes the chief of a large department, he assumes a new constituency of workers and bureaus, authority and appropriations. His natural urge, reinforced by the need to keep the loyalty of his subordinates, is to maintain his domain relatively intact and to minimize disruption and controversy. Thus, the Department of Labor under President Johnson fought against the poverty program, with some success, simply because it felt that it was the proper repository of such an effort. Examples could be multiplied. It would be a great mistake to misjudge the rapidity with which new men develop loyalties to old patterns, or the ability of an established bureaucracy to frustrate the most determined of Presidential designs. That is why the fundamentals of structure must be determined before operations begin if there is to be a serious and effective effort to chart new directions for public policy. This is little more than counsel to "think big," not in terms of huge expenditures or sweeping new programs but in terms of the hardest kind of innovation: liberating the public imagination from old categories, concepts, and structures. Our present inclination to look upon every national ill as a subject for federal action within the framework of existing departments is like trying to devise a way to go to the moon by putting a man in an automobile. We need not only new institutions but a fresh sense of which matters are appropriate to public action, and of where, within the federal system, responsibility and power should be vested.

Beyond such concrete and practical acts, there is a need to explore the deeper causes of our discontent. Again, as in the eighteen-fifties, we can sense that we are at the beginning of a new age—or, rather, a new way of living—which is forcing its values and demands on a society not equipped to cope with them. This kind of dislocation, this gap between realities and custom, is characteristic of revolutionary historical periods. To pursue this analogy, the insulation and barrenness of the modern suburb are counterparts of the misery that enveloped the mid-nineteenth-century factory, and Mayor Daley is at one with the Southern agrarian in defending a system that history will find not to have been an unmixed evil. Without judging the efforts of men like Marshall McLuhan to abstract a single, seminal cause from the complexities of social change, we can agree with many that the ascendancy of technology is a principal feature of modern society. To that we must add growth, both of population and of our physical artifacts, such as houses, factories, and roads. The problem, however, is not technological but ideological. We are threatened not by our creations but by our beliefs. In another place, I have written, "All nations . . . are governed on the basis of ideas and values . . . which are not derived either from the necessities of nature or the command of God. If a man snatches his hand from a hot stove, that is not ideological. If he then decrees there shall be no more hot stoves in order to prevent burning, he has imposed an ideology (and one wholly alien to our own)." There is, for example, nothing in the development of the automobile which makes the clogging of our cities and the poisoning of our air logically inevitable. It is simply that we have preferred these consequences—perhaps without anticipating them—to restrictions on the use of automobiles.

No one has more bluntly stated the inward passion of the time than Lewis Strauss, who summed up the faith of two centuries when he was asked if nuclear physics might not have overstepped itself. "No," he answered. "I would not wipe out any part of it, not the bomb nor any other part of it, if I could. I believe everything man discovers, however he discovers it, is welcome and good for his future. In me this is the sort of belief that people go to the stake for." This is not a reasoned formula but an affirmation of an ideological belief verging on the mystical. Guided by such a belief, our society has developed virtually no mechanism for weighing technological change against the social consequences and enforcing its judgment. Only the great religious institutions engage in a similar process, and then, as in the case of Pope Paul and the pill, they are condemned because the values they seek to defend have lost their hold on men. This is not the place to pursue such philosophical abstractions. Yet they are at the heart of the problem. In political terms, we are barred from much effective action because we have not regarded human values—except for those related to survival, civil liberty, and prosperity—as appropriate objects of public protection. This reluctance to allow government to become concerned with the quality of individual life has its historical roots in a healthy fear of the state and a desire to insure secular liberty. It now works against us, having been outdistanced by our material circumstances. Thus, traditional principles of private enterprise join with modern construction technology to create suburban blight. But there is no inherent reason a builder should not be under as much compulsion to provide open spaces, parks, and community centers as he is to provide safe wiring and sound structures. We can also maintain that clear air and freedom of movement are as important to us as the economic advantages of urban concentration. On a broader scale, we need to reëxamine all our institutions in order to determine whether what they do *for* people is worth what they do *to* them. This is not an easy job, especially since we must often match abstract or felt values against the formulations of logic and numbers. How, for example, does one explain an instinctive revulsion against the idea of a national computer center to store all the available information about every citizen, except to say that neatness and system and organization can be oppressive in themselves, and to draw upon our experience of human weakness to assert that increasing the capacity for control will increase the likelihood of control?

This kind of ideological reformation will not be easy for a people as little inclined to theory as our own. It will come, if it does come, in the context of relieving particular afflictions. Still, there is no other way that we can guide ourselves between the twin perils of uncontrollable turbulence and repression. We will be strengthened by the fact that such change corresponds to deeply felt human wants, many of which are manifesting themselves in our present disorders.

3

The Presidency: The Nature of the Office

For almost 150 years, in peace and in war, the American people have turned to their presidents for national leadership. In the process they have heaped upon the presidency enormous authority. From the days of Andrew Jackson—tribune of the people—through Lincoln, Theodore Roosevelt, Woodrow Wilson, and Franklin D. Roosevelt, we have idolized the power-seeking presidents and dismissed the Pierces, Buchanans, and Hardings as men who were unworthy of the office and thus of the American people. Our praise of "strong" presidents and the consequent dismissal of the "weak" presidents has been somewhat justified. Generally the strong presidents have been those who increased presidential powers to satisfy popular demands for a more democratic and just society. Indeed the failure of presidents to seek increased powers has become the single most important criterion for judging presidential weakness. When the Union was imperiled on the eve of the Civil War, we faulted Buchanan for saying that there was nothing he could constitutionally do to preserve the Union. Similarly, we faulted Hoover for his palliatives during the Depression in 1932. Again and again Americans have made it clear that they want a strong president, one who will promote their causes against the vested domestic interests— the "hydra-headed monsters" and "economic royalists" against whom Jackson and FDR so successfully flailed. In foreign affairs the rise of presidential power has been even more spectacular. Who can forget the glorious assertions of an independent presidential power in foreign affairs—Jefferson and the Louisiana Purchase, the Monroe Doctrine, McKinley and the Boxer Rebellion, Wilson's forays against Pancho Villa, FDR proclaiming the Atlantic Charter, the Truman Doctrine, and the Eisenhower Doctrine? Even a president's losses in foreign affairs can leave him with honor; witness the ignominious defeat of Woodrow Wilson by a "little group of willful men."

There have been negative critics of the expanding presidency, but by and large they have been dismissed either as cranks or because their motives were suspect. For example, it was difficult to accept seriously the charges of possible executive tyranny as a justification for denying presidential programs aimed at solving the economic plight of the farmer in the 1930s. Occasionally, respected scholars raised fundamental questions about the extent of presidential power, for example, the late Edward S. Corwin. However, the limited scholarly attention devoted to the presidency within the past twenty-five years has generally mirrored the confidence and trust of the American people in the office. Former President Johnson's view of the presidency, presented here, is not atypical of the nonpresidential views of what constitutes a strong and popularly oriented modern president. Though the rhetoric is sometimes heavy, Lyndon Johnson's message is clear—the president is the embodiment of the American people and is the steward of present and future generations; Johnson seemed to believe all the hopes of Americans could be heard and acted on by the president. This is in sharp contrast to Nixon's preelection view of the office: While he noted that the president alone represented all of the American people, still he warned that a president should be more realistic and presumably more circumspect about the promises he makes to the people. While as president he has continued the traditions of strong presidential leadership in foreign affairs, Nixon's preelection view of the office was a reasonably accurate forecast of his more limited view of the presidency on the domestic scene.

While the personal ideology of an incumbent president may well help to shape his particular view of presidential power, Thomas E. Cronin's article suggests that regardless of who is president there is an oversimplified notion that a president stands at the very center of power. Cronin's analysis of the office raises serious questions about the confidence and trust we have traditionally placed in the presidency. While he does not appear to be calling for a wholesale retreat from presidential government, he does point out the constraints within which a president necessarily acts.

Cronin's article suggests that it is no longer fashionable to uncritically recite a litany of presidential powers. This may imply some erosion in popular confidence in the presidency. Surely the war in Vietnam and the subsequent publication of the so-called Pentagon Papers raise serious questions about the independence and accountability of the president, particularly in foreign affairs. The contrasting positions are fully detailed in the testimony and statements of Nicholas deB. Katzenbach, Senator William Fulbright, and Representative Paul McCloskey. At the heart of the issue is the assumed constitutional competence of the presidency to operate secretly and independently of the Congress and the public, a competence that mere men can rarely be expected to possess. Indeed, George Reedy, former White House advisor to President Johnson, suggests that the atmosphere of the White House even under the strongest presidents is dangerously similar to a king's court, with all the attendant isolation from political and social reality. Such an isolated atmosphere is hardly the proper place to locate independent and unaccountable authority, particularly if the authority can commit the vast human and economic resources of the nation.

Some believe the presidency faces a crisis of confidence today. The crisis will not, however, result in the dismantling of the institution; the president will not become a mere appendage of Congress, and it is not likely that the office will decline in importance. On the contrary, if the past is prologue, the presidency will continue to enlarge. As we continue to confer new authority on the president and make additional expectations of the office, we ought to reflect that the White House has been populated far more by the Buchanans, Arthurs, Hardings, and (Andrew) Johnsons than it has been by the Washingtons, Lincolns, and Roosevelts. Americans have never taken kindly to Lord Bryce's comment in 1883 that we only infrequently select great men as presidents. Yet over the next decade, as the presidency expands, Lord Bryce's observation ought to be remembered.

Lyndon B. Johnson: The Presidency and the People

On the thirtieth day of April, in the year Seventeen Hundred and Eighty-nine, on the balcony of the Federal Hall in New York City, George Washington took the oath as the first President of the United States of America.

In the one hundred and seventy-five years since that occasion, thirty-five other Americans have sworn that same oath and entered that same office to discharge in seamless continuity the duties prescribed by the Constitution.

Individual incumbents are remembered individually according to the challenges and responses of their tenure. But the office itself has long since come to transcend its occupants. The Presidency has made every man who occupied it, no matter how small, bigger than he was; and no matter how big, not big enough for its demands. It has served as symbol of the spirit,

Excerpts from a Presidential Proclamation, April 30, 1964; remarks at Wilkes-Barre, Pennsylvania, October 14, 1964; and at a reception for the American Society of Newspaper Editors, April 17, 1964. *Public Papers of the Presidents of the United States: Lyndon B. Johnson,* Vols. 1–2, Government Printing Office, 1965.

purposes and aspirations of the American nation in this land and in lands far beyond these shores.

Ordained to serve a nation of fewer than four million inhabitants, the American Presidency will before its two hundredth anniversary be serving a country of more than two hundred million inhabitants, living together in the most successful society yet created and sustained on this earth.

In this achievement, it has been the will of the people that the office of the American Presidency be used in the work of perfecting our national unity, establishing justice, insuring domestic tranquility, providing for the common defense, promoting the general welfare, and securing the Blessings of Liberty to ourselves and our posterity by seeking a world of peace, freedom and opportunity.

The office of the Presidency is, as one President described it, "preeminently the people's office." The President himself is, in the words of another President, "the steward of the public welfare." While it has become custom, outside the original concept of the Constitution, for Presidents to be chosen from candidacies offered by political parties, the office itself and the conduct of that office remain today, as at the inception, national and not partisan, serving all the people without regard to party affiliations or philosophical persuasions.

Americans know that the Presidency belongs to all the people. And they want the President to act and be President of all the people.

Something else is very clear. The source of the President's authority is the people. A President who refuses to go out among the people, who refuses to be judged by the people, who is unwilling to lay his case before the people, can never be President of all the people.

The people want to see their President in person. They want to hear first-hand what he believes. They want to decide if he can act for them.

And unless the President goes to the people, unless he visits and talks with them, unless he senses how they respond as he discusses issues with them, he cannot do the President's job. The voice of the people will be lost among the clamor of divisions and diversities, and the Presidency will not become a clear beacon of national purpose.

As long as I hold it, I will keep the office of President always close to all the people. I think I know what it is the people want, and I make that as a solemn pledge.

I am the President of the United States, the only President you will have, God willing, until January of next year. One of the hardest tasks that a President faces is to keep the time scale of his decisions always in mind and to try to be the President of all the people.

He is not simply responsible to an immediate electorate, either. He knows over the long stretch of time how great can be the repercussions of all that he does or that he fails to do, and over that span of time the President always has to think of America as a continuing community.

He has to try to see how his decisions will affect not only today's citizen, but their children and their children's children unto the third and the fourth generation. He has to try to peer into the future, and he has to prepare for that future.

If the policies he advocates lack this dimension of depth and this dimension of staying power, he may gain this or that advantage in the short term, but he can set the country on a false course and profit today at the expense of all the world tomorrow. So it is this solemn and this most difficult responsibility, and it is always hard to interpret confidently the future patterns of the world.

We intend to seek justice because that is what the Nation needs. We intend to create hope because that is what the Nation needs. We intend to build opportunity because that is what the Nation deserves. And we intend to pursue peace relentlessly because that is what the world demands.

These are the simple aims of our purpose. These are the forward thrusts of our objective. But to start on this adventure, we must begin and we ought to begin today. Justice is a universal beginning for a great society. Justice is undone and untended in too many in our land.

We cannot deny to a group of our own people, our own American citizens, the essential elements of human dignity which a majority of our citizens claim for themselves. Civil rights are not a luxury to be accorded the many. They are an obligation under our Constitution that is owed to all. . . .

I want to repeat here today again, again, and again for the record what I said at Gettysburg last year: One hundred years ago Lincoln freed the Negro of his chains, but he did not free his country of its bigotry, for until education is blind to color, until employment is unaware of race, emancipation will be a proclamation, but it will not be a fact.

We are trying to preserve our national resource of humanity, also. Some call it, and choose to refer to it, as a war on poverty. Well, it is a war, and poverty is the enemy. But the real objective is the preservation of our most precious asset—over 9 million American families at the bottom of the heap. It is not a program of giveaway. It is not a program of doles. It is a program that is concerned with skills and opportunities, with giving the tools for the job of growth, in making taxpayers out of tax-eaters. We are investing in opportunity and giving them the skills to seize it.

For the first time in America's history, poverty is on the run and it is no longer inevitable and its elimination is no longer impossible, because it is right. We are fighting this war because it is wise. We are committed to winning it, and our strategy is to reach deep to the core and to the cause of the poverty and, having confronted it, then destroy it.

The world is no longer the world that your fathers and mine once knew. Once it was dominated by the balance of power. Today, it is diffused and emergent. But though most of the world struggles fitfully to assert its own initiative, the people of the world look to this land for inspiration. Two-thirds of the teeming masses of humanity, most of them in their tender years under 40, are decreeing that they are not going to take it without food to sustain their body and a roof over their head.

And from our science and our technology, from our compassion and from our tolerance, from our unity and from our heritage, we stand uniquely on the threshold of a high adventure of leadership by example and by precept. "Not by might, nor by power, but by my spirit, saith the Lord."

From our Jewish and Christian heritage, we draw the image of the God of all mankind who will judge his children not by their prayers and by their pretensions, but by their mercy to the poor and their understanding of the weak.

We cannot cancel that strain and then claim to speak as a Christian society. To visit the widow and the fatherless in their affliction is still pure religion and undefiled. I tremble for this Nation. I tremble for our people if at the time of our greatest prosperity we turn our back on the moral obligations of our deepest faith. If the face we turn to this aspiring, laboring world is a face of indifference and contempt, it will rightly rise up and strike us down.

**Richard M. Nixon: The Presidency:
A New Realism**

The next President must unite America. He must calm its angers, ease its terrible frictions, and bring its people together once again in peace and mutual respect. He has to take hold of America before he can move it forward. . . . The first responsibility of leadership is to gain mastery over events, and to shape the future in the image of our hopes. The President today cannot stand aside from crisis; he cannot ignore division; he cannot simply paper over disunity. He must lead. . . .

Condensed from a September 19, 1968, radio address by Richard M. Nixon.

The President is trusted (by the people), not to follow the fluctuations of the public-opinion polls, but to bring his own best judgment to bear on the best ideas his administration can muster. There are occasions on which a President must take unpopular measures. But his responsibility does not stop there. The President has a duty to decide, but the people have a right to know why. The President has a responsibility to tell them—to lay out all the facts, and to explain not only why he chose as he did but also what it means for the future. Only through an open, candid dialogue with the people can a President maintain his trust and leadership. . . .

When we debate American commitments abroad, for example, if we expect a decent hearing from those who now take to the streets in protest, we must recognize that neither the Department of State nor of Defense has a monopoly on all wisdom. We should bring dissenters into policy discussions, not freeze them out; we should invite constructive criticism, not only because the critics have a right to be heard, but also because they often have something worth hearing.

And this brings me to another, related point: The President cannot isolate himself from the great intellectual ferments of his time. On the contrary, he must consciously and deliberately place himself at their center. The lamps of enlightenment are lit by the spark of controversy; their flames can be snuffed out by the blanket of consensus.

This is one reason why I don't want a Government of yes-men. It's why I do want a government drawn from the broadest possible base—an administration made up of Republicans, Democrats, and independents, and drawn from politics, from career Government service, from universities, from business, from the professions—one including not only executives and administrators, but scholars and thinkers.

While the President is a leader of thought, he is also a user of thought, and he must be a catalyst of thought. The thinking that he draws upon must be the best in America—and not only in Government. What's happening today in America and the world is happening not only in politics and diplomacy, but in science, education, the arts—and in all areas a President needs a constant exposure to ideas that stretch the mind. . . .

When we think of leadership, we commonly think of persuasion. But the coin of leadership has another side. In order to lead, a President today must listen. . . . The President is the only official who represents every American—rich and poor, privileged and underprivileged. He represents those whose misfortunes stand in domestic focus and also the great, quiet forgotten majority—the nonshouters and the nondemonstrators, the millions who ask principally to go their own way in decency and dignity, and to have their own rights accorded the same respect they accord the rights of others. Only if he listens to the quiet voices can he be true to this trust. This I pledge, that in a Nixon administration, America's citizens will not have to break the law to be heard, they will not have to shout or resort to violence. We can restore peace only if we make government attentive to the quiet as well as the strident, and this I intend to do. . . .

The Presidency has been called an impossible office. If I thought it were, I would not be seeking it. But its functions have become cluttered, the President's time drained away in trivia, the channels of authority confused. When questions of human survival may turn on the judgments of one man, he must have time to concentrate on those great decisions that only he can make. One means of achieving this is by expanding the role of the Vice President—which I will do. I also plan a reorganized and strengthened Cabinet and a stronger White House staff than any yet put together. The people are served not only by a President, but by an administration, and not only by an administration, but by a Government. The President's chief function is to lead, not to administer; it is not to oversee every detail, but to put the right people in charge, to provide them with basic guidance and direction and to let them do the job. . . . This requires surrounding the President with men of stature, including young men, and giving them responsibilities commensurate with that stature. It requires a Cabinet made up of the ablest men in America, leaders in their own right and not merely by virtue of appointment—men who will command the public's respect and the President's attention by the power of their intellect and the force of their ideas. . . .

Another change I believe necessary stems directly from my basic concept of government. For years now, the trend has been to sweep more and more authority toward Washington. Too many of the decisions that would have been better made in Seattle or St. Louis have wound up on the President's desk. I plan a streamlined federal system, with a return to the states, cities and communities of decision-making powers rightfully theirs. The purpose of this is not only to make government more effective and more responsive, but also to concentrate federal attention on those functions that can only be handled on the federal level.

The Presidency is a place where priorities are set and goals determined. We need a new attention to priorities, and a new realism about goals. We are living today in a time of great promise—but also of too many promises. . . . A President must tell the people what cannot be done immediately as well as what can. Hope is fragile, and too easily shattered by the disappointment that follows inevitably on promises unkept and unkeepable.

Thomas E. Cronin: Our Textbook President

Franklin D. Roosevelt personally rescued the nation from the depths of the great Depression. Roosevelt, together with Harry Truman, brought World War II to a proud conclusion. Courageous Truman personally committed us to resist communist aggression around the globe. General Eisenhower pledged that as president he would "go to Korea" and end that war—and he did. These are prevailing idealized images that most American students read and remember. For convenience, if not for simplicity, textbooks divide our past into the "Wilson years," the "Hoover depression," the "Roosevelt revolution," the "Eisenhower period" and so forth.

Presidents are expected to perform as purposeful activists, who know what they want to accomplish and relish the challenges of the office. The student learns that the presidency is "the great engine of democracy," the "American people's one authentic trumpet," "the central instrument of democracy," and "probably the most important governmental institution in the world." With the New Deal presidency in mind the textbook portrait states that presidents must instruct the nation as national teacher and guide the nation as national preacher. Presidents should be decidedly in favor of expanding the federal government's role in order to cope with increasing nationwide demands for social justice and a prosperous economy. The performances of Harding, Coolidge, and Hoover, lumped together as largely similar, are rejected as antique. The Eisenhower record of retiring reluctance elicits more ambiguous appraisal; after brief tribute to him as a wonderful man and a superior military leader, he gets categorized as an amateur who lacked both a sense of direction and a progressive and positive conception of the presidential role. What is needed, most texts imply, is a man with foresight to anticipate the future and the personal strength to unite us, to steel our moral will, to move the country forward, and to make the country governable. The vision, and perhaps the illusion, is that, if only we can identify and elect *the right man,* our loftiest aspirations can and will be accomplished.

From "Superman, Our Textbook President," by Thomas E. Cronin, *The Washington Monthly,* Vol. 2, October 1970. Copyright by *The Washington Monthly.* Mr. Cronin is a research political scientist at the Brookings Institution. Reprinted by permission.

With little variation, the college text includes two chapters on the presidency. Invariably, these stress that the contemporary presidency is growing dramatically larger in size, gaining measurably more responsibilities (often referred to as more hats) and greater resources. Students read that more authority and policy discretion devolve to the president during war and crises; and since our country is now engaged in sustained international conflict and acute domestic problems, presidents are constantly becoming more powerful. One text points out that "as the world grows smaller, he will grow bigger."

Then, too, writers tend to underline the vast resources available for presidential decision-making—the array of experts, including White House strategic support staffs, intelligence systems, the National Security Council, the Cabinet, an Office of Science and Technology, the Council of Economic Advisers, and countless high-powered study commissions. To the student, it must appear that a president must have just about all the inside information and sage advice possible for human comprehension. A casual reading of the chapters on the presidency fosters the belief that contemporary presidents can both make and shape public policy and can see to it that these policies *work as intended*. Textbooks encourage the belief that the "president knows best" and that his advisory and information systems are unparalleled in history. The capacity of the presidency for systematic thinking and planning is similarly described as awesome and powerfully suited to the challenges of the day.

Clinton Rossiter wrote one of the most lucid venerations of the chief executive. In the *American Presidency,* he views the office as a priceless American invention which has not only worked extremely well but is also a symbol of our continuity and destiny as a people:

> Few nations have solved so simply and yet grandly the problem of finding and maintaining an office or state that embodies their majesty and reflects their character. . . .
> There is virtually no limit to what the President can do if he does it for democratic ends and by democratic means. . . .
> He is, rather, a kind of magnificent lion who can roam widely and do great deeds so long as he does not try to break loose from his broad reservation. . . .
> He reigns, but he also rules; he symbolizes the people, but he also runs their government. . . .

Recently written or revised government textbooks emphasize the importance of personal attributes, and there is little doubt that dwelling on the president's personal qualities helps to capture the attention of student learners. Not surprisingly, this personalization of the presidency also is reflected in a great deal of campaign rhetoric. Presidential candidates go to a considerable length to stress how personally courageous and virtuous a president must be. Nelson Rockefeller's (1968) litany of necessary qualities is as exaggerated as anyone else's:

> The modern Presidency of the United States, as distinct from the traditional concepts of our highest office, is bound up with the survival not only of freedom but of mankind. . . . The President is the unifying force in our lives. . . .
>
> The President must possess a wide range of abilities: to lead, to persuade, to inspire trust, to attract men of talent, to unite. These abilities must reflect a wide range of characteristics: courage, vision, integrity, intelligence, sense of responsibility, sense of history, sense of humor, warmth, openness, personality, tenacity, energy, determination, drive, perspicacity, idealism, thirst for information, penchant for fact, presence of conscience, comprehension of people and enjoyment of life—plus all the other, nobler virtues ascribed to George Washington under God.

The Lion's Transformation

The personalized presidency is also a central feature of contemporary political journalism, and no journalist does more to embellish this perspective than Theodore White. His "Making of the President" series not only enjoys frequent university use but additionally serves as presidency textbooks for millions of adults who savor his "insider" explanations of presidential election campaigns.

White's unidimensional concentration on the presidential candidates, their styles, and personalities promotes a benevolent if not reverential orientation toward the American presidency. His narrative histories of American political campaigns have an uncanny way of uplifting and seducing the reader to watch and wait an election's outcome with intense concern—even though the books are published almost a year after the event. His style ferments great expectations and a heightened sense of reverence for the eventual victor. At first there are seven or eight competing hopefuls, then four or five, penultimately narrowed down to two or three nationally legitimized candidates and finally—there remains just one man. Clearly the victor in such a drawn-out and thoroughly patriotic ritual deserves our deepest respect and approval. White subtly succeeds in purifying the victorious candidate: in what must be a classic metamorphosis at the root of the textbook presidency image, the men who assume the presidency seem physically (and implicitly almost spiritually) to undergo an alteration of personal traits.

On JFK's first days in the White House, 1961:

It was as if there were an echo, here on another level, in the quiet Oval Office, of all the speeches he had made in all the squares and supermarkets of the country. . . . He had won this office and this power by promising such movement to the American people. Now he had to keep the promise. He seemed very little changed in movement or in gracefulness from the candidate—only his eyes had changed—very dark now, very grave, markedly more sunken and lined at the corners than those of the candidate.

On Richard Nixon soon after his ascendency, 1969:

He seemed, as he waved me into the Oval Office, suddenly on first glance a more stocky man than I had known on the campaign rounds. There was a minute of adjustment as he waved me to a sofa in the barren office, poured coffee, put me at ease; then, watching him, I realized that he was not stockier, but, on the contrary, slimmer. What was different was the movement of the body, the sound of the voice, the manner of speaking—for he was calm as I had never seen him before, as if peace had settled on him. In the past, Nixon's restless body had been in constant movement as he rose, walked about, hitched a leg over the arm of a chair or gestured sharply with his hands. Now he was in repose; and the repose was in his speech also—more slow, studied, with none of the gear-slippages of name or reference which used to come when he was weary; his hands still moved as he spoke, but the fingers spread gracefully, not punchily, or sharply as they used to.

What, then, constitutes the recent textbook version of the American presidency? As always, any facile generalization of such a hydra-like institution is susceptible to oversimplification, but, on balance, more consensus than contention characterizes literature on the American presidency. Four summary statements may be singled out without doing great violence to the text literature. Two of these accentuate a dimension of presidential omnipotence, and two others emphasize an expectation of moralistic-benevolence. Taken together, this admixture of legend and reality comprise the textbook presidency of the last 15 years.

Omnipotence

1. The president is the strategic catalyst in the American political system and the central figure in the international system as well.
2. Only the president is or can be the genuine architect of United States public policy, and only he, by attacking problems frontally and aggressively and interpreting his power expansively, can be the engine of change to move this nation forward.

Moralistic-Benevolence

3. The president must be the nation's personal and moral leader; by symbolizing the past and future greatness of America and radiating inspirational confidence, a president can pull the nation together while directing us toward the fulfillment of the American Dream.

4. If, and only if, the right man is placed in the White House, all will be well, and, somehow, whoever is in the White House is the right man.

The "Selling of a Textbook"

Radio, television, and the emergence of the United States as a strategic nuclear power have converged to make the presidency a job of far greater prominence than it was in the days of Coolidge and before. While this is readily understood, there are other factors which contribute to runaway inflation in the attributed capabilities of White House leadership.

A first explanation for the textbook presidency is derived from the basic human tendency toward belief in great men. Most people grow up with the expectation that someone somewhere can and will cope with the major crises of the present and future. Since the New Deal, most Americans have grown accustomed to expect their president to serve this role. Who, if not the president, is going to prevent the communists from burying us, pollution from choking us, crime and conflict from destroying our cities, moral degradation from slipping into our neighborhood theaters? Within the complexity of political life today the president provides a visible national symbol to which we can attach our hopes. Something akin to presidential cults exists in the United States today just as hero-worship, gerontocracy reverence, and other forms of authority-fixation have flourished in most, if not all, larger societies. Portraits of Washington, Lincoln, the Roosevelts, and Kennedy paper many a classroom wall alongside of the American flag. While deification is presumably discouraged, something similar is a common side product during the early years of schooling.

On all but two occasions during the past 17 years, the president of this nation has won the Most Admired Man contest conducted annually by the Gallup polls. The exceptions in 1967 and 1968 saw President Johnson lose out to former President Eisenhower. Mentioning this pattern of popular response to a recent conversation partner, I was informed that "If they were not the most admired men in the country they wouldn't have been elected president!" And his response is, I believe, a widely respected point of view in America. On the one hand we are always looking for reassurance that things will work out satisfactorily. On the other hand we admire the dramatic actions of men in high places who are willing to take action, willing to cope with the exigencies of crisis and perplexity. Political scientist Murray Edelman writes quite lucidly about this problem:

> And what symbol can be more reassuring than the incumbent of a high position who knows what to do and is willing to act, especially when others are bewildered and alone? Because such a symbol is so intensely sought, it will predictably be found in the person of any incumbent whose actions *can* be interpreted as beneficent.

A second explanation of recent textbook orthodoxy is unmistakenly related to the commercial and political values of most text writers. Market considerations are hard to ignore and several text authors unabashedly cite commercial remuneration as a major incentive. The "selling of a textbook" may not be unrelated to a book's function and ideological orientation.

Most textbook authors are motivated by the goal of training "good" citizens just as much as by the goal of instructing people about the realities of the highly competitive and often cruel world of national party and policy politics. But the training of citizens often seems to require a glossy, harmonious picture of national politics, which inspires loyalty but conflicts with reality. When this occurs, as one text writer told me, "the author almost invariably emphasizes citizen training, usually at the expense of instruction."

Building the Great Cathedral

A Franklin Roosevelt halo-effect characterizes most of the recent treatments of the presidency. Writers during the 1950s and well into the '60s were children or young adults during the Depression years. Not infrequently, they became enlisted in one way or another in executive branch service to help fight or manage World War II. These times were unusual in many ways—including an extraordinary amount of attention paid to the way in which President Roosevelt employed the powers of the presidency. Moreover, in the arena of national and international leadership, FDR upstaged all comers as he magnified the personal role and heroic style of a confident, competent leader in the context of tumultuous times. The mantle of world leadership was passing to the U.S., beginning what some writers refer to as the American Era. Understandably these developments, especially the dramaturgy of the New Deal presidency, affected soon-to-be written interpretations as well as popular images of the presidency.

A final reason for the textbook presidency lies in the very nature of the American political and electoral system. We elect a president by a small margin, but after election he is supposed to speak for *all* the people. Textbook and school norms suggest that one can vigorously question a presidential candidate, but after the election it is one's duty to unite behind the winner. It is as though the new president were the pilot of an aircraft with all of us as passengers, whether we like it or not. Hence, we all have a stake in his success.

To be sure, this institution of ritualistic unification serves a need: it absorbs much of the discontinuity and tension promoted in our often hectic and combative electoral campaigns. Then there is the typical first-year grace period in which serious criticism is generally considered off limits. This presidential honeymoon is characterized by an elaborate press build-up in which it appears as though we are trying to transform and elevate the quite mortal candidate into a textbook president.

Other methodological factors also contribute to idealized versions of presidential leadership. Overreliance on case studies of presidential behavior in relatively unique crises is part of the problem. Textbook compartmentalization of problems and institutions is yet another. Both the student and the average citizen may quite reasonably get the impression that national policy is almost entirely the product of a president and a few of his intimates, or alternately of a few select national officials along with the president's consent. Only the presidents can slay the dragons of crisis. And only Lincoln, the Roosevelts, Wilson, or men of that caliber can seize the chalice of opportunity, create the vision, and rally the American public around that vision. The end result may leave the student quite confused, if not ignorant, about the complex transactions, interrelationships, and ambiguities that more correctly characterize most national policy developments.

In all probability we pay a price, however unwittingly, for the way we have over-idealized the presidency. Although this price is difficult to calculate, I shall suggest some of the probable consequences of the textbook presidency—beginning with the dangers of our unwarranted expectations of the president's power and of his capacities as a spiritual reservoir.

Most Americans now believe, along with Theodore and Franklin Roosevelt's celebrated assertions, that the presidency is a "bully pulpit" and preeminently a place for moral leadership. Few of our citizenry wince at James Reston's observation that "the White House is the pulpit of the nation and the president is its chaplain." British Prime Minister Harold Macmillan, on the other hand, could quip, "If people want a sense of purpose, they should get it from their archbishops."

We are accustomed to regarding our "sense of purpose" and pious presidential pronouncements as nearly one and the same. Accordingly,

Richard Nixon invoked God five times in his presidential inaugural and talked often of spirit and the nation's destiny: "To a crisis of the spirit, we need an answer of the spirit. . . . We can build a great cathedral of the spirit. . . . We have endured a long night of the American spirit. But as our eyes catch the dimness of the first rays of dawn, let us not curse the remaining dark, let us gather the light. . . . Our destiny offers not the cup of despair, but the chalice of opportunity."

But the trappings of religiosity, while temporarily ennobling the presidential personage, may run the risk of triggering unanticipated and undesirable consequences. Some presidents apparently feel the need to justify a particular strategy on the grounds that it is the moral and righteous course of action. But this moral emphasis can become elevated to overblown courses of behavior. For example, Wilson's attempts to help set up the League of Nations became imbued with a highly moralistic fervor, but the moral environment that generated the commitment was allowed to expand, as Wilson's own role as the nation's preacher expanded, until there was virtually no room for a political negotiator, a non-moralist Wilson to transform the idea into a reality. Perhaps Herbert Hoover's apolitical moral and ideological commitment to rugged individualism similarly inhibited alternative approaches in response to the Depression. Similarly, President Johnson's drumming up of moral and patriotic support for our Vietnam commitment probably weakened his subsequent efforts at negotiations in the languishing days of his Administration.

Part of the problem is related to the way campaigns are conducted and to the intensive hard sell—or at least "oversell"—seemingly demanded of candidates. Necessarily adopting the language of promise and sloganism, candidates and their publicists frequently pledge that they will accomplish objectives that are either near impossible or unlikely. Recall the early declaratory intentions of the War on Poverty, Model Cities, the Alliance for Progress, the war on behalf of safe streets, and an ambitious Nixon promise to underwrite "black capitalism."

The Cost of Elevation

The textbook presidency image may also influence the quality of civic participation. The moral-leader-to-layman relationship is quite often viewed as a one-way street. If the president is our national chaplain, how do we cultivate a democratic citizenry that is active and not passive, that may, on selective occasions, responsibly dispute this national moral eminence? Having been nurtured in the belief that presidents are not only benevolent but also personally powerful enough to end war, depression, and corruption, it is difficult for most average citizens to disagree strongly with their president, no matter what the circumstances. Students are instructed that it is proper to state one's differences in a letter to congressmen or even to the White House. But beyond these rather limited resources, the citizen-student is left alone and without a sense of personal efficacy. Due to the almost assured deference and relative lack of opposition, American presidents can expect at least a five-to-one favorable ratio in their telegram and mail response, and usually a three- or two-to-one ratio in national opinion poll responses about their handling of the presidency.

Most popular is the choice of quietly (if not silently) rallying around the president and offering him permissive support, hoping by such action to strengthen his and the nation's resolve against whatever real or apparent challenges confront the nation. Another pattern of behavior, that of apathy and indifference, is selected by sober citizens who feel secure in the belief that "presidents know best." Thus, a president can usually take it for granted that when major difficulties are faced, most Americans will support and trust him, at least for a while, often tendering him even increased support. It is difficult sometimes for Americans to differentiate between loyalty to president and loyalty to nation. As a result, presidential public support comes not only from those who feel the president is right, but is measurably inflated by those who, regardless of policy or situation, render support to their president merely because he is their president, or because he is the only president they have.

Few people are inclined to protest the actions of their president, but for those selecting to dissent, the textbook wisdom seems to encourage a direct personal confrontation with the president. If he alone is so powerful and independent, it appears logical to march on the White House and, if necessary, "break" or "dump" the president in order to change policy. But this may be one of the least economical strategies, for, as we have seen, breaking or changing presidents does not ensure any major shift in the execution of national policies.

The point here is that on both sides of the presidential popularity equation his importance is inflated beyond reasonable bounds. On one side, there is a nearly blind faith that the president embodies national virtue and that any detractor must be an effete snob or a nervous nellie. On the other side, the president becomes the cause of all personal maladies, the originator of poverty and racism, inventor of the establishment, and the party responsible for a choleric national disposition.

If the textbook presidency image has costs for the quality of citizen relationships with the presidency, so also it can affect the way presidents conceive of themselves and their job. To be sure, the reverence and loyalty rendered to a new president are a rich resource and no doubt are somewhat commensurate with tough responsibilities that come along with the job.

But, at the same time, an overly indulgent citizenry can psychologically distort the personal perspective and sense of balance. Former presidential press secretary George Reedy's acrimonious criticisms of the monarchical trappings of the contemporary White House deserve attention:

> The atmosphere of the White House is calculated to instill in any man a sense of destiny. He literally walks in the foosteps of hallowed figures —of Jefferson, of Jackson, of Lincoln. . . . From the moment he enters the halls he is made aware that he has become enshrined in a pantheon of semi-divine mortals who have shaken the world, and that he has taken from their hands the heritage of American dreams and aspirations.
> Unfortunately for him, divinity is a better basis for inspiration than it is for government.

The quality of advice, intelligence, and critical evaluation necessary to balanced presidential decision-making can also be adversely affected by too respectful an attitude toward the chief executive. If presidents become unduly protected or insulated, and if White House aides and Cabinet members tender appreciation and deference in exchange for status and accommodation, then the president's decision-making ability is clearly harmed.

The relatively sustained 15-year ascendancy of the textbook presidency's idealized image of presidential leadership may be coming to an end. The general American public probably still believes in a version of the New Deal presidency caricature, but the near monopoly of this view is under challenge from a growing list of critiques of liberal presidential government. We are currently witnessing an apparent recrudescence of an interpretation of the presidency, which holds that no one national political leader can galvanize our political system toward the easy accomplishment of sustained policy change or altruistic goals.

Toward Revision

Contemporary policy studies suggest that the more we learn about presidential policy performance, the more it appears that presidents (in both domestic and foreign policy) only rarely accomplish policy "outcomes" that can be credited as distinct personal achievements. More realistically, the presidency serves as a broker for a few party priorities and as a strategically situated and important participant among vast numbers of policy entrepreneurs and policy-bearing bureaucrats. More often than not a president's personal policy views are essentially moderate and only vaguely refined. When in office, however, he finds himself constantly surrounded by people who have "high-energy" interest and investments in specific policy options. Both the president and these elites, however, are in turn surrounded by what Scammon and Wattenberg call the real majority—the large majority of American voters in the center.

In a sample of recent in-depth interviews with 30 White House staffers who served Presidents Kennedy and Johnson, I found that a majority of these presidential advisers feel that the president exercises selective or relatively little power over policy matters. There are some who say that "he [the president] has a lot of influence on those problems he is willing to spend time on," but more responded that "he has far less than people think he has, he is far more constrained than popularly thought." In fact, many even express the somewhat restrained and almost anti-textbook presidency view that presidents can accomplish a limited number of projects and hence should carefully measure their requests and energies. Emphasizing this point were the following two respondents:

> I think the White House under Johnson was excessively activist—there was an impulsive need to do something about everything RIGHT NOW! There was always the feeling [given by the president] that we should fix this and fix that and do it now! Overall I think it went too far—there are definite costs and liabilities in that type of excessive aggressive activism. . . .

And a second staffer:

> Except in times of emergencies, presidents cannot get much accomplished. . . . In some areas a president can have a psychological influence, a psychological effect on the nation, for example by speaking out on crime concerns. And in an eight-year period a president can start a shift of the budget and of the political system, but it takes a lot of pressure and a lot of time. Basically, the thing to remember is that a presidential intention takes a very long time to get implemented.

On balance, of course, it is true that under certain circumstances a president can ignite the nuclear destruction of a substantial portion of the world or commit U.S. troops into internationally troubled crisis zones. But the American president is in no better position to control Bolivian instability, Chilean Marxism, or Vietcong penetration into Cambodia than he can make the stock market rise or medical costs decline. It is misleading to infer from a president's capacity to drop an A-bomb that he is similarly powerful in most other international or domestic policy areas. The more we learn about the processes of government, the more it becomes apparent that presidents are rarely free agents when it comes to effecting new policies—or dismantling policies which they have inherited.

George E. Reedy: Presidential Isolation

From the president's standpoint, the greatest staff problem is that of maintaining his contact with the world's reality that lies outside the White House walls. Very few have succeeded in doing so. They start their administrations fresh from the political wars, which have a tendency to keep men closely tied to the facts of life, but it is only a matter of time until the White House assistants close in like a pretorian guard. Since they are the only people a president sees on a day-to-day basis, they become to him the voice of the people. They represent the closest approximation that he has of outside contacts, and it is inevitable that he comes to regard them as humanity itself.

Even the vision of so earthy a politician as Lyndon B. Johnson became blurred as the years went by. He mistook the alert, taut, well-groomed young men around him for "American youth" and could never comprehend the origins of the long-haired, slovenly attired youngsters who hooted at him so savagely when he traveled (and eventually made most travel impossible) and who raged and stormed outside the White House gates. To him, they appeared to be extraterrestrial invaders—not only non-American but nonearthly. Certainly, they did not fit the pattern of young men and young women whom he had assembled so painstakingly and who were so obviously, in his eyes, the embodiment of the nation's dream.

The man who resisted this temptation most strongly, and who maintained his political skill longer than any other president, was Franklin D. Roosevelt. He understood thoroughly the weaknesses of the staff system in the White House. He saw to it that under no circumstances could the people in his immediate vicinity control his access to information. Every staff assistant from the New Deal days recalls the experience of bringing a report to FDR and discovering, in the course of the conversation, that the president had gained from some mysterious, outside source knowledge of aspects of the project of which the assistant himself was not aware. No assistant, with the possible exception of Harry Hopkins, ever felt that his position was secure. And none of them would have dared to withhold any information. The penalties were too swift and too sure to permit what would anyway have been a futile exercise.

It is difficult, however, for a president to maintain sources of information outside his immediate staff. It requires a positive effort of will. This situation arises from the general nature of the presidency.

Every political leader, of course, must have assistants and close associates in whom he can repose absolute confidence. The political life is a life of struggle in which a man is surrounded by enemies who will take advantage of any show of vulnerability. Only a band of people unified in a common purpose and determined to follow their leader through fire and storm can possibly survive. But for most politicians, there are day-to-day tests of each individual member of his following. He is told—immediately and unpleasantly—whenever any of his subordinates has made a bad "fluff" or has overstepped what is generally regarded as the bounds of legitimate warfare.

For many years, a corporation sold a popular mouthwash to the American people on the basis that it would inhibit bad breath. The slogan under which the product was merchandised—"Even your best friends won't tell you"—meant that the subject was too delicate to mention and that a person could exude the foulest odors without being aware of the fact. As far as the mouthwash was concerned, the slogan was somewhat misleading —not only your best friends but your worst enemies will tell you if you have bad breath. But the concept that "even your best friends won't tell you" about unpleasant things applies with tremendous force to the president.

As noted, an essential characteristic of monarchy is untouchability. No one touches a king unless he is specifically invited to do so. No one thrusts unpleasant thoughts upon a king unless he is ordered to do so, and even then he does so at his own peril. The response to unpleasant information has been fixed by a pattern with a long history. Every courtier recalls, either literally or instinctively, what happened to the messenger who brought Peter the Great the news of the Russian defeat by Charles XII at the Battle of Narva. The courtier was strangled by decree of the czar. A modern-day monarch—at least a monarch in the White House—cannot direct the placing of a noose around a man's throat for bringing him bad news. But his frown can mean social and economic strangulation. And only a very brave or a very foolish man will suffer that frown.

Furthermore, an outsider has a sense of diffidence in approaching a president to tell him "the facts of life" about his staff. It is in the same class as telling a father about the shortcomings of his son. The only people who will do it are boors, whose opinion is little valued under the best of circumstances. Consequently, a president can go through an entire term without knowing that some of his most trusted assistants have created resentments that have undermined his political position. He will, of course, read occasional articles in the newspapers describing the activities. These he is bound to regard as merely attacks by a jealous opposition, and the effect upon his thinking will be the reverse of what was intended.

A "strong" president, if strength is defined as determination to have one's own way, paradoxically is more liable to suffer from the operations of the White House staff system than one who is "weak." The strong man has a propensity to create an environment to his liking and to weed out ruthlessly those assistants who might persist in presenting him with irritating thoughts. It is no accident that White House staffs under the regime of a forceful president tend to become more and more colorless and more and more nondescript as time goes on. Palace-guard survivors learn early to camouflage themselves with a coating of battleship gray.

The "weak" president, on the other hand, is more susceptible to conflicting currents and less ready to eliminate strong-minded people from his immediate vicinity. The mere fact that he is somewhat "wishy-washy" at least assures that he will keep some avenues of approach open and that the courtier who has been cast out may find a way back in.

It is possible for a president to assemble a staff of mature men who are past the period of inordinate ambition that characterizes the courtier. But this is only a possibility—rarely, if ever, consummated. The White House is a court. Inevitably, in a battle between courtiers and advisers, the courtiers will win out. This represents the greatest of all barriers to presidential access to reality and raises a problem which will plague the White House so long as the president is a reigning monarch rather than an elected administrator.

Nicholas deB. Katzenbach and William Fulbright: Congressional and Presidential Powers in Foreign Affairs

---

The committee met, pursuant to notice, at 10 A.M., in room 4221 New Senate Office Building, Senator J. W. Fulbright (chairman) presiding.

Present: Senators Fulbright, Gore, McCarthy, Hickenlooper, Carlson, Mundt, Case, and Cooper.

United States Senate, Committee on Foreign Relations. Hearings, *U.S. Commitments to Foreign Powers*. 90th Congress, 1st Session, Government Printing Office, 1967.

Opening Statement

The Chairman: The committee will come to order.

We meet today to begin a series of hearings on the state of Congress' constitutional role on the making of American foreign policy. The occasion is Senate Resolution 151 which purports to define a national commitment as an undertaking carrying in one form or another the endorsement of Congress. Our purpose which goes beyond the present resolution is to evaluate the responsibilities and current roles of Congress and of the Executive in the making of foreign policy, the changes which have taken place in the respective roles of the two branches in recent decades, the reasons for these changes, and their effects upon our constitutional system . . .

Our witness today, who undoubtedly will enlighten the committee further as to the State Department's conception of the extent and sources of American commitments abroad, is the Honorable Nicholas deB. Katzenbach, former Attorney General.

Mr. Katzenbach, we are very pleased to have you this morning. We appreciate your taking the time and trouble to come before the committee. Do you have a prepared statement, sir?

Mr. Katzenbach: I do, Mr. Chairman.

The Chairman: Would you proceed.

Mr. Katzenbach: Mr. Chairman and members of the committee, despite its brevity, the resolution before this committee grapples simultaneously with two of the most important, most enduring, and most complex issues of state in American history.

One of these issues is the allocation of governmental powers, as shaped by our Constitution and by nearly 200 years of experience.

The second issue is the changing role of this Nation in the affairs of a changing world.

It is not possible to comment intelligently on the proposed resolution in only a current context. I would like, therefore, to begin my statement of the Administration's views with a few thoughts on the nature and history of both of these issues.

The framers of the Constitution recognized the impossibility of compressing the idea of the separation of powers into a simple formula. They did not attempt to engrave clear lines of demarcation.

With respect to diplomacy, they recognized the complexity of foreign affairs even in the far calmer climate of our Nation's childhood—a time when we took as our watchword Washington's declaration that, "It is our true policy to steer clear of permanent alliances, with any portion of the foreign world."

Hence the Constitution contains relatively few details about how foreign policy decisions shall be made and foreign relations conducted. It recognized that the voice of the United States in foreign affairs was, of necessity, the voice of the President. Consistent with that basic necessity, it also provided for the participation of Congress in a number of ways, direct and indirect.

John Jay observed in The Federalist that the Presidency possesses great inherent strengths in the direction of foreign affairs: The unity of the office, its capacity for secrecy and speed, and its superior sources of information. . . .

But if the constitutional formula of flexibility was not an easy one, it has surely proved to be a practical and useful one. It has always seemed to me that the genius of our Constitution rests on the recognition of its drafters that they could not provide precise resolution for all future problems, foreseen and unforeseen. And I think that the conduct of foreign affairs demonstrates the validity of this approach.

Despite occasional differences and debates, history has surely vindicated the wisdom of this flexibility—of this essentially political approach to the conduct of our foreign affairs.

In the world we now live in, answers have not become easier. And yet the constitutional allocation of powers continues to work well today.

Our Changing Role in a Changing World

Let me turn to the nature of our foreign policy and the role of the United States in the world today—to the commitments of this Nation in foreign affairs.

The basic objective of our foreign policy is the security of the United States and the preservation of our freedoms. How this objective is achieved obviously depends upon the kind of world in which we live and the extent to which we can bring American power and influence to bear upon it.

For most of our history, we had only spasmodic foreign business. We lived in relative isolation, content to allow the European powers to maintain the balance of power on which, in fact, our national security depended.

In recent years, there has been a revolutionary change in the political structure of the world—and of the relative importance of foreign affairs to the United States. What has been perceived by all—by Presidents, by the Congress, and by the people—is that our independence and our security can no longer be assured by default. They depend in large measure on our capacity to lead in the achievement of a system of assured world peace. Within the broad horizons of such a framework—and only within such horizons—can American democracy and American society be safe.

This framework, I believe, rests on three propositions. The first is that events elsewhere can have critical effects on this country; hence our security is bound up with that of other countries.

The second is that we must heed more than power politics. For if we are true to our domestic ideals and are concerned for our domestic security, we cannot ignore the conditions in which people around the world must live—conditions which can and do fuel reverberating political explosions.

The third is that we cannot and should not meet these first two needs alone, any more than we could or should seek unilaterally to establish a pax Americana. We must develop international instrumentalities to help provide collective security and to help create social progress and eliminate the flammable conditions of misery that embrace so much of the world's population.

The United States has made serious, substantial, and enduring efforts to act on all three of these propositions. I do not think it is susceptible of proof, but I firmly believe that the crises we have avoided as a result of imaginative military and political action are at least as important as the crises we have survived.

Coordinate Action by the Congress and the President

The progress in our efforts has been substantial—and it has been the result of a national commitment. And this has been possible in large measure because of two factors.

This commitment has not been one of administration or of party, but of bipartisanship. One of the remarkable aspects of American foreign policy in the past 20 years is that it has become bipartisan. Partisan politics have, in fact, stopped at the water's edge.

The second factor is the consistent, coordinate action of the Executive and Legislative branches, each in their proper sphere, to propose and dispose, to create and carry out a national commitment. . . .

Constitutional Quality of
Commitments

Let me emphasize the constitutional quality of these commitments. By their nature, they set only the boundaries within which the United States will act. They cannot and do not spell out the precise action which the United States would take in a variety of contingencies. That is left for further decision by the President and the Congress.

In short, none of these incur automatic response. But they do make clear our pledge to take actions we regard as appropriate in the light of all the circumstances—our view that we are not indifferent to the actions of others which disturb the peace of the world and threaten the security of the United States.

Congress has been a full partner, as well, in the great national effort to accelerate the pace of economic and social progress elsewhere in the world. . . .

Formal and Informal Consultation
between the Two Branches

Finally, there is the central fiscal power. In the exercise of its annual appropriations functions, the Congress reviews and debates the foreign policies of the administration.

Beyond these formal methods of congressional participation in foreign policy, there is the process of informal consultation between the Executive and the Congress. There are literally thousands of contacts each year between officers of the Executive branch and Members of Congress.

Not only do the Secretary and other high officials of the Department of State consult regularly and frequently with congressional leaders and committees; the President has often conducted such consultations personally and extensively.

The Importance of Coordinate Action

As I noted at the outset, the drafters of the Constitution recognized that the voice of the United States in foreign affairs was that of the President. Throughout our history the focus has always been upon the Presidency, and it is difficult to imagine how it could be otherwise. Jefferson put it succinctly: "The transaction of business with foreign nations is Executive altogether."

I think it is fair to say, as virtually every commentator has in fact said throughout our history, that under our constitutional system the source of an effective foreign policy is Presidential power. His is the sole authority to communicate formally with foreign nations; to negotiate treaties; to command the armed forces of the United States. His is a responsibility born of the need for speed and decisiveness in an emergency. His is the responsibility for controlling and directing all the external aspects of the Nation's power. To him flow all of the vast intelligence and information connected with national security. The President, of necessity, has a pre-eminent responsibility in this field.

But to say this is not to denigrate the role of Congress. Whatever the powers of the President to act alone on his own authority—and I doubt that any President has ever acted to the full limits of that authority—there can be no question that he acts most effectively when he acts with the support and authority of the Congress.

And so it is that every President seeks in various ways—formal and informal—the support of Congress for the policies which the United States pursues in its foreign relations.

Constitutional Powers of President and Congress

In part, the Constitution compels such support. It gives the President the responsibilities for leadership. It also gives the Congress specific powers which can on the one hand frustrate and distort and on the other hand support and implement.

Obviously, then, there are great advantages to the Nation in the conduct of its foreign policy when circumstances permit the President and the Congress to act together. The commitments of this Nation to the United Nations Charter and to our allies are more than a matter of constitutional process. It is essential that these basic commitments should be clear, both to our friends and to our potential adversaries. Fitfulness of policy and unpredictability of action make for serious international instability, disorder, and danger.

In short, our safety and our success depend in large measure on the confidence of other nations that they can rely on our conduct and our assurances.

It is, therefore, as important that the Congress fill its constitutional role as it is that the President fill his. The Congress is and must be a participant in formulating the broad outlines of our foreign policy, in supporting those fundamental and enduring commitments on which the conduct of day-to-day diplomacy depend.

But to say this is not to say that the Congress can or should seek to substitute itself for the President or even to share in those decisions which are his to make. . . .

Conclusion

I see no need to revise the experience of our history, or to seek to alter the boundaries of Presidential or congressional prerogative regarding foreign affairs. The need, as always, is to make the constitutional scheme and the experience of history continue to work.

"For myself," President Johnson has observed, "I believe that this is the way our system was intended to function—not with Presidents and Congresses locked in battle with each other—but locked arm in arm instead, battling for the people that we serve together."

Thank you, Mr. Chairman.

Department of State Opposes Enactment of Senate Resolution 151

The Chairman: Thank you, Mr. Secretary. It is not clear to me from your statement and I wonder if you could make it more precise: Does the Department support or oppose the enactment of Senate Resolution 151?

Mr. Katzenbach: I could not support the resolution, Mr. Chairman, because it seems to me that, if I understand it correctly, perhaps I do not, if I understand it correctly, it seems to me that it tries to do precisely what the Founding Fathers of this country declined to do in writing the Constitution, in that it purports to take a position, through a Senate resolution, on matters that it seems to me have worked out successfully, in terms of distribution of functions between the executive branch and the Congress. And it seems to me that it could be interpreted to seek to join the Congress with the President on those matters which I think the President, in his capacity of conducting foreign relations of the United States has the constitutional authority to do. . . .

The Chairman: Then, in short, you oppose its enactment?

Mr. Katzenbach: That is correct. I thought I made that clear, Senator.

The Chairman: No, it wasn't very clear. I confess it was not very clear; I wanted to try to make it clear. You are opposed then to the Senate acting upon this resolution or one similar to it?

Mr. Katzenbach: I would of course have to see some other resolution.

The Chairman: I understand.

Mr. Katzenbach: Yes, that is correct.

The Chairman: That is a good starting point. It joins the issue in any case. There are a few statements that maybe we should examine a little more closely. . . .

Congressional Declaration of War

The Chairman: Let us see if we can develop a few of the specific points. You make a statement that in speaking of the President—

His is a responsibility borne of the need for speed and decisiveness in an emergency. His is the responsibility of controlling and directing all the external aspects of the Nation's power.

How do you fit this in with the constitutional provision as to the declaration of war by the Congress?

Yesterday we had one of the Nation's leading authorities, Professor Bartlett before us. He interprets the Constitution as meaning that the Congress has the exclusive power to initiate war. He used the word "initiate" rather than "declare" but "to declare" are the words of the Constitution. He feels this has been eroded by practice, particularly beginning about the turn of the century. Do you agree with his interpretation as to the meaning of the Constitution on the question of declaration of war?

Mr. Katzenbach: I believe that the Constitution makes it very clear that a declaration of war is the function of Congress. I believe our history has been that the wars we have declared have been declared at the initiative and instance of the Executive.

The function of the Congress is one to declare. It is not one to wage, not one to conduct, but one simply to declare. That is the function of Congress as expressed in the Constitution.

The Chairman: To declare the war and to authorize the war, I guess.

Mr. Katzenbach: To declare it.

The Chairman: Not to conduct it.

Mr. Katzenbach: That is true.

Conduct of Foreign Policy
Different from
Formulation

The Chairman: You refer to the President as "the voice of policy."

Mr. Katzenbach: Yes.

The Chairman: I gathered from the discussion yesterday, citing Jefferson and others who were involved in the creation of the Constitution, Jefferson referred to the Presidential power as the power to "transact the business." That refers to the conduct of the policies, but the conduct of it is not the same as the making of policy or the formulation of the overall policy, is it? They are two different things.

Mr. Katzenbach: That is correct, and Congress has, as I noted, participated in the formulation of our policies, and many of the specific powers of Congress come into play in their conduct and operation. . . .

The Chairman: The voice of policy, it seems to me, is the Congress in the crucial matter of declaring war or carrying on a war, as opposed, for example, to the repelling of an attack, which is quite different, or of rescuing citizens who are stranded in a place which is in a state of emergency, and usually contemplates a limited participation. These latter actions are opposed to the kind of war that we are now engaged in that has been going on for a number of years. That is a full-fledged war. It seems to me there is a very important distinction between whether or not we go to war or whether or not we respond to an emergency. There is a real difference between the conduct, that is the carrying out of the policy and the creation, the formulation of policy. I am trying to develop your views about the nature of this problem. I think the Constitution contemplated that the Congress should make the decision of whether or not we should engage in war. Don't you agree to that?

Mr. Katzenbach: Yes, Mr. Chairman, I agree that the Congress should, except in the case of emergencies, participate in major decisions of that kind.

Let me say, that indeed in the war to which you refer it did participate. It did participate in that. Now, let me elaborate my statement in that regard and see if I can make myself clear, because I think it is important. And, Mr. Chairman, I think this issue is a difficult one, one on which I think the Congress and the Executive should work together, as indeed I think they have.

Clarifying Use of the Phrase
"To Declare War"

The point is this. The use of the phrase "to declare war" as it was used in the Constitution of the United States had a particular meaning in terms of the events and the practices which existed at the time it was adopted and which existed really until the United Nations was organized. The phrase came from a context that recognized "war" to be an instrument of implementing the acceptable policy, but which is not acceptable in the climate today, which rejects the idea of aggression, which rejects the idea of conquest. The phrase came from the earlier context.

Now, it came for a function. As you rightly say, it was recognized by the Founding Fathers that the President might have to take emergency action to protect the security of the United States, but that if there was going to be another use of the armed forces of the United States, that was a decision which Congress should check the Executive on, which Congress should support. It was for that reason that the phrase was inserted in the Constitution. . . .

Now, with the abolition of the use of force for all but a small number of purposes, by the commitment expressed in the U.N. Charter with respect to aggression, the question arises as to how the Congress can and should participate in the decision to use force; (1) where there is an emergency, and (2) beyond that, in a matter such as Korea where I think there was a genuine need for speed, or in the current instance in Vietnam?

A declaration of war would not, I think, correctly reflect the very limited objectives of the United States with respect to Vietnam. It would not correctly reflect our efforts there, what we are trying to do, the reasons why we are there, to use an outmoded phraseology, to declare war.

Is Declaring War Outmoded?

The Chairman: You think it is outmoded to declare war?

Mr. Katzenbach: In this kind of context I think the expression of declaring a war is one that has become outmoded in the international arena.

But I think there is, Mr. Chairman, an obligation on the part of the Executive to give Congress the opportunity, which that language was meant to reflect in the Constitution of the United States, to express its views with respect to this. In this instance, in the instance, if you will, of Vietnam, Congress had an opportunity to participate in these decisions.

Congress ratified the SEATO treaty by an overwhelming vote, which expressed the security concerns and the general obligation of the United States in accordance with its constitutional process to attempt to preserve order and peace and defense against aggression in Southeast Asia. That was debated, that was discussed, and it was affirmed by two-thirds of the Senate, and in fact confirmed by an overwhelming vote.

The Chairman: You are talking about the SEATO treaty?

Mr. Katzenbach: I am talking about the SEATO treaty. That is not all that happened.

The Chairman: You mentioned that as a basis for the Tonkin Gulf resolution?

Mr. Katzenbach: Congress participated in that. Congress made important decisions with respect to the interests of the United States in Southeast Asia and undertook important obligations to other signatories of that treaty. That is not all that happened.

As the situation there deteriorated, as American ships were attacked in the Tonkin Gulf, the President of the United States came back to Congress to seek the views of Congress with respect to what should be done in that area and with respect to the use of the military of the United States in that area, and on those resolutions Congress had the opportunity to participate and did participate, as you well remember, Mr. Chairman. The views of the Congress I think were very clearly expressed. That resolution authorized the President of the United States, by an overwhelming vote, with only two dissents in both Houses of Congress, two together, to use the force of the United States in that situation. The combination of the two, it seems to me, fully fulfill the obligation of the Executive in a situation of this kind to participate with the Congress to give the Congress a full and effective voice, the functional equivalent of the constitutional obligation expressed in the provision of the Constitution with respect to declaring war. Beyond that Mr. Chairman—

The Chairman: They did not ask for a declaration of war. They do not have one yet.

Mr. Katzenbach: That is true in the very literal sense of the word.

Gulf of Tonkin Resolution Presented as an Emergency Measure

The Chairman: It is quite true, not only literally, but in spirit. You haven't requested and you don't intend to request a declaration of war, as I understand it.

Mr. Katzenbach: As I explained—that is correct, Mr. Chairman, but didn't that resolution authorize the President to use the armed forces of the United States in whatever way was necessary? Didn't it? What could a declaration of war have done that would have given the President more authority and a clearer voice of the Congress of the United States than that did?

The Chairman: This is exactly one of the principal criticisms of Professor Bartlett yesterday about the imprecision of the resolution. It was presented as an emergency situation; the repelling of an attack which was alleged to have been unprovoked upon our forces in the high seas. It looked at the moment as if it was a wholly unprovoked, unjustified, and an unacceptable attack upon our armed forces. He criticized the language of that resolution yesterday as a mistake, but he went on to say that "the conditions in which it was submitted to the Congress" made it, I believe he said, enormously difficult to resist it.

The circumstances partook of an emergency, as an attack upon the United States which would fall within the procedures or the principles developed in the last century of repelling attacks temporarily as opposed to a full-fledged war like the one which we are in. And he was, I thought, quite critical of that, and the circumstances were such that we were asked to act upon this resolution very quickly. As a matter of fact, the President had already responded, before the resolution was approved, to the attack upon the sources of the PT boats.

It has been interpreted as equivalent to a declaration of war. I think it is a very critical difference as to how we regard it.

I had a debate on the floor with Senator Russell about whether or not this kind of resolution is now accepted as a substitute for a declaration of war. I don't think it is properly such, especially having been made under conditions of great emergency. It wasn't a deliberate decision by the Congress to wage war in that full-fledged sense against a foreign government. I think that has been one of the difficulties now, that we are not quite sure which government we are waging the war against although it seems to me it is fairly evident.

Resolution Drafted in Executive Branch

Mr. Katzenbach: May I comment on that, Mr. Chairman?
The Chairman: Yes. I thought you had commented on it. Go ahead.
Mr. Katzenbach: I would like to comment on it more specifically.
The Chairman: Yes, sir.

Mr. Katzenbach: It seems to me that if your complaint is the drafting of the resolution of Congress it ill becomes—

The Chairman: That resolution was drafted by the Executive and sent up here. We didn't draft it, but we did, under the impulse of the emergency, accept it.

Mr. Katzenbach: Mr. Chairman, it wasn't accepted without consideration.

The Chairman: Yes; it was, largely without any consideration.

Mr. Katzenbach: Mr. Chairman, how much debate was there on that resolution as compared with a declaration of war when President Roosevelt sent that up? How quickly did the Congress respond? If you say there was pressure, there was the urgency. Maybe people regret afterward a declaration of war or a vote for it, but that situation inherently is one of urgency, it is one of commitment.

Representative Paul McCloskey:
The War Power and Congress

If I may, I would like to discuss for a moment the possibility that through habit or neglect, the House of Representatives has gradually abandoned some of its key constitutional responsibilities with respect to the executive branch of Government. In reviewing the history of major policy decisions in America, I am struck by the fact that some of our gravest policy errors have been attended by the near-unanimous support of the Congress itself and the American people. A unanimity of opinion at any given time is no guarantee that the chosen course of action is correct. Some examples of error might well include the deportation of Japanese-Americans in 1942, the McCarthyism furor of the early 1950s, the Gulf of Tonkin resolution of August 1964.

In reviewing the historical prerogatives of the legislative branch, it is apparent that the framers of the Constitution gave the war power to Congress because of a healthy fear and concern over its misuse by the executive branch. . . .

This is not to derogate the powers of the President as Commander in Chief of the Armed Forces of the United States as to the conduct of a war once embarked upon by congressional authorization. However, as to the

---

Congressional Record, House of Representatives, February 18, 1971, pp. H 796–799. Condensed.

question of whether or not wars should be fought, whether other countries are to be invaded, and what expenditures will be authorized to support such wars, Congress not only has the sole power, but the sole obligation under the Constitution.

Against this background I would like to discuss some specific areas where it might be said that Congress has allowed its constitutional powers with respect to the war in Southeast Asia to be usurped and eroded.

First

We have repeatedly allowed the administration to conceal from both Congress and the American people facts which were highly relevant to our own decisionmaking process and the support of our constituents. For years, we permitted the administration to conceal the fact that we were bombing in Laos well beyond the area of the Ho Chi Minh Trail; American ground combat forces have been sent into Laos and told to conceal the fact; the present operation "Dewey Canyon II" is an expanded version of a former operation into Laos by American combat troops called "Dewey Canyon I"; the wives of American pilots shot down over Laos were instructed by our Defense Department not to reveal that their husbands had been shot down over Laos; we have pursued the fiction that American combat operations directed by the U.S. Ambassador and civilian employees of the Central Intelligence Agency in Laos did not really constitute American combat activity at all.

Perhaps, most amazingly of all, we have permitted the administration to conceal from most of us in the Congress the precise amount of the Defense Department appropriations necessary to conduct the war in Vietnam and Laos. Understandably, an administration which wants to retain popular support for a war in Southeast Asia may not want the American people to know how much that war is costing. That is no excuse, however, for the failure of the House of Representatives to insist that the administration disclose both to us, and to our constituents, the true cost of the war and the diversion of defense funds authorized for other purposes which we might have felt could be more appropriately used other than in the rice paddies and jungles of Southeast Asia.

Second

As a corollary to our acceptance of the concealment of Vietnam war costs during our consideration of Defense Department budget requests, we have permitted our strategic weapons strength and research and development to lag behind that of our real Communist opponent, Soviet Russia.

Shortly before his death, our distinguished colleague, Mendel Rivers, made an impassioned speech in this Chamber, suggesting that the United States had never been in graver peril because of the deterioration of our comparative strategic position vis-à-vis the Soviet Union. Mr. Rivers stated that the three basic reasons for this deterioration lay in our great expenditures in Vietnam over the previous 5 years, the inflation of which such expenditures were the primary cause, and increased domestic priorities. In his remarks, Mr. Rivers made it clear, to many of us for the first time, that in order to conduct the war in Vietnam, this country had cut back many essential defense programs of construction, repair and particularly in the field of research and development.

The magnitude of Russia's gain from our Vietnam involvement is reflected by the fact that while we have spent well over $120 billion in Vietnam over the past 5 years, the Soviets have spent less than $10 billion. Since their defense budgets are roughly similar to ours in size, say in the $70 billion range, the $110-plus billion saved by them has presumably gone into missiles, naval vessels, submarines and research and development which last year surpassed our own.

The Soviets must feel they are receiving a great deal of aid and comfort every day that we remain in Vietnam.

Third

We have tacitly permitted the United States to gradually adopt methods of waging war which are repugnant to our highest traditions of military history and honor. Having lost the stomach for fighting this war and suffering the casualties involved, we have grown to accept the idea of hiring mercenaries to do our fighting for us. . . .

Fourth

We likewise seem to have fallen into the view, now so vigorously espoused by the President, that it is all right to destroy the villages and people of small countries like Laos and Cambodia, if we only do it through airpower, rather than in head-to-head ground combat where those who pull the triggers actually see the people they are killing. . . .

Fifth

We seem to have likewise fallen into an acceptance of the nomenclature thrust on us by the public relations experts of DOD and the White House—that the peasant soldiers against whom we fight are all "Communists," that somehow they are "wrong" to be fighting to reunite their homeland; that we are "right" in seeking to permanently divide Vietnam into a South Vietnam and a North Vietnam, this in spite of our acquiescence in the Geneva Accords of 1954 where the Viet Minh were promised that Vietnam would be reunited as one country within 2 years—and further in spite of our growing understanding that the most dangerous sources of world war III may well be those countries divided against the will of their peoples, Korea, Germany and, perhaps, the Mideast.

Sixth

We might also reflect on the secondary burdens that this continuing war has imposed on the basic military potential and strength of this country. We have managed to convince most of our young people that a Congress, as an institution, is unresponsive to their desire to refrain from killing people they do not hate, in a cause in which they do not believe. . . . In years to come, the United States will be in desperate need of professional military men who are the equivalent of our best minds in science, the professions and the business community. Our military establishment will need the pride and esprit de corps that have characterized it since Lexington and Concord. By turning away from the pleas of our young people to end this war now, we may be depriving our future military forces of the ability to attract men of the necessary dedication and abilities, no matter what pay raises we may choose to later give them from a Treasury already suffering a chronic deficit. . . .

Seventh

In addition to the secondary military problems caused by our continued involvement in Vietnam, what of the threat to our economic stability? In order to afford the costs of this war, we are embarking upon a new concept, that of a $30 billion budget deficit over the next 2 years, concealed beneath the label of a "full employment budget." Inflation may or may not be under control, but the impacts of inflation have been disastrous to date, and as I have listened to the comments of my older and wiser colleagues during the past 2 years, I have gathered the impression that competent economists feel that Government deficit spending has been a primary cause of inflation. This was the primary argument advanced by the President last year when he asked us to sustain his vetoes of several hundred extra million dollars over his housing and education budget proposals. I have been accustomed to hear my Republican colleagues refer to the historic virtue of "fiscal responsibility" as a desirable congressional goal. If this is so, might we then not deliberate with some seriousness over whether we can afford to continue this war at the tremendous cost which the administration is so reluctant to specify in its otherwise carefully detailed budget? . . .

In conclusion, I wonder if perhaps our primary duty in the Congress is not to show the Nation some leadership in the basic thought that we should be big enough to admit our mistakes. Clearly the administration is not about to admit something which nearly all of us now admit—that it was a mistake to have ignored the admonitions of Generals MacArthur and Ridgeway that we should not become involved in a land war on the Asian continent, considering the history and terrain of Vietnam—that it was a mistake to have stayed in as long as we did—and that it is a mistake to think that somehow we can now wrest victory out of defeat if we will only hang in a little longer and kill every possible North Vietnamese and Vietcong that we can find anywhere in Indochina, using only bombs, napalm, and strafing runs where the enemy has chosen to mix in with the native population.

There are a great many good things to do in America—building houses and rapid transit systems, doing research in medicine, high energy physics and better education methods, cleaning up our air and water. I should think that the chances of achieving a "generation of peace" might actually be enhanced if we could bring ourselves to stop participating in the killing of people in Southeast Asia and leave it to the Vietnamese themselves as to how they decide to govern themselves and possibly even reunite a country which, in times of peace, is one of the most beautiful in the world.

4

The Presidency: Emergence of the Candidates

The American presidency makes incredibly imposing demands on the man in the White House. The office calls for a man who has the dignity of a monarch, the sagacity of an elder statesman, the adroitness of a professional politician, and the physical stamina of a track star. The question discussed in this chapter is: How do we find the man to meet the demands of the office? The answer is that "we" do not find the man, but rather that a political party at its national convention "finds" a man who claims to be able to meet the challenges of the office. The central problem, then, is to examine this method of selecting presidential candidates, viewing it against the nature of the presidential office.

The national conventions date back to the early 1830s as a product of Jacksonian democracy. Prior to this time, a small group of party and congressional leaders, "King Caucus," determined who would be the presidential candidate. Along with the increase in suffrage that accompanied Jacksonian democracy came demands for a nominating method that would allow a far greater number of people to participate directly in the selection of the nominees. Thus the convention system was born.

However, the convention system has long been under attack. Many have asked just who the delegates represent. Others have questioned the appropriateness of its circus atmosphere. In the words of one critic, it is a "colossal travesty of popular institutions." Dissatisfaction with the system grew to such proportions that toward the end of the last century many states adopted the presidential-preference primary. By this method, the voters of a state select the delegates to the national convention. These delegates are pledged to support a specified candidate—at least on the first ballot. Today, approximately twenty states have some form of preference primary; but the majority of the delegates continue to be selected by state or district conventions or by the state party committees. Even in the states that use the primary, some people criticize the primaries as hardly more than popularity polls. Yet, popularity is not necessarily a meaningless term in a democratic society.

Despite this doubt, the presidential primary has taken on added dimensions that probably have been strengthened by the coming of television. As indicated in Theodore H. White's article, for Senator John F. Kennedy in 1960 the hard primary route was his only means of competing for the nomination. He entered a series of contests culminating in a "showdown" primary in West Virginia against Hubert Humphrey. The California primary played an important part in Barry Goldwater's bid for the GOP nomination in 1964. Goldwater's California victory demonstrated popular support for his nomination and, perhaps more significantly, it ended the candidacy of his principal opponent, Nelson Rockefeller.

The 1968 Democratic presidential primaries were complicated by a series of events. Senator McCarthy entered the March 12 New Hampshire primary, running against a Johnson ticket. McCarthy's "moral" victory— 42 percent as against Johnson's 49 percent, but capturing most of the delegates—may have prompted Senator Robert Kennedy to declare his candidacy on March 13 for the nomination, and it may have influenced President Johnson to announce on March 31 that he would not seek re-election. This was followed by Vice-President Humphrey's announcement on April 27 that he would seek the Party's nomination but would not enter any primaries. Presumably McCarthy's candidacy was not, at least through the end of March, a serious bid for the nomination but rather an attempt to influence President Johnson's Vietnam policy. On the other hand, Senator Robert Kennedy's candidacy was from the outset a serious bid for the nomination as well as an attempt to influence policy. The route of the primaries provided both Kennedy and McCarthy with the kind of serious national political forum that relatively unknown contenders require if they are to influence the delegates at the conventions. Richard M. Scammon and Ben J. Wattenberg contend that the primary victories of both Kennedy and McCarthy proved little because their main opponent, Vice-President Humphrey, never officially entered a primary and didn't even mount a serious write-in campaign. Hence the Democratic primaries presented the anomalous situation that one of the principal—if not the leading—contenders for the nomination did not run.

The Republican primaries of 1968 presented just the opposite situation. From 1964 to 1968 Richard Nixon slowly rebuilt his base of support within the party. By late 1967 no one had emerged as a strong opponent to challenge him in the primaries. Michigan's Governor George Romney declared his candidacy in November 1967, but he fell behind in public opinion polls and withdrew from the race shortly before the March New Hampshire primary. The only other serious candidate, Governor Rockefeller of New York, first announced in March 1968 he would not seek the nomination and then on April 30, after winning a write-in primary in Massachusetts, announced he would enter the race, yet he never mounted an official primary race against the leading contender, Richard Nixon. Still, the Republican primaries of 1968 were significant because they afforded the major contender, Richard Nixon, an opportunity to overcome his "loser" image—he had not won an election on his own since 1950. In March through June he entered and won six major primaries, and additionally he won write-in primaries in Illinois, Pennsylvania, and New Jersey.

Primaries thus can serve as important platforms for policy announcements, as they did for Senator McCarthy; they can also serve as a method for relatively unknown candidates—for example, Senator John F. Kennedy in 1960—to gain wide television and press exposure; and finally they can serve the useful purpose of subjecting the front-runner—Richard Nixon in 1968—to popular preconvention tests.

The growing importance of polls, both pre- and post-primary polls, in presidential elections should also be mentioned. As noted above, George Romney's bid for the presidency was cut short by his weak showing in the polls before the New Hampshire primary. In recent years, professional politicians in and out of office have begun to rely increasingly on polling techniques to apprise them of their various strengths and weaknesses. Indeed, good polling has become an essential first step in the management of successful election campaigns. The public, the candidates and their opponents, and, of course, convention delegates, pay a certain respect to independent national and regional polls.

In any given presidential-election year only a limited number of potential candidates appear. In a broad sense, there is a natural political aristocracy; membership in this group of white males is equivalent to "availability" for the nomination. These political aristocrats have certain features in common: a middle- to upper-class social and economic status; residency in a large urban state; an unblemished family life; and some political experience. Formerly, the unwritten rules of availability excluded non-Protestants. Kennedy's election broke that tradition, as well as the tradition favoring candidates of English, Scotch, or German background. How soon a Jew, an Italian, or a Negro will break the rule against his candidacy is unknown.

The most "available" candidate for any party's nomination is a White House incumbent. Thus the 1972 Republican nominee is probably a foregone conclusion. The 1972 Democratic nominee will be selected from fewer than a dozen available candidates—McGovern, Humphrey, Muskie, Hughes, Kennedy, Bayh. All are politicians, all are members of the upper socioeconomic group, all are white, and all come from Christian backgrounds.

While primaries can help to shape later political events, still they have not replaced and do not seem likely to replace the national nominating conventions. These conventions, with their popular origins and subsequent antidemocratic trappings, have been under attack for years. The fear of the "smoke-filled room" of the Harding era will loom again in 1972. One of the earlier and more acid attacks on the system was made in 1902 by a European observer, M. Ostrogorski. Yet for all of their seemingly antidemocratic qualities, Herbert McClosky finds conventions superior to their alternatives.

Preconvention primary battles can mean that the national conventions serve only as rubber-stamps—to ratify the previously fought popularity contests. On the other hand, a convention where smoke-filled rooms dominate the scene could imply that conventions are controlled by the party elite, the bigwigs. The question is whether either alternative is consistent with the nature of the presidency or responsible government.

Theodore H. White: The Art of the Primary

A primary fight, at any level, is America's most original contribution to the art of democracy—and, at any level, it is that form of the art most profanely reviled and intensely hated by every professional who practices politics as a trade.

In theory a primary fight removes the nomination of candidates from the hands of cynical party leadership and puts it directly in the hands of the people who make the party. When, indeed, theory matches fact (for, in some states, primaries are absurdly meaningless), primary contests result in disastrous and unforgettable explosions. A genuine primary is a fight within the family of the party—and, like any family fight, is apt to be more bitter and leave more enduring wounds than battle with the November enemy. In primaries, ambitions spurt from nowhere; unknown men carve their mark; old men are sent relentlessly to their political graves; bosses and leaders may be humiliated or unseated. At ward, county or state level, all primaries are fought with spurious family folksiness—and sharp knives.

Bosses and established leaders hate primaries for good reason; they are always, in any form, an appeal from the leaders' wishes to the people directly. Primaries suck up and waste large sums of money from contributors who might better be tapped for the November finals; the charges and countercharges of primary civil war provide the enemy party with ammunition it can later use with blast effect against whichever primary contender emerges victorious; primary campaigns exhaust the candidate, use up his speech material, drain his vital energy, leave him limp before he clashes with the major enemy.

And whatever ill can be said of local primaries can be multiplied tenfold for the Presidential primaries. For the amount of money used in a series of Presidential primaries across the breadth of this land is prodigious; the stakes of the Presidency are so high and dramatic that a horde of self-winding citizens and amateurs suddenly insists on participation; and the wreckage that a primary usually leaves of a well-organized local machine is as nothing compared to the wreckage that two political giants from alien states can make of an instate organization, whose private ambitions they abuse and whose delicate local balances and compromises they completely ignore as they strive for power to command the whole country.

Yet, when all is said, there remains this gross fact: were there no Presidential primaries, the delegates sent to the National Conventions would be chosen by local party bosses, and the decision of the Convention, made blind by inability to measure candidates' voting strength, would rest in the back room, with the bosses. When, for a period of thirty-five years, from 1865 to 1900, the choice of Presidential candidates was left to the bosses in convention assembled, their selections resulted in such mediocre leadership of this country that it could be truly written that "No period so thoroughly ordinary had been known in American politics since Christopher Columbus first disturbed the balance of American society." It was only with the turn of the twentieth century that the Presidential primary was introduced, soon to spread over the union. Many states in the next half-century experimented with the Presidential primary—some making it a permanent feature of their politics, some finally abolishing it, most of them altering its rules from decade to decade. By 1960, only sixteen states still retained a legal, open primary, in which all seekers for the Presidency of the United States, of either party, might offer themselves to the people directly. These sixteen states were as diverse in their politics and sociologies as the diversity of American civilization itself; they had been chosen by no superior reason or plan. Altogether to the foreign eye they must have seemed the most preposterous field of battle on which men who aspire to the leadership of American freedom and control of its powers should choose to joust. Yet these states were, and remain, vital to the play of American Presidential politics.

For John F. Kennedy and Hubert Humphrey there was no other than the primary way to the Convention. If they could not at the primaries prove their strength in the hearts of Americans, the Party bosses would cut their hearts out in the back rooms of Los Angeles. Thus, as they approached their combat, they had a sense of multiple audience—first, the folksy audience of the primary state to be won directly, along with the local delegates that could be harvested in the primary victory (this, of course, was the least of their considerations); next, the national audience, as the nation first paid its attention to the combat and assessed the men; and, at last, there were the bosses of the big Eastern states and the smaller organized states who would coldly watch the race to observe the performance of political horseflesh.

Of the sixteen primary states, Hubert Humphrey had by late winter chosen five as his field of battle; of the same sixteen, John F. Kennedy had similarly chosen seven. And they were first to clash head-on in Wisconsin on April 5th. . . .

By Tuesday, April 5th, as Wisconsin prepared to vote, it was (or so the prognosticators felt) a walkaway.

The fact that it was not a walkaway, as shown by the actual result of the voting, was to shape all the rest of Kennedy's strike for the Presidency, from then until November.

. . . Within two hours after the polls had closed the profile of voting had become apparent. He was to lose the Western tier conclusively—the Third, Ninth, Tenth—whether because they were farm districts or Protestant districts he could not judge. He was to lose the Second equally heavily—whether because it was Protestant or loved Humphrey or was Stevensonian again he could not judge. He was to carry the Seventh narrowly; the Sixth and Eighth (heavily Catholic, old Joe McCarthy country) substantially; the First District and Milwaukee's Fourth and Fifth (again heavily Catholic) decisively. No one could tell whether Humphrey's districts had voted against Kennedy because they were Protestant or because they were farmland closest to Minnesota; nor whether Kennedy had won his own six districts because they were heavily Catholic or because they were heavily industrial. The returns had shown their character by eight o'clock; by then, the entire message was clear to him.

"What does it mean?" asked one of his sisters.

"It means," he said quietly yet bitterly, "that we have to do it all over again. We have to go through every one and win every one of them— West Virginia and Maryland and Indiana and Oregon, all the way to the Convention." . . .

If Kennedy received his six-district-to-four margin as a setback, Humphrey received the short end of 4 to 6 almost as a victory.

Humphrey had expected defeat, had accepted the prognosis of the experts as certain tidings of devastation. Yet here he now was, having run a tight race, finding in the figures hope, cheer and comfort. . . .

He emerged from this inner scene of homespun gaiety to greet the TV cameras and the press briefly. Exuberant, he told them, "You can quote me as being encouraged and exhilarated and sorry it's all over." He quipped for a few minutes, then said he was going directly back to Washington the next day and on to West Virginia.

It is quite clear now, in retrospect, that John F. Kennedy owes his nomination as much to Hubert Humphrey's decision that night in Milwaukee as to any other man's decision except his own. . . .

If, realizing this, Humphrey had withdrawn at that moment, Kennedy would have faced zero opposition in the West Virginia primary; thus, any Kennedy victory there would have proved nothing and been meaningless in terms of bargaining power vis-à-vis the big Eastern bosses. . . .

In American life political patterns are rarely determined by geography, and the states of the union group themselves in distinct political families more by past history than by simple neighborliness.

Only 640 miles separate Madison, the capital of Wisconsin, from Charleston, the capital of West Virginia. Yet centuries of time and tradition, immeasurable gulfs of culture, separate these two states. If one were to choose as a proud grouping those American states whose politics are probably the most decent and worthy of respect, one would group Wisconsin, certainly, with Minnesota, California and Connecticut. And if one were to choose those states whose politics (excluding the baroque courthouse states of the South) are the most squalid, corrupt and despicable, then one would add West Virginia to that Jukes family of American politics that includes Indiana, Massachusetts and Texas. . . .

Over the past thirty years coal has molded West Virginia politics. Starting with the era of Franklin D. Roosevelt (who let John L. Lewis organize the miners against an industrial savagery unique in American industry), West Virginia became a Democratic state; the Mine Workers Union became a force in politics equal to the United Automobile Workers in Michigan or the clothing workers in New York.

When coal began to die some fifteen years ago, West Virginia began to die with it. Technology helped kill coal. . . . High union wages also helped kill coal employment—as the union shoved wages up and up, it became not only cheaper but also imperative for the operators to automate their mines with the superb new machines of the postwar era. Gradually, as these pressures made themselves felt, the miners were dismissed, then they hungered. . . .

West Virginia had long attracted the interest of John F. Kennedy— perhaps longer than any of the other states in the union outside his own. Two years before, while running for re-election as Senator from Massachusetts, he had retained Louis Harris to make the very first probe of public opinion outside his home state—in West Virginia, in June of 1958. (The result of the poll then was 52 for Kennedy, 38 for Nixon, balance undecided.) . . .

By April of 1960, however, after the Wisconsin primary, it was uncertain whether it was Humphrey who was caught in the trap or Kennedy himself. For between February and April the political atmosphere of the country had begun to heat. The Wisconsin primary had attracted the attention of the national press and the national television networks; and the nation had become aware that a religious issue was beginning to develop in its national politics for the first time since 1928; men and women from West Virginia to Alaska were slowly learning the identity and religion of the major candidates; and the tide in West Virginia had turned against the Boston candidate. Sampling in Charleston now, three weeks before the primary voting day of May 10th, Harris discovered that the citizens of Kanawha county—which includes Charleston, the capital—had shifted vehemently in sentiment. They were now, he reported, 60 for Humphrey, 40 for Kennedy. When Kennedy headquarters inquired of their West Virginia advisers what had happened between his 70-to-30 margin of December and the short end of the present 40-to-60 split, they were told, curtly, "But no one in West Virginia knew you were a Catholic in December. Now they know." . . .

As usual with the Kennedy operation, solutions proceeded at two levels—one strategic and one organizational. . . . The organizational solution was, of course, O'Brien's. After ten years in the service of John F. Kennedy, Lawrence F. O'Brien is certainly one of the master political operators of the new school.

What distinguishes the new school from the old school is the political approach of exclusion versus inclusion. In a tight old-fashioned machine, the root idea is to operate with as few people as possible, keeping decision and action in the hands of as few inside men as possible. In the new style, practiced by citizens' groups and new machines (Republican and Democratic alike) the central idea is to give as many people as possible a sense of participation: participation galvanizes emotions, gives the participant a live stake in the victory of the leader. . . .

A first meeting in the morning for the northern chairmen took place at the Stonewall Jackson Hotel in Clarksburg. A second meeting for the southern chairmen took place that afternoon at the Kanawha Hotel, 100 miles away, in Charleston.

Jobs to be done:

Organization of volunteers for door-to-door distribution of the Kennedy literature.

Rural mailings.

Telephone campaign. (The West Virginians explained the problem of telephoning in a state where the party line still reigns, but O'Brien insisted nonetheless.)

Receptions to be organized. (And since tea and coffee receptions were too effete for West Virginia, it was all right to call receptions an "ox roast" in the northern part of the state, a "weenie roast" in the southern part.)

Finally, all county chairmen were told which members of the Kennedy family (plus Franklin D. Roosevelt, Jr.) would be available to tour in what areas on which day.

Above all: work.

. . . But beyond organization was the raw stuff of American politics: those things blurted out by simple people that show their emotion, their misgiving, their trust. And there could be no doubt about the issue that bothered these people . . .

The issue, it was clear, over and beyond anything O'Brien's organizational genius could do, was religion: the differing ways men worshiped Christ in this enclave of Western civilization.

All other issues were secondary. The Kennedy tacticians had already refined several minor lines of attack on Humphrey. They had begun and continued to stress the war record of John F. Kennedy, for in West Virginia, a state of heroes and volunteers, the stark courage of the Boston candidate in the Straits of the Solomons in the Fall of 1942 found a martial echo in every hill. ("To listen to their stuff," said an irate Humphrey man, "you'd think Jack won the war all by himself.") The Kennedy men continued to hammer at Humphrey as being "front man" for a gang-up crowd of Stevenson-Symington-Johnson supporters who refused to come into the open. They stressed their candidate's sympathy and concern for the hungry and unemployed. Humphrey, who had known hunger in boyhood, was the natural workingman's candidate—but Kennedy's shock at the suffering he saw in West Virginia was so fresh that it communicated itself with the emotion of original discovery. Kennedy, from boyhood to manhood, had never known hunger. Now, arriving in West Virginia from a brief rest in the sun in the luxury of Montego Bay, he could scarcely bring himself to believe that human beings were forced to eat and live on these cans of dry relief rations, which he fingered like artifacts of another civilization. "Imagine," he said to one of his assistants one night, "just imagine kids who never drink milk." Of all the emotional experiences of his pre-Convention campaign, Kennedy's exposure to the misery of the mining fields probably changed him most as a man; and as he gave tongue to his indignation, one could sense him winning friends.

Yet the religious issue remained, and as the days grew closer to the voting the Kennedy staff divided on how it must be handled. . . . It was up to the candidate alone to decide. And, starting on April 25th, his decision became clear. He would attack—he would meet the religious issue head on. Whether out of conviction or out of tactics, no sounder Kennedy decision could have been made. Two Democratic candidates were appealing to the commonalty of the Democratic Party; once the issue could be made one of tolerance or intolerance, Hubert Humphrey was hung. No one could prove to his own conscience that by voting for Humphrey he was displaying tolerance. Yet any man, indecisive in mind on the Presidency, could prove that he was at least tolerant by voting for Jack Kennedy.

Up and down the roads roved Kennedy names, brothers and sisters all available for speeches and appearances; to the family names was added the lustrous name of Franklin D. Roosevelt, Jr. Above all, over and over again there was the handsome, open-faced candidate on the TV screen, showing himself, proving that a Catholic wears no horns. The documentary film on TV opened with a cut of a PT boat spraying a white wake through the black night, and Kennedy was a war hero; the film next showed the quiet young man holding a book in his hand in his own library receiving the Pulitzer Prize, and he was a scholar; then the young man held his golden-curled daughter of two, reading to her as she sat on his lap, and he was the young father; and always, gravely, open-eyed, with a sincerity that could not be feigned, he would explain his own devotion to the freedom of America's faiths and the separation of church and state. . . .

The orchestration of this campaign infuriated Humphrey. Once the issue had been pitched as tolerance versus intolerance, there was only one way for a West Virginian to demonstrate tolerance—and that was by voting for Kennedy. Backed against the wall by the development of an issue for which there was no conceivable response either in his heart or practical politics, Humphrey fell back on the issue of money. ("There are three kinds of politics," he would say. "The politics of big business, the politics of the big bosses, and the politics of big money, and I'm against all of them. I stand for politics of the people.") . . .

Strangled for lack of money (Humphrey's expenditures in West Virginia were to total only $25,000—nothing, in the scale of American politics), knowing himself in debt, aware of the nature, depth and resources of this final Kennedy drive, as the final weekend approached Humphrey became a figure of pathos. He needed advertising, he needed workers, above all he needed TV to show himself across the state.

West Virginia voted on May 10th, a wet, drizzly day. By eight o'clock the polls were closed. With 100 names on some of the local ballots, all of them more important as jobs to West Virginians than the Presidency, the count was very slow. Shortly before nine o'clock, however, came the first flash: Old Field Precinct, Hardy County, Eastern Panhandle, a precinct acknowledging only twenty-five Catholic registered voters, had counted: For Kennedy, 96; for Humphrey, 36.

The count dragged on. By 9:20, with ten precincts out of 2,750 in the state having reported, the first faint trend became visible: Kennedy, 638; Humphrey, 473—a 60-to-40 break. Yet these were from northern West Virginia, the sensitized civilized north. How would the candidate do in the fundamentalist, coal-mining south? By 9:40 the count read Kennedy, 1,566 and Humphrey, 834; and someone in the Humphrey headquarters muttered, "We're dead." . . .

The Senator's eyes gleamed with tears in the bright lights that television had installed to catch the surrender. It took him a moment to get his voice under control.

"I have a brief statement to make," he said. He read the words, "I am no longer a candidate for the Democratic Presidential nomination."

. . . The first of the seven had been scratched from the list of candidates for the Presidency of the United States by the people of the hills. In the morning, when Hubert Humphrey woke, the Presidential image had evaporated. Outside the Ruffner Hotel his parked bus had overnight been given a ticket for illegal parking.

Richard M. Scammon and Ben J. Wattenberg: The Prove-Little Primaries

The remaining contested primaries showed much the same pattern as the Indiana primary: a highly publicized intramural confrontation between two left-of-center Democrats, largely running against each other on the basis of personality. While this was going on, the real battle of 1968—the battle between the ministerialists and the oppositionists, between the ins and the outs, waged in part on the basis of the Social Issue—was slowly taking shape off the front pages. This major battle had seen more premature and somewhat distorted testing in New Hampshire and Wisconsin. When Johnson withdrew, when Humphrey did not enter the primaries, with Nixon and Wallace not really subject to test, the real substance of the campaign lay publicly dormant for many months.

To recall the situation in the spring of 1968: In polls among Democrats, Humphrey continued to lead Kennedy by a little and McCarthy by a lot. In the primaries Kennedy beat McCarthy everywhere but in Oregon, while a third entry in the race, usually identified by the press (but not by the authors) as an administration slate, ran well back.

On the Republican side, no real candidate opposed Nixon, and he just kept winning "meaningless" victories. That at least is what his opponents called them. In fact, these victories were loaded with meaning: They meant that Nixon was not "a loser," as his opponents described him, and they built a national base behind the idea that "Nixon's the One," as his campaign slogan went.

George Wallace kept up a fairly steady speaking schedule, and his organizers saw to it that the necessary legal steps were taken to get his name on the ballot in each of the fifty states. Just as the McCarthy kids were giving new definition to the role of participatory democracy, so, too, were the Wallace workers: raising money; collecting petitions; staging rallies. Both the Wallace and the McCarthy movements showed far greater political effectiveness than most observers would have thought possible.

For the record, and for a few brief psephological lessons, we can glance quickly at the results of the remaining spring primaries.

The Nebraska primary showed fine results from the Kennedy point of view. In a state where only 1% of the population is black and less than 20% are blue-collar workers, Kennedy decisively beat a Midwestern farm-oriented Senator:

Democratic Preference Vote, Nebraska, 1968

Robert F. Kennedy	52%
Eugene J. McCarthy	31%
Lyndon B. Johnson	6%
Hubert H. Humphrey write-ins	7%
Other write-ins	4%

There was no Roger Branigin in the Nebraska election, no one campaigning with any effectiveness as an anti-Kennedy/McCarthy candidate. As always, the voters chose essentially from those who were actively running and actively campaigning. The two active national candidates were Kennedy, who campaigned heavily in the state, and McCarthy, who conducted a rather desultory effort, Kennedy won.

Now for a change. Nixon won again. But Reagan, while on the ballot, did not appear in the state, allowing pundits to note that Mr. Nixon's victory was "meaningless."

The Republican results:

Republican Preference Vote, Nebraska, 1968

Richard M. Nixon	70%
Ronald Reagan	21%
Others	2%
Nelson Rockefeller write-ins	5%
Other write-ins	2%

McCarthy's candidacy reached its apogee in the Oregon primary, two weeks later, when he solidly beat Kennedy:

Democratic Preference Vote, Oregon, 1968

McCarthy	44%
Kennedy	38%
Johnson	12%
Write-ins	12%

The strength of that showing should not be denied, as has been done, by deprecating Oregon as an atypically wealthy, white, and untroubled state, untarnished by the crisis of cities or other modern ailments. Be that as it may, it is by far outweighed by the fact that Somebody Beat a Kennedy Somewhere (first time anywhere, anytime). The fact that this same somebody had earlier beaten the incumbent President of the United States in a primary and that only six months earlier this somebody was a nobody is cause for a retrospective, retroactive, unencumbered, unmodified laurel wreath to be placed on Senator McCarthy's brow.

There was some talk at the time of the Oregon election that Humphrey supporters were urging their supporters to vote not for Johnson (who was on the ballot), but for McCarthy in order to help a "stop Bobby" movement. But like most such grand political machinations that the press finds so fascinating, the results among rank-and-file voters was probably somewhat less than small. It's a rare voter who will be directed *away* from a Johnson vote *to* a McCarthy vote in order to *stop* Kennedy and *help* Humphrey. Too cute. Far too cute to work. McCarthy won fair and square.

At the same time, it must also be stressed again that Senator McCarthy beat Senator Kennedy, not Vice President Humphrey. In national polls at about the time of the Oregon primary, Humphrey was beating McCarthy 56%–37% in a two-man race among Democrats.

That other fellow also won again. Governor Reagan was on the ballot, but he did not openly campaign in Oregon. Accordingly, Reagan's supporters were able to say that the contest was "meaningless" because Nixon was unopposed. But in fact, Nixon *was* opposed. Reagan, unlike Humphrey, *was* on the ballot. Reagan, unlike Johnson, by the time of the Oregon primary *was* a *de facto* candidate for President. If Oregon Republicans wanted to go the route of a right-wing candidate all they had to do was pull the little lever. They didn't. The fact that they didn't was to be clearly reflected at the Republican Convention in Miami.

The results:

Republican Preference Vote, Oregon, 1968

Nixon	73%
Reagan	23%
Rockefeller write-ins	4%

California. Same electoral story, with a different Democratic candidate the victor and terminated by a tragedy that changed the history of American politics.

After the defeat in Oregon, it was imperative for Robert Kennedy to win the preference primary (and California's 172 elected convention votes) in the most populous state of the Union. He did—barely.

Again, Kennedy's competition came from McCarthy and an amorphous third line on the ballot headed by Attorney General Thomas Lynch, who chose to vacation in Hawaii for two weeks just prior to the primary. The Lynch candidacy in California was further complicated by the fact some of the delegates on the Lynch slate announced publicly that they were in support of Kennedy or McCarthy. By our reasoning, Attorney General Lynch represented, in California, what Governor Branigin represented in Indiana: a noncandidate for President, generally nonidentified by the voters with a real candidate for President. There was one essential difference: Branigin *campaigned* in his role as noncandidate; Lynch did not. Furthermore, Branigin had some help from a strong Democratic Party organization in Indiana; on the other hand, California is an organization man's nightmare.

The results:

Kennedy	46%
McCarthy	42%
Lynch	12%

The popular political mythology concerning California deals with its atypicality, and the impression is frequently gained that every second California voter wears a button labeled "I Am a Kook." Such voters, as we are informed, are interested in yoga, vegetarianism, or cryogenics. Many are said to be little old ladies in tennis shoes who consider Ronald Reagan a leftist and the John Birch Society as a middle-of-the-road group of political activists. More recently, to the much publicized roster of screwball Californians, there have been added gun-toting Black Panthers and shaggy, sandaled students whose political rhetoric deals with four-letter words, of which "vote" is not the most conspicuous.

It's a nice story, it makes good copy, and, of course, there are a lot of strange types in California (as elsewhere).

Yet California, viewed psephologically, is not really atypical, screwballs notwithstanding.

To begin with, the largest state—with more than 10% of the nation's total population—is unlikely to be very atypical, although there are no "typical" states. California, compared to other states, is slightly more urban, somewhat more wealthy, substantially more Mexican-American and Oriental-American, slightly less black, and it has proportionately fewer people residing there who were born in the state. It has first- and second-generation foreign stock and foreign born in proportions not very different from the nation as a whole.

Beyond that, in the small world of election analysts, California is known as an excellent *barometric* state. Among large states, Illinois and California are the two that vote most consistently like America as a whole. Since 1948 California had never been more than two percentage points away from the final national percentage for the Presidential winner.

It is important to note this as we watch how the three main notions of American elections were hard at work in the 1968 California primary. The California electorate was about as unyoung and unblack as elsewhere and only slightly more unpoor. One of the key issues of the election was the Social Issue. And despite the blossoming phrase "New Politics," the politicians were demonstrating the same old political tropism to that same old political center. . . .

The results of both the District of Columbia Democratic primary and the South Dakota Democratic primary were largely eclipsed by far bigger primaries that were held on the same day: The D.C. primary was held at the same time as the Indiana primary; the South Dakota race was held simultaneously with the California primary.

The District primary provided the only point in the campaign where a slate of pro-Kennedy delegates directly faced a slate of pro-Humphrey delegates. (A pro-McCarthy slate withdrew from the race in favor of the pro-Kennedy slate.)

Kennedy clobbered Humphrey:

*Vote for Democratic National Committeeman,
District of Columbia, 1968*

Rev. Channing E. Phillips (pro-Kennedy)	62%
E. Franklin Jackson (pro-Humphrey)	36%
Byron N. Scott (independent pro-Humphrey)	2%

As an example of Kennedy electoral power, however, the results of the District primary were not of particular value to his candidacy.

The majority of the population of the District of Columbia in 1968 was black, compared to 11% for the country as a whole. What the District primary showed was great Kennedy strength among blacks—hardly a surprise.

It was in South Dakota that Robert Kennedy showed his most impressive political muscle of the 1968 campaign. Running in a proportionately whiter, more rural, more Protestant state even than Nebraska, Kennedy polled 50% in a three-slate race. Again Humphrey's name was *not* on the ballot, but South Dakota *was* his birthplace, and it was next door to Gene McCarthy's home state.

The vote:

Kennedy slate	50%
Johnson slate	30%
McCarthy slate	20%

These South Dakota results would probably have been valuable to Kennedy in a stretch run to the convention. Viewing these South Dakota returns along with the relatively weaker California results, one can only say that Robert Kennedy was shot at a moment when his political future was uncertain.

Aside from the great personal tragedy involved, two political thoughts about the assassination occur.

The first is that one of the key factors in electoral politics is that we can never know all the key factors. After Herbert Hoover was landslided into office in 1928, it was "clear" to all the experts that the Democratic Party was finished in America—and then came the Depression. Mr. Scammon recalls a 1961 Washington dinner party at which some of the wisest political observers in the nation's capital sat around over cigars and brandy speculating on the forthcoming 1964 Presidential race between John Kennedy and Nelson Rockefeller.

The second thought is tangential to the first. Because the rule is "Expect the Unexpected," there is little real sense in playing the political "what if?" game—except that it is addictive. As addicts to this fruitless pastime, we ask the question: *What if* Robert Kennedy had not been killed; would he have been nominated in Chicago? Our answer, resounding and emphatic, delivered with all the courage we can muster is: "Probably not, but—"

Kennedy had won some primaries with substantial numbers of delegates, notably California and Indiana, but he had not beaten his main opponent, Humphrey, face-to-face in any direct competition. In point of fact, from the time the Vice President announced his candidacy *Humphrey led RFK among Democrats in each of the public opinion polls up until Kennedy's murder.* The last poll showed Democrats voting 40%–31%–19%, for Humphrey, Kennedy, McCarthy, in that order. *Furthermore, Humphrey was shown to run strongest against Nixon in those same polls.* The importance of these data cannot be underestimated, particularly in light of what happened in Chicago later. Here are the early May Gallup data:

Nixon–Humphrey–Wallace "Test Election"
May, 1968

Nixon	Humphrey	Wallace	No Opinion
39%	36%	14%	11%

Nixon–Kennedy–Wallace "Test Election"
May, 1968

Nixon	Kennedy	Wallace	No Opinion
42%	32%	15%	11%

Humphrey's lead in the polls was reflected by his delegate strength in those states that did not have open and contested Presidential preference primary elections. Although there have been much subsequent comment and testimony about how "undemocratic" the no-primary system is, it has, in fact, been a rather good barometer of party sentiment over the years.

Because the system—if one chooses to dignify institutionalized helterskelterism with the word "system"—is so complicated, it is hard to say exactly *why* and *how* it ends up as responsive as it is. Some states have beauty contests and unbonded delegates. Some states have no beauty contest but elect pledged delegates. Some states choose delegates by caucus or convention. Some delegates in some states are chosen directly by the state committees. Some states have hybrid mixtures of these systems. Some states have all the mechanisms available for an open, contested primary but never reach a "democratic" choice because two competing candidates do not enter the contest. Some nonprimary states went to McCarthy, many more to Humphrey. Some nonprimary states went by a unit rule totally to Humphrey; some primary states went by unit rule totally to McCarthy; some states split their vote.

What can be said about the delegate selection system is this: Somehow it works. All the delegates are *elected* or, if not, are *selected* by people who *were elected* popularly, or, in some cases selected by people who were selected by people who were elected popularly at one time or another. There is, then, a democratic process, if far removed, behind each delegate. That there is also a good deal of democratic slippage in the system is unquestioned. Still, in convention after convention, the choice the delegates ultimately make is the choice of the tens of millions of party voters. This will be examined at greater length in the next chapter.

When we consider why Hubert Humphrey was ahead of Kennedy and McCarthy in the polls, it is wise to remember (again) who votes in America and what these voters were mostly disturbed about. The voters are unyoung, unpoor, unblack; they are middle-aged, middle-class; they wanted a conservative for the next Supreme Court Justice; they were concerned about crime, race, kids, disruption, and dissent, as well as with Vietnam.

Now, it is true that both Kennedy and McCarthy were against the established order, as were tens of millions of the electorate. But they were against things as they were from a direction that was probably not in tune with mainstream thinking. McCarthy and RFK were perceived as somewhat more liberal than Humphrey and more liberal than the Establishment at a time when liberalism was declining in popularity as a political label. The voters generally were to the ideological *right* of things as they were, certainly on the Social Issue. Both McCarthy and Kennedy were generally perceived to be the ideological *left* of things as they were. Humphrey was in the middle, which, as we have noted, is a very good place for a politician to be. He was perceived as more representative and more responsive to the aspirations and fears of that Democratic lady from suburban Dayton. The polls show it.

Humphrey's problem was that while he was in the middle of the Democratic Party, it turned out that when *all* the candidates were in the poll—and all the voters, not just Democrats, were voting—he was not in the center, but a little off to the left.

But because of the way the campaign fell into place, it left the New Politics ideologues with the feeling that they had been euchred out of a fair shake in the psephological marketplace. First, Johnson withdrew, robbing them of someone to run against; then Humphrey opted not to run in the few primaries he could have entered, and he was not a candidate early enough to be pushed into running in the so-called force primaries; finally, their most potent candidate was slain, eliminating their best hope to marshal public opinion behind their banner.

The conclusion drawn by the New Politicians was that the system was rigged and that the "bosses" denied the "people" the man they wanted or at least that the people never had a chance to pick their man. In the judgment of the authors, that is not what happened. The "people" did have a very eloquent, very powerful way of making their opinions felt. The advent of the accurate and speedy public opinion poll has probably done more to advance the responsiveness of the democratic process than any invention since the secret ballot and the direct primary. When the Gallup pollster and the Harris pollster visited that machinist's wife in suburban Dayton, they were hearing the voice of the people, and a week or two later her voice thundered its message to politicians across the land. Had the Gallup Poll in May shown Kennedy clearly ahead of Humphrey among Democrats, had the Gallup Poll in July shown McCarthy clearly ahead of Humphrey among Democrats, then it is entirely likely the Democratic delegates would have (1) been different people, or (2) not selected Humphrey. But it was Humphrey who was ahead—and it was Humphrey who was selected.

In one sense, the New Politics operation may actually have received more power and attention from the system than its public support merited. Suppose Humphrey *had* run in some of those spring primaries and *won* against either Kennedy or McCarthy or both of them—as the polls indicated he would have. Suppose something else. Suppose George Wallace *and* Humphrey entered the Democratic primaries. Wallace, let us remember, captured 34% of the Wisconsin primary vote and 30% of the Indiana vote in *1964,* long before the full flowering of the Social Issue. Suppose Wallace ran in Indiana and took 30% of the primary vote and Humphrey took another 35%, leaving Kennedy and McCarthy to split up the remaining 35%. Suppose there was a Wallace–*Johnson*–McCarthy race in New Hampshire. The against-things-as-they-were voters might well have split between Wallace and McCarthy, leaving Johnson with the 50% write-in vote he actually received and letting Wallace and McCarthy split up the rest.

Such speculations can go on indefinitely and can prove almost anything. That is why the speculations about RFK's ultimate success must remain only speculations about imponderables.

M. Ostrogorski: The American Convention System

At last, after a session of several days, the end is reached; the convention adjourns *sine die*. All is over. As you step out of the building you inhale with relief the gentle breeze which tempers the scorching heat of July; you come to yourself; you recover your sensibility, which has been blunted by the incessant uproar, and your faculty of judgment, which has been held in abeyance amid the pandemonium in which day after day has been passed. You collect your impressions, and you realize what a colossal travesty of popular institutions you have just been witnessing. A greedy crowd of office-holders, or of office-seekers, disguised as delegates of the people, on the pretence of holding the grand council of the party, indulged in, or were the victims of, intrigues and manœuvres, the object of which was the chief magistracy of the greatest Republic of the two hemispheres —the succession to the Washingtons and the Jeffersons. With an elaborate respect for forms extending to the smallest details of procedure, they pretended to deliberate, and then passed resolutions settled by a handful of wire-pullers in the obscurity of committees and private caucuses; they proclaimed as the creed of the party appealing to its piety, a collection of hollow, vague phrases, strung together by a few experts in the art of using meaningless language, and adopted still more precipitately without examination and without conviction; with their hand upon their heart, they adjured the assembly to support aspirants in whose success they had not the faintest belief; they voted in public for candidates whom they were scheming to defeat. Cut off from their conscience by selfish calculations and from their judgment by the tumultuous crowd of spectators, which alone made all attempt at deliberation an impossibility, they submitted without resistance to the pressure of the galleries masquerading as popular opinion, and made up of a *claque* and of a raving mob which, under ordinary circumstances, could only be formed by the inmates of all the lunatic asylums of the country who had made their escape at the same time. Here

---

From *Democracy and the Organization of Political Parties* by M. Ostrogorski, pp. 278–279. New York: The Macmillan Company, 1902.

this mob discharges a great political function; it supplies the "enthusiasm" which is the primary element of the convention, which does duty for discussion and controls all its movements. Produced to order of the astute managers, "enthusiasm" is served out to the delegates as a strong drink, to gain completer mastery over their will. But in the fit of intoxication they yield to the most sudden impulses, dart in the most unexpected directions, and it is blind chance which has the last word. The name of the candidate for the Presidency of the Republic issues from the votes of the convention like a number from a lottery. And all the followers of the party, from the Atlantic to the Pacific, are bound, on pain of apostasy, to vote for the product of that lottery. Yet, when you carry your thoughts back from the scene which you have just witnessed and review the line of Presidents, you find that if they have not all been great men—far from it—they were all honorable men; and you cannot help repeating the American saying: "God takes care of drunkards, of little children, and of the United States!"

Herbert McClosky: Are Political Conventions Undemocratic?

No feature of American politics has so aroused the disdain of political purists as our Presidential nominating conventions. Raucous, windy, tumultuous, festive, noisy—to the casual observer they seem as rowdy as a Tammany saloon, as stylized as a Kabuki drama, as ritualized as a professional wrestling match. Overripe in their rhetoric, inelegant in their proceedings, a combination Mardi Gras and clambake, they suggest a carnival rather than a deliberative body charged with the momentous task of nominating a Presidential candidate and shaping a party program. Some observers consider them an offense against dignity, reflection, and sensibility. Others, wearied by their interminable talk, find them irksome and boring.

The standard description of the convention's decision-making process is scarcely more flattering: In back rooms and hotel suites, candidates, delegation leaders, functionaries, and "bosses" meet clandestinely to arrange the convention's business and to work out agreements and accommo-

From "Are Political Conventions Undemocratic?" by Herbert McClosky, *The New York Times Magazine*, Aug. 4, 1968. Copyright © 1968 by the New York Times Company. Reprinted by permission.

dations favorable to their mutual interests; "deals" are made, bargains are struck, principles are compromised, and beliefs are sacrificed to expediency. This description, however widely voiced, is caricature. Like most caricature, it contains elements of truth, but it is far from being either generous or entirely accurate. This year such comments on our Presidential nominating process have increased, and there have been urgent calls by many prominent in public affairs for the abolition of the national convention. These doubtless reflect the unparalleled events of the past five years: the assassination of three of our most gifted and venerated public men; the horror, dashed hopes and frustrations caused by Vietnam; dramatic and disconcerting changes in the ecology of our cities; uprisings and disorder in the ghettos and universities; the reversion in many quarters to "confrontation" politics in place of democratic civility and mutual accommodation. All these matters have profoundly shaken the national consensus, provoked what some regard as a crisis of legitimacy, and brought into question many of our institutions, including, of course, our procedures for nominating the nation's Chief Executive.

Events specific to the present campaign have increased the misgivings many voters feel not only about the national convention as an institution but about the particular two conventions being held this month. Some have even been led to the conviction that the electoral process has miscarried this year and has deprived many voters—especially young people—of an effective voice in the shaping of their own, and the nation's, affairs.

Some of these charges, of course, are typical of the complaints voiced in political campaigns by the "outs" against the "ins." Nevertheless, one must concede that the existing method of nominating Presidential candidates is, from the point of view of democratic theory, less than ideal. Some of its deficiencies are inherent in all complex forms of political organization, while some are peculiar to the party system as it evolved under American conditions.

One consequence, for example, of combining a Presidential form of government with a Federal two-party system is that it puts the parties under severe pressure to bring together a coalition of state delegations large enough to nominate the one nationwide candidate who will represent the party in a general election. In contrast to multiparty, cabinet systems of government, more emphasis is put on attaining a majority than on calling attention to the diverse views within the electorate. Little effort is made in party conventions to expose, much less heighten, the cleavages that divide the country; instead, the emphasis is on unity and on the search for a candidate who can reconcile the often conflicting interests of party members and voters from different parts of the society.

The warning sounded by critics that each of this month's conventions may seek in its proceedings to minimize the national conflicts over Vietnam, the cities, law and order, etc., is a realistic expectation. In the face of crisis, and the bitter election struggle it is likely to evoke, party leaders will be especially concerned to soften existing differences, or at least to keep them from being paraded before the eyes of millions of television viewers and newspaper readers. The American parties are loose confederations of state parties, and this not only reduces their motivation to publicly debate divisive national questions, but also affects the degree to which party members across the nation are adequately represented. Whether a state's delegates are chosen by a primary, state convention, caucus, state central committee, or some variation or combination of these, no special effort is made to represent the state's party membership in proportion to their beliefs or preferences.

Primaries, in fact, sometimes turn out to be the least representative, since they assign the entire state's delegations to the Presidential candidate who gets a plurality. Certain state parties are strongly dominated by the governor or some other official, and these leaders are often more concerned with the strength and unity of the organization than with its representativeness.

Once a majority forms at a convention, or is on the way to becoming a reality, its usual impulse is to take command. It may stop short of actually trampling on the minority, but considerable forbearance is required for it to refrain from exploiting its strength to enlarge its advantage. The candidates who appear to be running behind in the delegate count are at a disadvantage, for they are less likely to win the close ones.

When a group of party leaders sense that they have, or are likely to have, a majority at the convention, some of them will surely try to force the appearance of unity upon the party by shutting out the minority in any way they can—the more so if they happen to perceive the minority as dissident or disloyal. Thus, in the present contest for the Democratic nomination, a number of factors may conspire to place the McCarthy forces at an even greater disadvantage than they would suffer from the mere fact of having attracted a smaller number of delegates to begin with.

The entire drama, however, need not go in this direction, for there are counteracting considerations which lead one to believe that the conventions are, or may be, less tightly dominated than one might suppose. The incentive of the majority to command, for example, is to some extent counteracted by a commitment Americans share about the "rules of the game." These include the sense of fair play and the respect for minority rights.

Then, too, while the party leaders of key states can, if they combine, move large numbers of key delegates, it is an oversimplification to assume that the convention delegates are mere pawns in a political chess game played out by masters. Not all delegations are dominated by a leader or unified in their preferences. Some delegations are the handiwork not of a single "machine" but of competing machines. Some contain dissident factions that challenge the leaders at every turn. Nor is the influence in one direction only, for even strong political leaders can retain their power only if they know when to bend to the wishes of the delegation.

We would also be mistaken to assume that the convention leaders always see eye to eye. Some are rivals or even enemies. They are not a syndicate or a clearly defined oligarchy, but rather a loose, unstable coalition, volatile and, except for a few of its members, surprisingly uncool. Behind the formal structure, especially among Democrats, one discovers a bewildering assortment of factional, class, geographic, ethnic, and ideological interests—the state of affairs that led Will Rogers to his famous comment that he belonged to no organized party, for he was a Democrat.

While some leaders or delegates have more power than others, one ought not to conclude that *more* power equals *absolute* power, or that *less* power equals *no* power. Like all men who are eager to win, they are weakened by their ambitions. Their desire, for example, to avoid a bloody public squabble may lead them to make concessions (these may involve changes in the platform, opportunities for certain individuals to address the convention, the seating of contested delegations, or in extreme cases, the Vice-Presidential nomination). Few party professionals want to drive the minority out of the party. The predominant motivation is to achieve unity, and it is this, rather than oligarchic usurpation, that most often leads to "deals" and accommodations.

It should be noted that the minority plays the same game as the majority, but enjoys the advantage, as a minority, of appearing the more virtuous. McCarthy supporters, for example, have been no less active than Humphrey's in trying to line up the support of party leaders and delegates. For Humphrey, there is no way to emerge unscathed: if he is nominated on the first ballot, he (or the "organization") will be said to have rigged the convention beforehand; if he wins only after several ballots, he (or the "organization") will be said to have successfully manipulated the convention in Humphrey's favor; and if he loses the nomination to McCarthy or some other candidate, he (or the "organization") will be said to have been overturned by an uprising of the "people."

In short, the degree to which partisans favor or oppose the nominating convention notoriously reflects the vicissitudes of the political contest. It is not uncommon for the losers in a political struggle to propose the structural reforms of the institution which denies them victory.

The circumstances of the Republican contest differ from those of the Democratic, but similarities can be detected. The Rockefeller camp, aware that Nixon enjoys a considerable initial edge in delegate strength, points to the national opinion polls to prove its claim that Rockefeller is the preferred candidate of the voters. Owing to Rockefeller's fumbling and indecision in first withdrawing from the race, and his reentry when it was too late to compete in the primaries, his associates cannot complain about the inappropriateness of the convention system or extol the superiority of a national Presidential primary. Nevertheless, they too have sought to circumvent the convention as an instrument of decision-making by asking, in effect, for a national plebiscite to be officially conducted by the Republican party, the results of which would presumably guide if not actually bind the delegates at Miami Beach.

The assumption behind both objections to the convention system is that the selection of the Presidential candidates ought properly to be lodged with the voters themselves and not with a body of party practitioners. A national primary, its proponents claim, would correct the deficiencies that now attend the Presidential nominating procedure. It would not only be democratic, allowing all party supporters to participate in the choice, but would also draw on the people's wisdom, remove the party from the hands of the political bosses and mountebanks and return it to the governed, restore a sense of individual participation in the shaping of one's destiny, awaken voter interest, and permit the electorate to register its preferences for urgently desired changes.

The recommendation is well-meaning; it is also, however, misguided, for many of its assumptions are false, and the cure would, in any event, be worse than the disease.

The mystique that surrounds elections in a democracy has been carried over by the proponents of the Presidential primary to bolster their claim for its superior wisdom. If the assumption of *vox populi, vox dei* holds for general elections, why should it not also hold for primaries?

One difficulty with this assumption, however, is that voters often differ sharply in their views, and unless God speaks in many and conflicting tongues, their claim to superior wisdom becomes difficult to sustain on this ground. Nor do voters always exhibit sagacity in their choice of rulers, for they have elected men of malignant as well as benevolent aspect. Nothing in the electoral process insures that wise, just, prudent, and compassionate men will be preferred to stupid, cruel, and irresponsible ones. Voters have elected despots and democrats, Fascists and Communists, totalitarians and libertarians, liberals and conservatives, the virtuous and the vicious, men of honor and integrity as well as liars and cheats.

On what grounds, then, should we expect the electorate to exhibit greater insight when it participates in a Presidential primary? Indeed, since a primary removes party differences and other familiar guides that are ordinarily available to the voter in a general election, the danger is increased that he will fall victim to demagogues and crowd-pleasers, matinee idols and publicity seekers, familiar names and celebrities. Primaries are, to an even greater degree than general elections, popularity contests. Men of minor talent who, by ostentatious display, are able to call attention to themselves, enjoy an unusual advantage in the primaries over men of greater gifts, but of more sober demeanor.

No defender of the convention system needs to apologize for the overall quality of the men who have been nominated for the Presidency. During the present century, the conventions have turned up, among others, Woodrow Wilson, William Jennings Bryan, Theodore Roosevelt, William Howard Taft, Charles Evans Hughes, Franklin Roosevelt, Herbert Hoover, John F. Kennedy, Harry Truman, Thomas Dewey, Richard Nixon, Wendell Willkie, and Adlai Stevenson. A few of the nominees may have fallen short of Presidential caliber, but the list on the whole is an impressive one.

Nor does the historical record show that the men chosen by the conventions were less able and deserving than the men they rejected. How many distinguished and supremely qualified men can one name who would have been nominated by a national Presidential primary but who were passed over by the conventions? In some instances conventions have turned up men of extraordinary quality and distinction who were not widely known to the electorate and who would certainly have been unable to win a national Presidential primary. Woodrow Wilson is one example, and Adlai Stevenson is another. It was the "organization" and the convention system that discovered Stevenson, recognized his brilliance, integrity, and high-mindedness, and nominated and renominated him for the nation's highest office.

The delegates' ability to recognize and nominate superior candidates is not fortuitous. Through comparative research on the characteristics of party leaders and voters, we have learned that convention delegates are much better prepared than ordinary voters to assess the attributes of candidates. They are more interested, aware, and concerned about political outcomes. Ideologically they are far more sophisticated and mature than the average voter. Despite their differences, the delegates to the two conventions constitute, to a far greater extent than their rank-and-file supporters, communities of cobelievers. Not only does each of the party delegations tend to converge around identifiable belief systems, but they also tend to diverge from each other along liberal–conservative lines. Their respective followers, however, tend to look alike.

Thus, it is not the delegates of the two parties but the mass of their supporters who can more appropriately be described as Tweedledum and Tweedledee. Whereas the delegates are prone to search out and select candidates who embody the party's values, the mass of Democratic and Republican voters, participating in a national Presidential primary, would be likely to select candidates who are ideological twins. Nomination by primary, in short, might well afford the electorate less of a choice than nomination by convention.

We have grown so accustomed to the stereotype of convention delegates as Babbitts who wear funny hats and engage in juvenile hijinks that we often overlook the fact that they are a relatively sophisticated group of people. Most of them are above average in education, have participated in politics for many years, have usually held public or party office, are active in their local communities, and associate with the men who lead and manage affairs in almost every segment of society.

Our stereotypes of politicians and convention delegates have done them (and us) the disservice of misleading us about the pride many of them feel about the political vocation. Like physicians, journalists, professors, or carpenters, most of them are concerned to do a good job and to uphold acceptable standards. No matter how drastically the political vocation changes, we persist in imagining the delegates as city-hall hacks and self-servers, ignorant and coarse.

Convention delegates actually are found to be not only less cynical politically than the average voter, but they have higher political standards and make greater demands on the performance of their colleagues. Many of the delegates who pursue politics mainly as an avocation hold important positions elsewhere in society. They are trade-union leaders, businessmen, editors, physicians, writers, civil-rights leaders, lawyers, professors, engineers, or have other jobs that require education or the ability to perform effectively in organizational roles. Many are conscientious citizens who belong to good-government groups, foreign-policy associations, organizations of women voters, and other voluntary bodies concerned with the public welfare. In sum, it is difficult to see by what logic or evidence convention delegates can be derided as morally shabby and intellectually inferior to the voters who participate in primaries, or as less qualified to assess the claims of the would-be candidates.

Consider also that the convention delegates often know the candidates personally, or have had opportunity to observe them at close quarters. The average primary voter, by contrast, has only superficial and indirect knowledge of the candidates, is poorly informed about even the simpler issues, has little special information concerning who in the party has worked industriously, shown originality or proved himself trustworthy, intelligent, or responsible. His concern with politics and with the party's welfare is marginal, and he generally lacks the motivation and knowledge to relate his opinions to a larger belief system.

The depths of misinformation among primary voters is sometimes astonishing. Surveys conducted in this year's Oregon primary, for example, confirmed that more than three-fourths of the voters who favored Kennedy or McCarthy were either unable to identify, or completely misidentified, the Vietnam views of the two men, although for many weeks the campaign had been fought over this very issue.

One must not, on the other hand, overstate the qualifications and wisdom of convention delegates. Not all of them meet the standards demanded of a society of philosophers, astrophysicists, or the League of Women Voters. But if the delegates fall short of the ideal, how much greater is the distance between the ideal and the average primary voter. The contrast holds not only for their knowledge of candidates, but also for their understanding of the requirements and deeper meanings of political democracy. The delegates are ahead of the average voter in this respect as well. What is even more startling is that they prefer, to a greater extent than the voters do, parties that divide by ideology, that stand for something, and that distinguish themselves from each other.

One also hears that conventions are inherently "conservative" and designed to defend the status quo, while direct primaries are "progressive" and open the system to new ideas. Even a moment's reflection, however, will confirm that conventions have nominated a large number of imaginative and forward-looking men (as well as some conservatives), and that the electorate has nominated and elected numerous conservatives and reactionaries (as well as many liberals).

Nothing about the primary process gives it an inherent advantage over the convention process in opening candidates to new ideas. Indeed, as much research bears out, one is more likely to find tendencies toward innovation and experimentation among active party members and leaders than among voters. On many questions, notably civil rights, tolerance, constitutional liberties, openness to "change," conformity and conventionality in opinions and life-styles, the delegates of the two parties are usually more enlightened than the ordinary citizen. What determines "progressiveness" is less the formal nominating device than the purposes to which it is addressed and the manner in which it is employed. To insist otherwise is to value appearance over substance.

Although the conventions tend to select candidates who represent the party's dominant ideological position and thus afford the voters a genuine choice, they are, oddly enough, less likely to confront the electorate with political extremists. There is no contradiction in observing that a convention will choose a candidate who can be ideologically differentiated from the opposition while maintaining that he is unlikely to be an extremist. Forces toward convergence and divergence are simultaneously at work in the conventions. The usual outcome is that one of the conventions (the Democratic) selects candidates who are somewhat left of center but not radical extremists; while the other convention (the Republican) chooses candidates who are somewhat right of center but not reactionary extremists.

One observes in the convention the pull of ideology in the one direction, and a desire to win, and therefore to attract the middle range of voters, in the other. Some people argue that the desire to win is so overwhelming that everything is sacrificed to that objective, and that the pull toward the center invariably prevails. But these observers overlook the genuine political convictions of the party activists. The delegates want to win, of course, but they hope to do so on something resembling their own intellectual terms. Strongly held beliefs are not the sole motivation for active political involvement, but neither are they entirely absent from the political activity of thoughtful men.

The nomination of candidates is for most voters only a small matter. They read, talk, and reflect upon politics much less often than the delegates do, and most voters see elections as having little relevance to their daily lives. The extent of their indifference is evident from the size of primary turnouts. It is not unusual for primaries to involve as few as 25 to 40 percent of the electorate. Since the election of governors, senators, and other important officials is frequently at stake, one may doubt that a national Presidential primary would activate many of the voters who now neglect to participate.

One of the most serious drawbacks of a national Presidential primary, however, is the damaging effect it would have on the operation of our political parties. Primaries are profoundly antagonistic to the achievement of a responsible party system, for they deprive the party of its most important functions, the right to select candidates and to formulate programs on which those candidates are to stand.

Candidates selected by primary rather than party have won their positions by plebiscite, and have little reason to feel obligated to any organization. They can refuse to support the party's candidates and even flirt with the opposition without fear of being disciplined.

A party that consists of totally autonomous individuals, none of whom bears any ideological or fraternal relationship to any other, is the equivalent of no party system at all. It is extremely difficult to derive from such an arrangement a coherent, integrated set of policies. Without a responsible party, every representative works only for himself, thinks only of his own political safety and advantage, and cannot be depended upon to behave in predictable ways.

In such a system, not only is a legislative program difficult to attain, but the voters are left in confusion. Party labels mean little. Under such conditions when voters choose someone who calls himself a Democrat or Republican, they have no idea what policies he is likely to follow. Thus, what seems on its face to be a more democratic and representative arrangement turns out in the end to be less representative, because more capricious and less predictable, than is possible under a more orderly, responsible system of party organization. In modern societies, with their vast and complex problems, the need for responsible political parties is greater than ever before.

Many political observers believe that the American parties are already too diffuse and too weak to impose discipline on their members or hold them to a political line. Even now, each survives as a party by the sheerest good fortune, with 50 state party units and no effective national office, no continually functioning executive committees, no clear criteria for membership, not even regular national newspapers or magazines to communicate with the rank and file, and no effective power to punish or reward members.

The parties can scarcely afford further impediments to their ability to function as national organizations. What holds them together now is in some measure a common set of beliefs, a sense of fraternity, informal personal and organizational ties and, perhaps most of all, a big, splashy, quadrennial meeting in which each tries to work out a common program, select national leaders, heal divisions, and unite in a common effort to elect party candidates. A national Presidential primary would be a step in the wrong direction: it would seriously weaken the chances of producing a strengthened, more responsible, more meaningful party system.

Despite all the flimflam about national primaries, the charge that bosses "put over" their own hand-picked candidates in disregard of the popular will, and that the "true" party leaders are seldom chosen, the two candidates most likely to emerge victorious from the Democratic and Republican conventions (Humphrey and Nixon) are by almost every criterion the leaders of their respective parties, who, if they win the nomination, will have earned it.

Both Humphrey and Nixon embody rather closely the ideological tendencies (liberal the one case, conservative in the other) of their parties. Both have the largest followings among party activists throughout the nation. Both have devoted themselves to their respective parties. Both are among the most experienced leaders of their parties, having served for more than two decades in party and government offices. Both have been Senators and Vice-Presidents, and have gained extensive experience in national and international politics beyond that of most (perhaps all) other contestants for the nomination. Both have expended much energy and time in raising funds and promoting their parties' causes and candidates. Both are men of unusual intelligence and political savvy. Both are energetic, active, lively, and effective politicians. Both have long been recognized as high among the highest-ranking leaders of their parties, and have long been thought of as qualified Presidential candidates. Even Rockefeller, who comes closest of all the other candidates to having comparable experience, does not have better credentials for the nomination than Nixon or Humphrey.

It is ironic, in light of their considerable achievements and records, that the convention system should now be challenged on the grounds that Humphrey and Nixon are likely to be the nominees. What would one say about the effectiveness of a party system which excluded or bypassed men of their qualifications?

The recommendation to eliminate the national convention and to nominate Presidential candidates by direct popular primary is a manifestation of that misplaced democratic zeal that has led to such absurdities as the election of sheriffs, dog-catchers, assessors, and coroners. Nothing about democracy requires that every official be elected. Like most virtues, democratic participation can be carried to excess and perverted by the very ubiquity or capriciousness with which it is employed. To elect certain officials in a large representative democracy is essential, but to subject every office to election is to impose impossible demands upon the electorate's ability to judge wisely. We would all be kept so busy with politics that we would have no time to read books, enjoy music, watch baseball, or make love.

A few state primaries in the course of a national campaign might conceivably be useful as warm-ups or to help candidates to estimate the effectiveness of various appeals. But the costs of these and other benefits are excessive.

The use of primaries lengthens the course of the campaign, and may serve, in the end, to diminish rather than increase voter interest. Primaries also add enormously to the cost of campaigns, and permit men of large fortunes an even greater advantage than they enjoy in general elections (the Rockefeller campaign this year—expensive, flamboyant, and lavish beyond belief—affords a dramatic example of the power of wealth to return a candidate from relative obscurity to the forefront of the political arena).

In discussing these and other shortcomings of Presidential primaries, Nelson Polsby and Aaron Wildavsky ("Presidential Elections") have observed that a national primary would invite the candidacy not merely of two or three participants, but of many, perhaps 10 or 12, with none coming close to a majority. This would necessitate a second or "run-off" primary which would add further to the length and expense of a campaign procedure that is already absurdly grueling and expensive.

Some of the arguments against primaries can, of course, be made against elections as well. One deludes himself in thinking that elections are in any sense ideal devices for the selection of rulers; they are simply the least bad of all the devices we have been able to think of so far. If we knew a way to recognize and appoint philosopher–kings, it would be mere fetishism on our part to continue to elect public officials. But we are, alas, fallible, and no method of appointment has so far been discovered that assures the selection of political leaders who are noble, fair, just, honorable, generous, compassionate, beneficent, strong, courageous, sensible, refined, prudent, and wise.

None of the alternative methods so far employed to select political leaders—hereditary title, oligarchic selection, military conquest, seniority, appointment by cooptation, charismatic revelation, ruthlessness, and the ability to climb over and eliminate rivals, etc.—have demonstrated a systematic capacity for producing leaders of superior virtue and solicitude for the governed. We use free elections because they offer us an opportunity to hold leaders responsible. When rulers govern without opposition or fear of removal, the temptation to oppress their subjects, to destroy rivals, to usurp power, and aggrandize themselves is too great for most of them to resist.

But if elections are essential to democracy, national Presidential primaries are not. Conventions are not only an acceptable but superior alternative, entirely in keeping with the democratic idea. Doubtless they could be improved. They could be made smaller, more deliberative, less chaotic, more representative, and less oratorical.

It is not clear, however, that either the parties or voters want the conventions reformed. Like the circus to which they are sometimes compared, they are among the greatest shows on earth. Tune in to Miami and Chicago and see for yourself.

5

The Presidency: The Process of Persuasion

Is a presidential campaign really a national soap opera, or is it a national effort to educate and inform the public about the political issues confronting the nation? Has Madison Avenue invaded political parties to the degree that the process of persuasion is simply the systematic manipulation of the mass mind? Has television basically altered the nature of campaigns, or are they today essentially the same as in 1860?

If we could turn the clock back to Lincoln's first presidential campaign, the four-party race of 1860, we would watch a number of campaign tactics that are still in use today. The nation was bitterly divided over the slavery issue, the aftermath of which is still an issue in 1968. The recently born Republican Party smelled victory in the winds. Out of caution, their nominee assumed a lofty, noncommittal pose. An old campaigner, William Cullen Bryant, advised Lincoln to make no speeches, write no letters as a candidate, and enter into no pledges. Why alienate large groups of voters already committed to Lincoln, for the sake of a few uncommitted voters? Lincoln stayed in Springfield during the entire campaign and never made a single campaign speech.

Thus, Lincoln's strategy in 1860 was what has been described as the "front-porch" campaign: he waited in Springfield for the press and the party workers to visit him—and they did. The campaign had wide press coverage, and Lincoln's party had most of the Northern press "sewed up" —a press which at least on the editorial page is still largely committed to the same party one hundred years later.

But Lincoln's principal opponent, Senator Stephen A. Douglas, could not afford to conduct a "front-porch" campaign. The "Little Giant" had to carry his cause to the people. Undaunted by imminent defeat, Douglas conducted a "whistle-stop" campaign. Harry Truman, laboring under similar odds, achieved different results when, in 1948, he decided to "give 'em hell" via a whistle-stop campaign.

137

Although the 1860 campaign was sobered somewhat by the threat of secession, still it had its ballyhoo and color. Republican speakers made an estimated 50,000 speeches, and the people flocked to political rallies all over the nation. There are few torchlight parades today, yet a lot of martial music, political rallies, and stomping of feet still exist. Another Senator from Illinois, Paul Douglas, one hundred years later, said that there is nothing to replace this old strategy of meeting the voters face to face.

What has changed since 1860? It does not seem likely that a front-porch campaign is still possible. The various constraints of modern campaign strategies as outlined by Nelson W. Polsby and Aaron B. Wildavsky seem to preclude such a strategy. One central fact develops, however, from studies of recent presidential campaigns: their heavy dependence on modern technology, particularly television, and the consequent soaring costs of elections. From this, two problems emerge. First, what role should a rational discussion of policy issues play in presidential campaigns? Some contend that television and Madison Avenue package presidential candidates much as toothpaste is packaged for mass audiences. One implication of Gene Wyckoff's study of image candidates is that presidential candidates might be selected in the future, at least in part, for their television appeal rather than for their presidential abilities.

The impact of television and professional public relations on democratic elections has been a concern since the early 1950s. Without regard to party, candidates for the presidency have tended increasingly to rely on the kind of television format suggested by E. S. J. Productions' television scripts for Richard Nixon in the 1968 campaign. What the professional public relations people are telling candidates is that political television must compete for audiences; they must present a lively program. In 1968, Vice-President Humphrey ended his campaign on election eve with a $675,000 telethon starring popular entertainment personalities. Yet for all of the concern that has been expressed about the possible negative impact of this approach on rationalism in elections, the reader should recall the position of V. O. Key, Jr., in Chapter 1, that voters are not fools and thus presumably are not fooled by Madison Avenue–Hollywood style political television.

The second problem that emerges out of the realities of modern presidential campaigns involves the soaring costs of elections and the consequent implications for a healthy democratic society. By 1968 total spending by all candidates at all levels reached $300 million. In presidential campaigns alone, the estimated cost per vote rose from 19 cents in 1952 to 60 cents in 1968. One of the most careful studies of campaign costs, the Twentieth Century Fund's 1969 study, concludes that media costs, particularly television costs, have contributed most to the sharp increase in campaign expenses. A democratic presidential campaign is presumably based on the premise of the widest possible dissemination of information about the candidates and their parties; yet current costs raise the question of whether access to the electorate is based largely on the ability to pay. Given the cost situation, candidates must turn to a variety of sources for money, including small as well as large donors. It is the latter that causes the greatest concern. The Citizens' Research Foundation study of the 1968 elections revealed that 15 individuals gave over $50,000 each to the parties in 1968. One of the donors was reported to have given an estimated $500,000 to the Republican Party in 1968, the bulk of it for the presidential campaign. Indeed, the same donor—W. Clement Stone of Chicago— told a reporter that he contributed $812,000 to 50 candidates in the 1970 elections.

It is probably unrealistic to expect presidential campaigns to be conducted in the style appropriate to a debate society or a college classroom. On the other hand, can a democratic society remain viable if it is expected to raise millions of dollars for presidential campaigns that focus largely on the candidates' television images?

One final observation about American presidential elections: We still retain the eighteenth-century system of presidential electors, the so-called Electoral College. The system has long been under attack as antidemocratic. Following the narrow victory of President Nixon in 1968, the movement to abolish the Electoral College in favor of direct election gained added momentum. The testimony and statements of Theodore H. White, journalist and student of presidential elections, and William Gossett, of the American Bar Association, present some of the arguments for and against reforming the present system.

It is unlikely that the reform movement will gain congressional support sufficient to alter the electoral system in the immediate future. Under the leadership of Senator Bayh, a divided Senate committee did favorably report a direct election proposal in 1970, but the proposal died due to a filibuster led by a coalition of small-state and Southern senators. Under the committee proposal, electors and the winner-take-all system would have been abolished. The committee proposal would have replaced the electoral system with a direct popular vote, requiring the winning candidate to receive at least 40 percent of the popular vote. Tie votes or the failure of any candidate to receive the required minimum plurality would have resulted in run-off elections. The principal arguments against the proposal were a fear of its negative impact on the two-party system; a concern that direct elections would result in an increase in voting fraud; Southern fears that it would lead to federally imposed voting requirements; and, finally, the small states anticipated that they would lose most of their already minimal influence in presidential elections.

**Nelson W. Polsby and Aaron B.
Wildavsky: The Campaign**

Once the conventions are over, the two Presidential candidates "relax" for a few weeks. On Labor Day they ordinarily begin their official campaigning. From that date onward they confront the voters directly, each carrying the banner of his political party. How do the candidates behave? Why do they act the way they do? And what kind of impact do their activities have on the electorate?

For the small minority of party workers, campaigns serve as a signal to get to work. How hard they work depends in part on whether the candidates' slogans, personalities, and visits spark their enthusiasm. The workers may "sit on their hands," or may pursue their generally unrewarding jobs—checking voting lists, mailing campaign flyers, ringing doorbells—with something approaching fervor. They cannot be taken for granted; activating them and imbuing them with purpose and ardor is perhaps the first task of the candidate.

For the population at large, much of which is normally uninterested in politics, campaigns call attention to the advent of an election. Some excitement may be generated and some diversion provided for those who were not aware, until they turned on the TV, that their favorite program had been preempted by a political speech. The campaign is a great spectacle. Talk about politics increases, and a small percentage of citizens may even become intensely involved as they get caught up in campaign oratory.

For the vast majority of citizens in America, campaigns do not function so much to change their minds as to reinforce their previous convictions. As the campaign wears on, the underlying party identification of most people rises ever more powerfully to the surface. Republican and Democratic identifiers are split further apart (polarized) as their increased awareness of party strife emphasizes the things that divide them.

Three-quarters of American adults identify with a party. Among these, the Democrats enjoy a 3 to 2 advantage. But Democrats tend to turn out less often. Given these facts, the outstanding strategic problem for Democratic politicians is to get their adherents to turn out and to vote for

Democratic candidates. No need to worry about Republicans or Independents if Democrats can do their basic job. Democrats stress appeals to the faithful. They try to raise in their supporters the old party spirit. One of their major problems as we have seen is that most citizens who identify with them are found at the lower end of the socio-economic scale and are less likely to turn out to vote than are those with Republican leanings. So the Democrats put on mobilization drives and seek in every way to get as large a turnout as possible. If they are well-organized, they scour the lower income areas. They try to provide cars for the elderly and infirm, baby sitters for mothers, and, occasionally, inducements of a less savory kind to reinforce the party loyalty of the faithful. The seemingly neutral campaigns put on by radio, TV, and newspapers to stress the civic obligation to vote, if they have any effect at all, probably help the Democrats more than the Republicans.

The Republicans face a different strategic problem. They must, to be sure, try to get out their party adherents. But even if they do this well, it will not be enough. They must not only encourage people with Republican leanings to register and vote, they must also attract more than their share of the uncommitted, and they must persuade at least some of the Democratically inclined to forego their usual preference. This means playing down partisan appeals. Republicans ask voters to vote for the man and not for the party, since this gives the party its best chance of winning.

For Republicans involved in Presidential nominating politics, the most important fact of life is that their party is without question the minority party in the United States. What is more, the Republicans can claim the allegiance of what seems to be a minority of citizens that has shrunk steadily over the last twenty-five years.

Percentage of Adults Identifying Themselves as:

	Republican	Democratic	Other
1940	38	42	20
1950	33	45	22
1960	30	47	23
1964	25	53	22

Source: AIPO News Release, November 8, 1964.

The Survey Research Center at the University of Michigan has found repeatedly that about three-quarters of those in its samples eligible to vote claimed a party identification; of these, three-fifths were Democrats.

In Presidential elections in which considerations of party are foremost and allowing for the greater propensity of Republicans to turn out and vote, it has been plausibly argued that the Democrats could expect to win with around 53% or 54% of the vote.

This is close enough to kindle hope justifiably in Republican breasts; despite the clear Democratic majority in this country, it must be assumed that either major party can win a Presidential election. But over the last thirty years it has generally been necessary for the Republicans to devise a strategy that could not only win, but win from behind.

With the handwriting so plainly on the wall, the strategic alternatives available to Republicans can hardly be regarded as secret. They can be boiled down to three possibilities. First, Republicans can attempt to de-emphasize the impact of party habit as a component of electoral choice by capitalizing upon a more compelling cue to action. The nomination of General Eisenhower, the most popular hero of the Second World War, overrode party considerations and is a clear example of the efficacy of this strategy. Efforts to play upon popular dissatisfaction in a variety of issue areas also exemplify this strategy, but these dissatisfactions must preexist in the population and must be widespread and intense before they will produce the desired effect. When issues do come to the fore in a compelling way, the payoff to the advantaged party is sometimes enormous, because these are the circumstances under which new party loyalties can be created.

Another possible Republican strategy, similar in some ways to the first, also seeks to depress the saliency of party in the minds of voters by blurring the differences between the parties, by seeking to efface certain of the stigmata that have been attached to the party over the years as stereotypes having general currency (e.g., "party of the rich"). This strategy gives full recognition to the arithmetic of Democratic superiority and also to the unit rule of the Electoral College, which weighs disproportionately votes cast in the large states that so often contain the heaviest concentrations of traditional allies of the Democratic party. Although it has been used often by Republican nominees such as Willkie, Dewey, and Nixon, with results that always fell short—sometimes barely short—of victory, this "me-too" strategy has over the years become increasingly controversial among Republicans. The fact that no Republican candidate has actually been able to win with it has created doubts about its efficacy. The "me-too" strategy may entail the advocacy of policies generally favored by most American voters, but this approach apparently does not correctly mirror the political sentiments of Republican activists. Critics of the "me-too" approach have argued that this strategy merely alienates potential Republican voters while failing to attract sufficient Democrats. Alienated Republicans, so goes this argument, seeing no difference between the policies espoused by the major parties, withdraw from politics into apathy.

Thus, a third strategy, whose claim of victory is based upon the presupposition of a hidden Republican vote, can be identified. This was the strategy pursued by the Goldwater forces in 1964. It has as its main characteristic the attempt to sharpen rather than blur party lines on matters of substantive policy.

Theory and Action

The contents of election campaigns appear to be largely opportunistic. The swiftly changing nature of events makes it unwise for candidates to lay down all-embracing rules for campaigning which cannot meet special situations as they arise. A candidate may prepare for battle on one front and discover that the movement of events forces him to fight on another. Yet on closer examination, it is evident that the political strategist has to rely on some sort of theory about the probable behavior of large groups of voters under a few likely conditions. For there are too many millions of voters and too many thousands of possible events to deal with each as a separate category. Keynes pointed out years ago, quite rightly, that those among us, including politicians, who most loudly proclaim their avoidance of theory are generally the victims of some long dead economist or philosopher whose assumptions they have unknowingly assimilated. The candidates must simplify their picture of the political world, or its full complexity will paralyze them; the only question is whether or not their theories, both explicit and implicit, will prove helpful to them.

What kind of organization shall they use or construct? How shall they raise money? Where shall they campaign? How much time shall they allocate to the various regions and states? What kinds of appeals shall they make to what voting groups? What kind of personal impression shall they seek to create or reinforce? How far should they go in castigating the opposition? These are the kinds of strategic questions to which Presidential candidates need answers—answers which necessarily vary depending on their party affiliations, their personal attributes, whether they are in or out of office, and on targets of opportunity that come up in the course of current events. Let us take up each of these questions in turn, taking care to specify the different problems faced by "ins" and "outs" and by Democrats and Republicans. For purposes of illustration, we shall turn often to the 1960 contest between John Kennedy and Richard Nixon and the 1964 Barry Goldwater–Lyndon Johnson battle.

Ins and Outs

In choosing a campaign strategy much depends on whether the candidate is an incumbent or is trying to dislodge a man who is already in office. The man in office has the advantage of having had huge amounts of publicity. For better or for worse, he is probably better known than any challenger can be. He is experienced, and people have learned to depend upon him. While he is in office, he may be in a position to take actions which will help him, such as acting decisively in foreign affairs, as Johnson did in the Bay of Tonkin incident, taking "nonpolitical" trips to drum up support, and little things like making sure that veterans' administration checks get mailed out promptly or even a little ahead of time.

The incumbent also has to face a number of disadvantages inherent in his position. Inevitably, Presidents have to do things which dissatisfy some people. Resentments build up. Should economic or military conditions appear to change for the worse, the President seeking re-election may well be the victim of a protest vote. Herbert Hoover felt the sting of this phenomenon deeply when the people punished the "ins" for a depression which Hoover would have given much to avoid. Moreover, the incumbent has a record. He has or has not done things, and he may be held to account for his sins of omission or commission; not so the man out-of-office, who can criticize freely without always presenting viable alternatives or necessarily taking his own advice once he is elected. The "missile gap" turned out to be something of a chimera after Kennedy got into the White House and he never found it possible to act much differently toward the Matsu–Quemoy situation than did Dwight Eisenhower, despite their over-publicized "differences" about this question during the campaign. The incumbent is naturally cast in the role of the defender of his administration and the challenger as the attacker who promises better things to come. After all, we would hardly expect to hear the man in office say that the other fellow could probably do as well or to hear the challenger declare that he really could not do any better than the incumbent, although both statements may be close to the truth.

The challenger has his own problems. He may not be well known and may find that much of his effort must be devoted to publicizing himself. All the while, the President is getting reams of free publicity and is in a position to create major news by the things he does—an administrative action to help Negroes, a call to the summit, an announcement of a new advance in space research.

The candidate aspiring to office may find that he lacks information, which puts him at a disadvantage in discussing foreign policy and defense issues. On the other hand, he may deliberately forbear from finding out too much for fear that he be restrained in his criticism by an implied pledge not to use information the President has furnished to him. Perhaps the major advantage the challenger possesses is his ability to criticize policies freely and sometimes in exaggerated terms, whereas the incumbent is often restrained by his current official responsibilities from talking too much about them. Obligations to other nations, for example, may restrain a President from talking about changes in foreign policy or from tipping his hand in a case like Cuba.

One of the most difficult positions for a candidate is to try to succeed a President of his own party. He loses many advantages of incumbency—huge publicity resources, ability to make decisions, a going organization—while taking on many of the disadvantages. No matter how hard he tries to avoid it he is stuck with the record made by the President of his own party. If he tries to disavow portions of this record, as Adlai Stevenson did when he tried to follow Harry Truman, the results can easily be disappointing. He may lose some support the current President has without gaining much for himself. He may actually turn public attention to allegedly bad aspects of the incumbent's record through his attempts to disassociate himself. As it turned out, Stevenson was badly hurt by allegations of corruption and failure to end the war in Korea under the Truman Administration. Richard Nixon faced an easier task in attempting to succeed the far more popular Dwight Eisenhower. Indeed, he attempted to wrap himself in Eisenhower's mantle whenever the opportunity presented itself. Yet Nixon increasingly found himself on the defensive as Kennedy talked about getting the nation moving again and acting more energetically. Nixon said we *were* moving, but he could hardly promise to do too much more and make things too much better, since that would have implied a disavowal of President Eisenhower.

Friends, Volunteers, and Professionals

While the incumbent has a going organization, molded and tested through years in office, the challenger has to build one piecemeal as he goes along in the frantic days of the campaign when there is never enough time to do everything that has to be done. Should he have a man of his own run the show without much of a nod to the professionals? They may resist, if not sabotage, his efforts. Should he enlist the cooperation of the old party men knowing that he may thereby lose some control over his campaign? Should there be two centers of campaigning with the inevitable duplication and problems of coordination? There is apparently no costless solution to this problem. There always seems to be grumbling from party professionals and the candidate's own men about their relationship.

All candidates seek special volunteer organizations to help attract voters who prefer not to associate themselves with the party organizations. The distaste with which some middle and upper class people regard the rather earthy and predominantly lower class party organizations is difficult to overcome. It is easier to construct new organizations in which they can feel ennobled by attachment to an Eisenhower or Stevenson rather than (as they may feel) associating with a group of vulgar politicians. The danger here is that the volunteer organizations will take on lives of their own and attempt to dictate strategy and policy to the candidates. A few of the volunteers may transfer to the regular party and this may lead to serious internal dissension as happened in the successful move to oust Carmine DeSapio of Tammany Hall in New York City. The candidates need the volunteers, but it is advisable for them to follow the lead set by Kennedy and Nixon in keeping tight reins on them to assure reasonable coordination of efforts and to avoid being captured.

The mechanics of electioneering are no simple matter; they cannot be entrusted wholly to amateurs. Not only must the candidate get to his various speaking engagements when he is supposed to, but he also needs to have some good idea of whom he is speaking to and what kind of approach to take. In the hurly-burly of the campaign, where issues and plans may change from day to day, where yesterday's ideas may have to end up in the wastebasket to make room for today's problems, where changes of schedule are made in response to the opportunities and dangers suggested by private and public polls, a poor organization can be severely damaging. The troubles of Adlai Stevenson present a case in point. His apparent distaste for the niceties of organization in 1956 hurt him badly. He was excessively rushed going from one place to another so that he lost the valuable assets of composure and thoughtfulness which should have been his stock in trade. If he continually made speeches which were inappropriate for his audiences, it may have been because he was badly informed about who his audience would be, not because he was talking "over people's heads." For instance, he once went to New Haven during the 1956 campaign, and made a speech redolent with allusions to Yale and Princeton, with punch lines depending on knowledge of what the "subjunctive" was, to an audience which happened to be composed largely of old-time Democratic party workers from around Connecticut. To be sure, some mixups, if not a few outright fiascoes, are inevitable given the frantic pace and the pressure of time. Resilience is not the least qualification of a Presidential candidate.

Where To Campaign

In deciding where to campaign, the candidates are aided by distinctive features of the national political structure which go a long way toward giving them guidance. They know that it is not votes as such that matter but electoral votes which are counted on a state-by-state basis. The candidate who wins by a small plurality in a state gains all the electoral votes there are for that state. The candidates realize that a huge margin of victory in a state with a handful of electoral votes will not do them nearly as much good as a bare plurality in states like New York and California with large numbers of electoral votes. So their first guideline is evident: Campaign in states with large electoral votes. There is, however, not much point in campaigning in states where a candidate is bound to win or to lose. Thus, states which almost always go for one party receive only perfunctory attention. Hence, the original guideline may be modified to read: Campaign in states with large electoral votes which are doubtful. In practice, a "doubtful" state is one where there is a good chance for both parties to capture the state, and politicians usually gauge this chance by the extent to which the state has delivered victories to both parties at some time in recent memory. Republicans and Democrats thus spend more time in the large doubtful states, such as New York, Ohio, Texas, and California, than they do in the deep South which will probably go Democratic or upper New England which will probably go Republican. And even if one or two of these one-party states should change in one election, the likelihood of such an event is too slim and the payoff in terms of electoral votes too meager to justify extensive campaigning when time might better be spent elsewhere. As the campaign wears on, the candidates take soundings from the opinion polls and are likely to redouble their efforts in states where they believe a personal visit might turn the tide.

Here we once again come across the pervasive problem of uncertainty. No one really knows how much value in changed votes or turnout is gained by personal visits to a particular state. Most voters have made up their minds. Opponents of the candidate are unlikely to go to see him anyway and one wonders what a glimpse in a motorcade will do to influence a potential voter. Yet no one is certain that whistle-stop methods produce no useful result. Visiting localities may serve to increase publicity because many of the media of communication are geared to "local" events. It also provides an opportunity to stress issues like public power or race relations which may be of special significance to citizens in a given region. Party activists may be energized by a glimpse at, or a handshake with, the candidate. New alliances, such as the one that emerged in 1964 between Goldwater and many long-time Democratic sectors of the deep South, can be solidified. And so rather than let the opportunity pass, the candidates usually decide to take no chances and get out on the hustings. They hedge against uncertainty by doing all they can.

Consider the case of John Kennedy in Ohio. He traversed that pivotal state several times in the 1960 campaign and exerted great physical effort in getting himself seen traveling across the state. But when the votes were counted, he found himself at the short end. The future President professed to be annoyed and stumped at why this happened. An analysis of the voting returns showed that Kennedy's vote was correlated in a high and positive degree with the percentage of Catholic population in the various counties. Kennedy made a considerable improvement over the Democratic showing in 1956, but that was not enough to win. Despite evidence of this kind, which suggests that personal appearances may well be overwhelmed by other factors, visits to localities will undoubtedly continue. Who can say, to take a contrary instance, that Kennedy's visit to Illinois did not provide the bare margin of a few thousand votes necessary for victory?

There was a time when Presidential nominees faced the serious choice of whether to conduct a front porch campaign or to get out and meet the people. A candidate like Warren Harding, who his sponsors felt would put his foot in his mouth every time he spoke, was well-advised to stay home. More hardy souls like William Jennings Bryan took off in all directions only to discover that to be seen was not necessarily to be loved. An underdog, like Harry Truman in 1948, went out to meet the people because he was so far behind. A favored candidate, like Thomas Dewey in 1948, went out to meet the people to avoid being accused of complacency. Everybody is doing it probably because it is the fashion, and the spectacle of seeing one's opponent run around the country at a furious pace without following suit is too nerve-wracking to contemplate. That no one knows whether all this does any good is beside the point. Some future candidate might want to consider running a different kind of campaign, taking account of the fact that radio and television make it possible to reach millions, without leaving the big metropolitan areas. Such a candidate might fix upon something like a half or a full dozen regional centers and make his appearances and speeches in these places. The added time for reflection and the additional reserves of energy he would gain over the previous method might do something to improve the quality of his campaign. And should he happen to be elected, he might become the only President-elect in recent history not to be utterly exhausted on Election Day.

Gene Wyckoff: A Concept of Image Candidates

What is unique about the personal image of a political candidate that television conveys to its viewers? An important clue to the answer of this question is found in the recent findings that *all* viewers tend to see the same personal image of televised candidates although the influence of that image on viewers may vary.

According to now-classic studies of American voting behavior, this should not happen. Voters are supposed to formulate varying mental images of the candidates according to their (the voters') *political predispositions.* To define that term, voters' political predispositions are tendencies, growing out of their habitual preference for the candidates of one party and their habitual rejection of opposition party candidates, to seek out and favorably interpret information leading to impressions of favored candidates and to avoid, misinterpret, distort, or forget information and impressions of opposition candidates. Wilbur Schramm has summed up the conventional wisdom about political predispositions with respect to television.

> WILBUR SCHRAMM: Man is far from a *tabula rasa,* or clean slate, for mass communication to write on. . . . He has built up a sense of values which lead him to react positively or negatively to much of what the candidate will say. . . . The voter will have a strong sense of belongingness. . . . Perhaps he will have a sense of how the people in his "set" or his union or his luncheon club evaluate the candidate. In other words, before he even sits down to the television set, he is prepared to react in a preset way to whatever comes out of it.

But, such scholarly opinion notwithstanding, this sort of selective distortion of candidate images as seen by television viewers failed to happen in a number of recent elections. A study by the Cunningham and Walsh advertising agency during the 1958 gubernatorial campaigns in New York concluded that voters, regardless of political affiliation, tend to see similar television images of the candidates. Respondents characterized the Republican challenger, Nelson A. Rockefeller, as dynamic and personable. The universal opinion of incumbent Governor W. Averell Harriman added up to a "strained and stiff" image.

In 1960, Joseph and Marian McGrath studied members of Young Republican and Young Democratic clubs as a sample of politically predisposed television viewers, assuming that "if any group is liable to distort the images of a favored candidate, one would expect a highly partisan group to do so." Yet after these two groups had witnessed the televised "great debates" between the Republican and Democratic presidential candidates, they characterized the two candidates in similar terms: "Kennedy was seen by both parties as more ambitious, aggressive, striving, active, dynamic, rebellious, etc. Nixon, in contrast, was seen by members of both parties as less ambitious, more easy-going, contented, passive, relaxed, conforming, etc."

This unexpected phenomenon may be explained without denying established findings about the distorting influence of a voter's political predispositions by accepting the concept that all voters, as television viewers, have some other mental predisposition that influences them to react in a preset way to whatever comes out of their television set and, further, that this other mental predisposition is so firmly fixed as to overwhelm and obliterate a partisan distortion of candidate images due to political predispositions.

This other and stronger mental influence on viewer perception of candidate images might be called *media predispositions*.

> HARVEY WHEELER: Television . . . has created its own symbolic language: what one's face looks like, how one's face corresponds to television's laboriously created stereotypes for good guys and bad guys becomes crucial. . . .
>
> The moment the television viewer takes his place before his set, he brings with him a series of invisible visual values which have a strong political significance regardless of the viewer's conscious desire.

Furthermore, television's stereotyped dramatic characters, with their "invisible visual values" that condition viewers on a year-round, year-after-year basis, embody personifications of universally admired (or detested) characters in the popular American culture, the culture shared by all voters regardless of their political affinities.

> PSYCHIATRIST'S OPINION RE NONPARTISAN AFFINITY FOR A FATHER-IMAGE CANDIDATE: [An] authority vacuum in the home and transfer of the directive roles from the father to the mother are reflected in the increasing interest in many levels of our government for a more authori-

tarian and paternalistic government, one featuring a maximum of security and a minimum of hazard. This may result in a tendency on the part of many people to secure such a state by vote.

SOCIOLOGIST'S OPINION RE NONPARTISAN AFFINITY FOR A SINCERE-IMAGE CANDIDATE: Sincerity means performance in a style which is not aggressive or cynical, which may even be defenseless, as the question-answering or press conference technique of some politicians appears to be. The performer puts himself at the mercy of both his audience and his emotions. . . . It would not be fair to be too critical of the person who has left himself wide open and extended the glad hand of friendliness.

Forced to choose between skill and sincerity, many in the audience prefer the latter. They are tolerant of bumbles and obvious ineptness if the leader tries hard.

All television viewers, to a greater extent than they might suppose, would seem to have mental picture galleries in their heads, the walls of which are hung with portraits of heroes, lovers, villains, stooges, fathers, statesmen, politicians, comedians, and the other stereotype characters in television's commedia dell'arte. With little conscious effort—or perhaps in spite of conscious effort—viewers probably match the images in their mental picture galleries against the images of candidates seen on television and derive an impression of the candidates' characters accordingly.

The Theatricality of Campaign Coverage on Television

Not only may the great preponderance of theatrical entertainment on television condition viewers to perceive political campaign coverage as a theatrical experience, but certain production techniques commonly used in television news programs may serve to heighten an illusion that the campaign is a "political drama" and the candidates are players therein who should be judged as dramatic characters.

The Reaction Shot

Kurt and Gladys Lang were early observers of television's tendency to dramatize news coverage into a theatrical experience. The Langs' study revolved about one news event: a "farewell" visit made by General Douglas MacArthur to Chicago in 1951, shortly after he had made his colorful "Old Soldiers Never Die" speech on returning to the United States from Korea. The Langs were interested in finding out if, and how, the reaction of eyewitnesses who saw the parade and public ceremonies honoring the general differed from the reaction of viewers who had seen these events on television.

Television, the Langs concluded, had magnified instances of public enthusiasm over MacArthur to the proportions of an "impersonal absolute force" that had an "overwhelming" effect upon home viewers: "Selectivity of the camera and the commentary gave the event a personal dimension non-existent for particular participants in the crowds." Whereas General MacArthur was in fact a controversial militarist who had to be removed from his Korean command by President Truman for fear that he would, on his own, take overt military action against Red China, from this television coverage the general appeared to be a conquering hero idolized by the American public.

Although the Langs did not use the technical term *reaction shots,* their findings indicated that selected scenes of parade watchers applauding and cheering the passing general intercut and hence juxtaposed with close-ups of the general was the prime technique that made a theatrical experience out of the television coverage and a face-value hero character out of General MacArthur.

[W]ith reference to the Nixon *Ambassador of Friendship* film, reaction shots are so typically a technique of film and television drama that their use in news coverage may (1) increase the emotional intensity of the coverage to the point of obscuring rational consideration of the subject matter, and (2) increase the illusion that the coverage is drama and not reality.

On September 26, 1960, Ted Rogers—as Richard Nixon's television adviser—fought out and lost a dispute with CBS television director Don Hewitt over the use of reaction shots on the first of the "great debate" programs. Possibly because he knew that his candidate looked awful in comparison with the healthier, handsome John F. Kennedy, Rogers demanded that reaction shots of one candidate listening to the other be barred. Rogers feared that reaction shots would dramatize the image contrast between the two presidential candidates and take the focus off the substance of their dialogue.

But director Hewitt ruled that to eliminate the reaction shot was "cheating the audience" and that it was wholly natural for the viewer watching the discussion to want to see the reaction of the other participants from time to time. In what sense would the elimination of reaction shots have "cheated the audience"? Certainly the average person sitting in an auditorium where a platform debate between presidential candidates was in progress would hardly be close enough to observe the effect of one candidate's words on the other as revealed by the nuances of the listening candidate's facial expressions. Rather, the expectation of reaction shots—

and the sense of being "cheated" when they are not used—is probably something cultivated in television viewers by continued exposure to reaction-shot drama and news coverage.

The Rigid Time-Period Factor

Television's slavish devotion to the stopwatch may also serve to reduce the substance of political statements to incidental dialogue between dramatic characters in conflict. Newscasts typically edit a candidate's SOF remarks to the most pithy and provocative sentences and, without elaboration or evaluation of the condensed statement, juxtapose it with a contrary statement by the opposition. Time considerations and the desire for a fast "pace" can reduce face-to-face confrontations between candidates on news-feature programs to a travesty of political debate. For example, on Saturday evening, October 29, 1966, Station WABC-TV in New York City gave an hour of air time and facilities to put on a face-to-face confrontation between the four most prominent gubernatorial candidates: Governor Nelson A. Rockefeller, Republican; Frank D. O'Connor, Democrat; Franklin D. Roosevelt, Jr., Liberal; and Paul L. Adams, Conservative. The format of the program was rigid: each candidate was asked two questions on campaign issues by the program moderator. Each candidate had 90 seconds to answer. Each of the three other candidates had 60 seconds to rebut the answer. Between the rebuttals, the candidate giving the original answer had 30 seconds for re-rebuttal. The potential governors of a state in which 18 million people lived were given the following air time for discussion of important public questions: 90 seconds, 60 seconds, 30 seconds. What sort of comprehension of alternative proposals could viewers gain from such a flash exposure? Most probably only an impression, an impression based not on substance of argument but on style.

Editorial Abstention by Television Journalists

Even when candidates are given more time to answer and rebut answers of questions about campaign issues, viewers may be forced to judge style rather than substance of the arguments because candidates are often in serious disagreement as to the basic facts and such disagreements are rarely (if ever) set straight by the professional television journalists conducting the program. This failure should not be dismissed with the comment that the professional journalists might not be prepared to inform the viewer where the truth lies. Technically it is quite feasible (and hardly more expensive) to record candidate confrontations on videotape and delay broadcast twenty-four or forty-eight hours until the facts cited by the candidates can be authenticated and appraised by inserted remarks by the program moderator.

But however feasible in a technical sense, any appraisal of political candidates or their remarks by television newsmen would constitute a cardinal sin against the medium's most holy commandment: *Thou shalt not offend.*

> JACK GOULD (TELEVISION CRITIC): You don't slap a customer in the face.
> ... All the major advertising agencies have testified at F.C.C. hearings that this is the basic policy of television: you do not offend.

A station that offered information, no matter how valid, that sharply contradicted a political candidate would run the risk of offending that candidate's supporters. That station might become "controversial" and scare away the advertising agencies, whose dollars are the lifeblood of television.

A few more courageous (and affluent) television stations have begun to endorse favored candidates in separately programmed and clearly identified editorial announcements by a spokesman for station management who is *not* a regular newscaster. (For example, WCBS-TV endorsed Republican John Lindsay for mayor of New York in 1965.) In accord with the FCC's "fairness doctrine," these stations are obligated to seek out rebuttal from (spokesmen for) other candidates, a step beyond the usual equal-time stricture.

But editorials aside—and they are aside from newscasts and news-features programs—television's professionals follow a strict policy of letting political candidates stand at face value. This editorial abstention from campaign coverage may encourage viewers to appraise candidates on face value, which is what most viewers appear to do.

Face Value

According to the Cunningham and Walsh study of the 1958 gubernatorial campaigns, although television viewers generally agreed that they were more favorably impressed by Nelson A. Rockefeller than by incumbent Governor W. Averell Harriman, few viewers could identify anything that either candidate had said on television. Commonly, the viewers remarked that the candidates were "just talking politics."

Elihu Katz and Jacob J. Feldman did a study of studies, reviewing thirty-one separate research projects concerned with the 1960 Nixon-Kennedy television debates. Katz and Feldman concluded that viewers had not learned enough from what was said by the candidates to cause any change of opinion on campaign issues but that the viewers had "learned something about the candidates themselves. They discovered how well each candidate could perform in a debate and they formed images of each candidate's character and abilities."

Such scholarly findings indicate what may be one of the most important—and least acknowledged—aspects of candidate appearances on television: *the rational import of what they say may be a minimal part of the sentiment that they arouse in viewers.*

Images into Image Candidates

The image characterizations of candidates conveyed to viewers by television *can* vary significantly from images of the same candidates conveyed to listeners by radio and to readers by the print media.

The potential contrast between television and newspaper images of candidates is fairly obvious. . . . A newspaper, if it chooses, can put selective emphasis on coverage that reflects favorably on the favored candidate and describes the opposition candidate as an ineffective failure or worse. But newspapers can only describe; they can only write a continuing and possibly biased political novel to stimulate the imagination, the mind's eye of the reader. The newspaper-stimulated image of a candidate can be largely fiction and differ sharply from the television image, or the newspaper-stimulated image can be largely the truth and differ sharply from the television image. It is the literary-fiction image that appears to be obliterated in voters' minds by the televised image when both media are fully covering the candidates. There are several reasons for this. Television most closely simulates intimate personal persuasion between candidate and voter, and personal persuasion has been found to be the most effective influence on voting. Further, television images are universally perceived, whereas newspaper images, especially the more highly fictitious images conveyed by the more intensely partisan papers, achieve a limited exposure. . . . When the newspaper-stimulated image of a candidate differs sharply enough from the television image and is largely the truth and is generally reported by all the printed media, it may well prevail in the minds of television viewers. The 1964 Republican presidential primary in New Hampshire . . . provided an apparent example of this situation. Newspapers had provided all the intimate details of Nelson Rockefeller's divorce from a wife of thirty years and of his subsequent remarriage to a much younger woman who had to give up legal custody of her four children to gain her own marital freedom. Before Nelson Rockefeller appeared on New Hampshire television screens, viewers held a striking characterization of him that was too recent to be readily obliterated by Governor Rockefeller's personable television image. In a similar manner, the printed media were generally describing Barry Goldwater's impulsive and rash pronouncements on important public questions, a personal characteristic that apart from the substance of his statements may have created a striking image of Goldwater as a "dangerous" candidate, an image that served to obscure Goldwater's most attractive appearance and demeanor on New Hampshire television.

The potential contrast between a newspaper image and a television image of the same candidate may be commonly recognized, but not the potential contrast between a radio image and a television image of the same candidate.

> DR. ITHIEL DE SOLA POOL: Television humanized Eisenhower by revealing him to be somewhat more sensitive and withdrawn than the iron soldier the public had previously imagined. TV did not improve the image of Stevenson, though it certainly helped him become known. Radio was the medium that conveyed an overwhelmingly favorable image of Stevenson.

In 1960, political reporter Earl Mazo observed a sharp contrast between radio and television images of a candidate. The night of the first Nixon-Kennedy debate, Mazo had been covering the Southern Governors' Conference in Hot Springs, Arkansas. Because the Hot Springs station was not directly on the network cable, the assembled governors heard the first debate on radio an hour or so before they saw it on television.

> EARL MAZO: Before the encounter on radio was half finished, every Kennedy partisan in the room was disparaging the idea of a fine, upstanding young man like Senator Kennedy having to clash verbally with a crusty old professional debater like Vice President Nixon. But the attitude changed immediately when the magic lantern of television came on.

On radio, Mazo observed, Nixon's deep resonant voice conveyed more conviction, command, and determination to the listening governors than Kennedy's high-pitched voice, with its Boston-Harvard accent. On television, Kennedy looked sharper of the two, more in control, more firm, more the image of a President who could stand up to Khrushchev.

In summary, television apparently does more than just present political candidates. Television transfigures candidates into personal images or characterizations that can be quite unique to the medium. Thus, it is necessary to have a term to describe this unique image, a term such as *image candidate.*

In summary, an image candidate is a leading character in the political drama presented by television before an election. His characterization tends to be universally perceived, regardless of viewers' political predispositions, due to viewers' media predispositions to see the candidates in terms of television's stereotyped desirable and undesirable characters, stereotypes that may in themselves be projections of characters valued or detested in the United States culture at large.

Such television production techniques and policies relevant to campaign coverage as the use of reaction shots and editorial abstention by the medium's journalists may work to enhance the viewer's illusion that he is watching a theatrical drama rather than political reality and that the image candidates are to be judged as characters in that drama. Most image techniques employed by political propagandists to enhance the appeal of their client-candidates seek to exploit television's inherent theatricality and viewers' tendencies to see the candidates as dramatic characters. By controlling the presentation or theatrical setting of candidates on paid political programs and commercials, propagandists can encourage viewers to perceive a favorable characterization of the client-candidate.

A candidate's appearance and demeanor appear to provide viewers with the most substantial clues to his character. The rational import of what the candidate says on television, as long as it is not blatantly offensive to the great central cluster of the electorate, appears to have very little influence on viewers' perception of image.

E. S. J. Productions, Inc.: Television Scripts, 1968

On the pages that follow are the complete scripts of a representative sampling of the spot commercials made by E.S.J. Productions, Inc., for Richard Nixon.

E.S.J. #2 "Order"

Video	Audio
1. Opening network disclaimer: "A Political Announcement."	
2. Fadeup on rapidly moving sequence of rioting, urban mob motivating to crowds taunting police authorities.	SFX up full. SFX under.
3. Flaming apt. house dissolving to police patrolling deserted streets in aftermath of violence.	R.N.: It is time for some honest talk about the problem of order in the United States.
4. Perplexed faces of Americans.	R.N.: Dissent is a necessary ingredient of change. But in a system of government that provides for peaceful change—
5. Sequence of shots of people moving through battered streets ordered by destroyed shops and homes.	—there is no cause that justifies resort to violence. There is no cause that justifies rule by mob instead of by reason.
6. Eloquent faces of Americans who have lived through such experiences, climaxed by single shot of charred crossbeams framing a riot ruin. In center of picture is battered machine on which can still be seen in red letters the word "Change." Fadeout.	Music up and out.
7. Fadeup Title: "This Time Vote like Your Whole World Depended on It."	
8. Dissolve to title word "Nixon." Zoom to CU. Hold. Fadeout.	

Video	Audio
9. Closing network disclaimer: "The Preceding Pre-Recorded Political Broadcast Was Paid for by the Nixon–Agnew Campaign Committee."	

E.S.J. #5 "Crime"

1. Opening network disclaimer: "A Political Announcement."

Video	Audio
2. Fadeup on pan into lonely policeman at call box. Motivate suddenly to series of shots of explosive criminal actions with police response ending on image of a bullet-shattered automobile window, which spins into a blur. Dissolve. Pan up row of weapons—then continue tilt up "Kennedy Rifle" and finally to huge CU of hand holding an open jackknife.	Music up and under.

Music under.
R.N.: In recent years crime in this country has grown nine times as fast as the population. At the current rate, the crimes of violence in America will double by 1972. We cannot accept that kind of future. |
| 3. Cut to montage of faces of Americans. They are anxious, perplexed, frightened. | We owe it to the decent and law-abiding citizens of America to take the offensive against the criminal forces that threaten their peace and security— |
| 4. Sequential story briefly illustrating crimes that plague the ordinary citizen: the dilemma imposed upon us by increase of drug sales to the young; victim of mugging; youths fighting police; capture of robbery suspect by police. | —and to rebuild respect for law across this country. |

Video	Audio
5. Dolly in MLS on line of hand-cuffed criminals standing by brick wall, their faces concealed by their hands or coats. Fadeout.	R.N.: I pledge to you that the wave of crime is not going to be the wave of the future in America! Music up and out.
6. Fadeup title: "This Time Vote Like Your Whole World Depended on It."	
7. Dissolve to title word "Nixon." Zoom into CU. Hold. Fadeout.	
8. Closing network disclaimer: "The Preceding Pre-Recorded Political Broadcast Was Paid for by the Nixon–Agnew Campaign Committee."	

E.S.J. #6 "Wrong Road"

1. Opening network disclaimer: "A Political Announcement."	
2. Dolly down LS empty road across western area. Dissolve to match movement pan—tilt in on dejected man asleep on park bench. Then into scenes of both urban and rural decay.	Music up and under. R.N.: For the past five years we've been deluged by programs for the unemployed—programs for the cities—programs for the poor. And we have reaped from these programs an ugly harvest of frustrations, violence and failure across the land.
3. Motivates into sequence of faces of America—all races, all backgrounds. There is a quality	R.N.: Now our opponents will be offering more of the same. But I say we are on the wrong road. It

Video	Audio
of determination to them, but they appear sorely tried.	is time to quit pouring billions of dollars into programs that have failed.
They are the hungry of Appalachia—the poor of an urban ghetto—the ill-housed members of a family on an Indian reservation. Slowly but firmly the picture leads toward a scene of frustrated anger, which is expressed in their faces.	
Sign on streets which says, "Government Checks Cashed Here."	R.N.: What we need are not more millions on welfare rolls—but more people on payrolls in the United States.
4. Series of quick, effective cuts of constructive work scenes— a ship unloading—a tower being raised—a factory line—a building erected.	I believe we should enlist private enterprise, which will produce, not promises in solving the problems of America.
5. Dissolve to shot of children standing in the mud of Appalachia. They stare at the camera. Tilt down for match movement dissolve to silo of little Negro boy (back to camera) as he looks out window. Hold. Fadeout.	Music up and out.

Twentieth Century Fund: Campaign Costs

Every four years American citizens make a momentous choice: Who is to be President of the United States? Perhaps no more important public act occurs in this nation than the motion of the hand that marks the X

From *Voters' Time:* Report of the Twentieth Century Fund Commission on Campaign Costs in the Electronic Era. Copyright © 1969 by The Twentieth Century Fund, New York. Reprinted by permission. Edited and footnotes deleted.

on a presidential ballot or pulls the lever on a voting machine. For on the decision of the American electorate hangs the fate of millions at home and abroad. That decision, indeed, may answer the very question of war or peace, of human survival.

What influences the voter in making his choice?

Many things. Party loyalty. Family tradition. A candidate's record. The record of the incumbent administration—national prosperity or depression. Outside events in midcampaign—the sudden outbreak of war (or peace), the fall of a foreign government. The opinion of others—his union shop steward, his closest friend, his fellow commuter. Columnists and commentators, political reporters and editorial writers. Precinct captains, volunteer workers. Billboards. Newspaper advertising. And campaign broadcasting.

No one knows just how important television and radio are in determining the outcome of an election. A voting decision is the result of so many influences that it is all but impossible to isolate one, such as electronic campaigning, from the others.

The use of television in presidential campaigns is only seventeen years old. It may be many more years before we know what it is doing to politics, or to society. We may never know.

Nevertheless, the power of political broadcasting is assumed by large numbers of politicians and broadcasters alike. According to some political scientists and sociologists, a sizable number of people felt that the 1960 television-radio debates between John F. Kennedy and Richard M. Nixon helped them to make up their minds. And certainly at the time there was widespread public sentiment, reflected in the studies, that Kennedy "won" these confrontations by showing that he was a match for his older, more experienced opponent. These facts taken together have led many people to suspect that the debates gave Kennedy his slim margin of victory.

Other researchers, including some studying the same evidence, have held that broadcasting has only a reinforcement effect on many people already committed to one candidate or the other. Others have adopted the term "cumulative effect" to suggest that people are influenced by the images they receive from the broadcast media, especially television, over long periods of time. They contend that the impressions that enter into a voting decision are gradually built up through the years and that broadcasting plays a large part in shaping this political imagery.

All agree that the media that takes a candidate's voice and individual traits into a voter's home make his message powerfully personal and are bound to have an effect at the ballot box . . .

Broadcasting and Politics

These facts about broadcast media had enormous significance for a candidate in the 1968 presidential campaign because, almost alone among aspirants for high political office throughout the world, he could "buy" time on the air.

With a single message lasting one minute, presented within one program, on one television network, he could reach as many as 23 million viewers of voting age—a number equal to almost a third of the votes cast in the 1968 election. With the most intensive old-fashioned whistle-stop campaign, a candidate could have reached only a small fraction of that audience.

Politicians believe, even without scientific proof, that the broadcast media provide the best way in certain campaigns to get their messages to the people. Consequently, broadcasting has had an enormous influence on our political affairs. Television, particularly, makes political life more fluid and more volatile. It affects the tempo of campaigning. Adroit candidates —or their staffs—plan morning events that will gain free coverage in the evening newscasts. In fact, campaign strategists devote a great deal of effort and ingenuity to getting free television coverage for their candidates. It has put a stronger emphasis on the personality and appearance of candidates. It has helped to nationalize political life. The sum is a revolution in political campaigning.

A telling measure of the importance of both television and radio for many candidates is the rise in political broadcasting expenditures since the 1956 presidential campaign, when a basis for comparison became available. . . . In 1956, total broadcasting charges for presidential and vice presidential candidates in general election campaigns were $4.6 million. They were 11 million in 1964 and rose to $20.4 million in 1968. Thus they quadrupled in twelve years.

When professional politicians say, as many do, that broadcast campaigning is decisive in a presidential race, they mean it. Some would go so far as to predict that before long presidential campaigning will be done almost entirely by television and radio. This Commission does not go so far; there may be less here than meets the eye. But the fact that many politicians believe that broadcasting is of major importance tends to make it so. Certainly it has resulted in an impressive increase in the use of the broadcast media by presidential candidates and their running mates. And this in turn has led to an impressive increase in the total cost of presidential campaigning—which is one of our concerns.

The Citizens' Research Foundation estimates that in 1968 total political spending by all candidates and committees at all levels in the United States reached $300 million. This was 50 per cent higher than the total of $200 million estimated for 1964. . . .

Television Costs

Television has contributed greatly to the growth in presidential campaign expenditures.

Television is ideally suited to reaching a national constituency, and presidential candidates have regularly accounted for a high percentage of total political spending on television in general election campaigns. Furthermore, the growth in campaign television spending has shown little sign of abating, as some once expected. In 1968, half of all political television costs in the general election period were charged to candidates for the Presidency and Vice Presidency. . . .

Further evidence that television has driven up costs of presidential campaigning can be found in the growth of national-level expenditures since 1952, a growth that has gone far beyond past historical patterns.

When television first became a serious tool in political campaigning, it was expected to displace some of the money formerly spent on radio (just as radio had displaced some of the money spent on newspapers) rather than increase costs. But after 1952, when television emerged as a dominant form of communications in presidential campaigns, the estimated cost per vote took a sharp upward turn. From 19 cents in 1952, the cost per vote rose to 29 cents in 1960 and to 35 cents in 1964. In 1968 it jumped to 60 cents.

Many factors contributed to the big 1968 rise. Wallace's campaign alone added about 10 cents per voter. The consumer price index rose 12 per cent between 1964 and 1968. And parties made more use of costly new tools, such as computer technology and jet travel, in 1968. But no single one of these factors seems to have had television's explosive effect on the cost of each vote.

Candidates for public office use broadcasting because it offers unprecedented opportunities to reach the electorate—an electorate that is growing rapidly, growing beyond the power of candidates to reach by other means. Broadcasting requires candidates to raise large sums of money for buying time on the airwaves and for the production of programs using that time.

Problems of Financing

Raising money for political campaigns in America has never been easy. Television has exacerbated the problem, for now that the candidate can reach almost all of the people, he wants to do so over and over again. And to do that he must spend heavily.

In the early years of this century, money seemed to be the key to winning elections. In 1904 and 1908 the Republicans spent 75 per cent and 72 per cent of all direct expenditures made by the national committees of both parties, and the Republicans won; in 1912 and 1916 the Democrats outspent them with 51 per cent and 53 per cent, and the Democrats won. Then through the 1920's the Republicans consistently outspent the Democrats, with 75 per cent in 1920 and 1924 and 56 per cent in 1928, and they won consistently. The correlation was very strong, the case seemed proved.

But the correlation was less marked and the case collapsed in the 1930's and 1940's. In 1932 the Democrats spent 49 per cent of the total reported by both national committees, yet won. In 1936 they spent 41 per cent; in 1940, 35 per cent; in 1944, 42 per cent; and in 1948, only 39 per cent—yet they won every time. Money, it appeared, might talk without winning. It is doubtful that Herbert Hoover could have been re-elected in 1932 had he spent many times what Franklin D. Roosevelt did. . . .

Money may not win elections today, but candidates lacking access to large amounts of money cannot buy broadcasting time and are thus denied full access to the major means of communication in this era. This fact has reinforced the notion that "politics is a rich man's game." True, in 1968 neither Nixon nor Humphrey was a rich man. But their personal finances made no difference. Their parties raised large sums for them, the Republicans much more than the Democrats; and they spent large sums on broadcasting for them, the Republicans much more than the Democrats: $11.5 million and $5.5 million respectively. Without such broadcast expenditures, the campaign managers of both parties thought that their candidates had little chance to capture the full attention of the American voter.

To be sure, there are those who are not alarmed by the rise in presidential campaign expenditures, pointing out that even now they are only a small fraction of the sums regularly spent on advertising autos, cigarettes, or soap. But they ignore the possibly degrading effect on candidates of the need to wheedle large contributions from individuals. They also ignore the possibility that a presidential candidate will feel obligated to his campaign's financial benefactors. And they forget that any suspicion that money buys elections and that contributors buy candidates undermines the credibility of our political system.

The popular suspicion that "politics is a rich man's game" adds to public cynicism about politics itself. Its prevalence is suggested by such research as a poll conducted by the Louis Harris organization in 1967. More than 60 per cent of those interviewed in the poll expressed the belief that politicians take graft and that very few of them are dedicated public servants. However unfair this judgment may be, it is abetted by the loopholes and violations of the reporting laws and occasional scandals.

Even if an average citizen would like to support his favorite candidate's campaign, the amounts of money required may lead him to conclude that only big business or big labor can foot the bill—a conclusion with its own dividend in cynicism. Possibly as a result, many people tend to avoid financial participation in politics. The percentage of people who give to any campaign is low. It has ranged from 6 to 12 per cent of the adult population since 1956.

Ordinarily, once a candidate is nominated by one of the two major parties he can expect to raise money, somehow. But there are exceptions. Humphrey, in fact, was one. He had great problems in raising money in September 1968, not because he was poor but because, among other things, so many potential contributors judged—along with the polls—that he was a sure loser following the Democratic convention in riot-torn Chicago that was so fully covered on television. . . .

Problem of Reform

Nearly everybody believes these inequities should be corrected. Some, confronted with the intricacies of the problem, have simply proposed that all candidates be prohibited by law from purchasing television time. The Commission not only feels that this proposal may be unconstitutional but also considers it unacceptable to most broadcasters, politicians, and elected officials. Television is a fact of life, and one way or another it will continue to influence elections. In our view, it ought to be transformed into a positive influence.

The problem of money and politics has been with us almost since our beginnings as a republic. But it has taken on a new dimension and heightened urgency with the emergence of television and its high—and rising—costs.

John F. Kennedy expressed concern about the problem of money and political television in 1959. He was quite clear on the decisive role played by the medium and on the possible impact of the large contributions that now make campaign broadcasting possible. As he put it:

> If all candidates and parties are to have equal access to this essential and decisive campaign medium, without becoming deeply obligated to big financial contributors from the world of business, labor or other major lobbies, then the time has come when a solution must be found for this problem of TV costs.

Concern about the influence of money on politics has led to a variety of legislative restrictions to limit campaign expenditures and contributions.

The federal Corrupt Practices Act of 1925 requires political committees operating in two or more states to file reports of their receipts and expenditures. It also sets campaign expenditure limits of $25,000 for candidates for the Senate and $5,000 for candidates for the House of Representatives.

The Hatch Act of 1939 places a limit of $3 million on the expenditures of any committee operating in two or more states. It limits to $5,000 the amount of money that an individual may contribute to any candidate or political committee.

Most states require public reporting of campaign disbursements and thirty-three have spending ceilings, but only seven limit individual contributions. All too often these attempts at regulation are evaded or simply ignored. . . .

Undoubtedly the weaknesses in our legislation are a main reason for the cynicism about money in politics. As President Dwight D. Eisenhower once observed:

> It does mean, in effect, that we have put a dollar sign on public service, and today many capable men who would like to run for office simply can't afford to do so. Many believe that politics in our country is already a game exclusively for the affluent. This is not strictly true; yet the fact that we may be approaching that state of affairs is a sad reflection on our elective system.

The trends in the use of paid broadcast time may not serve as much as they should to allay public cynicism. When television began to be widely used by political candidates, some observers suggested that its extraordinary intimacy would improve the quality of campaigns. Television, it was thought, would give voters a sharper personal impression of the candidates and a deeper understanding of the issues. The voter, watching and meditating before his set, would arrive at a more informed and intelligent choice than he would by attending a political rally, where he might be swayed by partisan hysteria. But the degree to which television has met this ideal is questionable.

Use of Television

Two main kinds of paid political broadcasts are widely used today. One is the "spot," similar to a commercial, lasting for a minute or less (a related variety is the short message lasting up to five minutes). The other is the program lasting a half-hour or an hour (it sometimes stretches over several hours, as in "telethons"). Candidates have shown increasing preference for "spots."

The tremendous growth in the popularity of "spots" has occurred for two major reasons: they enable a candidate to reach a large number of viewers at a relatively low cost per viewer, and they allow him to address people he could not reach by any other means.

In October 1968 a presidential candidate might have bought a one-minute network "spot" in "Gunsmoke" at almost $50,000 (not including the cost of producing the "spot"). It would have entered an estimated 13 million homes and been seen by approximately 19 million people of voting age. A thirty-minute network program scheduled at a similar time would have cost more than $80,000 in time charges (plus a sizable expenditure for production) and could have been expected to reach an audience of 6 to 8 million homes. Thus the longer program would have been a far more expensive purchase in relation to the number of homes—or viewers—reached.

Some campaign strategists, however, believe that the longer programs are decidedly useful. Although the viewers who remain might consist largely of the candidate's partisans, whose minds are already made up, they cite the reinforcement effect already mentioned—the motivation to work harder for the party's candidate.

Even so, a political "spot" in a high-rated program can attract the attention of many viewers who would not watch a half-hour political program. Its audience is a much better cross-section of the voting—and nonvoting—public, since it can be assumed to contain a much higher proportion of uncommitted voters. And in a year such as 1968, when the margin of victory was narrow (about a million votes—1.5 per cent of those cast), these uncommitted voters can hold the balance.

Political candidates in general election campaigns during 1968 chose to spend more than three-quarters of their total television budget on "spots," and they spent nearly twice as much for this purpose as the candidates in 1964. . . .

Candidates are under increasing pressure to get maximum return for their money. And broadcasters prefer to sell campaign time in small segments, since they are more profitable than longer programs and less disruptive of schedules. In the absence of counterpressures, the proportion of short messages can be expected to increase.

The Public Interest

This Commission does not question whether television is the appropriate instrument for informing the electorate. But it does believe that ultimately the voter has much to lose from present arrangements. For the democratic process requires open forums for political ideas and the widest possible dissemination of information. Letting ability to pay determine access to the great audience and fostering the development of commercial-like campaign spots rather than rational political discussions may in time subvert the democratic process.

The first and most essential aim of this Commission, therefore, is to make recommendations for changes in public policy relating to campaign broadcasting that will primarily assist and benefit the American voter, not the broadcaster or the candidate. To accomplish that aim the Commission has identified these specific goals:

1. To guarantee that there is basic access to the broadcast media for all significant candidates for President and Vice President.
2. To help relieve the financial pressures of broadcast campaigning on presidential and vice presidential candidates.
3. To promote rational political discussion in presidential campaigns, thus exposing as many voters as possible to candidates and issues within a rational context.
4. To stimulate effective citizen participation in the processes of democratic government by encouraging small contributions to political campaigns.

Theodore H. White and William Gossett: Electoral College Reform

Mr. White: Thank you very much, Mr. Chairman.

I have no prepared remarks. I have a few notes. Then I am open to questions.

I would submit that this Senate will consider no more important question in this decade than the matter of how we elect our President. This is the essence of the game. This is the question of leadership in a modern society. This is where I think politics and history join.

In modern times, other nations have tried direct election of presidents. Germany did. They tried it by a direct unitary vote of the nation, and they got Hitler.

You have the French now experimenting with direct unitary elections of presidents. And I have very little hope for that prospect. The longest lived experiment in direct popular vote in a republic was that of the Roman Republic which voted, where the people voted in electoral units very much like our own. Rather than 50 States and electoral voting, the 35 tribes voted.

Now, I believe that this country needs to reform its electoral laws, and immediately. But I believe the method suggested in this amendment is a direct invitation to chaos. You only have to project this scheme against the last two elections to realize that it will only compound and multiply the instabilities in our system.

I spend time covering presidential elections. The election of 1960 was carried by one-tenth of 1 percent of the popular vote.

It may amuse you to know in all the years since then I have never been able to get an official count of John F. Kennedy's margin over Richard Nixon. One count says 113,000, the Clerk of the House says 119,450; there is another count of 112,000, another count of 122,000. There is no way now of collecting a direct official vote in the United States of America.

I want to approach the problem in the most sordid way and not in the high minded manner you gentlemen have been speaking in. I want to talk of crooks in elections.

From United States Congress, Senate Judiciary Committee, Hearings, *Electoral College Reform,* April 1970, and *Electing the President,* March 1969. Government Printing Office.

I believe that you cannot steal in any State of the Union more than 1 percent of the vote, but when elections get hot, votes are stolen. I would wonder whether the Senator from Indiana completely trusts the count of Lake County, out of Gary.

I know that in my own town of New York last year we canceled an election, a very minor election for the Democratic nomination for the presidency of a borough because there were 1,000 irregularities in those machines and a slight margin of 100 votes between them, so we called that election off and we ran it over.

I wonder here whether anybody trusts the vote in Duval County, or remembers the 87 votes of the 1948 election which made Lyndon Johnson Senator.

I could go right around the Union to Philadelphia, to Kanawha County, to South Boston, and wonder whether we really want to trust the election of Presidents to a direct pool of votes where the arts and skills of those few people who do steal votes are magnified.

Right now, what you have in the country is a system of self-sealing containers. Again, I speak the language of the press. If the crooks in Illinois, if the crooks in Cook County are going to steal votes and the crooks in upstate Illinois are going to steal votes, each State has built up some sort of antibody system so that it seals the theft, the stealing, the rigging of elections. There are certain States like Minnesota or Connecticut, California, Oregon, where I think the votes are counted with scrupulous honesty. But if the margins are going to be as thin as they were in 1960 and 1968, I can see the honesty of the majority of honest States crumbling just like that.

I have sat on election nights both at political headquarters and in national TV studios. I wonder whether you can imagine what the scenario of election night might be with the entire Nation hanging awake for the returns if we had another election as close as 1960 or 1968 with no one knowing what was happening?

You all remember how in 1960 when the Connecticut vote was coming in strong for John F. Kennedy, Eisenhower took to the air to plead with the people in California to get out there and vote. Connecticut closes 3 hours earlier than California; I think about 8 hours earlier than Hawaii. Once those eastern votes start piling up from the big cities one way or the other the pressure to steal, the urge to cheat becomes unbearable if it is a close election. You can't steal a real election, a real majority, but, if it is a close election, that election night would be an invitation to have militia out guarding the ballot boxes the next morning.

There is an almost unprecedented chaos that comes in the system where the change of one or two votes per precinct can switch the national election of the United States.

Now we have 180,000 voting boxes, or precincts, in the United States; and, if by 10 or 11 o'clock it is going to be as close as 1960 or 1968, I hesitate to think of what is going to happen in the western precinct boxes and some of the southern precinct boxes.

I would like to go on from this sordid consideration of fraud to the more serious considerations of history. And I would like to use as my text a remark made by John F. Kennedy of Massachusetts on March 5, 1956, in Senate debate. He was discussing an amendment similar to this. He began by saying that on the whole, our system has given us "able Presidents, capable of meeting the increased demands upon our society. No urgent necessity for change has been proven."

And then he said the point I want to make which is that "When all these factors are considered, it is not only the unit vote for the Presidency that we are talking about but a whole solar system of Government power. If this proposal changes the balance of power in any one of the elements of the solar system, it is necessary to change all of them."

Our country has been structured in balances of parties and States and Congress and Senate; and indeed on the realities of minority and ethnic groups, which are as much a part of the structure of American politics as anything else. So I would like to pass first in discussing the structural changes to what happens to minorities.

It has amused me very much to see southern conservatives taking up the struggle against this amendment and northern liberals being for it. Any plebiscite form of vote that we have had in the United States of America works directly and brutally against our black population. That goes for California's proposition 14. It goes for New York's Police Review Board. Whenever you give the voters a chance to make a clear-cut choice, the vote goes antiblack. I can see a clear-cut antiblack force in the next election under this proposal.

The protection of the minorities—and I submit to you, sir, that they are as much a part of our system as any of us—rests upon their clotting and coagulation in the big cities of our States. You cannot think of Massachusetts or New York or Illinois without thinking of the great ethnic minorities which inhabit them. They are underrepresented in the Congress and in the Senate of the United States of America. Where they swing their clout is in the big States, because their votes move the great States with the great clusters of electoral votes.

When you change the way you elect the President to a direct addition of digits, you erase the identity of all these people.

You change the strategy of campaigns. The presidential candidate right now—we all know it—puts a coalition together by pleasing as many people as possible. He cannot preach one thing in the South and another thing in the North. He has to have a national policy.

Under the new system I think the real big bosses in this country would become the men of Madison Avenue. We would market candidates the way Ford markets its new products. Ford spends $50 million marketing new automobiles every year. That is about what it costs to market a President in a major campaign. You will have candidates who need not assemble the vote of South Carolina and New York and California and Indiana but media masters and market analysts who will give you cleavages that run right across the country. . . .

I have not yet seen how, under this new amendment, candidates will get on the ballot. The effort of George Wallace to qualify in 50 States of the Union was a spectacular one. He qualified everywhere except in the District of Columbia. It was one of the most amazing phenomena of the 1968 election.

Will some candidates run only regionally or will any candidate who enters the list for President of the United States of America be on the ballot of every State of the Union? If so, does the Federal Congress determine the qualifications? Do you have to go around collecting signatures, say a million signatures to get on the ballot in 20 States of the Union?

I do not see how you qualify unless you permit any number of regional and ideological candidates.

Finally, in politics, I believe there are things that are more important than statistics and vote counting. There are communities. We live in a world of communities which have been balanced and put together by our federalized American system. I believe it is good and right that when somebody goes to the polls in Boston, Mass., he feels he is doing something about the Massachusetts vote, and when the Tar Heel from North Carolina goes to the polls he feels he is doing something for North Carolina.

I would not want to strip this sense of identity from the great historic communities of the United States of America in which each man feels he has a role to play in the larger role of his community for a role which makes him just one more digit, one of those electronic figures that will come cascading in at 70 to 80 million votes in a 6-hour period some November night in which he has no identity whatsoever.

Where I believe this amendment has its thrust and its force is the real need now for the abolition of the electoral college and as soon as possible. We have lived under a two-party system for a long time. We live in the real presence of a third party right now. It was Wallace last time. I don't know who it will be this time.

To leave the manipulation of the final results in a contested election to such third party candidates in so impossible an organization as the electoral college seems to me to be a dereliction of duty. I believe that what must be done immediately is the immediate purging of the electoral college as such from the Constitution of the United States of America. I believe thereafter the electoral vote may be preserved. If no clear-cut, sound digital majority occurs in that electoral college, I believe the election should go to the House and the Senate sitting jointly with the representatives of the people doing for them what they would do by themselves.

William Gosset: Mr. Chairman, we are grateful for the privilege of appearing before this distinguished Committee of lawyer members of the Senate to express the views of the American Bar Association on the great issue of electoral reform.

Mr. Chairman, although there is a general consensus that the Electoral College system should be reformed, there are those who oppose the direct popular election method. The principal burden of my statement today is to analyze and respond to some of those objections including the alternatives advanced by the opponents.

Professor Bickel, who appeared before the Committee on Wednesday, agreed that electoral reform is essential; but he would limit it to the elimination of the "faithless elector," and to the substitution of an election by a joint session of Congress for the present one state–one vote election in the House, in the event of a deadlock in the electoral vote contest.

Although he confessed that "there is a certain ideological chastity in the proposal for popular election, which one can wonder at, and even ruefully admire," to use his words, he prefers the electoral system, modified as he suggests. Why?

First, he contends that "The two-party system would not likely survive the demise of the electoral college." The electoral college deters national minor-party challenges, he argues, because unless a minor party candidate has a substantial regional base, his popular vote will not register in the electoral college, except as a spoiler; indeed, the "Electoral College makes it impossible for a third-party candidate to have any sort of impact," said Professor Bickel.

But, Professor Bickel continues, in a popular election with a run-off possibility, "The major party nomination would count for much less than it now does . . . coalitions would be formed not at the conventions but during the period between the general election and the run-off, and the two-party system would not long survive."

The question of the possible effect of a popular vote arrangement upon the two-party system occupied much of the discussion at meetings of the ABA commission, and its position was adopted with confidence that a direct election would carry no serious risk of producing a multi-party system. In the light of subsequent discussion of that subject in the House hearings and in the debate, we will strongly support that view. Indeed, it is our opinion that the two-party system has survived in spite of rather than because of the electoral college system; and that is the view of distinguished authorities on the subject. Professor Paul A. Freund, professor of Constitutional Law at Harvard Law School (a member of the ABA commission), made the following statement before the House Judiciary Committee:

"This provision for a run-off is important not only as a democratic solution to the problem of a deadlock, but as a deterrent to the rise of splinter parties. Some critics of a direct popular vote have feared that by giving effect to every vote in the final tally, the plan would foster the growth of minor parties and would jeopardize the two-party system. If, however, the only achievement that such splinter parties could hope for would be to force a run-off between the two leading candidates, their gain would probably not seem to be worth the candle in the first place, and there would be an incentive to come to terms with a major party, as at present."

"The two-party system, in addition, is buttressed by more than the unit count of the present electoral system; it rests on the foundations of the party system in Congress and the states, and there is no solid reason to expect that these foundations would be shaken by the direct election of the President."

The present system (including Professor Bickel's proposed alteration of it) offers special incentives to third-party candidates and can easily give them power disproportionate to their numbers.

Direct election would fully cure the defects in our system which the Wallace candidacy—and others in 1912, 1924 and 1948—sought to exploit. It would also remedy other faults that could magnify third-party efforts. Close analysis proves that direct election will actually strengthen the two-party system—not weaken it—by removing special incentives to third parties and equalizing all voters throughout the nation. . . .

A candidate rarely, if ever, is able to deliver a block of voters who supported him. On the other hand, he often can deliver the electors; and that is exactly what George Wallace wanted to do and apparently was prepared to do had a deadlock occurred. There would seem to be little incentive for the creation of third parties when they know they have no chance of winning—that the maximum product of their effort would be to require a run-off election; and in any such election, they would have little or no control over those who voted for them. Negotiation for the votes of electors and behind-the-scenes bargains on that level are quite feasible; but dickering for the support of the general public is quite another matter.

The ABA commission considered also the writings of ten political scientists who had given special attention to the foundations and functions of political party systems. We learned that no single factor accounts for the two-party system and that there is considerable disagreement as to its major origins.

The experts are virtually in agreement on one point, however. It is that election of legislators and executives by plurality votes from single-member districts is the chief cause of two-partyism. This is the one element which all two-party systems have in common.

No one proposes to alter our practice of electing members of Congress and state legislators, governors and mayors on this basis. To the extent that these elections undergird our two-party system, that support will continue. Moreover, our proposal essentially places presidential elections on the same basis and thus perfects and extends that feature which best serves the two-party system.

Nonetheless, we were sufficiently concerned by the possibility of weakening the two-party system that a major provision of our proposal is directed largely at supporting it. This is the provision requiring run-off elections when no candidate obtains 40 percent of the popular vote. This avoids the peculiar evils of a majority requirement on the one side and simple plurality requirement on the other.

In summary, then, we emphasize that the two-party system is likely to be preserved by perfection of that feature of the present system which is most conducive to two parties: plurality election by a single constituency. Thus, the functioning of our two-party system on a national basis will be greatly strengthened.

Under the electoral college system, the decision of the people is inoperative unless it is approved by, in effect, another electorate. Such a barrier between the people and their President is both anachronistic and abhorrent.

The electoral college system violates fundamental democratic principles in other ways:

The winner-take-all feature of the system suppresses at an intermediate stage all minority votes cast in a state. The winner of the most popular votes in a state, regardless of his percentage of the votes cast, receives all of that state's electoral votes. The votes for the losing candidates are, in effect, discarded while those for the winner are multiplied in value.

As Senator Thomas Hart Benton said in 1824: "To lose their votes, is the fate of all minorities, and it is their duty to submit; but this is not a case of votes lost, but of votes taken away, added to those of the majority, and given to a person to whom the minority is opposed."

The present system discriminates among voters on the basis of residence. While a small state voter might seem to enjoy an electoral vote advantage because his state receives two electoral votes regardless of size, a large state voter is able to influence more electoral votes, and it is in the large industrial states that presidential elections are usually won or lost.

There is no sound reason why every citizen should not have an equal vote in the election of our one official who serves as the symbol and spokesman for all the people.

Some opponents of the direct election plan argue that a benefit of the electoral system is that it minimizes the risks of voting frauds and other irregularities. Said Professor Bickel, "Since most often a shift in popular votes, even if it should change the result in a state, will not affect the national outcome, claims of voting irregularity are most frequently dropped, having been dealt with locally. But if everything depended on the total popular vote, would we not likely face in each close election, as Professor Brown has said, 're-examination of every ballot box and voting machine in the country, not to mention also the records of registration and qualification of voters'?"

It is our view that voting irregularities and demands for recount are much more likely to arise under the electoral college system than under a direct election arrangement. In large states especially, fraud and other voting irregularities involving relatively few popular votes could deliver an entire block of electoral votes. But in a national, direct election, where 70 million votes are involved, a much larger shift of votes, on a multi-state basis, would be required. Professor Freund, in his statement before the House Judiciary Committee, discussed voting frauds and recounts:

Professor Bickel defends the present electoral system "as one of countervailing centers of power . . . It has meant," he argues, "that each of our major parties is really two parties—a congressional party, moderate-to-conservative in orientation and rooted in the less populous, less urbanized, more homogeneous states, and in the equivalent sectors of the large states; and a presidential party which is oriented more toward urban regions, liberal ideology, and minority groups. The system, in short, builds into the President an incentive to be a counterweight to Congress and, while a national leader, a particular spokesman for the urban and minority groups."

That argument encounters serious difficulties as applied to a number of presidential elections, including that of 1968. Indeed, to quote Professor Freund, the argument "may be backward looking to the time when New York was the crucial state to carry. With the spread of urbanization and the shift of population, there are now six states with twenty-five or more electoral votes, and these states have tended to cancel each other out in the electoral count. President Nixon gained his victory carrying just three of these states (California, Illinois and Ohio), with a total of 92 electoral votes, while Mr. Humphrey carried New York, Pennsylvania and Texas, with 100 electoral votes. Of these six states, only one—Illinois—has been in the winning column in all three of the recent closely contested national elections; in 1948, 1960 and 1968. The large states will get their due share of attention under a popular vote. Where the nectar is thickest, there will the bees foregather."

In response to the argument that the countervailing tensions between rural residents and urban areas provides necessary leverage for minority groups in presidential elections, Professor Freund expresses doubt "on principle and in practice whether the voice of minority groups, whether black voters or others, is best expressed through this kind of magnification." A more appropriate and an effective way would be to give vitality to similar votes in states where they are now ineffectual under the winner-take-all method of counting. And this is the view of such political leaders of the black community as Congressman John Conyers of Michigan.

Referring to the proposed modified electoral system espoused by Professor Bickel as a "minimum proposal," Professor Freund concludes that while the proposal would get rid of some of the most egregious faults of the system, it would "perpetuate others." Said he:

"It would not end the risk of electing a candidate who stood second in the popular vote."

"The distortions of leverage would remain."

"By continuing to base the result on electoral votes, the plan would still prefer population to actual voter turnout as the critical factor in a state's weight. In states having a dominant party, there would be no incentive for voters of the minority party to go to the polls; if they did, their votes would not be included in the state's tally."

"Our federalism, like our two-party system, rests on more impregnable foundations than the survival of the unpredictable contrivance known as the electoral college."

Part Two   The Issues

6   Social Disorder

There is more than a whiff of apocalypse in the air these days. It is a fevered, rancorous, tumultuous time for the nation. It is a time, also of much self-doubt about the nation's capacity to solve its problems or even to survive with its institutions and social structures recognizably intact. Many alienated young people scream their hatred for what they call "Amerika" in the most shockingly explicit and provocative language they can muster. Other young people, less explosively or vituperatively but with equal determination, are making statements of renunciation and rejection. They drop out, they turn on with dope, they embrace what they take to be the peer culture, they turn outlaw. Whatever form the renunciation may take, those who make it rejoice in thinking of themselves as strangers or aliens in this land. Nearly every form of established authority is challenged by the alienated; the authority of the general laws, of the political and social leadership, of the school, the church, the intelligentsia, and of the home. With those authorities challenged and swept away, the behavior of the alienated can seem shocking and illegitimate. The rage of the alienated inspires its counterpart among those who still live by the challenged authorities. Thus we are polarized, and the possibilities for discussion and reconciliation disappear with new manifestation of outrage.

It is similar with the blacks. In order to develop group cohesion sufficent for effective group politics, blacks must stress their common condition, drawing upon everything which produces the sense of apartness and distinctiveness; hence Black Pride, Black Power. The more blacks conceive of themselves in collective terms, the harder it is for them to conceive of the nation as two-hundred million individuals, each with his private interests and his vote to protect and advance him. With each advance of black self-consciousness, there comes a corresponding sense that the general laws and authorities are white laws and white authority and thus are not legitimate for black people. Black rage at subjection to law and authority that they cannot identify as their own also produces a counterpart rage among white people.

We have been taught that our nation is great and worthy of our love and loyalty because it leaves each individual free and secure to enjoy his liberty and goods. When millions of people either do not feel free or can feel no security in the enjoyment of their liberty and the fruits of their efforts, we can say that this national belief has been badly shaken. An alarmingly high proportion of young men and women and most blacks feel subject to illegitimate authority and hence, not free. The middling-to-conspicuously successful white person who believes that his talent and energy entitle him to what he has amassed cannot feel secure in his enjoyment of it because of the challenge of blacks and of alienated young people. The old belief is shattering, then, and we have not yet found anything to put in its place. In the meantime, it grows harder and harder for the various elements of the estranged and those committed to the established order to talk with one another. This fact, we think, lies at the bottom of the pervasive sense of disorder and pathology.

Our political mechanisms do not function well under such stresses. The system functions best when concrete social or economic interests form and generate concrete legislative demands (farm price supports, the right of labor to organize and bargain collectively, the introduction of greater flexibility in the money supply, and so on.) It is not that these deep philosophical and psychological stresses do not find their way into political debate. They do, but in obscure and imperfect fashion. They tend to be expressed in slogans about law and order, changing the system, and abolishing racism and imperialism. Such language, such discussion (if it can be called that) may arouse some, but it persuades few. In the congressional elections of 1970 there was much furious sloganeering, but it seems to have had little effect on the voters and little effect in changing the terms of legislation within the Congress chosen in that election. In 1972 these underlying disorders in society are not getting direct and clear expression from the mechanisms of conventional politics, either. We believe, nevertheless, that those issues really do pervade the atmosphere of this election year. The selections in this chapter are an attempt to better illuminate some of them.

Robert Brustein's hilarious yet chilling account of a famous incident at a symposium sponsored by the Theatre for Ideas in New York City seems to us to embody most of the elements of the current social pathology. Brustein, a distinguished director and critic and dean of the Yale School of Drama, sought with his own remarks in the symposium to define and then invoke the authority of theatrical tradition, including the traditions of skill and discipline of the various crafts that comprise the theatre: he was explicating an order. The young hecklers, in contradiction to their values of personal expressiveness and spontaneity, vented their rage against the confines of the tradition upheld by Brustein. Their expressiveness and their rage truly disrupted the event, but also provoked a counterrage in the audience who largely shared Brustein's values. The result was a shambles. Neither group could speak to the other. Of course, in such a circumstance one must say that the world of the theatre is in a state of crisis.

"When constabulary duty is to be done, the policeman's lot is not a happy one." There is a lot of constabulary duty to be done in this country today, and the conclusion is obvious. Who could begin to catalog the problems of the police? What is clear about them as a group is that they are in the center of social unrest. They are viewed as the symbol and agency of oppression by the alienated; as the symbol of order and protection by the majority. That is part of the trouble, of course; they may be symbols, but they are also men and citizens. We believe that Robert Coles' subtle and poignant recapitulation of his interviews with the "ordinary cop" brilliantly illuminates part of the character of today's unrest and also goes a long way toward restoring to the policeman, himself, a measure of his own authenticity as a person and citizen as well as a symbol.

The staff paper of the President's Commission on Campus Unrest included here offers a dispassionate and not unsympathetic view of what we now call the "youth culture" or "counterculture." Coles' sergeant acknowledges that it is the college kids and other long-haired, dissident youths who produce the real rage in him, who make him feel like smashing things or people. It is no defense of the youth culture and its often fatuous expressions to believe that adults have a greater obligation to try to understand their own young people—to meet rage, gullibility, and plain juvenile foolishness with sobriety and responsibility and, above all, sympathetic knowledge. In any case, we don't think one can claim any understanding of the condition of unrest in the country without some knowledge of the grounds of youthful alienation.

Finally, Bernadine Dohrn's article is a typical expression of the most severely alienated yet politically active of the younger people. We do not offer the statement by Weatherman underground for its analytical powers or for the doctrinal and programmatic content that it offers, but rather for its expressiveness, for its depiction of belief and mood among a segment of relatively well-educated middle-class young people. The language of the young Weatherman activists is more subdued than it was in 1969 and 1970. They seem less certain about their goals and their tactics. They have apparently rejected the random violence that led to the bombings and self-detonations of 1970. They are uncertain of their relationship to the working class and even to the militant blacks. Yet who can mistake the evidence here of relentless and total rejection of the existing social and political order?

Robert Brustein: Monkey Business

As a benefit for itself, the Theatre for Ideas, a private group which arranges symposiums on a variety of subjects, organized last month a symposium called *Theatre or Therapy*. In the expectation of a large turnout, the group hired a former Friends' Meeting House near Gramercy Park, now preserved as a New York landmark. The white auditorium, in which both participants and audience were arranged in pews, provided what seemed a good atmosphere for rational discussion. The director of the Theatre for Ideas, Shirley Broughton, had invited Julian Beck and Judith Malina of the Living Theatre, Paul Goodman, and myself to participate in the symposium, and I had accepted, in spite of an instinctive distaste for symposiums and a deep sense of foreboding.

I had recently published an article on the Living Theatre in these pages in which I criticized the company, along with some elements of the radical young, for mindlessness, humorlessness, and romantic revolutionary rhetoric. The meeting looked to me like a good opportunity for more extended debate on the subject, as well as for exploring the differences between those who practiced the "new theatre" and those more skeptical about its aims and aspirations. On the other hand, I had been hearing rumors that attempts would be made to disrupt this symposium. Since I don't function well under disruptive conditions, I thought it wise to make some notes, rather than run the risk of trying to extemporize during a heckling session.

Because of difficulty with the sound system—a difficulty never adequately repaired—the symposium began a half hour late. I passed the time chatting with Nat Hentoff, the moderator, Goodman, and with the Becks, whom I had not seen since their visit to Yale last fall. The Becks seemed amiable, though a little breathless, and talked about their American tour, then in its final week. Non-violence was in trouble, they said. The "revolution" was going beyond pacifism on the assumption that only violent overthrow of the Establishment could cure its insanity and corruption. I wondered if the Becks, too, had rejected the non-violence which they always declared to be the basis for their anarchistic program.

Hentoff worried about the proper order of speakers, Goodman about the meaning of the topic. We decided to limit our statements to ten minutes apiece, then to debate each other, and then to throw the debate open to the audience. We also decided to make some effort to interpret the vague topic title in the course of our statements. I was to speak first, Goodman second, and the Becks last.

We entered the hall past an audience that was growing restive. I caught sight of a number of friends in the house, as well as several members of the Living Theatre company stationed in the balcony and the orchestra. Hentoff started to introduce the discussion—into a dead mike; when it finally seemed in comparatively good working order, we were able to begin. Hentoff reflected on the confusing nature of the subject we were discussing, and asked me to attempt a definition. I did so, speaking from my notes, after mumbling some apology for the insecurity that had prompted them:

"Theatre or Therapy is a rather loaded topic title," I said, "but it does begin to indicate the kind of controversy that is occupying the theatre today where the central question seems to be: To what extent should a production be oriented toward the audience, to what extent toward the actors, and to what extent toward the playwright. One's answer to this is affected by one's attitude toward some important issues of our time: Freedom versus responsibility, activist theatre versus non-activist theatre, free improvisation versus disciplined skill, process versus presentation, and so forth."

A voice from the balcony: "What the hell is disciplined skill?"

A voice from the orchestra: "Shut up, you twerp."

From the balcony: "Fuck you, I'm asking him a question."

From the orchestra: "We'll listen to you later. He's doing the talking now."

"My own position quite simply stated is this," I continued. "I believe the theatre to be served best when it is served by supremely gifted individuals possessed of superior vision and the capacity to express this in enduring form. In short, I believe in the theatre as a place for high art."

The heckler: "We're all supremely gifted individuals."

Brustein: "I doubt that very much."

The heckler: "Up against the wall."

I decided to skip the repartee and get through the statement. "I do not believe the theatre changes anybody, politically or psychologically, and I don't believe it should try to change anybody. While necessarily concerned with social-political as well as psychological-metaphysical issues, the theatre cannot be expected to resolve these issues. . . . Chekhov, one of those supremely gifted individuals I spoke of, has said . . . "

"Fuck Chekhov!"

" . . . that the correct presentation of problems, and not the solution of problems, is what is obligatory for the artist." I elaborated on this notion, describing how democratic America—and now "revolutionary" America— had always been uncomfortable with the concept of high art because of its elitist and aristocratic implications. Now the practitioners of the "new theatre" have joined the old Philistines in the scandalous American contempt for art.

I concluded: "We are at the tail end of Romanticism when the spectators are on the stage, and actors are refusing to play roles that are not sufficiently close to their own personalities. The rationale behind this reluctance is a refusal of external limitations—limitations which are now called 'authoritarian.' This direction was already anticipated in the work of the Actors Studio, whose members were encouraged to examine not the lives of the characters they played but rather their own psychic eccentricities with the result that the actors invariably played themselves rather than their roles. Under such conditions, why use actors at all? This is an extension of America's love of amateurism, and looks forward to a time when there will be no more spectators, only performers—*arrogant, liberated amateurs, each tied up in his own tight bag.*" I aimed these last phrases at the heckler in the balcony, though he had been relatively silent during the last part of my statement.

Paul Goodman spoke next—without notes. He reminisced affectionately about the past work of the Living Theatre company, particularly its productions of *The Connection,* of Brecht, and of his own plays. He had enjoyed my article, he said, but he couldn't understand what I was so "hot and bothered" about—he confessed that he had seen none of the work of the Living Theatre on its recent tour. Goodman then proceeded to create an analogy between contemporary unrest and the Protestant Reformation.

"Don't think you're like the Christians in the catacombs," he said. "You're not going to destroy the institutions, you're going to reform them. You talk like there's a cataclysm coming, but there isn't . . . . The institutions will survive . . . ."

"No, they won't," shouted Rufus Collins, a black member of the company who had suddenly materialized on the floor of the hall. "Because we're going to destroy them."

"You're not going to destroy them," replied Goodman, goodhumoredly. "You can't destroy them. And you won't even reform them unless you can think up some ideas. I've lived through movements like this before, and I'm always struck by the poverty of ideas. In two thousand years, there hasn't been a single new revolutionary idea."

"We'll destroy them," Collins screamed. "We'll create a cataclysm."
"You're not powerful enough. You're just an idiosyncratic fringe group like the Anabaptists. You don't have the capacity even to close down the universities."

"Close them down, close them down," Collins shouted. "Fuck the universities!"

"If you start to do that," Goodman said, still maintaining his sweet reasonableness, "they'll just put you on a reservation somewhere and keep you quiet."

"They're going to put us on reservations and kill us," Collins said, his voice now cracking with fury. "They're going to exterminate us, just like the Indians—the racists, the genocides. They're going to kill all of us."

"No, they won't," Goodman answered. "They'll just feed you some LSD and keep you pacified."

Norman Mailer chose to make his entrance at this point, lumbering down the aisle to his seat just as Goodman was replying to one of Rufus Collins's assaults on America's machine culture.

"Don't blame everything on technology," Goodman said. "It's too easy. Just the other day, I listened to a young fellow sing a very passionate song about how technology is killing us and all that. . . . But before he started, he bent down and plugged his electric guitar into the wall socket."

Collins began jumping up and down in fury. "That boy has thrown away his guitar. He's taken off his clothes. He's going up to the mountains where he's using only his voice and his feet. Fuck technology!"

"Why are you wearing glasses then?" asked a man sitting nearby.

"BECAUSE I CAN'T SEE," Collins screamed. "FUCK TECHNOLOGY. FUCK TECHNOLOGY."

Mailer applauded loudly and conspicuously. Goodman shrugged and sat down on the floor in front of his seat with his back to the audience. He lit his pipe, and seemed to be listening attentively to Judith Malina, who spoke next.

But the mike went dead. "Turn her microphone on," urged Hentoff to the sound man. "Yes," said Miss Malina, "turn me on." Pleased with her witticism, she repeated it several times. "Am I turned on? Okay. . . ."

"Bob Brustein said something about freedom and responsibility, like they were different things. This is all tied up with questions I don't want to get into tonight, like are we good or bad at heart. I do want to say that when people act freely, with complete freedom, they act creatively, beautifully. Everybody has it in him to be an artist—there's no such thing as special individuals who are supremely gifted. When the audience does its thing in *Paradise Now,* it does some wild, beautiful, creative scenes. Not

always, of course, but I've seen people do things as beautiful as I've ever
seen in the theatre. Better than us . . . better than Shakespeare or Euripides . . . ."

"Fuck Shakespeare, fuck Euripides," yelled the balcony voice.

"I dig Shakespeare sometimes," Miss Malina replied. "But I also want
to speak in my own voice, in my own person. I mean there's Hedda Gabler
and there's Judith Malina, and I want to be Judith Malina."

"Let's have five minutes of Hedda Gabler," shouted one of the spectators in the orchestra pews. "We've already had five minutes of Judith
Malina."

"I'll give you Hedda Gabler," yelled the heckler in the balcony, and,
in a mincing voice, " 'The candle is on the table.' That's Hedda Gabler.
Now I'll give you me: Fuck Ibsen. Fuck all liberal intellectuals and their
fucking discussions . . . ."

"Another thing," Judith Malina said. "The first night we did *Paradise
Now* at Yale—the night we got busted—we all came out of the theatre on
each other's shoulders and into the streets. It was a very beautiful and
joyous moment, everybody was feeling like something beautiful was happening. And Bob Brustein came up to me and said: 'Judith, I hate this
play. All this freedom, it could lead to fascism.' But I say, freedom is
beautiful. It can never lead to fascism, it can only lead to more freedom."

This remark was the cue for pandemonium; the entire Living Theatre
company proceeded to take over the Meeting House. A flamboyant actor
named Olé, dressed in yards of brightly colored silk, appeared on the platform where he began doing fashion model poses while sucking on a long
thin cigar. Rufus Collins was joined on the floor of the auditorium by
Stephen Ben Israel (the heckler from the balcony) both shouting obscen-
ities at the audience. The actress Jenny Hecht almost broke her neck
climbing down from the balcony, her electrified hair shooting wildly in
every direction. Other actors from the company began pounding on the
railings and screaming at the top of their lungs. And now the audience
began to scream back.

Shirley Broughton ran down the aisle in great agitation, to discuss
with Hentoff the possibilities of moderating the tumult or at least returning everybody's money. Hentoff leaned back to watch the spectacle. For a
few minutes Goodman attempted to discuss issues with the actors, the
audience, and the Becks. Shouted down, he walked calmly off the platform
and out of the hall, puffing on his pipe.

Rufus Collins was screaming: "You people all came here to have one
of your discussions. Ten dollars you paid to get in here. We'll give you
ten dollars worth."

"How did you get in? What about your ten dollars?"

"I got in for nothing. I don't pay for shit like this. Your money came out of my black skin and the skin of my black brothers. My own mother couldn't come here tonight. She called up and was told she couldn't attend your fucking meeting. That's when I decided to come . . . ."

After spitting into a spectator's face, Stephen Ben Israel ran to the center of the hall, holding a purse high over his head. "That lady over there hit me with her pocketbook—so I took it away from her. And this is what I am going to do with that pocketbook." He opened the purse, held it high over his head, turned it upside down, and emptied its contents on the floor.

A voice from the back, calm, sweet, and patient: "I just embraced eight members of the Living Theatre. I embraced them with love. And one of them took my wallet. You can keep the money, but would you kindly return the cards?"

"Credit cards? To buy things in this fucking money culture? Tear up the cards! Tear up the cards! Burn the money!"

Julian Beck's voice, above the din: "Get used to this. It's happening all over America, in every meeting house in America. Get used to this. This is what is going to happen from now on."

Ben Israel was now on the platform, chanting verses from R. D. Laing: "I'd like to turn you on, I'd like to drive you out of your wretched mind . . . ."

Collins was yelling into the microphone: "Do the Africans have theatre? When they beat their drums and do their dances? Do the Latin Americans have theatre? Do the Cubans have theatre? Do the Vietnamese have theatre? I want Brustein to answer yes or no."

"Yes," I shouted. By this time, I was off the platform and sitting with friends.

A woman in a fur wrap pushed her way to the platform toward Rufus Collins, shouting: "You're rude, you're stupid, and you're vulgar. People paid money to come here and listen to a discussion and you . . . ." A young man came up behind her and started pinning an obscene message on the back of her wrap. A spectator came up and started pulling the message off. She continued her conversation with Julian Beck, who asked her: "Why are you wearing that loathsome fur?"

"To keep me warm."

"You musn't wear the skins of animals," Beck answered. "It's disgusting," and he tore the fur from her shoulders.

"Tell your people not to wear sheepskins then," the woman said, and picked the fur up again.

"I tell them all the time," Beck replied, taking her hat off her head and throwing it on the floor. "What are you doing about Vietnam? What are you doing for the black people?"

"Today I marched in Newark," the woman said, in a tight voice. "I am a poet, and I am as outraged as you over the treatment of the blacks in this country."

"It's not enough, it's not enough," said Beck. He was shouting now.

The woman said quietly, "Today I feel more hate than I have ever felt in my life. I'm going home now. I'm going to write a poem about the hate I feel for you."

Now Richard Schechner, former editor of *The Drama Review,* was on the platform, fondling one of the mikes. He sat crosslegged, smiling. With his moustache, long hair, and striped tee shirt, he looked like an apache dancer. "You've all got to try to understand this," he said to the angry audience. "You've got to learn to groove with it. Let's all have five minutes of meditation to think about the beautiful thing that's happening here."

By this time the noise in the Meeting House was bouncing off the walls, like a bad mix in a recording studio. Everyone was wandering around the hall or shouting. I was beginning to enjoy myself. Two private cops, both of them black, came into the room, trying to look friendly and relaxed. They were mostly concerned with preventing any smoking in the hall.

Suddenly, the wave of bodies in the aisle parted. Norman Mailer had risen, and was strutting toward the platform, pitching and rolling like a freighter in a heavy sea. He was wearing a well-made dark blue suit with a vest, and his face was flushed. He grabbed one of the mikes.

"I was one of those that applauded when Mr. Black over there said 'Fuck Technology'—so I'm not going to use this thing." He laid the mike on the pew beside him. "I'm forty-six years old. I've got a strong voice, but I don't want to waste it. So I want you all to listen, and listen hard." Some of the tumult subsided.

"This is a tough town," Mailer continued, "the toughest town in the world. Because if you think you're tough, there's always somebody who's tougher. Remember that!" The tumult was beginning again. "Now I've got a message for Mr. Black over there. You've got no surprises, and you haven't had any since the French Revolution. I've seen all this *jacquerie* before, many times before. Get it? J-a-c-q-u-e-r-i-e—it's a pun in case you don't know it." This pun was lost on most of the audience, including me.

Ben Israel grabbed a mike: "You should have sent your suit up there Mailer, and stayed home yourself." Collins started to scream at him, but Mailer remained on the platform for a short while, a faint hard smile on his face, trying to stare down his noisy antagonists. Then he said, "I guess I lost Round One," and left the platform.

About a third of the spectators had drifted out by this time. Some wandered into the back room where drinks and sandwiches were being served. Paul Goodman had returned to the hall to be told by Rufus Collins: "I don't take drugs to escape from reality. I take drugs to reach reality." Hentoff remained on the platform, a weary witness. Saul Gottlieb, the producer of the Living Theatre's American tour, was talking gently into a microphone.

"I want Bob Brustein to say why he thinks the Living Theatre is fascist."

Saul is a portly, stooped man with a fuzzy beard, a veteran of many ideological wars. I went up to the platform and gave him a kiss.

Judith Malina, holding a microphone, was now walking back and forth in front of her husband, like a jaguar.

"I think what happened here tonight was beautiful and good," she said. "You've had an experience—like you've never had before. This is what we should all be discussing now, how beautiful this evening was. How many people here think it was beautiful?"

"It's *boring*, IT'S BORING," came a voice from the hall. "You may think it's beautiful, but it's not what we came for. The subject was Theatre or Therapy, and all we got tonight was therapy—Living Theatre therapy. When do we get to listen to some discussion about theatre?"

"This is better than discussion, better than theatre," replied Miss Malina. "It's spontaneous, it's authentic, it's real, it's beautiful."

Stanley Kauffmann, the critic, was on his feet, and it was the only time in my life I have seen him angry. "You're lying. The whole thing was *phoney!* You staged it. You and your stooges. You brought your stooges here tonight and staged the whole dismal affair."

"No, no," Judith Malina cried. "We allow our people to do just what they want to do. Everybody should be allowed to do what he wants. That's what's so beautiful about freedom."

"You talk about *freedom!*" somebody else shouted. "What about *our* freedom? We weren't allowed to have what we paid for. Your freedom is our repression!"

Julian Beck, who all this time had been sitting silent and withdrawn, suddenly stood up. "This is the future," he said. "It's happening all over the country. And it will happen again and again whenever you try to hold a meeting. This is the future."

In one of the Marx Brothers movies, there is a scene in which Harpo picks up a book, looks it over very carefully, and then goes into a blind fury, tearing the book to bits and jumping up and down on the pages and the binding.

Groucho: "What's the matter with him?"

Chico: "He gets angry because he can't read."

**President's Commission on Campus
Unrest: The Youth Culture**

In early Western societies, the young were traditionally submissive to adults. Largely because adults retained great authority, the only way for the young to achieve wealth, power, and prestige was through a cooperative apprenticeship of some sort to the adult world. Thus, the young learned the traditional adult ways of living, and in time they grew up to become adults of the same sort as their parents, living in the same sort of world.

Advancing industrialism decisively changed this cooperative relationship between the generations. It produced new forms and new sources of wealth, power, and prestige, and these weakened traditional adult controls over the young. It removed production from the home and made it increasingly specialized; as a result, the young were increasingly removed from adult work places and could not directly observe or participate in adult work. Moreover, industrialism hastened the separation of education from the home, in consequence of which the young were concentrated together in places of formal education that were isolated from most adults. Thus, the young spent an increasing amount of time together, apart from their parents' home and work, in activities that were different from those of adults.

This shared and distinct experience among the young led to shared interests and problems, which led, in turn, to the development of distinct subcultures. As those subcultures developed, they provided support for any youth movement that was distinct from—or even directed against—the adult world.

A distinguishing characteristic of young people is their penchant for pure idealism. Society teaches youth to adhere to the basic values of the adult social system—equality, honesty, democracy, or whatever—in absolute terms. Throughout most of American history, the idealism of youth has been formed—and constrained—by the institutions of adult society. But during the 1960's, in response to an accumulation of social changes, the traditional American youth culture developed rapidly in the direction

From *United States President's Commission on Campus Unrest.* Government Printing Office, Washington, D.C., 1970.

of an oppositional stance toward the institutions and ways of the adult world.

This subculture took its bearings from the notion of the autonomous, self-determining individual whose goal was to live with "authenticity," or in harmony with his inner penchants and instincts. It also found its identity in a rejection of the work ethic, materialism, and conventional social norms and pieties. Indeed, it rejected all institutional disciplines externally imposed upon the individual, and this set it at odds with much in American society.

Its aim was to liberate human consciousness and to enhance the quality of experience; it sought to replace the materialism, the self-denial, and the striving for achievement that characterized the existing society with a new emphasis on the expressive, the creative, the imaginative. The tools of the workaday institutional world—hierarchy, discipline, rules, self-interest, self-defense, power—it considered mad and tyrannical. It proclaimed instead the liberation of the individual to feel, to experience, to express whatever his unique humanity prompted. And its perceptions of the world grew ever more distant from the perceptions of the existing culture: what most called "justice" or "peace" or "accomplishment," the new culture envisioned as "enslavement" or "hysteria" or "meaninglessness." As this divergence of values and of vision proceeded, the new youth culture became increasingly oppositional.

And yet in its commitment to liberty and equality, it was very much in the mainstream of American tradition; what it doubted was that America had managed to live up to its national ideals. Over time, these doubts grew, and the youth culture became increasingly imbued with a sense of alienation and of opposition to the larger society.

No one who lives in contemporary America can be unaware of the surface manifestations of this new youth culture. Dress is highly distinctive; emphasis is placed on heightened color and sound; the enjoyment of flowers and nature is given a high priority. The fullest ranges of sense and sensation are to be enjoyed each day through the cultivation of new experiences, through spiritualism, and through drugs. Life is sought to be made as simple, primitive, and "natural" as possible, as ritualized, for example, by nude bathing.

Social historians can find parallels to this culture in the past. One is reminded of Bacchic cults in ancient Greece, or of the *Wandervoegel,* the wandering bands of German youths in the 19th century, or of primitive Christianity. Confidence is placed in revelation rather than cognition, in sensation rather than analysis, in the personal rather than the institutional. Emphasis is placed on living to the fullest extent, on the sacredness of life itself, and on the common mystery of all living things. The age-old vision of natural man, untrammeled and unscarred by the fetters of institutions, is seen again. It is not necessary to describe such movements as religious, but it is useful to recognize that they have elements in common with the waves of religious fervor that periodically have captivated the minds of men.

It is not difficult to compose a picture of contemporary America as it looks through the eyes of one whose premises are essentially those just described. Human life is all; but women and children are being killed in Vietnam by American forces. All living things are sacred; but American industry and technology are polluting the air and the streams and killing the birds and the fish. The individual should stand as an individual; but American society is organized into vast structures of unions, corporations, multiversities, and government bureaucracies. Personal regard for each human being and for the absolute equality of every human soul is a categorical imperative; but American society continues to be characterized by racial injustice and discrimination. The senses and the instincts are to be trusted first; but American technology and its consequences are a monument to rationalism. Life should be lived in communion with others, and each day's sunrise and sunset enjoyed to the fullest; American society extols competition, the accumulation of goods, and the work ethic. Each man should be free to lead his own life in his own way; American organizations and statute books are filled with regulations governing dress, sex, consumption, and the accreditation of study and of work, and many of these are enforced by armed police.

No coherent political decalogue has yet emerged. Yet in this new youth culture's political discussion there are echoes of Marxism, of peasant communalism, of Thoreau, of Rousseau, of the evangelical fervor of the abolitionists, of Gandhi, and of native American populism.

The new culture adherent believes he sees an America that has failed to achieve its social targets; that no longer cares about achieving them; that is thoroughly hypocritical in pretending to have achieved them and in pretending to care; and that is exporting death and oppression abroad through its military and corporate operations. He wishes desperately to recall America to its great traditional goals of true freedom and justice for every man. As he sees it, he wants to remake America in its own image.

What of the shortcomings of other societies, especially the Soviet Union? Why does the new culture denounce only the United States? On this question, Drs. Heard and Cheek said in a memorandum to the President:

> The apparent insensitivity of students to Soviet actions and to evils in the Soviet system is at least partly explainable by considerations like these: *First,* they feel that by the wrongness of our own policies, such as the war in Vietnam, we have lost our moral standing to condemn other

countries. *Second,* there is an obsession with our own problems, a feeling that our own crises should occupy all our attention. *Third,* the fear of Communism is less than existed a decade ago.

Students perceive the Czech invasion as one more evil action by a powerful imperialist government, but they don't perceive it as a threat to the United States. Since the Sino-Soviet split, they see Communism as consisting of different and often competing national governments and styles. The Russians appear to repress their satellite countries, but students see that fact as parallel to American domination in *its* sphere of influence (the Dominican Republic, Guatemala, economic exploitation, etc.). They see the Russians as no better than [ourselves], maybe not as good, but feel more responsibility for our actions than for those of foreign powers.

The dedicated practitioners of this emerging culture typically have little regard for the past experience of others. Indeed, they often exhibit a positive antagonism to the study of history. Believing that there is today, or will be tomorrow, a wholly new world, they see no special relevance in the past. Distrusting older generations, they distrust the motives of their historically based advice no less than they distrust the history written by older generations. The antirationalist thread in the new culture resists the careful empirical approach of history and denounces it as fraudulent. Indeed, this antirationalism and the urge for blunt directness often lead those of the new youth culture to view complexity as a disguise, to be impatient with learning the facts, and to demand simplistic solutions in one sentence.

Understandably, the new culture enthusiast has at best a lukewarm interest in free speech, majority opinion, and the rest of the tenets of liberal democracy as they are institutionalized today. He cannot have much regard for these things if he believes that American liberal democracy, with the consent and approval of the vast majority of its citizens, is pursuing values and policies that he sees as fundamentally immoral and apocalyptically destructive. Again in parallel with historical religious movements, the new culture advocate tends to be self-righteous, sanctimonious, contemptuous of those who have not yet shared his vision, and intolerant of their ideals.

Profoundly opposed to any kind of authority structure from within or without the movement and urgently pressing for direct personal participation by each individual, members of this new youth culture have a difficult time making collective decisions. They reveal a distinct intolerance in their refusal to listen to those outside the new culture and in their willingness to force others to their own views. They even show an elitist streak in their premise that the rest of the society must be brought to the policy positions which they believe are right.

At the same time, they try very hard, and with extraordinary patience, to give each of their fellows an opportunity to be heard and to participate directly in decision-making. The new culture decisional style is founded on the endless mass meeting at which there is no chairman and no agenda, and from which the crowd or parts of the crowd melt away or move off into actions. Such crowds are, of course, subject to easy manipulation by skillful agitators and sometimes become mobs. But it must also be recognized that large, loose, floating crowds represent for participants in the new youth culture the normal, friendly, natural way for human beings to come together equally, to communicate, and to decide what to do. Seen from this perspective, the reader may well imagine the general student response at Kent State to the governor's order that the National Guard disperse all assemblies, peaceful or otherwise.

Practitioners of the new youth culture do not announce their program because, at this time at least, the movement is not primarily concerned with programs; it is concerned with how one ought to live and what one ought to consider important in one's daily life. The new youth culture is still in the process of forming its values, programs, and life style; at this point, therefore, it is primarily a *stance*.

A parallel to religious history is again instructive. For many (not all) student activists and protestors, it is not really very important whether the protest tactics employed will actually contribute to the political end allegedly sought. What is important is that a protest be made—that the individual protestor, for his own internal salvation, stand up, declare the purity of his own heart, and take his stand. No student protestor throwing a rock through a laboratory window believes that it will stop the Indochina war, weapons research, or the advance of the feared technology—yet he throws it in a mood of defiant exultation—almost exaltation. He has taken his moral stance.

An important theme of this new culture is its oppositional relationship to the larger society, as is suggested by the fact that one of its leading theorists has called it a "counter-culture." If the rest of the society wears short hair, the member of this youth culture wears his hair long. If others are clean, he is dirty. If others drink alcohol and illegalize marijuana, he denounces alcohol and smokes pot. If others work in large organizations with massively complex technology, he works alone and makes sandals by hand. If others live separated, he lives in a commune. If others are for the police and the judges, he is for the accused and the prisoner. In such ways, he declares himself an alien in a larger society with which he feels himself to be fundamentally at odds.

He will also resist when the forces of the outside society seek to impose its tenets upon him. He is likely to see police as the repressive minions of the outside culture imposing its law on him and on other students by force or death if necessary. He will likely try to urge others to join him in changing the society about him in the conviction that he is seeking to save that society from bringing about its own destruction. He is likely to have apocalyptic visions of impending doom of the whole social structure and the world. He is likely to have lost hope that society can be brought to change through its own procedures. And if his psychological makeup is of a particular kind, he may conclude that the only outlet for his feelings is violence and terrorism.

In recent years, some substantial number of students in the United States and abroad have come to hold views along these lines. It is also true that a very large fraction of American college students, probably a majority, could not be said to be participants in any significant aspect of this cultural posture except for its music. As for the rest of the students, they are distributed over the entire spectrum that ranges from no participation to full participation. A student may feel strongly about any one or more aspects of these views and wholly reject all the others. He may also subscribe wholeheartedly to many of the philosophic assertions implied while occupying any of hundreds of different possible positions on the questions of which tactics, procedures, and actions he considers to be morally justifiable. Generalizations here are more than usually false.

One student may adopt the outward appearance of the new culture and nothing else. Another may be a total devotee, except that he is a serious history scholar. Another student may agree completely on all the issues of war, race, pollution, and the like and participate in protests over those matters, while disagreeing with all aspects of the youth culture life style. A student may agree with the entire life style but be wholly uninterested in politics. Another new culture student who takes very seriously the elements of compassion and of reverence for life may prove to be the best bulwark against resorts to violence. A student who rejects the new youth culture altogether may nevertheless be in the vanguard of those who seek to protect that culture against the outside world. And so forth.

As we have observed elsewhere in this report, to conclude that a student who has a beard is a student who would burn a building, or even sit-in in a building, is wholly unwarranted.

But almost no college student today is unaffected by the new youth culture in some way. If he is not included, his roommate or sister or girlfriend is. If protest breaks out on his campus, he is confronted with a personal decision about his role in it. In the poetry, music, movies, and plays that students encounter, the themes of the new culture are recurrent. Even the student who finds older values more comfortable for himself will nevertheless protect and support vigorously the privilege of other students who prefer the new youth culture.

A vast majority of students are not complete adherents. But *no* significant group of students would join older generations in condemning those who are. And almost *all* students will condemn repressive efforts by the larger community to restrict or limit the life style, the art forms, and the nonviolent political manifestations of the new youth culture.

To most Americans, the development of the new youth culture is an unpleasant and often frightening phenomenon. And there is no doubt that the emergence of this student perspective has led to confrontations, injuries, and death. It is undeniable, too, that a tiny extreme fringe of fanatical devotees of the new culture have crossed the line over into outlawry and terrorism. There is a fearful and terrible irony here as, in the name of the law, the police and National Guard have killed students, and some students, under the new youth culture's banner of love and compassion, have turned to burning and bombing.

But the new youth culture itself is not a "problem" to which there is a "solution"; it is a mass social condition, a shift in basic cultural viewpoint. How long this emerging youth culture will last and what course its future development will take are open questions. But it does exist today, and it is the deeper cause of the emergence of the issues of race and war as objects of intense concern on the American campus.

Robert Coles: A Policeman Complains

I have known the police sergeant who speaks here for five years. I have visited him again and again in his home and spent time with him while he does his work—in Boston. In the following selections from long, tape-recorded conversations I have tried hard to do justice to the range of his feelings, their ambiguity and complexity. I have wanted to learn how it goes for him in a difficult job, and he has been willing to let me know— he is, in fact, a passionate teacher.

No doubt many readers will find much of what he says objectionable, to put it mildly—even as others will emphatically cheer him on. I believe that he wants neither quick dismissal nor applause but an effort on the part of his fellow citizens—he himself often makes such an effort—to look

From The *New York Times Magazine,* June 13, 1971. Copyright © 1971 by The New York Times Company. Reprinted by permission.

at exactly what our society is like, at exactly what it is he and others like him must constantly defend, so often at the risk of their lives.

"Why does everyone say the police are against the Negroes? I'm sick of hearing that. *The police!* There are thousands and thousands of policemen, and they're individuals, just like everyone else. The same people who say they want us to recognize that Negroes are like other people— good and bad and not-so-good and not-so-bad—are the ones who call us every name in the book. We're bigots. We're pigs. We're killers. We're flunkies. We're storm troopers. We're ignorant and fascists—and on and on they go.

"Have you ever seen those college kids shouting at the police? I've never seen anything like them for meanness and cheapness. The language that comes out of their mouths; you begin to wonder whether you're in a mental hospital. I mean it; those kids go crazy when they see us. The uniform seems to trigger something in them. They become dirty, plain dirty. They use the worst language I've ever heard. They make insulting gestures at us. They talk about killing us. The girls make sexual overtures—when they're not swearing. Swearing, that's not the word for what you hear! Someone has never really taught those wise-guy kids good manners. They say they're out to help the poor; but I'll take a Negro kid to them any day. The Negroes have a lot to teach those college radicals.

"I laugh at times, though; I laugh at the radicals and I laugh at the Negro people. They think they're living under a dictatorship, and that the police are out to get them. The fact is that the poor policeman, he has to watch himself all the time. He can't do half the things the radicals claim he does; and he can't say what they say he says. The policeman's hands are tied. And so is his salary; he gets paid not much more than people on welfare. He's in constant danger. We lose men; they're shot, knifed, beaten up. It seems I'm always visiting a buddy in the hospital.

"And we don't get flowers from radicals, saying they sympathize with us, because 'if a man dies, the world is smaller.' You know where I heard that? From them, the students. They were protesting something: a Panther's death, which they said we caused, which we didn't, and we had to arrest them—after warning them a hundred times and listening to them dare us and tease us and swear at us and push themselves at us for three hours. In jail I tried to help them out. I had to get their signatures on some forms. They refused. All we wanted to do was keep their watches from getting lost. They kept on shouting: 'If a man dies, the world is smaller.'

"I got angry, but I tried to joke. I said maybe the world would be smaller in a day or two if they didn't shut up and let us do our work. They'd been calling us murderers all afternoon, but now they said I was a Nazi, the kind of man Hitler was. I thought they were fooling. I honestly did, at first. I'd even said 'please' to them, on the street and in jail. I *asked* them to be quiet and orderly. I *asked* them to move back. I *asked* them to clear away for the sake of pedestrians and cars. The nicer you are to them, the worse they get. God, they're a filthy-mouthed bunch of little bastards.

"I went to confession later and told the priest that I'd sworn back at them, I'd cursed them, and I was sorry, I really was. Did I hit them, strike at them, he asked me. I said no. Were they 'provoking' me, he asked me. I said yes, yes, Father, so help me God, they were. He said I shouldn't feel bad. He said that Christ had been afraid and worried while He was on the Cross; and if that was the case, we're all entitled to lose our tempers every once in a while. Then he said he wanted me to know, apart from his being a priest, that he was behind us in what we're trying to do, the police. I figured that if he was getting friendly, I'd be friendly, too. I said: 'Father, if you know what we're trying to do, I wish you'd let me know, and that would be two of us that knew.' I didn't hear a sound out of him. Then he asked me if I had anything more to tell him. I figured he thought I was being fresh, but I wasn't being like that.

"What *are* we doing, the police? We're like those students; we want to know whose fat we're pulling out of the fire. No one comes and talks to us, and asks us our opinions, not like they do with the college students and the Negro people. A day doesn't go by that I don't see a poll that says the students want this, or something else, and the Negroes, too—they want, want, that's all they're capable of, wanting.

"Well, we want some things, too. We want better salaries. We want more men on the force. We want the public to understand what we have to do, every day, to keep the city from becoming a jungle. It's not exaggerated, what you see on television. Between smart gangsters, all kinds of them, and dumb hoodlums, and the Negroes, and the drunks, and the college crowd and their demonstrations, and the crazy ones walking the street when they should be locked up—between all those, it's a miracle more of us don't get killed on the police force.

"I said to a television man once, after he took pictures of the college kids sitting all over the sidewalk near a high school, that he should let us speak to the American public. All people see is us arresting someone, or trying to clear away a mob. They don't know what we have to listen to and put up with. But if you can't take it, I suppose you shouldn't be a cop. I tell my men that. They laugh at me and tell me to stop. I mean it though; I'm not fooling. Sure, I lose my control. Sometimes I wish I could go and kill some of those demonstrators.

"And as for the Negroes, I wish the average American worker could see what we see: the stealing that goes on, and the knives they have, and the razor blades they pull on each other, and the way they all loaf and collect welfare, and the way the men move from woman to woman, and leave each one of them with kids. They don't care; they don't care how they live and what they do to the buildings! A lot of people feel sorry for the 'slum landlords,' that's what they call them. How many people have seen what those kids do to the buildings? And their parents don't give a damn. They just laugh. And let me tell you: sometimes that's all *I* can do, laugh—and talk to myself. I do a lot of that. I even carry on a conversation with myself!

"I say that a cop can only do the best he can, and he has to be honest and fair, as honest and fair as he can be, and the worst thing he can do is forget that. People say we're crooks, we're bribed left and right. People say we're working for the big corporations and the politicians. People say we're unsympathetic to the poor. Some cops *are* like that. But a lot aren't.

"I'll tell you who the police are. They're men from plain, ordinary families. They don't have rich, fast-talking parents. They don't have parents who make all kinds of money by climbing over other people until they get on top, then start feeling sorry for the poor Negro, or the poor Puerto Rican, or whoever it is. They're not full of a lot of big talk about how they want to change the world, and help everyone out, and bring us freedom and peace and all the rest. But I'll tell you something, they're good men, a lot of policemen; they work long hours, and they don't get rich, even if they do pick up a few extra dollars now and then, some of them. They go to church. They try to bring up their kids to respect older people and obey the law. They send their sons into the army, so the country will be the strongest on the earth, and they teach their daughters to be good wives and good mothers.

"You're going to say I'm building up the policeman, and I'm not mentioning that there are plenty of bad things they do. Look, in any organization you'll find no-good people. There are rotten apples right in my own backyard; our precinct has some crazy cops who are ready to use machine guns against the 'college kids and niggers,' that's how they are called. But for every cop like that I can find you two that you'd just have to admire. I really mean it, *admire*. Every day at work they save people's lives, and protect people, and help people. They help people cross the streets. They help people when they need a ride to the hospital. They help them when they're scared of something. They help them when they've been robbed or assaulted or there's been a fire or they need to know how to get some place and can't find their way.

"I've listened to those students talk about 'helping mankind,' and how much they 'love' people and how much they believe in 'giving' themselves to other people. I wonder how much they actually practice what they preach. They talk a lot, I know that. They march up and down advertising to the world how right they are and wrong everyone else is, and how much love they feel for humanity and how bad the cops are and most of the world, it seems. But do they ever really go and prove their good intentions?

"You'll say I'm prejudiced, but I honestly believe a lot of those long-haired radical students are spoiled brats from rich families who won't lift a finger for anyone who's not part of their own group. It's talk, talk, talk with them and dirty filthy talk, to be exact. The same goes for the civil-rights people, a lot of them. They're for the Negro they say; but the police are helping Negroes every hour, day and night.

"You look surprised. You see, that's the trouble! People just don't know. They don't stop and think. They forget that it's the cops who come and take sick Negroes to the hospital, and rescue them from killing each other. Have you ever seen the way those drugged-up niggers go after each other with knives and blades? It's unbelievable. I'm not prejudiced when I say that colored people have a lot of violence in them, like animals. The Irishman will get sloppy drunk and pass out. The Italian will shout and scream his head off. The Jew will figure out a way he can make himself a little more money, and get even with someone that way. But your nigger, he's vicious like a wild leopard or something when he's been drinking or on drugs. They throw lye at each other, and scalding water, and God knows what. I tell my men to stay away, stay away. It's a jungle. They drove the Jews out, and they're not storekeepers themselves; they don't know how to run a store. And now it's a ghost town, the colored section.

"The Negroes want more kids, to get more welfare money, and they want to push into new districts. You can get fed up with them; but you can feel sorry for them, too. They didn't ask to come here, did they? They were slaves, you can't forget that. And they treated them like animals, down there in the South, from what you read. They never let them even vote, or make a half-decent living. And they kept them separate, under the law. No Irishman or Italian or Jew ever had to live like that here in America! The average cop knows that, too. It's just that he's all the time seeing the results, not the causes of things.

"I wish the big, smart college people would get that through their heads, that someone has to be there on the firing line, protecting the whole of American society from what it's done wrong in the past. I believe that slowly things will get better, for the Negro I mean. I *don't* believe we'll see an improvement in the way the rich college kids behave, though. *There's* where I see our main trouble coming from in the next 10 years. The Negroes, a lot of them, will begin to feel more part of America; but those kids, they're another story. They hate this country. They're full of hate, the radical kids. The Negroes only want more of America. Some of the radicals want to blow the whole country up. They're lunatics, I believe.

"You're the doctor. Maybe you know what's bothering them. I listen to them; I should know. But I don't. I can't believe it's what they *say* it is, that they're just upset about injustice. There's something that's under their skin. They have a grudge against the world. They never smile, you know. They're mean. I've tried to get on with them, make a joke or two; but no, they hiss and spit and make faces and come out with the worst language I've ever heard in my life.

"Listen, I'm a cop, from poor people; and they had no education to speak of, my mother or my dad, and he was a longshoreman. But let me tell you, I get red in the face, I blush, when I hear those kids talk. And, it's not from being mad at them, either. I've just never heard such words come out, one after the other, and nonstop, all day and all night, so long as you stand and listen. It's those kids, and the other ones they depend upon—the lawyers, the teachers on their side—that we're going to have around with us for a long time. I don't get discouraged too much about our Negro people. They'll lift themselves up, a lot of them will, in time. But these rich, spoiled college kids, drugged up on all kinds of stuff, and with their parents waiting, ready to bail them out and give them money to loaf on, we'll have more and more of those kids around.

"The worst thing about them is that they've never really worked for more than a few weeks, here and there. And when they call a 'strike' on a campus, they're supposed to get clemency and be excused from exams and everything else. Do they know what a *real* strike is? Do they know the sacrifices that strikers make and *expect* to make and don't always brag about? I hear those college people talking about how they're different, they're not like everyone else, and they can't respect what the rest of us do. No wonder; they've never had to get up in the morning and go to work, and stay on the job, whether they like it or not, and pay their bills or try to pay them. Does anyone except the rich keep up with his bills, these days?"

Things run into one another eventually; and so the students eventually give way to inflation in a policeman's mind. He is a tall, rather heavy man, full of stories, and they are stories he has earned, stories he has lived through. He loves "the beat." He loves walking down a street, driving down a street, catching the sense of a neighborhood, feeling its rhythms. They are all different, those various neighborhoods, he lets his listener know, and goes on to tell why and how in direct language. He doesn't miss much while patrolling a street. His mind can be subtle, canny, practical and yes, open to change. That is, he can be dogmatic and bitter one minute, then come around to a longer, more reflective viewpoint. It is then that he summons history, recalls past events, speculates about the future. It is then that he sums up what he has gone through, what others have also gone through, what a whole world has had to experience.

To some extent he feels a little shy about revealing his considerable powers of observation and reflection. He doesn't want to be caught spinning a lot of fancy theories. He doesn't want to be like those wordy, brainy protesters and demonstrators and radicals. He doesn't want to sound like an "expert" on the one hand or an "agitator" on the other. He is tired of experts; they call themselves criminologists and sociologists and psychologists and they want to lecture to the police and tell them in fancy language what "any cop" knows out of his everyday, concrete experience. They go on and on, delivering those "lectures" he and his friends are ordered by "the Chief" to hear, and the men, most of them, get annoyed and angry. It is not that they feel they have nothing to learn; it is simply that "professors aren't practical, and they can't talk straight."

Nevertheless, there is a lot to worry about, a lot happening, and a lot of help is needed by policemen as well as other people. And there is the irony; sympathy and compassion are mobilized for blacks and Indians and Mexican-Americans by all sorts of thoughtful and well-educated people, but the police and their serious difficulties are often ignored by those same people. Why is it that some of us do that, overlook or try hard to "understand" the meanness and brutishness and open violence to be found among the poor (among other groups of people) but jump upon the police with a whole range of epithets, some of them openly nasty, some thinly disguised with a veneer of academic jargon? He asks that question again and again, in many different ways. Sometimes he can be self-pitying when he asks. Sometimes he can be angry. Often he is genuinely puzzled.

When the question is put back to him he pleads ignorance, or he becomes silent, or he talks and talks and talks. Yes, he acknowledges, some policemen are unthinking and crooked and even cruel. Yes, some are bigots, pure and simple. Yes, the police upon occasion lose their cool, wrongly go after people and at the same time shelter others considered friendly or "patriotic." But in any occupation, any profession, any group of human beings one will find a wide range of people, and he feels that the "so-called liberals" don't mobilize their considerable powers of compassion or understanding for everyone, "just certain people."

Over and over again he makes that point. He would like, one day, to talk with some of "them," the people who call the police so many bad names, who look upon them as the enemy, who say the ghettoes ought to be "freed of the pigs." On the other hand, he is afraid that were the occasion to arise he would be so enraged and provoked by the way "those people" look and talk, by their attitude toward him and his kind, that he would have to leave immediately; or if he did stay, he worries that he would be unable to state his case. Yet, he does want to talk about some of these matters, and by no means is he as sure of himself as others say he is, or as he himself sometimes says he is.

The sergeant more than anything else regrets the breakdown of old customs and habits. In addition he cannot understand what will replace those customs and habits, especially because things seem so unstable, so uncertain, so unpredictable. He senses all kinds of shifts in public opinion. He listens to people all day, and has come to realize how troubled and fearful they are, how buffeted by rising prices and the demands of our armed services for men and more men.

Many people read of such things, pride themselves on knowing what is happening in America, yet cannot comprehend (so he believes, so many policemen believe) the particular stresses that fall on those who are "caught in the middle." If he prefers any expression it is that one. He and others are destined to be caught in the middle, and he adds to those words three others meant to emphasize a certain finality in the predicament: "and that's it." If asked whether he sees any changes forthcoming, has any hope about the immediate future, he says "no" and repeats himself, says exactly what he has said before: "We're caught in the middle, and that's it."

But he will go on talking. He will declare emphatically his faith in America, in its institutions and its history. He will go back on his own remarks and refute them, acknowledge that he has been wrong and will be wrong. And is he not human? Has he not the right to "let off steam," he asks, and take to task a lot of "noisy people, in love with their own voices?"

He can criticize even that effort at self-justification. The police *are* different. In a way they don't have the rights others do, the right to take sides and show their alarm or rage or apprehension. If a man is to be a good policeman he has to be "neutral." He has to *feel* neutral. Naturally, it is impossible to do so, deny one's convictions and allegiances. Still, one has to try; and one can within limits succeed. Nor does he have in mind "a lot of talking." Nor does he favor "these groups you hear about." ("Sensitivity training groups" have been recommended for the police.) He does not want his men becoming too introspective, saying everything that's on their minds. "Hell, if we got to doing that, we'd have no time to do our work, and let me tell you, we'd be walking around like zombies, always wondering what someone else is thinking. That's no way to live."

He has been to "a couple of those things." He had been asked to take part in a "group" sponsored by a "human relations outfit, they called themselves." He went. He went because he wanted to learn something. He went because he was curious and also a little desperate. His men are under great strain, get thoroughly inadequate salaries, and at times seem on the verge of quitting en masse. He is a little older than some of them, a little younger "but wiser" than others. He wants to do what he can to "clear the air," make the men he works with "a little happier about their work." So he went, and found himself being asked one question after the other by people who smiled at him and told him they "understood" how he felt, but were, so he believed, "real strangers," by which he meant "always wanting to bury anything you say in a long afternoon of speeches."

Is he an "ordinary cop," as he once called himself? Is he a "boss," a "sergeant boss," as he refers to himself sometimes with mixed pride and embarrassment? Is he a "fascist pig," as he is called, among other things, by bright, vocal college students who are taking courses in sociology and psychology and political science and economics and urban affairs and law— and who prompt from him a wider range of responses than they might believe possible, for all their unquestionable awareness and sharpness of mind?

It is, of course, possible to list those responses, and yet somehow no list, however well drawn up and accurately phrased, quite seems to render truthfully a man's ideas as they come tumbling out in the course of talk after talk—all of which is rather obvious not only to "investigators" and "observers" doing their "research" but to those very able and sensitive and strong-minded and independent and mean-spirited and inefficient and awkward and generous and sullen and lighthearted and callous and kind people who are "interviewed."

More than anything else the police sergeant resents "propaganda" about the police, his way of describing "those articles about our problems." He is tired of them, tired of "dumb reporters" doing "quickie stories on the cops," and tired of "smart-aleck graduate students and their professors" who are always going to police headquarters and wanting to interview someone on the force. Can't they simply go strike up a conversation with a cop, buy him a beer, get to know him, learn "whatever in hell it is" they want to know *that way?* Can't they do anything without those folders and the questions, dozens and dozens of questions? Life for him is too complicated for a questionnaire. Life for him is hard to put into any words, "even your own, never mind someone else's."

It is easy to argue with him, or applaud him because he says what seems eminently sensible and correct. It is more important, perhaps, for all of us to understand that he is not so much against one or another "method" of research as he is doubtful that "a policeman or a fireman or a man who works on an assembly line of a factory" is going to get the compassion and fair treatment he deserves from people who make it their business to be known as compassionate and fair-minded: "The worst insults the police get is from the liberals and the radicals. A suburban housewife called up the other day and demanded to speak with 'the lieutenant.' She said she belonged to some committee, I didn't catch the name. She said we were the worst people in America, and if a Hitler ever took over here, we'd be marching people into concentration camps.

"Now, you know, that's not the first time I've heard that. Every time we get called to a college campus we get told things like that; and not only by the kids. Their teachers can be just as bad. I'd like to give each of them a jab to the stomach and a jab to the jaw. But I can't. And I tell my men that *they* can't, either.

"Very few people know what it's like to have the radicals shouting at you from one direction and the Negro people in the slums looking at you as if you hate each and every one of them, and the people in between, most white people, claiming you've failed them, too, because there's crime all over, and it's the fault of the police, *the police.* I go to work some days and tell myself I'm going to quit. The men all say that. I don't know a policeman who feels he's being treated right. We don't get nearly the money we should, considering the fact that every hour we take risks all the time and could be killed almost every minute of the working day. And even our best friends and supporters don't know what we do—the calls that come in for our help, the duties we have.

"You go and ask the average Negro in a Negro neighborhood about the police, and he won't talk the way the civil-rights people do. They call us all the time, Negroes do. I used to work in one of their districts. The switchboard was busy all day and all night. They fight and squabble with each other. They drink a lot. They lose themselves on drugs. They rob and steal from each other. They take after each other and kill. Then people say it's us, the police, the white man, that's to blame.

"I know I keep telling you all that, but people don't understand. I have one wish. I wish I could take some of those student radicals and send them out with some of my men that work in the Negro sections. I think it would open up their eyes, the students'—that is, if anything can. They'd see that if you pulled the police out of the Negro sections, like the white radicals say you should—*they* don't live there!—then the ones who would suffer would be the poor, innocent, colored people. They're always the ones to suffer. A lot of Negroes are like a lot of white folks—good people, real good people.

"I hear my men talking. They say what I do. I have a brother who's a fireman. He says the same thing: it's not the average colored man who's to blame for all the trouble we're having in this country. It's a handful; well, it's more than a handful of troublemakers. There are the crazy agitators, and the college crowd, the students and the teachers, and worst of all, if you ask me, the rich people who support them all, and come into the city to march and demonstrate and wave their signs.

"Maybe it's all for the good, though. I've given up figuring out the answers. There's a whole lot of injustice in America. I know that. I can't afford for anyone in my family to get sick, least of all myself. The rich get richer, and the poor ordinary man, he can barely buy his food and pay his rent. I feel sorry for the Negroes, I really do. People are prejudiced, most people are. You're almost born that way, don't you think? People like to stick together. The Irish want to live near the Irish. The same with the Italians or the others. Jews always stick together, even when they get rich, and a lot of them do. The poor Negroes, they want to get away from each other. They want to break out. I don't blame them.

"But when they break out, what will they find? They'll see that the Irish are no good, and the Italians and Jews and everyone. We're all no good. I believe you should know the man, not where his grandfather came from. I mean, people like their own, but that isn't the way it should be. My son comes home and tells me that his teacher says the world is always changing. Well, you know it *is* always changing. I can remember a different world, the one I grew up in. That's gone, that world. A Negro boy born today is growing up in a country really worried over his people. I think everyone accepts the fact that we've got to end poverty and give people an even break, whether their skin is black or brown or whatever color it is.

"When I was a kid of 25, I used to patrol a Negro section of this city. All was quiet then, no riots and no talk of revolution, and all the rest. I knew a lot of Negro people. They were poor, but they were polite and friendly. I'd get dozens of offers of coffee or a drink. We could talk, easy, real easy, with each other. Now all I hear is how no white man is trusted over there in that section. So, I asked one of my buddies, who's a sergeant like me, and over in the district I used to be in—I asked him how he could stand it over there. He said he was surprised at me talking that way. I said I was surprised at *him* talking that way. He said it wasn't the same all the time, because they'd had a small riot or two, but it was the same as it always was most of the time: women who have to be rushed to the hospital to deliver their babies, and fires, and robberies, and fights to help settle, and kids caught on a roof or hurt playing who need to go to the emergency ward—you know, a cop's job. Then I thought to myself that I was a real fool for not thinking like that in the first place. You let those news stories go to your head, and you forget that most Negro people are too busy for demonstrations; they go to work, like the rest of us.

"I'd like to see more Negro policemen. I have nothing against them. But I don't believe in hiring a man just because he's colored or white or Chinese or anything else. If a man is going to be a policeman these days he's got to be tough. The world is tough; it's tougher than it ever was. Sometimes I look at my kids and hope they'll be all right when they grow up. I hope they'll have a world to live in."

Bernardine Dohrn: Letter to the Movement: New Morning— Changing Weather

---

This communication does not accompany a bombing or a specific action. We want to express ourselves to the mass movement not as military leaders, but as tribes at council. It has been nine months since the townhouse explosion. In that time, the future of our revolution has been changed decisively. A growing illegal organization of young women and men can live and fight and love inside Babylon. The FBI can't catch us; we've pierced their bullet-proof shield. But the townhouse forever destroyed our belief that armed struggle is the only real revolutionary struggle.

It is time for the movement to go out into the air, to organize, to risk calling rallies and demonstrations, to convince that mass actions against the war and in support of rebellions do make a difference. Only acting openly, denouncing Nixon, Agnew and Mitchell, and sharing our numbers and wisdom together with young sisters and brothers will blow away the fear of the students at Kent State, the smack of the Lower East Side and the national silence after the bombings of North Vietnam.

The deaths of three friends ended our military conception of what we are doing. It took us weeks of careful talking to rediscover our roots, to remember that we had been turned-on to the possibilities of revolution by denying the schools, jobs, the death relationships we were "educated" for. We went back to how we had begun living with groups of friends and found that this revolution could leave intact the enslavement of women if women did not fight to end and change it, together. And marijuana and LSD and little money and awakening to the black revolution, the people of the world. Unprogramming ourselves; relearning Amerikan history. The first demonstration we joined; the first time we tried to convince our friends. In the wake of the townhouse we found that we didn't know much about each others' pasts—our talents, our interests, our differences.

From *Liberation*, November 1970.

We had all come together around the militancy of young white people determined to reject racism and U.S. exploitation of the third world. Because we agreed that an underground must be built, we were able to disappear an entire organization within hours of the explosion. But it was clear that more had been wrong with our direction than technical inexperience (always install a safety switch so you can turn it off and on and a light to indicate if a short circuit exists).

Diana, Teddy and Terry had been in SDS for years. Diana and Teddy had been teachers and both spent weeks with the Vietnamese in Cuba. Terry had been a community organizer in Cleveland and at Kent; Diana had worked in Guatamala. They fought in the Days of Rage in Chicago. Everyone was angered by the murder of Fred Hampton. Because their collective began to define armed struggle as the only legitimate form of revolutionary action, they did not believe that there was any revolutionary motion among white youth. It seemed like black and third world people were going up against Amerikan imperialism alone.

Two weeks before the townhouse explosion, four members of this group had firebombed Judge Murtaugh's house in New York as an action of support for the Panther 21, whose trial was just beginning. To many people this was a very good action. Within the group, however, the feeling developed that because this action had not done anything to hurt the pigs materially it wasn't very important. So within two weeks' time, this group had moved from firebombing to anti-personnel bombs. Many people in the collective did not want to be involved in the large scale, almost random bombing offensive that was planned. But they struggled day and night and eventually, everyone agreed to do their part.

At the end, they believed and acted as if only those who die are proven revolutionaries. Many people had been argued into doing something they did not believe in, many had not slept for days. Personal relationships were full of guilt and fear. The group had spent so much time willing themselves to act that they had not dealt with the basic technological considerations of safety. They had not considered the future: either what to do with the bombs if it had not been possible to reach their targets, or what to do in the following days.

This tendency to consider only bombings or picking up the gun as revolutionary, with the glorification of the heavier the better, we've called the military error.

After the explosion, we called off all armed actions until such time as we felt the causes had been understood and acted upon. We found that the alternative direction already existed among us and had been developed within other collectives. We became aware that a group of outlaws who are isolated from the youth communities do not have a sense of what is going on, can not develop strategies that grow to include large numbers of people, have become "us" and "them."

It was a question of revolutionary culture. Either you saw the youth culture that has been developing as bourgeois or decadent and therefore to be treated as the enemy of the revolution, or you saw it as the forces which produced us, a culture that we were a part of, a young and unformed society (nation).

In the past months we have had our minds blown by the possibilities that exist for all of us to develop the movement so that as revolutionaries we change and shape the cultural revolution. We are in a position to change it for the better. Men who are chauvinists can change and become revolutionaries who no longer embrace any part of the culture that stands in the way of the freedom of women. Hippies and students who fear black power should check out Rap Brown's *Die Nigger Die* and George Jackson's writings. We can continue to liberate and subvert attempts to rip off the culture. People become revolutionaries in the schools, in the army, in prisons, in communes and on the streets. Not in an underground cell.

Because we are fugitives, we could not go near the Movement. That proved to be a blessing because we've been everywhere else. We meet as many people as we can with our new identities; we've watched the TV news of our bombings with neighbors and friends who don't know that we're Weatherpeople. We are often afraid but we take our fear for granted now, not trying to act tough. What we once thought would have to be some zombie-type discipline has turned out to be a yoga of alertness, a heightened awareness of activities and vibrations around us—almost a new set of eyes and ears.

Even though we have not communicated about ourselves specifically before this, our actions have said much about where our heads are at. We have obviously not gone in for large scale material damage. Most of our actions have hurt the enemy on about the same military scale as a bee sting. But the political effect against the enemy has been devastating. The world knows that even the white youth of Babylon will resort to force to bring down imperialism.

The attacks on the Marin County Court House and the Long Island City Jail were made because we believe that the resistance and political leadership that is growing within the prisons demands immediate and mass support from young people. For all the George Jacksons, Afeni Shakurs and potential revolutionaries in these jails, the movement is the lifeline. They rebelled expecting massive support from outside.

Demonstrations in support of prison revolts are a major responsibility of the movement, but someone must call for them, put out the leaflets, convince people that it is a priority. We are so used to feeling powerless that we believe pig propaganda about the death of the movement, or some bad politics about rallies being obsolete and bullshit. A year ago, when Bobby Seale was ripped-off in Chicago and the movement didn't respond, it made it easier for the pigs to murder Fred Hampton. Now two Puerto Ricans have been killed by the pigs in the New York jails, in retaliation for the prisoner rebellion. What we do or don't do makes a difference.

It will require courage and close families of people to do this organizing. Twos and threes is not a good form for anything—it won't put out a newspaper, organize a conference on the war, or do an armed action without getting caught. Our power is that together we are mobile, decentralized, flexible, and we come into every home where there are children who catch the music of freedom and life.

The women and men in jails are POW's held by the United States. When an Amerikan pilot is shot down while bombing North Vietnamese villages, he is often surrounded by thousands of people who have just seen their family and homes destroyed by the bombs he was delivering. Yet the man is not attacked and killed by the Vietnamese but is cared for as a prisoner. Nixon is now waging a last ditch moral crusade around the treatment of these Amerikan war criminals to justify all his impending atrocities.

The demonstrations and strikes following the rape of Indochina and the murders at Jackson and Kent last May showed real power and made a strong difference. New people were reached and involved and the government was put on the defensive. This month the bombings could have touched off actions expressing our fury at double-talking Laird and his crew—war research and school administrators and travelling politicians are within reach of our leaflet, our rallies, our rocks. Women's lib groups can find in Nguyen Thi Binh a sister for whom there is love and support here. Her proposals for peace must be explained and Bloody Dick's plans to use more bombers to replace the GIs who are refusing to fight exposed as the escalation and genocide it is. Vietnamization Indianization limited duration protective reaction suppressive fire horseshit. It seems that we sometimes forget that in Vietnam strong liberated women and men live and fight. Not as abstract guerrilla fighters, slugging it out with U.S. imperialism in Southeast Asia, but as people with values and loves and parents and children and hopes for the future.

People like Thai, a fighter in the People's Liberation Armed Forces who was in Hue during Tet and at Hamburger Hill a year later, or Than Tra, an organizer in the mass women's organization and the students' movement in the cities, who had not seen her lover in nine years. They travelled for a month to come to Cuba to meet with us, to sing and dance and explain how it is in Vietnam. There is nothing brutal or macho about guns and bombs in their hands. We can't help thinking that if more people knew about them, the anti-war movement would never have allowed Nixon and Agnew to travel to so many cities during the past election with only the freaks at Kansas State and the people of San Jose to make our anger at his racism known to the world.

The hearts of our people are in a good place. Over the past months, freaks and hippies and a lot of people in the movement have begun to dig in for a long winter. Kent and Augusta and Jackson brought to all of us a coming of age, a seriousness about how hard it will be to fight in Amerika and how long it will take us to win. We are all beginning to figure out what Cubans meant when they told us about the need for new men and new women.

People have been experimenting with everything about their lives, fierce against the ways of the white man. They have learned how to survive together in the poisoned cities and how to live on the road and the land. They've moved to the country and found new ways to bring up free wild children. People have purified themselves with organic food, fought for sexual liberation, grown long hair. People have reached out to each other and learned that grass and organic consciousness-expanding drugs are weapons of the revolution. Not mandatory for everyone, not a gut-check, but a tool—a Yacqui way of knowledge. But while we sing of drugs the enemy knows how great a threat our youth culture is to their rule, and they employ their allies—the killer-drugs (smack and speed)—to pacify and destroy young people. No revolution can succeed without the youth, and we face that possibility if we don't meet this threat.

People are forming new families. Collectives have sprung up from Seattle to Atlanta, Buffalo to Vermont, and they are units of people to trust each other both to live together and to organize and fight together. The revolution involves our whole lives; we aren't part-time soldiers or secret revolutionaries. It is our closeness and the integration of our personal lives with our revolutionary work that will make it hard for undercover pigs to infiltrate our collectives. It's one thing for pigs to go to a few meetings, even meetings of a secret cell. It's much harder for them to live in a family for long without being detected.

One of the most important things that has changed since people began working in collectives is the idea of what leadership is. People—and especially groups of sisters—don't want to follow academic idealogues or authoritarians. From Fidel's speeches and Ho's poems we've understood how leaders grow out of being deeply in touch with movements. From Crazy Horse and other great Indian chiefs we've learned that the people who respect their tribe and its needs are followed freely and with love. The Lakotas laughed at the whites' appointing one man to be chief of all the Lakota tribes, as if people wouldn't still go with whichever leader they thought was doing the right thing!

Many of these changes have been pushed forward by women both in collectives with men and in all women's collectives. The enormous energy of sisters working together has not only transformed the movement internally, but when it moves out it is a movement that confuses and terrifies Amerika. When asked about the sincerity of Mme. Binh's proposals Ky says, "Never trust a woman in politics." The pigs refuse to believe that women can write a statement or build a sophisticated explosive device or fight in the streets. But while we have seen the potential strength of thousands of women marching, it is now up to revolutionary women to take the lead to call militant demonstrations, to organize young women, to carry the Viet Cong flag, to make it hard for Nixon and Ky to travel around the country ranting about POWs the same day that hundreds of women are being tortured in the prisons of South Vietnam.

It's up to us to tell women in Amerika about Mme. Binh in Paris; about Pham Thi Quyen, fighter in the Saigon underground and wife of Nguyen Van Troi; about Mme. Nguyen Thi Dinh, leader of the first South Vietnamese People's Liberation Forces unit uprising in Ben Tre in 1961; about Celia Sanchez and Haydee Santamaria who fought at Moncada and in the Havana underground; about Bernadette Devlin and Leila Khaled and Lolita Lebrun; and about Joan Bird and Afeni Shakur, and Mary Moylan here.

We can't wait to organize people until we get ourselves together any more than we can act without being together. They must go on at the same time. None of these changes that people are going through are rules and principles. We are in many different regions of the country and are building different kinds of leaders and organizations. It's not coming together into one organization, or paper structure of factions or coalitions. It's a New Nation that will grow out of the struggles of the next year.

7

The Crisis of the Cities

In our now almost wholly urban nation, who is there who truly loves his own city today? We still have arrestingly beautiful urban places in America. San Francisco—sea-girt, fog-washed, and glistening on its fabled hills—is a jewel among the cities of the world. One feels only delight and mounting excitement as he approaches The City. Even Europeans, who profess to be appalled by the raw, garish, brittle, and metallic ugliness of the average American city, acknowledge that San Francisco ranks with the most beautiful of the gracious European cities. But even San Francisco is deep into what we now call the "urban crisis," just as dozens of other medium- to outsized American cities are. New York City, Chicago, Washington, D.C., Los Angeles—monarchs all—are each still possessed of islands of heart-catching beauty in the midst of their tawdry glitter and decay. Each of those great cities can still suggest to us a measure of urbanity and ease, of challenge and pounding excitement. Yet we come to think of them all as passé, as ungovernable, as scenes of personal danger and soul-searing ugliness. Once the American cities were the symbols of both the promise and the achievement of this people. Now they are a problem, and serious men are ready to make the final surrender, to turn them from proud municipal corporations into kept wards of the central national government. It is no foolish lapse into hysteria, then, to speak of the "urban crisis."

But what is the urban crisis? In the immediate sense, there are two different urban crises. They are not unrelated, but they can be identified separately. First, a racial catastrophe is brewing. The cities have become the scene not of the greening but of the coming apart of America. The inner city of most great municipalities is becoming black as whites move to the suburbs. The blacks stew and choke in their ghettos and can do nothing to arrest the process of ghettoization of the inner city and the flight to the suburbs. As the inner cities grow more exclusively black they

215

grow impoverished and the services and amenities of urban life degenerate. The ghetto schools are nightmares. Their function has become custodial rather than educational. They are despised and feared by students, parents, and teachers alike. The police appear to the residents of the ghetto to be an occupying army. The cop in the ghetto feels himself to be on a combat mission in hostile territory. Next to the school and the police stands the welfare worker and the employment counselor as the visible embodiment of the state, of authority. They, too, are hated and feared rather than even passively tolerated. But ghetto residents are so demoralized that they do not generate an autonomous legitimate authority of their own. Communal life exists in an attenuated state. The community passes on the knowledge requisite for survival in that environment but it does not serve as a home, a sanctuary, and a matrix for individual growth and achievement. Within the ghetto, the black disabilities produced by centuries of enslavement and oppression feed upon themselves and multiply. Whites peer briefly at the realities of ghetto life, but the two races live in greater and greater separation and mutual hostility and dread. Our cities are becoming communalized. Multicommunal political and social systems tend to be stagnant when they are stable and positively murderous—as in Northern Ireland or East Pakistan—when they are unstable. Do we even have a grammar and a set of referents so we can discuss how to arrest this plunge toward disaster?

In the selection by Theodore J. Lowi, we see the road we have traveled to arrive at our own version of apartheid. Although Iron City is in the South, its essential characteristics have been repeated throughout the North as well. Enlightened, humane, progressive federal legislation in the fields of guaranteed housing loans, public housing for the poor, and urban redevelopment have, ironically, hugely contributed to the communalization of the cities. Lowi's article shows us also that various proposals for "local control" or "returning power to the local communities" do not guarantee that the local communities will display the will and capacity for solving this part of the urban crisis.

If there were no race problem, would there still be an urban crisis? The answer is certainly affirmative, although it would be foolish to try to separate the two entirely. But even if blacks shared the affluence of their white fellow-citizens, there would be grave problems of congestion, pollution, crime, education, and the viability of the major cities. Every mayor of a large and troubled city would agree with Mayor John V. Lindsay, of New York City, that inadequate revenue spells doom for the cities. As Lindsay notes, the property tax—the traditional revenue base for most cities—has been exhausted by the steep rises in the tax rate of the past two decades. Lindsay argues that New York cannot survive on the revenue that it may now legally generate and what it can coax or bludgeon from an often unsympathetic state government. Here he identifies an important policy conflict of the next few years: Should the federal government return to the states and communities a substantial block of income tax revenues? The need may seem clear to Mayor Lindsay, but Representative Wilbur D. Mills (Democrat, Arkansas), the powerful Chairman of the Appropriations Committee of the federal House of Representatives—the man who must be persuaded if there is to be federal revenue–sharing legislation—is not at all convinced. He describes the basic argument for those opposed to the President's revenue–sharing proposals. In doing so, Mills also delineates other aspects of the urban problem.

America has probably always suffered from some kind of urban crisis. Certainly in our founding times we thought of ourselves as an agrarian people, and the cities were viewed as centers of corruption and malignancy. In time, of course, the cities came to be viewed with pride as symbols of our collective conquest of the wilderness, of our common triumph over this awesome land. But in an important way, the cities were just another version of the wilderness. The wilderness was turned into cities by the accretion of private efforts. Each man was seeking his private fortune and happiness, and his efforts combined with those of thousands and then millions of others to subdue this continent and create a civilization. Men who were so motivated, then, loved the land and loved their country so long as both yielded to their private struggle. So it was with the cities. They were places where men struggled for private success in a different way than they had in the wilderness. Their value to Americans has always been instrumental value. That is, they have been valued for the private lives that men could lead in them, not for their sake as a public entity. We have no cathedral cities in America. Our cities have not been the birthplaces of our legends, and they have not nurtured our heroes. We have not had an Athens, a Rome—cities once valued for the quality of their public life rather than for the style of private life they afforded. James L. Sundquist suggests in his article that perhaps our cities are already too large to contain a true public sense. But he also notes with some urgency that we must develop a public philosophy about the cities, that laissez-faire will no longer do.

Our final selection is from Edward C. Banfield's *The Unheavenly City*. Here Banfield challenges the basic thrust of this chapter, that there is an urban crisis. Banfield contends that the so-called urban crisis is really the product of rising standards and expectations and thus not a crisis that is likely to lead to disaster.

John V. Lindsay: Only the Federal
Government Can Take the
Positive Steps . . .

Mr. Chairman, . . . New York is so large and so diverse that in some ways it is an economy unto itself. This strength and diversity have shielded the city from some of the worst effects of the disaster we call inflationary recession. On a percentage basis, personal income, corporate profits, and sales have held up a little better than the national average. And unemployment—though very high for New York at just over 4 percent—is well under the national rate now running above 6 percent.

Nevertheless, the damage has been severe. Some trends, particularly inflation, have been more pronounced in New York than elsewhere—and the impact on city finances has been especially harsh.

New York City, like most States and cities, does not have a single, consolidated budget. It has two sets of accounts—a capital budget for investment-type expenditures, and an expense budget for current operations. All construction, all equipment purchase, all land acquisitions are paid for through the capital budget, which is supported by borrowing. The expense budget—supported by local taxes and grants from other sources—contains only employee salaries and benefits, debt service, and some consumable supplies.

It is this expense budget which we must, by law, balance each fiscal year. There is no room for deficits, planned or unplanned. There are only the wages and salaries of people—of 32,000 policemen, 14,000 firemen, and 11,000 sanitation workers, of the teachers of more than 1 million schoolchildren, and the doctors and nurses in 18 municipal hospitals, and all the others who make the city fit to live in. Presidents choose whether and how to balance budgets. Like most mayors and Governors, we in New York only choose which vital services to do without.

A few simple numbers tell the story in New York. Our expense budget for the current fiscal year estimated expenditures of $7.7 billion. These were to be financed from four sources: City property taxes, $2.1 billion;

From United States Congress, 92nd Congress, 1st Session, Hearings before the Joint Economic Committee, "Economic Prospects and Policies," Part I, pp. 24–27, January 1971. Government Printing Office, 1971.

other city taxes, $2.5 billion; State aid, $1.6 billion; Federal aid, $1.3 billion; and other receipts, $0.2 billion; for a total of $7.7 billion.

However, it is now clear that the recession will deny us about $150 million of this revenue, while inflation is driving our costs $100 million higher. Additional shortfalls in receipts expected from the State lottery and the new off-track betting corporation will bring our total deficit in the current year to more than $300 million.

It is difficult to convey the meaning of a current-year deficit of this size in a city expense budget. It is less than 4 percent of our total budget and only 7 percent of city tax revenues. But consider it in human terms. It equals the salaries and benefits of 25,000 to 30,000 employees over a full fiscal year. They are employees who depend on the city for a living and upon whom the city depends for its life. When the deficit climbs into the hundreds of millions, the remedies multiply in pain and risk to the point that the quality of urban life hangs in the balance.

Moreover, there is no consolation in the outlook for next fiscal year, beginning July 1. Our next budget is only beginning to take shape, but it is clear even now that the gap between mandatory expenditures and anticipated revenues may approach a billion dollars.

This fiscal crisis has forced us to make drastic cutbacks.

In October, we clamped a freeze on filling vacant city jobs.

In November, we made extensive cuts in many city programs, including postponement of hiring of new policemen and firemen.

Later the same month, we laid off 500 employees, the first layoffs of city workers in New York since the depression.

In December, we announced that the city could not finance salary or benefit increases in new contracts with our police, fire, and sanitation unions except where justified by projected increases in the cost of living or measurable increases in productivity.

These were hard but necessary steps. At every stage, we made clear that more would be required unless the Federal and State Governments met their responsibilities.

There is a clear limit to the capacity of any community—no matter how determined—to deal with problems forced upon it by national conditions beyond its control. We have reached that limit in New York City. Just since 1965 we have absorbed a 100-percent increase in welfare rolls—equivalent, I may say, with the rest of the Nation—and in some parts of the country, it was substantially higher than that.

And we have taxed ourselves heavily:

A city tax on personal income with progressive rates up to 2 percent, and a lesser rate on the earnings of commuters;

A tax on transfers of stocks through all three exchanges; and

A substantial increase in assessed valuation, and thereby ineffective property tax rates.

These and other measures have doubled our taxpayers' contribution to the city budget. That contribution now stands at $4.4 billion.

Yet, even this is not enough. For our fixed expenditures tend to grow at 15 percent each year while our local revenue base grows at 5 percent. And we have virtually exhausted our taxing powers.

Here in Washington, this might sound like just another version of the same old story. You have all heard the pleas of the cities and their mayors before.

But this year things are different. This year the mayors have been joined by the Governors in an almost universal appeal for assistance. And this year we are not just asking for help to solve specific problems—housing, schools, mass transit. This year we have the more fundamental concern of survival itself, and I believe that survival is not too strong a word to describe our stake in the crisis that confronts us.

Across the Nation, cities, counties, and States face a widening gap between demands for services and available funds. Inflation has aggravated the problem. But each day brings increasing evidence that the fiscal system itself, which has served our Nation since its founding almost two centuries ago, is failing to meet the needs we face today. Financial collapse and the breakdown of basic services loom as a clear and present danger in 1971.

The primary resource for local governments is still the property tax, which was once the keystone of all governmental revenue. But the income tax yields far more—with almost all of that elastic revenue source going to the National Government.

At the turn of this century, State and local governments controlled some two-thirds of the revenue in the total Federal system. Today, the ratio has been reversed, with two-thirds of all moneys flowing to the National Government in Washington. Washington takes the Nation's most powerful financial resources, while the problems remain at the State and local level.

Our survival depends on ending this mismatch of revenues and responsibilities. This year we must be prepared to reshape the fundamental relationship between the Federal Government and its States and localities. That is the challenge of the current crisis—to provide a new framework for financing the States, cities, and suburbs of the Nation for many years to come.

We can accomplish that goal with the combined effect of two separate measures—revenue-sharing and welfare reform. Revenue sharing at a significant level would provide an elastic source of money to bolster local budgets. Nationally financed welfare reform would release local tax revenues to meet local needs. With welfare costs removed and revenue sharing added, State and local budgets might, for the first time, reflect an adequate match between revenues and responsibilities.

Much has been said about these programs. There is little time left to act upon both.

First, at least $10 billion in Federal revenues must be returned to our States and cities in unrestricted form beginning in 1971.

Many believe that $10 billion is too ambitious a figure.

Let's examine it for a moment.

It amounts to less than 5 percent of total Federal collections.

It adds about 10 percent to total States and local collections.

It translates into about $50 per user of the services State and local agencies provide.

It is less than half of the additional funds that States and localities will almost certainly need simply to maintain service levels in a sluggish, inflation-ridden economy.

Some ask whether we can afford so much. But can we afford to risk less? A revenue-sharing program financed at a lower level will not provide the stability we so desperately need. Neither will a program achieved by money-shuffling or empty numbers games do the job. To be meaningful, sharing must be real and it must be in addition to existing Federal programs.

Second, the Federal Government must move immediately to relieve States and localities of the crushing financial burden of welfare.

New York City is ordered by the State and National Governments to spend more than $600 million of its own tax dollars to support the Federal-State welfare system. And that amount is growing at about 20 percent per year. We have no choice. Eligibility requirements and benefit levels are mandated upon us. The law orders us to appropriate enough money to meet set levels, regardless of effects on other priority programs. Our role is purely that of harried clerk and unwilling banker.

That is why I recently rejected the welfare budget request mandated on us by the State and Federal Governments for the next fiscal year, which would have added more than $100 million to New York City's contribution to this disastrous program. That is also why I have instructed the city's corporation counsel to sue the State and Federal Governments to stop them from mandating welfare costs on our city's taxpayers.

Only the Federal Government can take the positive steps necessary to create a reasonable and effective national welfare program. This must include Federal takeover of the total costs of welfare and the establishment of uniform levels for benefit payments.

Mayors who testify in Washington have often been dismissed as chronic Cassandras. They always predicted disaster, but the cities always muddled through. But now there are new warning voices. In every part of America, Governors are talking like mayors.

This year, as never before, we look to Washington for there is no other place to go. The crisis of the Federal fiscal system has overcome traditional rivalries between States and their localities and has inspired us to do battle together for our common survival. Mayors and Governors will stand together, for all of us know we cannot survive alone.

Wilbur D. Mills: Revenue Sharing Is Bad in Principle

. . . Today I want to speak to you rather briefly on two quite important subjects, one of which will be voted on very soon in the House of Representatives and the other which I predict will not be voted on in the House.

Welfare Reform

The first of these subjects, and one on which the Committee on Ways and Means will soon report a bill, is comprehensive reform of the public welfare system, in which the Federal Government and the States over the years since its inception have assumed the role of partners.

Now clearly, everybody seems to agree that we need welfare reform; but agreement on just how welfare should be reformed is quite another matter. One of the reasons for the lack of agreement on how to do it is because we must reform not one, but 50 separate State welfare programs, involving large segments of our population and substantial resources of our State governments.

These separate State programs are very different in their characteristics and in the manner in which they are operated. This is one reason we find such a variety of complaints about the present program—particularly the Aid to Families with Dependent Children, or AFDC as it is called. Certainly, we find a growing lack of confidence on the part of the taxpaying public that assistance goes to those who need it and not to those who are

---

From United States Congress, 92nd Congress, 1st Session, *Congressional Record,* May 12, 1971.

indolent or ineligible. Moreover, there is understandable bitterness from those who in some areas must depend for help upon a system that in too many cases extracts self-respect as a price for even its temporary benefits. In other areas we find hopelessness on the part of those who have been trapped in a life on the dole from which the possibility of escape seems remote. In still other areas, we find contempt from those who all too easily obtain undeserved benefits from an antiquated, unstable, and lax welfare bureaucracy.

When we look at all the separate programs, there is a crazy quilt pattern of benefits and eligibility requirements that makes little sense in a highly industrialized and mobile society.

And, additionally, the economic incentives under the present programs seem to lead to more and more welfare, less and less work and to family disintegration.

But the overriding characteristic of AFDC is its out-of-control growth. From January 1970 to January 1971 there was a 30-percent increase in the number of recipients, rising to a total of 9.8-million people. Total money paid out increased by more than 40 percent in that same year rising to a total rate of about $½-billion a month. This is not a phenomenon of just the big States and the big cities. My own State of Arkansas had an increase of 38 percent in the number of recipients in that same year. Tennessee also is above the national average at 34 percent.

The Committee on Ways and Means is just completing the most thorough-going, extensive and intensive review and analysis which has ever been made of this program. We have worked very closely and harmoniously with representatives of the Administration and have improved and tightened up the President's basic proposal. The bill which the Committee is about to recommend to the House of Representatives will contain provision after provision designed to meet the myriad of problems which we have identified during our consideration of the subject. I cannot take your time now to go into all the details of the bill, for it is an extensive and complex subject, but I believe that it is legislation which will deserve the active support of every Member of the Congress and the support of State legislators like yourselves, who have had to deal with these difficult problems at the State or local level.

Our general approach to this problem has been to devise a program which is fair to the taxpaying public and to the people who will benefit from it. One general theme has marked the Committee's deliberations throughout in this matter. We wanted a system of welfare where it is *hard to get on* and *easy to get off*. We have spent much time and effort to insure that we would have an effective, efficient administrative mechanism which has both the confidence of the taxpayer and the respect and cooperation of those who must apply for the benefits. We will establish a system of in-

centives and requirements for *work* and *training*—both sticks and carrots
—which we believe will lead to many more people working themselves off
welfare.

We have developed systems and safeguards designed to avoid cheating
and fraud, and stiff penalties for those who are caught trying. We include
provisions for requiring deserting fathers to either support their children
or find that they owe Uncle Sam for whatever is paid to those children.
The bill makes it a crime for a person to cross a State line to avoid supporting his family. It includes a requirement that every welfare mother be
offered family planning services, and the government will pay for the
services if she takes it.

In line with the basic emphasis on work and training, families in which
at least one person is employable would be enrolled in what we call the
"Opportunities for Families" program that would be administered *not* by
the Department of Health, Education and Welfare, but by the Department
of Labor. Only those families without employable persons would be enrolled in the Family Assistance Plan, the part that would be administered
by HEW.

All adult family assistance recipients, except those specifically ex-
empted by the bill, would be required to register for work or training. The
exemptions from the registration requirements for work or training are
very limited.

In order to accomplish these objectives we intend to "federalize" welfare, both administratively and to a large extent financially. This will enable
us to provide a set of uniform national standards, uniformly applied and
effectively administered. The beneficial financial effects of these provisions
on the States will be quite substantial.

Federalization in this particular area, that is, public welfare, is the
proper course to achieve greater fairness and equity, desirable uniformity
and better control, economy, and enforcement of the program, and it will
provide very significant savings to the States amounting to hundreds of
millions of dollars. This is the way to improve the Federal–State partnership. We plan to continue to seek these specific areas on a program-by-
program basis and determine in a logical, rational, objective manner
whether a particular program would lend itself to full Federal responsibility.

Revenue Sharing

To be contrasted with this program-by-program, area by area, approach, which I am convinced will strengthen the Federal–State relationship, is the blunderbuss, general revenue sharing, "cure-all-ills" proposal

currently being ballyhooed across the country. I hear you may have heard something about it just recently.

Now I have made no secret of my opposition to "no-strings-attached" general revenue sharing. *It is very bad in principle. It would be capricious in its results. It assumes the existence of a non-existent surplus of revenues. It has the dangerous potential—indeed, probability—in my judgment, for destroying rather than strengthening our Federal system* and the independence of State and local governments. I predict it will not be approved by the Ways and Means Committee or the Congress. I surely hope it will not.

Now why do I say these things about a program which seems to be so popular? Let me enumerate just a few particulars, and I ask your most thoughtful consideration of these points.

It is extremely bad in principle because it separates the spending function from the revenue-raising responsibility. Throughout my entire period of public service, both as a country judge in Arkansas in the depression years and nearly three decades on the House Committee on Ways and Means, I have known firsthand the difficulties and political hazards of raising revenues. I remain convinced that this is a necessary discipline on any governmental authority, and I am not yet ready for a new American revolution that would remove this discipline from those who spend the revenues. I am not prepared to become a party to any revolutionary scheme that would encourage State and local governments to reduce and relegate themselves to an insipid and innocuous function of "representation without taxation." While this would be undoubtedly an incredibly delightful and utopian condition for politicians, I doubt that our Federal system of government could long survive this kind of new American revolution.

Second, the proposal assumes the existence of a surplus of revenues which is non-existent. For about 40 years, save for only a couple of years, we have had only deficits at the Federal level. Our Federal debt subject to the debt ceiling is now about $400-billion, while some States and localities have very little, if any, debt. We just raised the ceiling, at the request of this Administration, by an unprecedented 35-billion dollars. For the Federal Government to be granting largesse to State and local governments when we have to borrow to finance our own responsibilities simply adds more flames to inflation. This year our deficit is estimated at $25.5-billion and for fiscal 1972 it is estimated to be $23.1-billion. From 1961 to 1968 the Federal Government ran a string of deficits totalling over $78-billion, with the record-breaking $28-billion in 1968, $5.5-billion in 1969, $13.1-billion in 1970, and as I have said, $25.5-billion in 1971. How can anyone question that this string of deficits has not been a principal contributor to the rampant inflation which we have suffered? So what we would "share" would *not* be *revenues,* but *borrowed money.*

Now why do I say that this proposal carries with it the potential, if not the probability, that it would in time destroy the Federal system? Let us look down the road a little way. Let us assume that forces might be enough politically to bring about the passage of a program calling for no-strings-attached revenue sharing of 5 billion dollars now. Are any of us in this chamber today so naive as to believe that those same forces in time cannot have that 5 billion dollars swelled to 20 billion, 30 billion, or even 40 billion?

Then let us look at the question of turning power over to the local governments. What is there to prevent a future Congress or an Administration—either Democratic or Republican—somewhere down the road, when the Federal part of the total expenditures of the States grows to represent a sizable amount of their total spending, telling the States that they are rather backward? There are certain things that we would like for you to do—with respect to your judiciary, with respect to your legislature, with respect to your local governments, with respect to any State program you want to name—in order for us to justify continuing giving you this largesse out of the Federal Treasury. In fact, there is already one revenue-sharing proposal which would tie revenue sharing to increased efficiency in local government—efficiency determined *not* by you, but by someone else.

Now, to me, that is just the reverse of what the proponents say it is. It may give the illusion of temporary vitality to the State governments, but, in the long run, it makes them dependent entirely on the Federal Treasury and on whatever controls Congress or the President subsequently wants to impose.

Whenever the Federal Government gives out money, there is always the possibility of entrapment. And those who advocate revenue sharing today, in my opinion, are creating that old trap for their successors in the future, who are going to regret that their predecessors ever fell for any such scheme. It could become a massive weapon against the independence of State and local governments.

I also observed that the proposal would be capricious and inequitable in its results. It would have the unfortunate result of distributing aid in a haphazard manner without regard to the financial ability of State and local governments or their need for assistance. The formula would distribute the funds among the States primarily on the basis of their population, with a small adjustment for tax effort, but we all know that population in itself cannot be an adequate measure of the need for assistance since it does not take into consideration the fact that some States are wealthier than others and have larger tax resources or that some States have greater welfare and other costs than other States.

The revenue-sharing funds would also be distributed to the local governments in an unfair manner. The basic formula would allocate these funds on the basis of the respective amount of taxes collected by each governmental unit. It is true that each State and its local governments would have the option to adopt alternative methods of sharing the funds— but it is questionable whether these alternative formulas would produce very much different results from the tax collection basis. I want to stress that the amount of taxes collected by a particular local government is not a good measure of its need for assistance. This gives the greatest amount of aid to local governments which can raise substantial tax revenue because they have wealthy residents or a large industrial or commercial tax base. In contrast, the poorer communities with large unmet needs would get less revenue because they cannot raise substantial amounts of tax revenue. . . .

I know it seems to be a popular proposal among State and local officials, because it spells MONEY. But I have not and I will not support any measure just because it is popular if I think it is wrong in principle. I do not believe, when you really think about it, you will fall for any such dangerous proposal. I sincerely hope and predict that it will not be enacted by the Congress, but I also will assure you that this Congress *does* intend to provide relief to both State and local governments before we complete our endeavors. We will do it, however, in the right way.

I thank you.

Theodore J. Lowi: Apartheid U.S.A.

The United States is over 100 years away from an official apartheid policy. Yet, after more than 20 years of serious involvement by the federal government in the "urban crisis," the social condition of American cities could be little worse if the concerned federal agencies had been staffed all those years by South African agents. A close look at the actual results of federal urban policies gives wonder how there remains any national legitimacy and why the crisis of the 1960s has not been more violent.

The crisis of the 1960s signaled the end of the era that began in the 1930s. Lyndon Johnson was the Herbert Hoover of this moment of change. As Hoover presided over the wreckage of the depression, Johnson presided over the wreckage of the New Deal. In both crises, the sincere application of established criteria began to yield unexpected, unintended and unacceptable results.

The New Deal was founded on the principle of positive government made possible—that is, acceptable to Americans—by a very special form of decentralization. Ideally, federal funds are to be passed to state and municipal administrators to deal with their problems as they see fit. The legislature is expected to set up a program without giving the administrator any guidance whatsoever for fear of intruding upon state or municipal autonomy. As K. C. Davis puts it, "Congress says, 'Here is a problem. Deal with it.' " The result we generally call enabling legislation.

The New Deal was expected to work effectively and without arbitrariness by putting the new programs in the best of all possible worlds: responsibility will be imposed upon central bureaucrats and decisions will be made miraculously in the public interest merely through the pulling and hauling of organized interests; central government expands; local influence expands as well; everybody gains. It is the providential "hidden hand" of Adam Smith applied to politics.

This neat process has been the prevailing public philosophy for the past generation. Panglossian political scientists describe it with overwhelming approval as pluralism. The Supreme Court has enshrined the essence of the New Deal in American jurisprudence as delegation of power. Most recently, political rhetoricians embrace it as creative federalism, maximum feasible participation, and countervailing power. Thanks to the work of such unlikely comrades as Lyndon Johnson, Arthur Schlesinger, J. K. Galbraith, *Fortune* and the *Wall Street Journal,* the principle of decentralization through delegation became the consensus politics that celebrated the end of the New Deal era in 1968.

What follows is a simple case study of the implementation of the two major federal urban programs in a single city. The case goes far toward explaining why the national regime in the United States is no longer taken to be legitimate by so many black people and why this sense of illegitimacy was so likely to spread eventually to whites. Legitimacy, that elusive but vital underpinning of any stable regime, is that sense of the rightness of the general political order. It is that generalized willingness to view public error or corruption as the result of bad administration. There is probably no way practicably to measure legitimacy as such, but one can usually assess roughly the extent to which a regime is less legitimate today than yesterday—just as a doctor may not say precisely what a healthy body is but can know whether it is less healthy now than before.

In this spirit, one can fairly clearly detect a decline in the legitimacy of the regime by noting the rise of instances of repression of Left and Left-sounding activities; one can also detect it by noting the increasing number of political trials and political prisoners, and, more palpably still, the increased infiltration of Left organizations by paid informers. But other indications are not limited to the Left, as for example the increasing numbers of instances of defiance of federal laws—something Southerners have been leading the country in at least since 1954. One can therefore speak of problems of national legitimacy when he begins to sense a general unwillingness to submit political disputes to recognized channels of political settlement, when he sees mediation replaced by direct action.

This case suggests the extent to which the policies of the liberal state are producing its own downfall, and along with that the failure to achieve even a modicum of social justice. Also, in its perverse way, the case also illustrates the effectiveness of planning when governments do define their goals clearly and guide administrators firmly. Tragically the plan was for implementation of an evil policy, apartheid. But through the case perhaps liberals could learn a little something about how to plan for good ends.

Iron City is an urban-industrial area whose corporate boundary surrounds nearly 60,000 residents and whose true metropolitan area includes about 100,000. The history of the development plan of Iron City presents a single, well-documented case of the implementation of explicit racial goals. More than that, the nature of Iron City's official development plans and proposals upon which federal allocations were based serve to document beyond doubt the extraordinary permissiveness of federal urban policy.

Housing Policy in Iron City

The name of the city has been changed to protect the guilty. They are guilty as charged, but no more so than thousands of mayors, councilmen, planners, realtors and builders all over the country. The Iron City situation is extreme and unrepresentative, but it will soon be clear that it provides an ideal laboratory for discovering the nature and limitations of modern federal enabling legislation. Iron City is a southern city, and its development plan fostered racist goals, namely, apartheid, but in doing so its officials only stated the awful truth about the goals of land use development plans in cities all over the country.

In 1950 over 20 percent of Iron City's population was Negro, and they did *not* live in a ghetto. There were neighborhoods of Negroes in virtually every section of town. There was a narrow strip along the river, and there were several strips in the west central and western sections in easy walking distance from the steel and textile mills. There was a largely black neighborhood in the south central section, and there was a larger concentration in the north central section, "across the tracks." (Note the shadings on the map.) There was no Harlem; the implications of the very word suggest the nonsouthern origin of systematic housing discrimination.

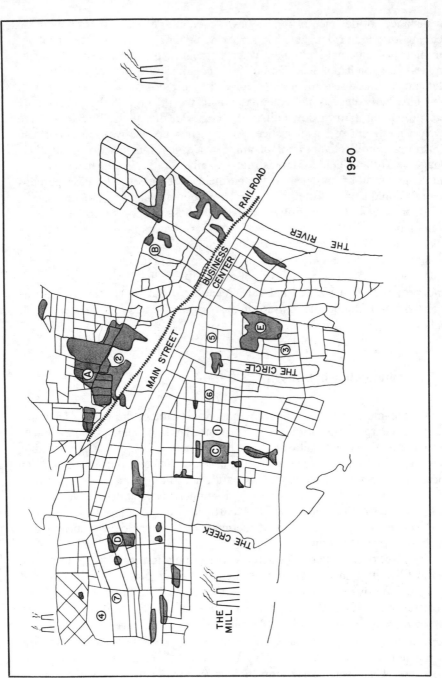

Iron City in 1950

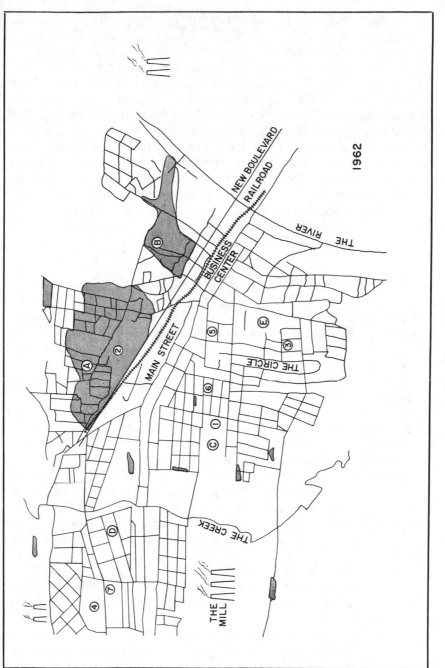

Iron City in 1962

Iron City's has been the typical Negro residential pattern in stable, middle-size southern cities. Rather than a single Negro section, there were interwoven neighborhoods of black and white. This patchwork pattern began in the 1920s with the slow but steady immigration of Negroes from outlying areas to the growing city. Access to industry and the needs of the wealthier whites for domestic servants made "close quarters" a desired condition. For example, the Negro neighborhoods east and north of The Circle were surrounded on three sides by the wealthiest homes in Iron City. But while the residents tolerated and encouraged in many ways the proximity of the races, it could not be said that Iron City constituted an integrated community. Each neighborhood was distinctly monochromatic. There were no black-white-black-white house patterns, although there were a number of instances when several Negro families lived directly across the street from or alley-to-alley with a larger number of white families.

They "Knew Their Place"

Negroes seemed to accept their back-of-the-bus status and the questionable privileges they had which were unavailable to whites. Crimes committed within the race were not, as a rule, investigated or prosecuted with utmost vigor. Black bootleggers (legal sale of liquor has for years been forbidden in the county) had freer rein to cater to the blacks and the insatiably thirsty white middle class. The raising of a pig or a goat was usually allowed, in violation of public health regulations. The rents tended to run considerably lower. And merchants and newsboys were more permissive in granting or extending petty credit to Negroes. This was the dispersed and highly status-bound social situation as recently as 1950.

Early in that decade, however, most Southerners could see a racial crisis approaching, and for them the problems inherent in the residential pattern were immediately clear. In Iron City each of the major public schools was within walking distance of at least one strip of Negro housing and its complement of school-age children. The map serves to make this graphically clear.

Central High School (1 on the map) offered 9th–12th grade education to the white children who lived east of The Creek. Rebel High (4) served white children living west of The Creek, including some areas not shown on the map. Washington High School (2) taught both junior and senior high school grades (7th–12th) to Negro children from both the entire city and the surrounding county. Note the proximity of Negro neighborhoods, hence eligible children, to the white high schools. Most vulnerable to any impending court order for integration would be Central High, attended by virtually all of the children of upper-middle and middle-class families. Note also how far a good half of the Negro children commuted to Washington High and also how many of them actually crossed the paths to Rebel and Central in the course of their journey. The same problem existed for the junior high (3 and 7) and elementary schools (5, 6, and 7).

The Plan

Into this situation stepped the Iron City Planning Commission in 1951. First, the commission analyzed housing, land uses, economic facilities and deterioration. In 1952 they produced a handsome and useful Master Plan, the emphasis of which was upon the need for measures ". . . for arresting beginning blight and correcting advanced blight." On the basis of the Master Plan, a more intensive investigation was ordered toward ultimate production of a Rehabilitation Plan to guide actual implementation and financing. The result of this careful study was a professionally designed, fully illustrated, three-color, glossy paper booklet entitled *Iron City Redevelopment*. The focus of this publication was three areas, designated A, B and E on the map, in which blight had made urban redevelopment necessary.

Upon closer scrutiny, however, the plan reveals itself less a scheme for urban renewal as much as a script for Negro removal. All of the projects proposed in the plan are explicit on this point. The underlying intent to create a ghetto is further highlighted by the inconsistencies between the design for Area E, which had relatively few Negroes, and that for Area A, which was predominantly Negro. The latter housing was as blighted as Area E, but, curiously, the standard of blighting was not applied. There the plan called for intensification of use rather than renewal.

The plan identified Area E as:

occupied by Negroes, but the number is too few to justify provisions of proper recreational, school and social facilities. . . . The opportunity to reconstitute the area as a residential district in harmony with its surroundings was the main reason for its selection as the number one redevelopment site.

The second, Area B, was chosen because "a relatively small amount of housing—standard and substandard—exists there"; therefore it would serve as a companion project to . . . [Area E] . . . thus affording home sites for those occupants of [Area E] who are not eligible for relocation in public housing or who, for reasons of their own, prefer single-family or duplex dwellings." Area A, as shown by the intensive survey and the maps published with the plan, contained as much dilapidated and blighted housing as Area E; but Area A was *not* designated an urban redevelopment area in the plan. Although "blighted and depreciating," it was the "center part of the area . . . growing as the focal point of Negro life." Along the main street of this area, extending into Area B, the plan proposed the building of an auditorium, a playfield and other public facilities "to serve [Iron City's] Negro community." Sites were inserted for the three Negro churches which would be removed by the redevelopment of Area E.

Before completion of *Iron City Redevelopment,* implementation projects had begun and were expanding as financing allowed. It was to be a showcase program, and enthusiasm ran high. The first steps, quite rationally, were to acquire housing for those families who were to be displaced. It was perfectly consistent with the city's view of these people that this housing would be public housing. There had been some public housing projects built under depression legislation, but the only meaningful projects were those begun in 1952 under The Housing Act of 1949. On the map the letters A, B, C and D represent the actual locations of these projects. There was never any controversy over the racial distribution of the occupants. Projects A and B were 100 percent Negro; Projects C and D were 100 percent white. By 1955 they were completed and occupied.

Public Housing Projects in Iron City

Project	Size (No. of Units)	% Negro in Project	Original Composition of Area	Development Cost
A	160	100	Negro	$1,491,000
B	224	100	Mixed	$2,491,000
C	146	0	Negro	$1,595,000
D	220	0	Negro	$2,300,000

Each public housing project was placed carefully. Project A was built in the middle of the largest Negro area. Project B was built in a sparse area, about 50 percent Negro, but marked out in the plan as the area for future expansion of the Negro community. In the area around Project B, the plan proposed sites for the three new "colored churches" and the "colored auditorium."

Project C, an exclusively white project, was built literally on top of the Negro area around it. While it was relatively inexpensive and contained the fewest number of units, it occupied an eight-square-block area due to its design. According to the executive director of the Greater Iron City Housing Authority, it was "a rather unique design, known in the architectural trade as a crankshaft design, thus providing both front and rear court-yards." This project was cited professionally as an outstanding example of good design. And no wonder! Its maximum utilization of space, although a low-rent project, made it a combination public housing, urban renewal and Negro removal plan par excellence. Project D was also built on top of a blighted Negro neighborhood. While it was a relatively large project, it was not solely responsible for eliminating every Negro from the area, as was Project C.

Meanwhile, renewal of the central city was proceeding at a slower pace; it wasn't until 1956 that implementation projects were fully designed. Two areas, designated by the shaded areas around B and E on the map, were selected for intensive renewal. Most important was Area E, a 56-acre area relatively tightly packed with rickety frame houses, outside toilets, corn or potato plots and Negroes. In the official plan, Area E included the unconnected Negro neighborhood just north of The Circle, as well as the entire shaded area due east of The Circle. Area B was relatively sparsely populated, containing a few shacks which needed removing. In some of these shacks were white unemployables.

Within three years the two urban renewal projects were declared 100 percent accomplished. In the official report to the Urban Renewal Administration, the results were as follows:

Completed Urban Renewal Projects in Iron City

Accomplishment	Activity	For Area E	For Area B
100%	Land Acquisition, No. of Parcels Acquired	168	39
100%	No. of Families Relocated	176	24
100%	No. of Structures De-molished (Site Clearance)	236	33

In Area E every trace of Negro life was removed. As the executive director of the Greater Iron City Housing Authority put it, "In this project, all of the then existing streets were vacated and a new land use map was developed." One entirely new street was put in, several of the narrow lanes (e.g., Saint James' Alley) were covered over, and through connectors were built for a dead-end street or two.

All of Area E has now become prime property. One large supermarket, several neighborhood businesses, and two apartment complexes are operating on renewal land purchased from the authority. To serve the 95 percent white area, an elementary school was constructed, as a consolidation of schools No. 5 and No. 6 which no longer exist. Its large playground and lighted ball field occupy most of the eastern sector of Area E. The renewal effort resulted in an equally impressive campus for the nearby junior high, No. 3. But most of the area was zoned for single family residences, and, as of 1968, the boom in construction of houses in the $25,000–$40,000 range was still in progress.

Area B now enjoys a new elementary school with a field house, lighted ball field, tennis court and playground. The city also built a swimming pool here, but it and the original municipal pool on The River were closed for several years to avoid integration of public facilities. Moreover, though redevelopment sites had been set aside in Area B for the three churches demolished in the redevelopment of Area E, each of the congregations chose locations elsewhere in the Negro community. Similarly, most of the relocating Negroes rejected Area B in favor of Area A, even though it was more densely populated and blighted. Except for the 224 units of new public housing, Area B remains underutilized. Furthermore, the major part of Area B extends north of Project B toward the mountain, where *Iron City Redevelopment* reports that although

> some of the terrain is steep, much of it is gently rolling and well drained. ... In most southern cities there is a scarcity of vacant land located close to schools and churches and shopping districts and served by city utilities and transportation, land that is suitable and desirable for expansion of Negro neighborhoods or creation of new ones. Area B is such an area.

Apparently the Negroes do not agree, and most of the area remains a graded, but raw, expanse of red southern earth on the side of the mountain. This was the one part of the plan that went wrong; this was the voluntary part, not financed by federal agencies.

Yet, as a whole, the plan was an overwhelming success. Well before the 1960 census the large Negro contingent in Area E had been reduced to 5.1 percent of the entire census tract, and this was comprised of a few shanties behind the bottling works and the western edge of the area along The River. In Area C the removal process immediately around Central High was completed with Public Housing Project C. After 1960 some 10 percent of the area was still nonwhite, but this was drying up still further. Removal from Area D was approaching totality. By 1964 removal from all areas west of The Creek was given further assistance by the completion of one federally supported artery running east–west through the city and the inauguration of Iron City's portion of the new north–south Interstate Highway. That brought the nonwhite proportion in the western sectors of the city down to about 3 percent of the total population of those areas.

This is how the situation stood by the end of 1967: west of The Creek and north of Main Street (all around Area D), there remained six Negro families. When a nearby textile mill was closed down some years before, they, as employees, were given the right to buy their houses, and they have chosen to remain. West of The Creek and south of Main Street (the area including The Mill), fewer than 5 percent of the housing units were occupied by Negroes. Virtually every one of these houses is located in isolated and sparse sections along The Creek and behind The Mill, where one can still plant a plot of sorghum, catch a catfish, and, undisturbed, let a 1948 Chevrolet corrode into dust. Closer to the center of things, east of The Creek and south of Main Street, the 1960 distribution of Negroes continues to be reduced. Every last shack is gone from Area E and the entire central section of the white city. Three small pockets remain in the western portion near Area C, and that is all that remains in all of the white city. The last remaining Negro neighborhood of any size, a group of shanties running along The River south of Main Street, was removed by the construction of a City Hall–Police Department–YMCA complex. Area B remains completely nonwhite and underdeveloped. Area A now fills the entire triangle pointing north. It is a ghetto.

The plan enjoyed strong consensus among officials and white citizens. It enjoyed at least the acquiescence and tacit consent of the Negroes whose landlords, in any case, were white. Consensus or not, the plan would have had little chance of success without outside financial assistance. That assistance came, abundantly, from federal programs. And, most importantly, the federal personnel who allocated these funds, and still do, also had access to all the project plans, including the Master Plan and the Renewal Plan. Despite Iron City's open approach to apartheid—nothing was kept secret—federal assistance was never in question. Relative to the population of Iron City and the size of its annual public sector budget, federal aid was quite substantial—amounting to 20 percent of the municipal budget for a few years. What we have seen here is an honest, straightforward job of federally sponsored physical and social planning. And the results were dramatic. Perhaps only New Haven, Connecticut, a city famous for its redevelopment, has had a higher per capita success ratio.

Direct federal assistance for public housing in Iron City amounted to slightly over $280,000 for the single fiscal year 1966. Each year since the completion of the four projects the city received a similar amount. This varying figure cannot be broken down among the four projects because it is computed on the basis of the "development costs" given above and granted as a lump sum. The Public Housing (recently changed to Housing Assistance) Administration of Housing and Urban Development (HUD) is authorized by law to grant *each year* to any housing authority the difference between expenses (governed by development costs) and income from public housing. Such a subsidy arrangement enabled authorities like Iron City's to borrow from private banks and to refinance through sale of relatively cheap Housing Authority bonds. What is even more significant is that, under the formula, Iron City is authorized to receive a maximum grant of nearly $305,000 per annum. It is a point of pride at the Greater Iron City Housing Authority that the full amount available under the law was never needed or requested. At a minimum estimate of $250,000 per year, federal grants to help carry the public housing have amounted to $3,000,000. And federal public housing grants are never-ending. Each year the total to Iron City goes up another $250,000 or more.

Subsidizing the Rich

Federal assistance for urban renewal, as differentiated from housing assistance, was another indispensable part of the plan. Between 1957 and 1961, by which time virtually everything but land disposition was completed, Iron City received just short of $1,600,000 from the federal government under the urban redevelopment laws. This amounts to an additional subsidy of $400,000 per annum.

The federal housing assistance was at least $300,000 for each year between 1954 or 1955 and 1957. Together with the urban renewal allotments, the total was at least $700,000 during the years of peak planning activity, 1957–1962. This money is the key to the plan's success.

But to this we must also add the resources made available through various other federal agencies. Federal highway assistance added an undetermined amount for new arteries and, incidentally, forced Negroes to move from the western edge of Iron City. The Federal Housing Authority and the Veterans Administration help to finance the lovely homes being built in Area E. It has not been possible to determine whether federal community facilities funds helped remove Negroes from The River where the new City Hall complex now stands. Nor has it been possible to determine if the local banks balked at extending FHA and VA home owner credit to Negroes seeking to build on the mountain side north of Area B. Answers would affect the meaning of the case only marginally.

Tarnished Legitimacy

First, the case bears out what many people have been saying for two decades, that slum removal meant Negro removal. But it goes further. It supports the even more severe contention that the ultimate effects of federal urban policies have been profoundly conservative or separatist, so much so as to vitiate any plans for positive programs of integration through alteration of the physical layout of cities.

Second, it supports the general thesis that a policy of delegation of powers without rule of law will ultimately come to ends profoundly different from those intended by the most libertarian and humanistic of sponsors. Moreover, it supports the unfashionable contention that some of the most cherished instruments of the liberal state may be positively evil—and that a criterion by which this evil can be predicted is the absence of public and explicit legislative standards by which to guide administrative conduct.

Third, the case of Iron City, especially the explicit nature of its racial policy, shows precisely how and why federal policy is ill equipped to govern the cities directly. The permissiveness of federal enabling legislation could do no greater harm to the social future of the cities than if harm were intended. The present disorder in the cities is explained properly by the failure of government and politics, rather than by the inferiority of Negro adjustment. The case demonstrates how national legitimacy can be tarnished to the degree that it is loaned to the cities for discretionary use and how the crisis of public authority is inevitable as long as a political process unguided by law climaxes in abuses such as those catalogued in Iron City. In sum, it helps show why liberal government based on current principles of delegation cannot achieve justice.

Every Negro in Iron City knew what was happening. Every Negro in Chicago and New York and Cleveland and Detroit knows the same about his city too. But since northern Negroes are not as docile, does that mean that federal imperium was used completely differently outside the South? True, planning authorities would never so deliberately pursue such obviously racial planning. It is also true that few social plans could be as relatively extensive or as successful as Iron City's. Nonetheless, it is undeniable that misuse of federal programs in ways indistinguishable in principle from the Iron City misuse has been widespread.

Martin Anderson, for example, estimated in 1964 that about two-thirds of all displacements resulting from urban renewal were Negro, Puerto Rican, or some other minority group. In public housing the record is even more somber. First, because the pattern is even clearer, and second, because these projects stand as ever-present symbols of the acts of discrimination by which they were created.

A study by Bernard Weissbrourd for the Center for the Study of Democratic Institutions concluded that ". . . most cities have followed a deliberate program of segregation in public housing. . . ." Until July 1967, many housing administrators followed a rule of "free choice" allowing eligible tenants to wait indefinitely for an apartment, which allowed them also to decline a vacancy on racial grounds. Still more recently it was revealed that the Chicago Housing Authority, with the full knowledge of federal agencies, cleared all proposed public housing sites with that member of the Board of Aldermen whose ward would be affected. Thus, while the whole story cannot be told from official statistics, we may conclude what every urban Negro knows—Iron City is not unique.

Separate but Equal?

According to HUD reports of 1965, only three of New York City's 69 public housing projects were officially listed as all nonwhite or all white in occupancy; but ten of Philadelphia's 40 projects were all nonwhite, and 21 of Chicago's 53, five of Detroit's 12, four of Cleveland's 14, and all of Dallas' ten projects were listed as either all nonwhite or all white. The rest of reality is hidden, because the Public Housing Administration defines an "integrated project" as one in which there are "white and more than one nonwhite, including at least one Negro family." Not only does this system of reporting make it impossible to determine the real number of truly integrated projects, it also serves to maintain local racial policies and prejudices.

The Civil Rights Act of 1965 was supposed to have put an end to such practices, but there is little evidence that it can or will improve the situation in public housing in particular or city housing in general. It was not until July of 1967 that the rule of "free choice" was replaced with a "rule of three," a plan whereby an applicant must take one of the first three available units or be dropped to the bottom of the eligible lists. All of this is undeniable testimony that the practices all along had constituted a "separate but equal" system of federally supported housing.

In June 1967, three years after the 1964 Civil Rights Act and after strenuous efforts by the Johnson Administration, two of Detroit's five segregated projects became "integrated" when one white family moved into each of two totally black projects. At the same time, at least 11 of New York's projects were classified as "integrated" when, in fact, fewer than 15 percent of the units were occupied by families of some race other than the race of the 85 percent majority in that project.

For 33 years the Federal Housing Authority has insured over $110 billion of mortgages to help whites escape, rather than build the city. This confession was made when the FHA instituted a *pilot* program to increase FHA support for housing finance in "economically unsound" areas. And it took the belated 1967 directive on public housing to get them to do that much. These remedial steps came five years after President Kennedy's famous "stroke of the pen" decision aimed at preventing discrimination in publicly supported housing and three years after the first applicable Civil Rights Act. Yet no such legislation or executive decisions can erase the stigma of second-class citizenship placed upon the residents of federal housing programs. Nor can more skillful administration of essentially separatist programs remove the culpability of federal participation in the American local government policy of apartheid. Rather, all of these efforts merely suggest that remedies and correctives are never going to help bad organic laws, because bad organic laws are, quite literally, congenitally defective.

Perhaps it is better to have no new public housing than to have it on the Iron City pattern and at the expense of national legitimacy. With the passing of the Housing Act of 1968 and union agreements to build modular units off-site, some will surely argue that the answers lie in the proper expansion of public housing. But unless steps are taken to prevent the duplication of the patterns reviewed here, more will hardly yield better. Other writers and officials have proposed various solutions. President Johnson suggested creating semipublic corporations to finance public low-cost housing, while Senator Charles Percy would offer incentives to private corporations. These proposals focus on the details of financing and offer further examples of the confusion shared by liberals today concerning forms of law versus essentially technocratic forms of administration for achievement of simple, ordinary justice. Regardless of the means of financing, these programs will produce no lasting social benefit without the rule of law that states unmistakably what administrators can and cannot do, what is to be forbidden, and what is to be achieved. That is the moral of the Iron City story.

James L. Sundquist: Where Shall They Live?

By the end of this century, 100 million people will be added to the population of the United States. That is as many people as now live in Great Britain and France combined.

Where shall they live?

If present trends continue—if they are allowed, that is, to continue—most of the 300 million Americans of the year 2000 will be concentrated on a very small proportion of the nation's land area. Projections of the Urban Land Institute place 60 per cent of the country's population—or

Reprinted from *The Public Interest*, No. 18, Winter 1970. (Copyright © National Affairs, Inc., 1970.) Mr. Sundquist is Senior Fellow at The Brookings Institution and writes frequently on the politics of public policy.

187 million persons—in just four huge urban agglomerations. One continuous strip of cities, containing 68 million people, will extend 500 miles down the Atlantic seaboard from north of Boston to south of Washington, D.C. Another, with 61 million, will run from Utica, New York along the base of the Great Lakes as far as Green Bay, Wisconsin. Some 44 million persons will live on a Pacific strip between the San Francisco bay area and the Mexican border. A fourth agglomeration, with 14 million, will extend along the Florida east coast from Jacksonville to Miami and across the peninsula to Tampa and St. Petersburg.

Most of the remaining 40 per cent of Americans will live in urban concentrations, too—and big ones. In this decade, the larger concentrations have been growing fastest; metropolitan areas over 150,000 grew faster than the national average of 9.8 per cent between 1960 and 1965, while the smaller areas grew more slowly, as the following data show:

Size of Urban Area	1960–65 Growth Rate (Per cent)
20,000– 50,000	7.6
50,000– 100,000	8.3
100,000– 150,000	8.4
150,000– 250,000	10.6
250,000– 500,000	9.8
500,000–1,000,000	11.8
over 1,000,000	9.8
All metropolitan areas	10.1
Nonmetropolitan areas	3.9

Source: Adapted by the Advisory Commission on Intergovernmental Relations from Rand McNally.

These trends, continued for the next three decades, would place 77 per cent of the coming 300 million Americans on 11 per cent of the land (excluding Alaska and Hawaii). Only 12 per cent of the population would be outside urban areas of 100,000 or more population.

Is this the way we want to live?

Two questions are presented. The first pertains to regional balance. Is it desirable that population be massed in a few enormous "megalopolises" along the seacoasts and lakeshores? The second relates to rural-urban balance (or, more accurately, the balance between metropolitan and nonmetropolitan areas). Is it in the best interest of the country, and its people, to continue indefinitely the depopulation of rural and small-town America and the building of ever bigger metropolitan complexes, in whatever region? In short, the 300 million can be highly concentrated in a few "megalopolises," or they can be distributed more evenly as among regions and dispersed in a more nearly balanced way among large metropolitan areas, middle-sized cities, and thriving small towns and villages. Which do we want?

But there is an earlier, and even more fundamental, question. Is population distribution a matter upon which the United States should have a policy at all?

Population Policy or Laissez-Faire?

The projections of the enormous population concentrations that are in prospect have appeared in the popular press, but they are presented as Sunday supplement curiosities—as glimpses into the inevitable and or-dained future—not as a subject for public debate and acceptance or re-jection. Yet surely the subject is one worthy of debate. How each family lives is profoundly influenced, even controlled, by the size of the popula-tion cluster in which it is embedded. The degree to which population is massed determines the amenity and congeniality of the whole environment in which adults and children live and grow and work. It affects their per-sonal efficiency, their sense of community, their feelings about the relation-ship between man and nature, their individual and collective outlooks on the world. The impact of size is most emphatic on the lives of the ghetto dwellers of the great cities, of course, but no one in a megalopolis is im-mune. The resident of Scarsdale or Winnetka is not wholly spared the stresses of big city life; the larger the metropolitan area, the greater the strains and irritations of commuting and the more inevitable that the environmental pollution that arises from population concentration will affect the most idyllic suburbs, too. In any case, the desirability of popula-tion concentration must be measured by its consequences for the majority of families who live at near-average or below-average levels, not upon the few who can insulate themselves in political and social enclaves.

So the question is, what kind of environment do we want to build? The nation, through its government, has established policies on matters of far less crucial import, yet the extent to which the country's population will be concentrated remains essentially laissez-faire. That would be all right, perhaps, if by laissez-faire one meant free choice by the individuals and the families that make up the population. But it is far from that. The movement of people from smaller to larger places is, to a large extent though no one knows the exact proportions, involuntary, forced migration. Young people going freely to the cities in search of adventure and opportunity make up part of the migrant flow, but only part; among the rest are millions of uprooted, displaced families who have little desire, and less preparation, for life in large cities and whose destination is often inevitably the city slums. These displaced families are simply forced into the migration stream by economic forces they cannot control.

The spatial distribution of population is determined, of course, by the distribution of jobs. With the exception of the limited numbers of the self-employed and the retired, people are not in reality free to live just anywhere. The vast majority are employees who must live where there are jobs, and the location of jobs is not their choice. The concentration of the country's population is the result of employer-created job patterns that the people have had to follow.

For the most part employers have not been free to create jobs just anywhere, either. They have been bound by considerations of economic efficiency—the location of raw materials and of markets, the transportation cost differentials of alternative locations, etc. As a result, the basic pattern of population distribution has been designed by the play of economic forces, not by men acting rationally as environmental architects; events have been in the saddle once again.

It need not be. In the past, population distribution has been a subject of conscious national policy and it can be again. In the first hundred years of the nation, the government pursued a deliberate policy of dispersing population westward. Motivated in part by desire to confirm its title to the empty continent, the government subsidized turnpikes, railroads, and river navigation, herded Indians onto reservations, and opened public lands to settlement.

Once the continent was spanned, governmental programs continued to encourage a balanced regional development—reclamation, navigation, and electric power projects traditionally, and more recently the more sophisticated and broader efforts authorized in the Appalachian Regional Development Act and the "depressed areas" legislation of the 1960's. The government enacted rural development programs specifically aimed at rural-urban balance, administered for the most part by the Department of Agriculture.

But there is apparently no clear sense of national purpose like that which motivated the early policies for western development. The present regional and rural development programs essentially are the product of legislative log-rolling—the chance balancing of political forces analogous to economic laissez-faire. Urban programs need rural votes so urban areas support rural programs. The west, or the south, or the Appalachian states can muster enough political strength to enact limited programs. But they are offset—more than offset, probably—by other programs that encourage population concentration, like the postwar housing programs that fostered suburban growth around big cities but were inoperative in most smaller cities and rural areas. Congress responds to the pressures of its various constituent regions more or less in proportion to their relative political strength, which means that future congresses will be less and less likely to tilt the benefits of its programs toward nonmetropolitan areas, that are declining in relative political importance, unless it is guided by a conscious policy of population distribution.

Perhaps it is enough to repeat the well-worn observation that a lack of policy is itself a policy. If the nation chooses not to have a population distribution policy, then it is, in effect, accepting the agglomeration that is in prospect, in preference to any alternative spatial distribution patterns that might be brought about by decisive intervention to influence and control the forces that shape the future.

Is it possible to develop a better population distribution pattern than the one in prospect, if the country's scholars, philosophers, and politicians were to put their minds to it?

Making a Population Distribution Policy

It is far easier to agree in the abstract on the logic of having a population policy than to agree upon the policy itself, which may be the most practical and telling argument for laissez-faire. But let us see what might be involved in such an exercise.

Two criteria are apparent. A population distribution pattern could be designed either according to what is considered good for people or according to what they want. (As we know from documents as early as the book of Genesis and as late as the Surgeon General's Report, those are not necessarily the same.) Unfortunately, in either case we must do our thinking without benefit of solid data because no one knows for sure either what is best for people or what they want. Nevertheless, there are many clues.

Even in the absence of quantified evidence, it seems reasonably clear that our largest urban concentrations have grown well beyond the point at which diseconomies of scale begin to show. The costs of moving people and things within large metropolitan areas are demonstrably greater than the costs of moving them in smaller population centers. Commuting distances are obviously longer, the time loss greater, the costs higher. The flight of industry from central cities to the suburbs is a reflection, in part, of the cost of transportation to and within congested areas. The cost of urban freeway construction varies directly with the population density of the areas affected, and subway systems are an enormous expense that only the larger metropolitan areas require. Such municipal functions as water supply and sewage and solid waste disposal are probably also subject to diseconomies of scale, for the simple reason that the water and the waste must be carried over longer distances. San Francisco, for example, had contemplated dispatching a 70 car train daily to carry its solid waste over 300 miles into the mountains on the Nevada-California border.

The diseconomies are ultimately measurable, at least in theory, in dollars and cents. Other disadvantages of scale are less measurable but no less real. Air pollution, for example, is a function of the dense concentration of automobiles. Similarly, water pollution is more amenable to control in areas where population is dispersed; there, given the will, the way is at least available.

One other factor that must be considered in any calculation of costs and benefits of urbanization is the social and economic cost of migration itself. To decide which new plant location is *really* most efficient, it is not enough to measure only the building and operating costs of the plant, although that has been the sole criterion of our laissez-faire philosophy. There are enormous costs, as well as appalling cruelties, in the forced displacement and migration of populations, whether it be Negroes from the south, mountaineers from Appalachia, or small businessmen from the declining regions of the Great Plains and the midwest. (In the 1950's, more than half of America's counties suffered a *net loss* of population.) Families lose their homes and savings and equities and property values along with their most deeply cherished associations; communities lose their tax base for public services; community institutions wither. Some of the migrants are too ill-prepared, too sick, or too poor to adjust to city life successfully; many of them wind up on welfare, and they burden every kind of institution. Yet these costs and losses are not borne by the industry locating the plant, but by people and communities, thereby entering no one's cost-benefit equation, no one's computations of efficiency. If they did so enter, then calculations of simple efficiency would no doubt show that, as a general rule, it is far from economical from the standpoint of the *whole* society to create new economic opportunities where the people are rather than allow existing communities to die while building other whole communities from the ground up in the name of "economic efficiency."

Moving from the physical to the social environment, hard data on disadvantages of scale are even more difficult to come by. Yet we know that as population in general is concentrated, so is poverty (large ghettos exist only in large urban concentrations) and crime, drug addiction, family breakdown and every other form of social pathology. It may be specious to argue that rural poverty is better than urban poverty when both are bad enough, yet the fact remains that the social evils associated with poverty tend to be mutually reinforcing when the poor are herded together in concentrated masses—as studies of public housing population, for example, have clearly shown. Racial tension and rioting are not limited to big cities, to be sure, but in their most terrifying aspects they seem to be. Perhaps most important of all, the problem of unemployment and underemployment of the urban poor appears all but insoluble in the largest urban complexes, because transportation systems just cannot economically link the inner cities where the poor live with the scattered suburban sites where the new jobs are being created. In smaller places, by contrast, people can even walk to work.

For all these reasons, it is not hard to accept as a hypothesis, at least, that our largest metropolitan agglomerations are less governable, less livable and economically less sound than smaller urban centers. If this is the case, then it should not matter whether the people like their agglomerations; in the public interest, they should be dispersed. However, what little evidence is available suggests that people do *not* like to live in unlivable places; they are there, in substantial proportion, against their will. A Gallup poll in 1968 showed that 56 per cent of Americans would choose a rural life, if they were free to choose, only 18 per cent a city and 25 per cent a suburb. Even a majority of the inhabitants of Paris—surely one of the most livable of large cities—were shown in a polling sample to prefer small town life. The polling methods may be suspect—the Parisians may have been comparing the city life they know to an idealized life in a romanticized rather than a real small town—but the results are indicative if not conclusive.

More important, from the standpoint of judging what people want, is the plain fact cited earlier that a high proportion of population migration is involuntary movement. Except for economic pressures, many, perhaps most, people would not move to the city in the first place. And they go home eagerly when the economic pressures shift. Each slump in the auto industry finds the Appalachians in Detroit heading back to the hills, and the first generation Puerto Ricans in New York City characteristically look upon themselves as transients who will return home as soon as they are financially able to do so.

It should be possible, within a reasonable time, to fashion a quantitative methodology that would supply at least some hard data on these questions—both on the economic costs and benefits of population concentration and on the reaction of human beings to the life styles they find themselves compelled to assume in centers of population density. Let us suppose that these data agree in confirming what intuition seems to tell us: that our largest metropolitan agglomerations have grown too far beyond the human scale, that their further growth should be arrested, and

248 The Crisis of the Cities

that their population should, if possible, be lessened. What then? Other countries have become concerned about population concentration—Great Britain, for instance, has been worried for two decades about the drift of people to the densely-settled south—without finding the means to check or reverse the concentration process. Is there any reason to think that the United States can do better?

Getting the Problem on the National Agenda

The first problem is one of gaining attention and getting interest. Henry David has remarked that, to keep its sanity, a society must practice "selective inattention"—it simply cannot attack all of its problems all at once. Population distribution is one of the problems that, until very recently at least, had been marked for inattention.

Over the last decade, only one leading figure in public life has made it his mission to sound the alarm on the question of population distribution policy. That was the recent Secretary of Agriculture, Orville L. Freeman. For the whole of his eight years in office, he led a personal crusade for what he initially called "rural areas development" and later came to call "rural-urban balance." Before a House Subcommittee in 1967, he said, "I say it is folly to stack up three-quarters of our people in the suffocating steel and concrete storage bins of the city, while a figurative handful of our fellow citizens rattle around in a great barn full of untapped resources and empty dreams." And then he got carried away: "The whiplash of economic necessity which today relentlessly drives desperate people into our huge cities must be lifted from the bleeding back of rural America."

Freeman's metaphors could be excused; no one listened to all his years of sober pleas and reasoned argument. True, President Johnson gave him moral support and himself made a speech or two on rural development and sent the Congress some minor measures, but the subject remained low on the president's priority list and even lower on the lists maintained by the Bureau of the Budget and other staff agencies that advise the president. As for the congressional committees on agriculture, who might have been expected to take some leadership, Freeman could not even get them to set up active subcommittees to consider rural development. Their concern for rural America extended to the price of agricultural commodities and the location of Department of Agriculture research stations, but not much further.

The nation's intellectual community, insofar as it was aware of the Freeman thesis, treated it with a disdain that blended into outright hostility. Teachers, writers, scholars, and editors for the most part live in cities; it is there that newspapers are published and television shows produced. The country's intelligentsia is wholly urban now; the voices that once sang of rural life, the Hamlin Garlands and Willa Cathers and Robert Frosts, are now stilled without replacement. One can stock a library with books on "the urban crisis," but try to fill a single shelf with works that deal in depth with the corresponding rural crisis!

A composite view of the urban intelligentsia toward rural America can be portrayed, with a touch of caricature, something like this: culturally, the cities have a monopoly, and have had since the Age of Pericles. Urban means urbane; rural means rustic. The theater, the concert hall, the museum are exclusively urban institutions; the countryside cannot produce the higher culture, and those who insist on living there are, by definition, both culturally unrefined and, what is worse, content to remain so. Economically, rural America is destined for decay; the economic forces that built the cities are too powerful to be reversed, even if it were desirable to do so. Freeman's "back to the farm" movement (which, for the record, is not what it was) is romantic nonsense that flies in the face of every economic reality. Sociologically, rural America is a backwater populated by misshapen characters out of Faulkner, given to choosing as their leaders men like George Wallace and Lester Maddox, and to hunting down civil rights workers and interring them on the banks of the Tallahoga river. Politically, it is time that rural America got its come-uppance; the farmers have been exploiting the cities far too long through outrageous programs that pay them enormous subsidies to cut production while the urban poor —and the rural poor as well—go hungry. Let the land grant colleges— the "cow colleges," that is—worry about the Podunks and the hicks and hayseeds who live there; we are an urban nation now.

This picture of the rural areas is not, unfortunately, wholly unrelated to reality. The fact is that the rural areas of the country *are* disadvantaged in many ways: they *are* culturally isolated (although their isolation has been drastically reduced by television and good roads); they *have* declined economically; their governmental and social institutions *are* often primitive and backward; racial exploitation *is* rife. But the cities are not all that superior. There is truth, too, in Freeman's counter-portrait of big cities as places of "congestion and confusion, crime and chaos, polluted air and dirty water, overcrowded schools and jobless ghettos, racial unrest . . . and riots in the streets."

But there are signs, now, that the intellectual world may at last be rediscovering rural and small town America and looking with fresh eyes upon the problem of rural-urban balance. Like so many other trends of current history, this one was set in motion in August 1965—in Watts. The analysts of that explosion, and those which followed, suddenly discovered that the problems they called urban had rural roots. "We're being overwhelmed," cried the urbanists. "Stop the migration. Get these people off our backs!" Joseph P. Lyford was among the first to see the rural-urban relationship. "Why," he asked in his study of a New York slum, *The Airtight Cage,* "do we treat the consequences and ignore the causes of massive and purposeless migration to the city? Why are we not developing new uses for those rural areas that are rapidly becoming depopulated? Why do we still instinctively deal with urban and rural America as if they were separate, conflicting interests when in fact neither interest can be served independently of the other?"

So the rural and the urban interest may have converged, finally, and it is out of such convergence that effective political coalitions are born and problems attain their place on the national agenda. The prospects for such a coalition are expressed most sharply in, of all places, the 1968 Republican platform. "Success with urban problems requires acceleration of rural development in order to stem the flow of people from the countryside to the city," reads the GOP's plank. The language is not without irony for the party of small town America and the party that enacted the Homestead Act. Should development of rural America be accelerated because rural people are suffering economically and, as God-fearing Americans, deserve a better fate? No. Should it be accelerated because rural development is a worthy goal on its own merits? Not at all. The whole subject is treated under the heading, "Crisis in the Cities"; rural development should be accelerated because the problems of the big cities, where the Democrats live, must be solved.

The leadership for a rural development coalition, also ironically, will have to come from those very cities. Groups with names like the Urban Coalition, the Urban Institute, and the Urban League will have to assume the burden of worrying about rural America, because there is no rural coalition, no rural institute, no rural league. Nobody has ever organized to speak for rural and small town people in the nation's councils as the United States Conference of Mayors, say, and the Urban Coalition speak for city people. Farm groups exist, to be sure, but their interest is the economic interest of farmers as producers, and most rural Americans— whatever the definition of the word "rural"—are not farmers but small town and small city dwellers. And they are not organized at all.

When rural America is saved, it is clear, it will be for the wrong reasons and under the wrong leadership. But that is better than not being saved at all.

The Outlines of a Program

The first requirement of any program to cope with America's population distribution ills—and the greater ills that are in prospect—must be a research component. As I observed earlier, those who would cope with the question have hardly any data at all on the consequences of population concentration, on the diseconomies and disadvantages of scale. (What data exist are summarized in the excellent 1968 report of the Advisory Commission on Intergovernmental Relations, *Urban and Rural America: Policies for Future Growth,* from which the figures used earlier in this article were taken.) Criteria do not exist for deciding how many people in a metropolitan area are too many or, at the other extreme, how much dispersal is too much dispersal.

Nevertheless, the country cannot afford to wait until all the analyses have been completed and all the facts are in. Action normally must precede research; it takes the actuality or imminence of action to attract scholars, and the funds required for their support, to an issue. The objective must be to move toward an ideal population distribution pattern while at the same time perfecting its design. And that is possible; in driving to the Pacific, one need not have a map of the entire route to know that he begins by heading westward.

We can begin by defining one objective—to bring to a halt, as nearly as possible, all involuntary migration. The purpose of governmental policy, then, would be to permit people to live and work where they want to live and work; if they prefer to move to the big city, well and good, but if they want to remain where they are the objective should be to bring the jobs to them. That would serve the dual end of protecting the big cities against the unwanted influx of the displaced poor, and of taking from the shoulders of the poor themselves—and the involuntary migrants who may not be poor—the burden of paying through their own hardship and economic loss for the adjustments in employment patterns brought about by technological advance.

This proposal will be confronted at once by the objection that some rural areas are too remote, too backward to be salvageable in any circumstances—that no matter how much they are subsidized they are beyond the reach of economic opportunity. I hide behind the qualifying phrase; forced migration should be brought "as nearly as possible" to a halt, and where a rural community lies beyond the possibility of redevelopment (the Appalachian "head of the hollow" communities come to mind) then it is by definition impossible to help. However, the number of people living in such communities is far smaller than is usually believed, if one understands that the jobs to be provided need only be *near,* not *at,* the community concerned. Commutation is a fact of life in this automobile age in rural areas as well as on Long Island, and rural people commonly travel daily to jobs within a radius of 25 to 50 miles. Circles with 25 mile radii drawn around small cities that have a proven economic potential—proven by the fact that they are growing now—cover the vast majority of the country's rural population east of the high plains, and if the circles are extended to 50 mile radii they blanket almost the whole country but for a few sparsely-settled sections of the Western mountains and the plains.

In the administration of the Appalachian Regional Development Act and the Public Works and Economic Development Act, growth centers are designated, and investment is concentrated in those places to stimulate the growth not just of the centers themselves but of the hinterlands they serve. Usually every rural settlement in an area being assisted is within reasonable commutation distance of a growth center. The commutation radius can be greatly increased, of course, by the improvement of road transportation, which is part of the rationale behind the heavy emphasis in the Appalachian program upon the construction of "developmental highways."

A population distribution policy, then, would seek to encourage an accelerated rate of growth in the smaller natural economic centers of the country's less densely populated regions, as the alternative to further concentration of population in the larger metropolitan areas. To effectuate such a policy, the present approaches would have to be extended in both breadth and depth. First, they would need to be expanded beyond Appalachia and the other presently-recognized redevelopment areas to cover all areas that are sources of out-migration. Second, they would need to be greatly improved in potency, so that they have a decisive impact upon the migration stream. Present federal programs are limited to public investment—roads, hospitals, vocational training schools, and so on—to strengthen the "infrastructure" of the nonmetropolitan areas, and loans and loan guarantees to encourage private investment. To these would have to be added the policy instrument of tax incentives that has proved so effective in stimulating and channeling investment both for war production and for peacetime economic growth. If an extra investment tax credit were available for defined types of new industry located in the places where the national population distribution policy called for it to be located, then jobs would be created where the people are rather than in places to which they have to migrate. Specific legislation to aid the development of new cities would also be helpful, although for the most part existing smaller cities should be the nuclei for urban growth. *Urban and Rural America: Policies for Future Growth* carefully catalogs a wide range of other possible program measures.

The rub will come, of course, when the Congress begins to write the language defining exactly the places eligible for benefits. While the objective of aiding sources of out-migration is simple enough in conception, the problem of drawing boundary lines is not. Specifically, growth centers that serve areas of out-migration would have to be included among the beneficiaries, even though the centers themselves were areas of in-migration. But only up to a certain point. A cutoff population figure would have to be established, at the point where a growth center is considered to have grown large enough, or at least to be able to attain its further growth under its own power. But given the old-fashioned booster psychology that still conditions the thinking of the leadership of even the largest cities, the Congress will find it difficult to designate any area, even the New York City area, as one that is destined—if national policy can bring it about— to stop growing. Real estate values still benefit from population increase, and wholesale and retail trade increase, no matter what the ancillary evils of population concentration. To most community influentials, bigger and bigger still mean greater and greater and richer and richer. A population distribution policy may therefore ultimately have to await a major shift in the national psychology.

When the country has to be jarred loose from a traditional outlook and shocked into a new one, the best means is often the institutional device that the United States has adopted from Great Britain—the royal commission. Such commissions have sometimes jarred us in the past; the Kerner commission, despite adverse circumstances, did so. Population distribution policy seems singularly appropriate as a subject for study by such a body. To its credit, the Senate passed a resolution in 1967 and again in 1969 to create a Commission on Balanced Economic Growth. It remains for the House of Representatives and the president to act.

Edward C. Banfield: The Unheavenly City

It is widely supposed that the serious problems of the cities are unprecedented both in kind and in magnitude. Between 1950 and 1960 there occurred the greatest population increase in the nation's history. At the

From *The Unheavenly City: The Nature and Future of Our Urban Crisis,* by Edward C. Banfield. Little, Brown and Company, Boston, 1968. Copyright © 1968, 1970 by Edward C. Banfield. Reprinted by permission.

same time, a considerable part of the white middle class moved to the newer suburbs, and its place in the central cities and older suburbs was taken by Negroes (and in New York by Puerto Ricans as well). These and other events—especially the civil rights revolution—are widely supposed to have changed completely the character of "the urban problem."

If the present situation is indeed radically different from previous ones, then we have nothing to go on in judging what is likely to happen next. At the very least, we face a crisis of uncertainty.

In a real sense, of course, *every* situation is unique. Even in making statistical probability judgments, one must decide on more or less subjective grounds whether it is reasonable to treat certain events as if they were the "same." The National Safety Council, for example, must decide whether cars, highways, and drivers this year are enough like those of past years to justify predicting future experience from past. From a logical standpoint, it is no more possible to decide this question in a purely objective way than it is to decide, for example, whether the composition of the urban population is now so different from what it was that nothing can be inferred from the past about the future. Karl and Alma Taeuber are both right and wrong when they write that we do not know enough about immigrant and Negro assimilation patterns to be able to compare the two and that "such evidence as we could compile indicates that it is more likely to be misleading than instructive to make such comparisons." They are certainly right in saying that one can only guess whether the pattern of Negro assimilation will resemble that of the immigrant. But they are wrong to imply that we can avoid making guesses and still compare things that are not known to be alike in all respects except one. (What, after all, would be the point of comparing immigrant and Negro assimilation patterns if we knew that the only difference between the two was, say, skin color?) They are also wrong in suggesting that the evidence indicates anything about what is likely to be instructive. If there were enough evidence to indicate that, there would be enough to indicate what is likely to happen; indeed, a judgment as to what is likely to be instructive is inseparable from one as to what is likely to happen. Strictly speaking, the Taeubers' statement expresses *their* guess as to what the evidence indicates.

The facts by no means compel one to take the view that the serious problems of the cities are unprecedented either in kind or in magnitude. That population growth in absolute numbers was greater in the decade 1950 to 1960 than ever before need not hold much significance from the present standpoint: American cities have frequently grown at fantastic rates (consider the growth of Chicago from a prairie village of 4,470 in 1840 to a metropolis of more than a million in fifty years). In any case, the population growth of the 1950's was not in the largest cities; most of them actually lost population in that decade. So far as numbers go, the migration of rural and small-town Negroes and Puerto Ricans to the large Northern cities in the 1950's was about equal to immigration from Italy in its peak decade. (In New York, Chicago, and many other cities in 1910, two out of every three schoolchildren were the sons and daughters of immigrants.) When one takes into account the vastly greater size and wealth of the cities now as compared to half a century or more ago, it is obvious that by the only relevant measure—namely, the number of immigrants relative to the capacity of the cities to provide for them and to absorb them—the movement in the 1950's from the South and from Puerto Rico was not large but small.

In many important respects, conditions in the large cities have been getting better. There is less poverty in the cities now than there has ever been. Housing, including that of the poor, is improving rapidly: one study predicts that substandard housing will have been eliminated by 1980. In the last decade alone the improvement in housing has been marked. At the turn of the century only one child in fifteen went beyond elementary school; now most children finish high school. The treatment of racial and other minority groups is conspicuously better than it was. When, in 1964, a carefully drawn sample of Negroes was asked whether, in general, things were getting better or worse for Negroes in this country, approximately eight out of ten respondents said "better."

If the situation is improving, why, it may be asked, is there so much talk of an urban crisis? The answer is that the improvements in performance, great as they have been, have not kept pace with rising expectations. In other words, although things have been getting better absolutely, they have been getting worse *relative to what we think they should be.* And this is because, as a people, we seem to act on the advice of the old jingle:

> *Good, better, best,*
> *Never let it rest*
> *Until your good is better*
> *And your better best.*

Consider the poverty problem, for example. Irving Kristol has pointed out that for nearly a century all studies, in all countries, have concluded that a third, a fourth, or a fifth of the nation in question is below the poverty line. "Obviously," he remarks, "if one defines the poverty line as that which places one-fifth of the nation below it, then one-fifth of the nation will always be below the poverty line." The point is that even if everyone is better off there will be as much poverty as ever, provided that the line is redefined upward. Kristol notes that whereas in the depths of the Depression, F.D.R. found only one-third of the nation "ill-housed, ill-clad, ill-nourished," Leon Keyserling, a former head of the Council of Economic Advisers, in 1962 published a book called *Poverty and Deprivation in the U.S.—the Plight of Two-Fifths of a Nation.*

Much the same thing has happened with respect to most urban problems. Police brutality, for example, would be a rather minor problem if we judged it by a fixed standard; it is a growing problem because we judge it by an ever more exacting standard. A generation ago the term meant hitting someone on the head with a nightstick. Now it often means something quite different:

> What the Negro community is presently complaining about when it cries "police brutality" is the more subtle attack on personal dignity that manifests itself in unexplainable questionings and searches, in hostile and insolent attitudes toward groups of young Negroes on the street, or in cars, and in the use of disrespectful and sometimes racist language . . . .

Following Kristol, one can say that if the "police brutality line" is defined as that which places one-fifth of all police behavior below it, then one-fifth of all police behavior will always be brutal.

The school dropout problem is an even more striking example. At the turn of the century, when almost everyone was a "dropout," the term and the "problem" did not exist. It was not until the 1960's, when for the first time a majority of boys and girls were graduating from high school and practically all had at least some high school training, that the "dropout problem" became acute. Then, although the dropout rate was still declining, various cities developed at least fifty-five separate programs to deal with the problem. Hundreds of articles on it were published in professional journals, the National Education Association established a special action project to deal with it, and the Commissioner of Education, the Secretary of Labor, and the President all made public statements on it. Obviously, if one defines the "inadequate amount of schooling line" as that which places one-fifth of all boys and girls below it, then one-fifth of all boys and girls will always be receiving an inadequate amount of schooling.

Whatever our educational standards are today, Wayland writes, they will be higher tomorrow. He summarizes the received doctrine in these words:

> Start the child in school earlier; keep him in school more and more months of the year; retain all who start to school for twelve to fourteen years; expect him to learn more and more during this period, in wider and wider areas of human experience, under the guidance of a teacher,

who has had more and more training, and who is assisted by more and more specialists, who provide an ever-expanding range of services, with access to more and more detailed personal records, based on more and more carefully validated tests.

To a large extent, then, our urban problems are like the mechanical rabbit at the racetrack, which is set to keep just ahead of the dogs no matter how fast they may run. Our performance is better and better, but because we set our standards and expectations to keep ahead of performance, the problems are never any nearer to solution. Indeed, if standards and expectations rise *faster* than performance, the problems may get (relatively) worse as they get (absolutely) better.

Some may say that since almost everything about the city can stand improvement (to put it mildly), this mechanical rabbit effect is a good thing in that it spurs us on to make constant progress. No doubt this is true to some extent. On the other hand, there is danger that we may mistake failure to progress as fast as we would like for failure to progress at all and, in panic, rush into ill-considered measures that will only make matters worse. After all, an "urban crisis" that results largely from rising standards and expectations is not the sort of crisis that, unless something drastic is done, is bound to lead to disaster. To treat it as if it were might be a very serious mistake.

This danger is greatest in matters where our standards are unreasonably high. The effect of too-high standards cannot be to spur us on to reach the prescribed level of performance sooner than we otherwise would, for that level is by definition impossible of attainment. At the same time, these standards may cause us to adopt measures that are wasteful and injurious and, in the long run, to conclude from the inevitable failure of these measures that there is something fundamentally wrong with our society. Consider the school dropout problem, for example. The dropout rate can never be cut to zero: there will always be some boys and girls who simply do not have whatever it takes to finish high school. If we continue to make a great hue and cry about the dropout problem after we have reached the point where all those who can reasonably be expected to finish high school are doing so, we shall accomplish nothing constructive. Instead, we shall, at considerable cost to ourselves, injure the boys and girls who cannot finish (the propaganda against being a dropout both hurts the morale of such a youngster and reduces his or her job opportunities) while creating in ourselves and in others the impression that our society is morally or otherwise incapable of meeting its obligations.

In a certain sense, then, the urban crisis may be real. By treating a spurious crisis as if it were real, we may unwittingly make it so.

8

Regulating the Economy

When it comes to the "dismal science" of economics, the layman is frequently at a loss to understand the sometimes esoteric economic theories. By the time he has mastered Adam Smith, he discovers he must go on to Keynes, Marshall, and then Samuelson, and then back to Milton Friedman. In the late 1960s and early 1970s, the layman was distressed and bewildered to find the nation, and not infrequently himself—as a consumer and worker—confronted by two seemingly contradictory forces: rising prices, the hallmark of an economic boom, and rising unemployment, the hallmark of an economic recession. No political battle cry is louder than "unemployment–recession"; when coupled with the cry of "inflation," it may turn the bewildered layman into an angry voter.

Major upturns and downturns in the economy are rarely in response to momentary fiscal and monetary policies. Blame for economic recession is no easier to assess than credit for prosperity. Yet a near certainty in American politics is that the voter will hold the man in the White House accountable. The Republican Party, long the stronghold of anti-inflationary monetary and fiscal policies, has had to live with the bitter memories of Democratic candidates running on the specter of "Hoover's Depression." To temper economic theory with political reality is not an easy choice, but by 1971 it was about the only choice available to Richard M. Nixon.

When Richard Nixon entered the White House in 1969 he inherited an economy over-heated by Vietnam deficits as well as by increasing expenditures for domestic programs, a deliberate policy of guns and butter. In short, Nixon was faced with the difficult task of ending an unpopular war, but ending it with prosperity and without runaway inflation. He chose to rely on traditional monetary and fiscal policies as the best method of cooling the economy. Under the leadership of Arthur Burns, Chairman of the Board of Governors of the Federal Reserve System, and with the cooperation of the Federal Reserve System itself, a tight money policy was adopted, the keystone of which was high interest rates on credit.

The early Nixon economic game plan also called for cooling off the economy by restraining the domestic side of the federal budget. However, the plan had both expected and unexpected results. There was an expected increase in unemployment, but there was also an unexpected rise in the consumer price index. Inflation continued to rise with rising unemployment. By 1971 unemployment had climbed to a recession level of six percent, and consumer prices were still going up, almost at the same rate as unemployment. By late 1970 the gross national product—the total volume of goods and services produced by the nation—had risen to over one trillion dollars, but in constant (uninflated) dollars, the GNP was declining. Industrial production declined throughout 1970. The negative balance of payments problem continued, but in April 1971, for the first time since the nineteenth century, we had a negative balance of trade. Finally the federal government ended the 1971 fiscal year with an approximate deficit of $20 billion, this in contrast to the initial estimate by the President of a $1.3 billion surplus.

By fall 1971 the prospects for fiscal 1972 were even gloomier. Corporate profits for early 1971 were down, and it was estimated that the 1972 federal budget would be in the red by about $28 billion, making it the largest peacetime deficit in American history. The game plan was not working.

Faced with such a dark economic picture, the Nixon Administration began to alter the plan. The President announced he was a "Keynesian" and promised a fiscal policy of pump-priming to stimulate the economy. Arthur Burns retreated from his earlier high interest rate position and began to move the Fed in the direction of increasing the money supply by reducing interest rates.

The new policies were too little and too late. Finally, on August 15, 1971, the President addressed the nation and announced a series of new economic policies, including a temporary 90-day freeze on wages and prices and the floating of the dollar in the international money market. The President had borrowed a page out of the works of liberal economist John Kenneth Galbraith.

Galbraith's position, as developed here in testimony before a congressional committee, endorses a permanent system of wage, price, and profit controls. But Galbraith proposes to control only that sector of the economy that does not respond exclusively to market conditions. In short, he adopts a position similar to that of Gardiner Means, who contends that inflation during an economic recession is caused by "administrative inflation." In testimony before the Joint Economic Committee in 1970, Means stated:

The most basic error underlying the Nixon game plan is the failure to recognize the reality of administrative prices and the consequent reliance on the conventional wisdom which says that the inflation of the last five or six years must have been the product of excess demand. . . . The second major error in assumption underlying the Nixon game plan grows out of the first. It is that, once excess demand is eliminated the basic inflation problem is one of momentum and that, if the momentum can be killed by a prolonged period of depressed operation, there can be a return to full employment without inflation.

I think no one would deny that with market prices, inflation generates a speculative momentum. . . . But this is short-lived and corrects itself when excess demand is avoided or eliminated.

The case of administrative inflation is quite different. It does not arise from the extra demand from customers or speculators. What can look like momentum to a classicist is not primarily momentum but something vastly more complex which does not grow out of an excess of demand by speculators or a sustained rise in prices. . . .

The reason administrative inflation can occur in the absence of excess demand and at less than full employment is quite simply explained. In our modern highly concentrated economy, management has significant discretionary power over prices, and labor has significant bargaining power over wages. In the more concentrated industries, market forces do not *determine* prices, they only limit the range within which prices and wages are set. . . . In the more concentrated industries, price administrators usually have the power to raise prices a few percentage points when there is no change in demand or costs. Likewise, organized labor often has the power to push wage increases a few percentage points beyond the level justified by increases in national productivity and living costs. These powers provide the basis for administrative inflation.

Since Galbraith rejects the break-up of our concentrated industries and unions as politically unrealistic, he recommends a permanent system of wage, price, and profit controls. In contrast to this position, President Nixon's 90-day freeze was temporary, although it was to be followed by wage and price stabilization. However, the wage and price stabilization was, according to the President, to be ". . . a way station on the road to free markets and free collective bargaining. . . ."

Public reaction to the President's August 1971 announcement was favorable. Yet important sectors of organized labor immediately questioned the equity of a freeze on the wages of workers without a corresponding freeze on the profits of management. Indeed, since the August announcement was coupled with a presidential recommendation of an investment tax credit for business, some labor leaders and economists concluded that the new economic policy was a narrowly drawn windfall for management. Economist Milton Friedman, considered close to the administration, applauded the President's tax proposals but characterized the wage and price freeze as cosmetic and not therapeutic, concluding that

"Sooner or later, and the sooner the better, it will end as all previous attempts to freeze prices and wages have ended, from the time of the Roman emperor Diocletian to the present, in utter failure and the emergence into the open of the suppressed inflation."*

The remaining articles presented in this chapter are from recent congressional testimony of Arthur F. Burns and George P. Shultz. While Burns has been a leading advocate of a tight money policy, his testimony indicates that he recognizes that monetary and fiscal policies alone cannot solve the dual problems of inflation and high unemployment. He reluctantly and cautiously recommends a mild incomes policy, but one without mandatory controls on wages and prices.

Shultz's testimony presents the Administration's basic fiscal policy, the annual federal budget. The 1972 budget request of $229 billion was called a "full employment budget." This is a term borrowed from economists and means that expenditures would equal revenues if the economy were at full employment. However, the federal budget for 1972 did not anticipate full employment and it projected a deficit of $11.6 billion, a deficit that was to more than double by the end of the fiscal year. Much of Shultz's testimony discusses the wisdom of relying exclusively on monetary and fiscal policies as methods for combating inflation and high unemployment. When the question of wage and price controls came up, Shultz was even less willing than Burns to recommend their adoption.

When a Republican president announces that he is a Keynesian, a chapter in American history has ended; so too, presumably, has one of the dividing lines between our two national parties. No longer will we debate whether it is appropriate for the federal government to assume a role in maintaining a healthy national economy. That role is now recognized as a responsibility. But the debate in 1972 will center around the degree of federal responsibility and around the most appropriate measures to achieve the goal of national prosperity. In dealing with the issue of administrative inflation, the Democrats would face formidable opposition from organized labor and the Republicans from the business community. Neither party is likely to meet this issue head-on.

---

* *Newsweek, Magazine* August 30, 1971, p. 22.

John Kenneth Galbraith: Wage
and Price Controls

Let me begin by summarizing matters relating to the economy as they now stand. First, unemployment is now at 5 percent of the labor force and in fact considering the lag in the statistics, and the nature of the statistics themselves, the underenumeration of those who are not seeking work, who have withdrawn from the labor force because they found the search for jobs hopeless, probably somewhat higher. Production has been stable or declining for many months. Inflation is at a record rate and duration since the years immediately following World War II. The housing industry despite a housing shortage is, as the chairman pointed out, deeply depressed. The financial markets have just had their most severe break in 40 years. This is held to be in accordance with the game plan of the administration or as one of the members of the Council of Economic Advisers said yesterday, to be slightly below the game plan. It is, I think we may safely conclude, not a good game plan.

We have this disenchanting combination of circumstances because a theory of economic management has been tried, fully tried and found wanting. It is always unwise to put theory to a test if it is unsound. The theory was that control of the monetary supply, as most eloquently advocated by Prof. Milton Friedman of the University of Chicago, could, if combined with a reasonable restrictive fiscal policy bring stable prices and without unduly depressive effects on the economy. This doctrine discounted the ability of large corporations and strong unions to shove up prices and wages under conditions even of severe monetary and fiscal restraint. The proponents of this view are men who believe deeply in the market. Not remarkably among men of deep belief, they substitute faith for reality. Though this may be theologically commendable, it can be very hard on the other people who must suffer for their faith.

Wages do shove up prices and prices do pull up wages in the modern highly organized economy. Monetary restraint, while it works rather ruth-

From "To Extend The Defense Production Act of 1965," Hearings before House Committee on Banking and Currency, 91st Congress, 2nd Session. June 1970. Government Printing Office, 1971. Mr. Galbraith is Warburg Professor of Economics, Harvard University.

lessly for the smaller businessman, works very well for the smaller businessman, and especially as I have noted for the home construction industry, does not so directly affect General Motors, General Electric, United States Steel or the other very large corporations. These firms have large cash flows, are favored visitors at the banks and can pass their higher interest rates on to the public. This is precisely the part of the economy which gives leadership on the wage-price spiral. As Dr. McCracken pointed out yesterday in Europe, farm prices, prices of services generally at the moment are stable or even coming down, but prices in the organized sector of the economy—prices in the sector of the economy where large corporations bargain with strong unions—are still going up. In saying a year ago last January that it had no concern for wages and prices the administration may well have done as much to promote inflation as it accomplished in the ensuing 18 months to control it.

The administration has taken extensive refuge in the fact that it inherited an inflation. Dr. McCracken again recurred to that theme yesterday in Europe.

While this is true, economic policy will become excessively easy and attract an inferior class of talent, if it is always possible to blame the failures of one administration through much or all of its life on the errors of the previous administration. Those who are responsible, unhappily, must assume responsibility. But the administration should not be blamed for everything. The financial markets to which they fell heir, to which the administration fell heir, were already in an advanced state of insanity.

The glamour stocks, the jerry-built conglomerates, the go-go funds, the conviction that God had arranged matters so that men of sedentary inclination could get rich sitting down in the branch office of a brokerage firm—all of these things invited an eventual day of reckoning. Some of the recent unemployment has been in the aerospace industries. We cannot criticize the administration for this unemployment, if one applauds as I have the need for cutbacks in military indulgence. Finally, the administration inherited an unnecessary war which makes everything much more difficult, although here Mr. Nixon does seem disposed to establish his own responsibility.

Within the framework of its approved measures, monetary and fiscal policy, there is nothing that the administration can now do. The inflation with its punishing impact on those with fixed incomes, on the public services, and on those who are promised a real dollar for dollar return on their savings, that punishment still continues. To ease interest rates and relax further on the budget—some relaxation of the budget is inevitable from falling revenues—would accelerate this inflation. To continue the present policy is to continue for some period the present remarkable combination of inflation and recession. We have long known, Mr. Chairman, that under some circumstances you can have your cake and eat it too. We are now learning from this combination of inflation and recession that you cannot have your cake and not be able to buy it either.

To tighten up sufficiently on money and the budgets to end inflation would, we now know, require a very serious recession. So, disagreeable as may be the prospect, there must be a search for a new line of policy. This new line of policy must be actual not oratorical, honest, not fraudulent. Those of us who have long argued that monetary and fiscal measures are insufficient can better aid this process, and do more to ease feelings generally by welcoming the redeemed sinners than by praising our own prescience. However, a certain number of the redemptions to date are of men who seem determined to pass from a wrong policy to a fraudulent one.

That, for example, tempers my own applause for the somewhat belated conversion of Dr. Arthur Burns to the belief that wage and price relationships are important for inflation.

Specifically the newest fraud is to say that wage price interaction causes inflation and that we must recognize this fact and then having established this fact to say that we must carefully do nothing about it and that we can call the resulting inaction an incomes policy. . . .

If the economic problem is serious, and it is, the responding action must be serious. Wage claims now in prospect provide for the present inflation the expected increase in inflation, a safety margin for unexpected inflation and beyond that for a hoped-for increase in real wages. These wage claims will be disinflated only if there is a firm promise to the unions of price stability. Nothing can now be accomplished by the most massive deployment of public oratory, whatever the added component of mild jawboning, strong jawboning, billingsgate or old-fashioned competitive hog calling. Nor are these dignified devices for conducting the affairs of the modern State. Nor do they become either useful or effective by calling them incomes policy, which is the present fashion.

The proper course is, under legislative authorization . . . to freeze all prices and wages as of some recent date. I think, myself, this should be for a period of about 6 months. . . .

This assures all concerned that the spiral, the wage price spiral has been brought to an end. Where prices and wages are set by the market rather than by corporate and union power, there is no need to continue the freeze. This means that all retail prices, all farm prices, all wages not covered by collective bargaining contracts, all prices of firms employing fewer than 100 or possibly even 1,000 workers should be promptly released from control. The point is important and I would like to stress it. Where neither corporations nor unions have power to shove up prices and wages, the Government obviously doesn't need to prevent the shoving. That is what we are concerned with here. Some of these prices and wages will rise, and some of them will fall, but that will be in response to a market decision.

One needs to control through public action those prices and wages that are subject to strong private control.

The 6 months should be used in working out with corporations and unions a more permanent system of restraint. Here I depart in my recommendation more than slightly from that in the legislation. This includes the elimination of inequities resulting from arbitrary imposition of any freeze. Different unions in particular will be caught in various contractual states in their bargaining and the difference between a union that has just completed bargaining for a wage increase and one that has not yet got it is indefensible. This sort of thing will have to be ironed out. There will have to be provision for the further wage increases that can be tolerated that are consistent with expected gains in productivity and therefore not damaging to price stability. From this stage on we should notice that the wage increases that the worker gets will be real. If the policy is to be equitable and even defensible there must also be provision in industries of exceptionally high profits for either price reductions or surrender of excess profits. One cannot have a policy that holds wages in line but does nothing about such profits.

I would also suggest that executive salaries should also be frozen and it would be good for the Congress to suspend the unfortunate bonanza which the last tax bill gave to earned income, as it is called, in the upper executive salary brackets.

Needless to say, all of this action needs to be combined . . . with a speedy liquidation of our adventure or misadventure in Indochina. This is necessary to restore confidence and our reputation for good sense. I would, of course, be opposed to a price control policy that was for the purpose of fighting this war more efficiently.

Once prices and wages are under control, interest rates can be drastically reduced. These interest rates now include a large percentage for expected inflation. When one sees an interest rate of 10 percent, 6 or 7 percent of that is for the expected increase in prices during the coming year, only 3 or 4 percent is for interest as we commonly think of it.

Especially as the end of the war comes in view, a modest deficit in the budget could also be tolerated. We notice that the end of the war would also release resources for the urgent civilian use and relieve pressures there. Price and wage controls are not pleasant. Life often involves a choice between unpleasant alternatives. There is no reason why economists should be spared.

The limited controls that I have advocated . . . will not be pleasant to administer—the administrative problem must be taken seriously. But these controls, when the public interest is weighed, are by far the least unpleasant, by far the most practical of the various courses of action available. They should not require a vast administrative organization in this limited form. One should notice that only a few hundred collective bargaining contracts and a few thousand larger corporations will be under surveillance.

Corporations can be accorded freedom for individual price adjustments within a general level of return. There are other simplifications of the same sort that are possible. Let me point out again that all one is concerned with here is stopping the gross spiral of large wage increases and large price increases to cover them. We are not concerned with establishing precise price stability.

For all of this, no great organization is needed. A few hundred people would suffice.

It is worth bearing in mind that it is comparatively easy to fix and keep surveillance over prices that are already fixed. That is true of the prices of steel; it is true of the wages in—say—the steelworkers' contract. Still, I do not want to minimize the task. It requires much more effort than doing nothing. But public officials are paid to work and try harder, especially where it saves in public suffering. My friends in the administration will have spared themselves the need for making those endless and terrible explanations as to why inflation continues, unemployment increases, but nothing should be done.

With these actions, limited control, easier interest rates, a greatly lessened reliance on monetary policy and, of course, liquidation of the Indochina mistake, the economic crisis will be largely over. There is nothing about our present economic situation that is unmanageable. Our trouble lies in the effort to manage the economy without having recourse to the obviously relevant remedies. If the results of this effort are bad we should not be surprised.

Mrs. Sullivan (presiding): Professor, you have given us very interesting testimony, spread through with your seriousness and humor. I have a few questions to ask.

Professor Galbraith, outside of money for such things as housing, or for any other purpose, at reasonable rates of interest, what is scarce enough to make price control work effectively?

Dr. Galbraith: Well, scarcity, Madam Chairman, is not I think the decisive factor. The decisive factor is that we have within the price system great corporate power. General Motors, Ford, Chrysler have extensive power over the prices they charge for automobiles, which they exercise in conjunction with the prices charged by the big foreign firms. And the UAW has extensive power in bargaining for wages. It is this interaction of prices and wages, not scarcity which is the source of the inflationary pressure.

Mrs. Sullivan: If you are going to set ceilings at the highest level prices have reached, all you are saying is that they just simply can't go any higher. But a price control program at this stage could not roll back prices or wages, could it?

Dr. Galbraith: I don't think so. I think you are quite right on that. At various times in the past rollbacks have been talked about but it is a hard thing to do. I certainly wouldn't recommend it. I do think there needs to be some provision for the special case of the industry which is making very high profits. Here it is very hard to tell the union, "You stay within the guidelines while the profits remain at these levels." The answer is to do one of two things. Either have an excess profits tax . . . or have a provision for passing some of those profits on to the public in the form of lower prices. That is the only exception to acceptance of past prices I would make.

Mrs. Sullivan: . . . [W]hat would you have to do about executive salaries and policeman's pay and everything else where the fellow may have been left behind on the so-called wage inflation?

Dr. Galbraith: . . . I would urge that there be simply a freeze on executive salaries. Better still, would be repeal of the very bad provision of the last tax act reducing their maximum tax to 50 percent. This was an outrageous bonanza. Whoever sold the Congress on the idea that corporate pay of half a million dollars a year was earned income was really too good a salesman.

Mrs. Sullivan: Now we get to the policeman's pay and everything else where the fellow may have been left behind on the so-called wage inflation, where they haven't caught up.

Dr. Galbraith: I wouldn't control those. I do not think there is any danger of any municipality in the United States overpaying its public employees. I wouldn't control those wages at all. . . .

Mrs. Sullivan: If you were the price administrator under this bill we are considering, what would you do first insofar as reducing inflationary pressures are concerned?

Dr. Galbraith: I would first, Madam Chairman, put into effect the immediate freeze, subject to the withdrawal action that I have mentioned. The immediate need is to break the whole structure of inflationary expectations. By which I mean the expectations that prices are going to go up 6, 8, 10 percent next year, therefore, you must have wage increases and interest rates that cover that kind of a price increase and must so plan your prices. Nothing else is going to break those expectations apart from serious depression. The game plan of the administration if I may use that somewhat fanciful term is not a cure. I said the other day—one is always in danger of repeating his own humor—that there has been no game plan like this since the Rose Bowl game of 1929, when a man by the name of Roy Riegle ran 75 yards to the wrong goal line.

These inflationary expectations are only going to be changed by the kind of action which we are talking about here this morning.

Mrs. Sullivan: Would it be possible if we just simply froze everything as is, to police that?

Dr. Galbraith: No, not indefinitely. I would urge doing it only for a short period of time, during this time you must also get rid of the inequities that you froze into the system as well as getting rid of the controls on all the prices and wages that you really do not need to fix.

Mrs. Sullivan: What consideration would you give to the unemployment consequences of any price control action?

Dr. Galbraith: I would attribute great importance to this aspect.

When you are no longer relying on these outrageous interest rates for your control then you can ease the housing market, you can ease up on loans for smaller businessmen; you can ease up on consumer credit terms; on municipal borrowing; you can also ease up on the budget and public employment. All of this will have a strongly favorable employment effect.

Price and wage restraint takes the problem of inflation control off the back of the unemployed—that, at least, is one way of putting it.

Mrs. Sullivan: I realize we are in the craziest kind of economic dilemma that I can remember, with high prices, rising unemployment both at the same time.

When you look at the Consumer Price Index you see that a good part of the increase in the past year has been the reflection of higher medical fees, higher hospital costs, higher public transportation and such, much higher homeownership costs reflecting the higher mortgage interest rates and local taxes.

What can price control do to bring these kinds of prices down?

Dr. Galbraith: I am awfully glad you mentioned this business about hospital costs. I should have had a paragraph in my prepared statement on that.

The higher hospital costs are not part of the general pattern of inflation in my view. They are related to two other factors. The first has been a catching-up going in this area, which has been going on a long time. I am not talking about doctors. I am talking about nurses, technicians, custodial personnel, janitors, and so on. It has been long a supposition that because those people were doing such good work, such fine compassionate work, they would be paid handsomely in the next world. So they could be paid low rates in this world. This doctrine no longer holds—perhaps not surprisingly.

So those wages, what we pay in the hospitals, what we pay for people who do the very important job of looking after the sick, have been catching up. It is time they did. There is also the very special problem arising from the shortage of medical personnel. This has led to a certain amount of profiteering under medicare and medicaid in regular practices and that has also affected medical costs. These are all causes of higher prices and of higher index levels. These prices would not be reached by anything I have suggested here this morning. You correctly put your finger on that.

One other factor, of course, is more expensive types of hospital care, better diagnosis and so forth. The remedy for the high cost of medical care is a better system of helping people pay their medical costs and better administration of medicare and medicaid. I think there would be wide agreement on the need for this. And one takes care of the problem of shortage of nurses and the shortage of technicians and particularly the shortage of doctors, by spending a lot more money on medical education.

Mrs. Sullivan: I gather from this that hospital, medical costs, and so forth could not come under any kind of a freeze.

Dr. Galbraith: I wouldn't touch it for a moment. There is no remedy for anything of that sort here.

Mrs. Sullivan: What about transportation costs?

Dr. Galbraith: I am addressing myself and to where one has the inter-action between strong unions and strong corporations and where this leads the inflationary spiral.

Mrs. Sullivan: I realize that. My $64 question is the one which has caused I believe every price controller untold agony and abuse. Do you impose price controls on food products when the raw agricultural commodity is still far below parity and if you wait until it gets up to parity and above it what price controller can get away with ceilings on potatoes, meat?

Dr. Galbraith: I wouldn't—again those would be excluded commodities.

Prices of farm products are set in the market. No individual farmer can fix the prices at which he sells his products. The Department of Agriculture has somewhat more authority in these matters but it isn't necessary to have price control authority to control the Department of Agriculture— or it shouldn't be necessary.

There being no market power this is not part of the area where one needs to intervene. Farmers have always gone to some length to insure that they don't have to deal with unions, either, as we know.

Mrs. Sullivan: I think one of the first things that people would want to see controls put on would be food. For instance, a box of cereal about 15 months ago cost 31 cents; today it is 45.

Dr. Galbraith: I would urge that in this part of the economy the proper action is fiscal and monetary restraint. Where the market works as it does generally for agricultural products, one should act through general measures.

Mrs. Sullivan: I think maybe you can remember back, and I do, too, to the Korean situation. The day troops were ordered into action, immediately the food costs went up, store managers changed every price on every can or box or item on their shelves and so did every other retailer. How are we going to stop this constant spiral with prices of these kinds of products—food, clothing—that people notice most of all?

Dr. Galbraith: As I say, again, there are those temporary effects, but I do not regard this as the initiating force in inflation.

Mrs. Sullivan: Thank you very much. . . .

Mr. Ashley: I have just two short questions if I may, Madam Chairman. On page 7 you say prices and wages are set by the market rather than by corporate—there is no need to continue the freeze. That means all retail prices and farm prices should be released from control, and so forth. Isn't there a distinction to be made between wages and prices at the commodity level in agricultural products, and wages and prices in the food processing industry which takes these raw materials and turns them into the foods offered to the public at the retail level? It would seem to me there certainly would be many firms particularly in the processing and retailing of food that would be included in the 100 or 1,000 firms that you suggest.

Dr. Galbraith: That is entirely possible.

Mr. Ashley: Finally, you say 6 months should be available for working out with the corporations and the unions a more permanent system of restraint. I am not sure I entirely understand why 6 months. I certainly don't understand fully the more permanent system of restraint. You alluded to the possibility of compulsory arbitration or something of that kind, didn't you?

Dr. Galbraith: No. The 6 months is arbitrary. I took that from Mr. Roosa, as a matter of fact. If I had to say why it should be 4 months or 6 months, rather than a year, I would have some difficulty.

Mr. Ashley: What happens during the time period?

Dr. Galbraith: During those 6 months, one does two things. One, first of all, irons out all the inequities in the wage structure that are a result of the particular timing of the freeze, the fact that some union gets frozen at the end of its contract period. This sort of thing has to be worked out. Beyond that, one works out jointly with labor and management to establish the improvement factor that can be allowed within a framework of stable prices. This becomes the rule that one adheres to from then on. I would like to be quite frank about one thing: I think if we are going to have full employment, stable prices, we must have some system of wage and price restraint on a continuing basis. That is the lesson of this recent flirtation with the free market, it doesn't work.

Mr. Ashley: Yes. I think I begin to see what you mean by continuing the system of restraint on both wages and prices. I do wonder who would be the umpire in such a system?

Dr. Galbraith: There is no doubt—it is the Government.

Mr. Ashley: And whether this wouldn't, in effect, lead to compulsory arbitration?

Dr. Galbraith: It is possible compulsory arbitration would have to be used on occasion here. I wouldn't exclude it. There is no question as to who the umpire is, the Government has to be the umpire.

Mr. Ashley: Thank you very much.

Dr. Galbraith: This is a system which puts added power in the state, let us not duck it, it does.

Mr. Ashley: I find myself in very substantial agreement with you. I just think we want to be perfectly clear on these matters. Thank you.

Mrs. Sullivan: Mr. Blackburn.

Mr. Blackburn: Thank you, Madam Chairman. I appreciate your candor in saying you always felt some form of wage and price controls were necessary. I was going to begin by asking you if there had ever been a year in which you didn't favor wage and price controls. Apparently, you think this is a permanent thing we need in our economy, is that so?

Dr. Galbraith: Yes. If you are going to reconcile price stability with high employment, which I believe most people want, you are not going to accomplish it by prayer, and it is not going to be accomplished by speeches about the market, and it is not going to be accomplished by Milton Friedman. It is only going to be accomplished by doing something about it. We are adult people, we should face the consequences. We should not deny that this means a larger exercise of public power.

Mr. Blackburn: I think we also look toward a productive society. Certainly our economy is on a par, if not above the economic well-being of other economies.

Dr. Galbraith: I thoroughly agree with you and this is one of the reasons for my recommendation. The present policy has given us declining production for a great many months. So I welcome your support on that score, too.

Mr. Blackburn: What I am trying to say is that our economy has been a free market economy essentially and those controlled economies have never been able to match our performance. So I am not so interested in dialog as I am in performance. Performance has certainly been above that of controlled economy. I am certainly amazed that someone should say we should move toward a controlled economy.

Dr. Galbraith: I would amend only one point. I would say that the control that we are talking about here really substitutes public control for what is now the private control by the corporations and unions. So that one is really changing one form of control for another. And while the productivity of the economy would be increased, the degree of control will not be substantially altered as it passes from private to public authority.

Mr. Blackburn: Let me first answer one of your observations, that the present policies have reduced our productivity. I think that is true. That is one of the purposes of our present policy. I don't like it, but that is one of the peripheral disadvantages of trying to combat inflation. You admit yourself that if we did have the power to immediately freeze all prices and all of the wages in the country—and of course, we are a Government of men and not of God—so if the man in the White House himself were to stand with you at his side and announce from henceforth and forever after there will be no increases in wages or prices for at least 6 months, the only way he can enforce that is with some police machinery. If the President were deluged with 50,000 complaints the week afterward, that prices were raised on a great myriad of things that we sell in our economy, it is going to mean the establishment of a very vast police machinery to control it.

Now, it is easy to say, let's freeze wages and prices, but what about the machinery necessary to enforce that freeze.

Dr. Galbraith: I have dealt with this previously, I do not think that the enforcement machinery would be all that difficult. As I said I would get rid of all the market controlled prices and all wages not covered by collective bargaining agreements. You don't have to worry about the individual farmer's prices. He can't raise his prices. He has to take what the market gives him. You know that as well as I do. So you are left with a manageable number of collective bargaining contracts and a manageable number of corporations. For this you don't need a vast organization.

Mr. Blackburn: Let me inject this question at this point—

Dr. Galbraith: Let me say just one word. I would hope, Congressman, you wouldn't want to describe the unemployment that comes from the present reduction in production, the present effort to pursue stability as wholly peripheral. When a million people lose their jobs I would like to persuade you that this is not a purely peripheral effect.

Mr. Blackburn: I was not describing unemployment as being peripheral. I was saying the loss of production was one of the peripheral losses that we have to suffer with. I am just as concerned about unemployment as anyone.

Would you suggest that there be some curbing of power on the part of the unions or management? You have the monopoly union power. Do you feel that perhaps a combination of business enterprises also constitutes some form of business monopoly?

Dr. Galbraith: Well, there is an old economic formula that a great many economists have adopted, they say: Sure, unions have the power to shove up prices, they have the power to get wage set limits that are a threat to prices, and corporations have the power to shove up prices which then invite union demands. The proper action is to cut loose with the antitrust laws—break up the unions, break up General Motors, and so forth. I regard this as pure romance. It isn't going to happen. Since I like to be practical, associate myself with things that should be done, I reject such nonsense out of hand. There is a function for the antitrust laws but they do not serve any purpose in this area.

Mr. Blackburn: When you say it is not going to happen as regards the breakup of big power, whether business or labor, you mean as a matter of practical politics?

Dr. Galbraith: That is right.

Mr. Blackburn: You are not arguing an abstract theory that a breakup of monopoly power in business or labor might not be desirable.

Dr. Galbraith: In the American economy about half of our production comes from 1,000 large corporations. The country doesn't suddenly one day decide that half its economy is illegal and break it up.

Since I consider this unlikely to happen, I am not going to advocate it as a solution. . . .

Richard M. Nixon: Our Best Days Lie Ahead

Good evening.

I have addressed the Nation a number of times over the past two years on the problems of ending a war. Because of the progress we have made toward achieving that goal, this Sunday evening is an appropriate time for us to turn our attention to the challenges of peace.

America today has the best opportunity in this century to achieve two of its greatest ideals: to bring about a full generation of peace, and to create a new prosperity without war.

This not only requires bold leadership ready to take bold action—it calls forth the greatness in a great people.

From *Weekly Compilation of Presidential Documents,* Monday, August 23, 1971, Vol. 7, No. 34, pp. 1168–1172. Government Printing Office, Washington, D.C., 1971. The above address was made by President Nixon in Washington, D.C., on August 15, 1971.

Prosperity without war requires action on three fronts: We must create more and better jobs; we must stop the rise in the cost of living; we must protect the dollar from the attacks of international money speculators.

We are going to take that action—not timidly, not half-heartedly, and not in piecemeal fashion. We are going to move forward to the new prosperity without war as befits a great people—all together, and along a broad front.

The time has come for a new economic policy for the United States. Its targets are unemployment, inflation and international speculation. This is how we are going to attack them.

First, on the subject of jobs. We all know why we have an unemployment problem. Two million workers have been released from the Armed Forces and defense plants because of our success in winding down the war in Vietnam. Putting those people back to work is one of the challenges of peace, and we have begun to make progress. Our unemployment rate today is below the average of the four peacetime years of the 1960s.

But we can and must do better than that.

The time has come for American industry, which has produced more jobs at higher real wages than any other industrial system in history to embark on a bold program of new investment in production for peace.

To give that system a powerful new stimulus, I shall ask the Congress, when it reconvenes after its summer recess, to consider as its first priority the enactment of the Job Development Act of 1971.

I will propose to provide the strongest short-term incentive in our history to invest in new machinery and equipment that will create new jobs for Americans: A 10 percent Job Development Credit for one year, effective as of today, with a 5 percent credit after August 15, 1972. This tax credit for investment in new equipment will not only generate new jobs; it will raise productivity and it will make our goods more competitive in the years ahead.

Second, I will propose to repeal the 7 percent excise tax on automobiles, effective today. This will mean a reduction in price of about $200 per car. I shall insist that the American auto industry pass this tax reduction on to the nearly 8 million customers who are buying automobiles this year. Lower prices will mean that more people will be able to afford new cars, and every additional 100,000 cars sold means 25,000 new jobs.

Third, I propose to speed up the personal income tax exemptions scheduled for January 1, 1973 to January 1, 1972—so that taxpayers can deduct an extra $50 for each exemption one year earlier than planned. This increase in consumer spending power will provide a strong boost to the economy in general and to employment in particular.

The tax reductions I am recommending, together with the broad upturn of the economy which has taken place in the first half of this year, will move us strongly forward toward a goal this nation has not reached since 1956, 15 years ago—prosperity with full employment in peacetime.

Looking to the future, I have directed the Secretary of the Treasury to recommend to the Congress in January new tax proposals for stimulating research and development of new industries and new technologies to help provide the 20 million new jobs that America needs for the young people who will be coming into the job market in the next decade.

To offset the loss of revenue from these tax cuts which directly stimulate new jobs, I have ordered today a $4.7 billion cut in Federal spending.

Tax cuts to stimulate employment must be matched by spending cuts to restrain inflation. To check the rise in the cost of government, I have ordered a postponement of pay raises and a 5 percent cut in government personnel.

I have ordered a 10 percent cut in foreign economic aid.

In addition, since the Congress has already delayed action on two of the great initiatives of this Administration, I will ask Congress to amend my proposals to postpone the implementation of Revenue Sharing for three months and Welfare Reform for one year.

In this way, I am reordering our budget priorities to concentrate more on achieving full employment.

The second indispensable element of the new prosperity is to stop the rise in the cost of living.

One of the cruelest legacies of the artificial prosperity produced by war is inflation. Inflation robs every American. The 20 million who are retired and living on fixed incomes are particularly hard hit. Homemakers find it harder than ever to balance the family budget. And 80 million wage-earners have been on a treadmill. In the four war years between 1965 and 1969 your wage increases were completely eaten up by price increases. Your paychecks were higher, but you were no better off.

We have made progress against the rise in the cost of living. From the high point of six percent a year in 1969, the rise in consumer prices has been cut to four percent in the first half of 1971. But just as is the case in our fight against unemployment, we can and we must do better than that.

The time has come for decisive action—action that will break the vicious circle of spiraling prices and costs.

I am today ordering a freeze on all prices and wages throughout the United States for a period of 90 days. In addition, I call upon corporations to extend the wage-price freeze to all dividends.

I have today appointed a Cost of Living Council within the Government. I have directed this Council to work with leaders of labor and business to set up the proper mechanism for achieving continued price and wage stability after the 90-day freeze is over.

Let me emphasize two characteristics of this action: First, it is temporary. To put the strong, vigorous American economy into a permanent straitjacket would lock in unfairness; it would stifle the expansion of our free enterprise system. And second, while the wage-price freeze will be backed by Government sanctions, if necessary, it will not be accompanied by the establishment of a huge price control bureaucracy. I am relying on the voluntary cooperation of all Americans—each one of you—workers, employers, consumers—to make this freeze work.

Working together, we will break the back of inflation, and we will do it without the mandatory wage and price controls that crush economic and personal freedom.

The third indispensable element in building the new prosperity is closely related to creating new jobs and halting inflation. We must protect the position of the American dollar as a pillar of monetary stability around the world.

In the past seven years, there has been an average of one international monetary crisis every year. Who gains from these crises? Not the workingman; not the investors; and not the real producers of wealth. The gainers are international money speculators. Because they thrive on crises, they help to create them.

In recent weeks, the speculators have been waging an all-out war on the American dollar. The strength of a nation's currency is based on the strength of that nation's economy—and the American economy is by far the strongest in the world. Accordingly, I have directed the Secretary of the Treasury to take the action necessary to defend the dollar against the speculators.

I have directed Secretary Connally to suspend temporarily the convertibility of the dollar into gold or other reserve assets, except in amounts and conditions determined to be in the interest of monetary stability and in the best interests of the United States.

Now, what is this action, which is very technical? What does it mean for you?

Let me lay to rest the bugaboo of what is called devaluation.

If you want to buy a foreign car or take a trip abroad, market conditions may cause your dollar to buy slightly less. But if you are among the overwhelming majority of Americans who buy American-made products in America, your dollar will be worth just as much tomorrow as it is today.

The effect of this action, in other words, will be to stabilize the dollar.

Now, this action will not win us any friends among the international money traders. But our primary concern is with the American workers, and with fair competition around the world.

To our friends abroad, including the many responsible members of the international banking community who are dedicated to stability and the flow of trade, I give this assurance: The United States has always been, and will continue to be, a forward-looking and trustworthy trading partner. In full cooperation with the International Monetary Fund and those who trade with us, we will press for the necessary reforms to set up an urgently needed new international monetary system. Stability and equal treatment is in everybody's best interest. I am determined that the American dollar must never again be a hostage in the hands of the international speculators.

I am taking one further step to protect the dollar, to improve our balance of payments, and to increase sales for Americans. As a temporary measure, I am today imposing an additional tax of 10 percent on goods imported into the United States. This is a better solution for international trade than direct controls on the amount of imports.

This import tax is a temporary action. It isn't directed against any other country. It is an action to make certain that American products will not be at a disadvantage because of unfair exchange rates. When the unfair treatment is ended, the import tax will end as well.

As a result of these actions, the product of American labor will be more competitive, and the unfair edge that some of our foreign competition has had will be removed. That is a major reason why our trade balance has eroded over the past fifteen years.

At the end of World War II the economies of the major industrial nations of Europe and Asia were shattered. To help them get on their feet and to protect their freedom, the United States has provided over the past 25 years $143 billion in foreign aid. This was the right thing for us to do.

Today, largely with our help, they have regained their vitality. They have become our strong competitors, and we welcome their success. But now that other nations are economically strong, the time has come for them to bear their fair share of the burden of defending freedom around the world. The time has come for exchange rates to be set straight and for the major nations to compete as equals. There is no longer any need for the United States to compete with one hand tied behind her back.

The range of actions I have taken and proposed tonight—on the job front, on the inflation front, on the monetary front—is the most comprehensive New Economic Policy to be undertaken by this nation in four decades.

We are fortunate to live in a nation with an economic system capable of producing for its people the highest standard of living in the world; a system flexible enough to change its ways dramatically when circumstances call for change; and most important—a system resourceful enough to produce prosperity with freedom and opportunity unmatched in the history of nations.

The purposes of the government actions I have announced tonight are to lay the basis for renewed confidence, to make it possible for us to compete fairly with the rest of the world, to open the door to a new prosperity.

But government, with all its powers, does not hold the key to the success of a people. That key, my fellow Americans, is in your hands.

A nation, like a person, has to have a certain inner drive in order to succeed. In economic affairs, that inner drive is called the competitive spirit.

Every action I have taken tonight is designed to nurture and stimulate that competitive spirit; to help us snap out of that self-doubt and self-disparagement that saps our energy and erodes our confidence in ourselves.

Whether this nation stays number one in the world's economy or resigns itself to second, third or fourth place; whether we as a people have faith in ourselves, or lose that faith; whether we hold fast to the strength that makes peace and freedom possible in this world, or lose our grip—all that depends on you, on your competitive spirit, your sense of personal destiny, your pride in your country and in yourself.

We can be certain of this: As the threat of war recedes, the challenge of peaceful competition in the world will greatly increase.

We welcome competition, because America is at her greatest when she is called on to compete.

As there always have been in our history, there will be voices urging us to shrink from that challenge of competition, to build a protective wall around ourselves, to crawl into a shell as the rest of the world moves ahead.

Two hundred years ago a man wrote in his diary these words: "Many thinking people believe America has seen its best days." That was written in 1775, just before the American Revolution, at the dawn of the most exciting era in the history of man. Today we hear the echoes of those voices, preaching a gospel of gloom and defeat, saying that same thing: "We have seen our best days."

I say, let Americans reply: "Our best days lie ahead."

As we move into a generation of peace, as we blaze the trail toward the new prosperity, I say to every American: Let us raise our spirits. Let us raise our sights. Let all of us contribute all we can to the great and good country that has contributed so much to the progress of mankind.

Let us invest in our nation's future; and let us revitalize that faith in ourselves that built a great nation in the past, and will shape the world of the future.

Thank you, and good evening.

Arthur F. Burns: Monetary and Fiscal Policies

Mr. Burns: Thank you very much, Mr. Chairman. Perhaps I can start first by reading my statement. Is that satisfactory?

Chairman Proxmire: Yes, sir. I might say if you abbreviate it in any way, the full statement will be printed in the record.

Mr. Burns: Thank you.

I appreciate the opportunity to meet with this committee once again to present the views of the Board of Governors on the condition of our national economy.

Our overall economic performance during the past year has left much to be desired. Unemployment rose to more than 6 percent of the civilian labor force by year end. Idle industrial capacity increased. Business profits deteriorated further. The price level continued to rise sharply. Our balance of payments remained in an unsatisfactory condition. These frustrations and disappointments cannot be overlooked; but they also must not be allowed to blind us to the progress that our Nation has been making toward the restoration of its economic health.

Underneath the surface of aggregate economic activity, major changes took place during 1970, and they have been—on the whole—in harmony with the aspirations of the Congress and the American people. Thus, the defense sector of our economy has continued to shrink, with employment in this sector—when the reduction of the armed forces is counted in— declining three-quarters of a million during the past year. Also, the protracted investment boom in business fixed capital—whose continuance would have necessitated a major retrenchment later on—has tapered off. Meanwhile, the homebuilding industry has in recent months been experiencing a great upsurge of activity. And our trade surplus—which had plummeted from 1965 to 1960—began to recover as our exports rose relative to imports. These several developments have imparted better balance to our national use of resources, and thereby promise to contribute to economic and social progress. . . .

From "The 1971 Economic Report of the President," Hearings before Joint Economic Committee, 92nd Congress, 1st Session, Part I, February, 1971. Government Printing Office, 1971. Mr. Burns is Chairman of the Board of Governors of the Federal Reserve System.

I can assure this committee that the Federal Reserve will continue to supply the money and credit needed for healthy economic expansion. But I also wish to reaffirm the assurance that I gave to this committee and the Nation a year ago—namely, that the Federal Reserve will not become the architects of a new wave of inflation. We know that the effects of monetary policy on aggregate demand and on prices are spread over relatively long periods of time. We are well aware, therefore, that an excessive rate of monetary expansion now could destroy our Nation's chances of bringing about a gradual but lasting control over inflationary forces.

We recognize also, as do an increasing number of students around the world, that the problems of economic stabilization policy currently plaguing us cannot be solved by monetary policy alone, nor by a combination of monetary and fiscal policies. Monetary and fiscal tools can cope readily with inflation arising from excess aggregate demand. But they are ill suited to dealing with a rising price level that stems from rising costs at a time of rising unemployment and excess capacity.

During the past year, despite an increase in unemployment of 2 million persons, we have once again witnessed advances in wage rates substantially above the growth of productivity. In industries such as retail trade and finance, wage-rate increases have slowed somewhat. In others, such as manufacturing and construction, the rate of advance in average hourly earnings has not diminished. Wage settlements granted in major collective bargaining agreements during 1970 were, in fact, considerably larger on the average than in the previous year. For the first year of the new contracts, they averaged 8 percent in manufacturing and 18 percent in the construction industry.

There have been earlier instances in our history when price increases have continued for a time despite weakness in business activity. But, as far as I know, we have never before experienced a rate of inflation of 5 percent or higher while the unemployment rate was rising to recession levels. Continuation of this situation much longer would, I am afraid, sap the confidence of the American people in the capacity of our Government and in the viability of our market system.

We are thus confronted with what is, practically speaking, a new problem. A recovery in economic activity appears to be getting underway at a time when the rate of inflation is still exceptionally high. The stimulative thrust of present monetary and fiscal policies is needed to assure the resumption of economic growth and a reduction of unemployment. But unless we find ways to curb the advance of costs and prices, policies that stimulate aggregate demand run the grave risk of releasing fresh forces of inflation.

In view of this new problem, it is the considered judgment of the Federal Reserve Board that, under present conditions, monetary and fiscal policies need to be supplemented with an incomes policy; that is to say, with measures that aim to improve the workings of our labor and product markets so that upward pressures on costs and prices will be reduced.

The administration has already taken significant steps in this direction. Public attention has been called pointedly to areas in which wage and price changes are threatening the success of our battle against inflation. Restrictions on the supply of oil have been relaxed. Part of the recent increase in prices of structural steel has been rolled back as a result of governmental intervention. And the President has clearly conveyed to the construction industry that the Government will no longer tolerate the runaway labor costs that are destroying construction jobs and depriving so many of our families of the opportunity to buy a home at a price they can afford to pay.

These steps have put our Nation's business and labor leaders on notice that the Government recognizes the character of the present inflationary problem, and that it is serious in its intent to find a cure. If I read the national mood correctly, widespread public support now exists for vigorous efforts to bring wage settlements and prices in our major industries within more reasonable bounds. Such efforts should bolster consumer and business confidence, and thus contribute materially to getting our economy to move forward once again.

Chairman Proxmire: Thank you very much, Mr. Burns.

Mr. Burns, you and the administration seem to differ sharply on what we need to stimulate the economy and get unemployment down to provide the jobs we need. In your statement, you seem to feel that there is a stimulus, significant and sharp stimulus, perhaps, in the fiscal policy of our Government. Now, when Mr. McCracken appeared before us, he told us that in his judgment, changes in the full-employment surplus from period to period, from year to year, is what is important. He told us further that there has been no change between 1970 and 1971. He said that the full-employment surplus was just about the same; therefore, the budget should have about the same stimulus in both years, with no change.

That is why it is hard for me to understand your statement, when you indicate that you think that the present fiscal policy is consonant with the requirements of an economy operating at high levels of unemployment. What is your answer to that? Where will the stimulus come from?

Mr. Burns: Senator, I think that the fiscal policy of the administration is a stimulative policy. I don't think it is a sharply stimulative policy, but it is a stimulative policy. The fact that the stimulus in the coming fiscal year may be no larger than the stimulus occurring this year does not alter the fact, as I see it, that the administration's fiscal policy overall is stimulative.

Now, the question you put to me is: Is it stimulative enough? Well, I do not know the answer to that question. It looks reasonable to me. I would watch developments; and depending on developments, I might want to see fiscal policy change. . . .

Chairman Proxmire: . . . Your position seems to disagree with that of Mr. Shultz, who indicated to us that he felt that a sufficiently stimulative monetary policy could do the job. Do you think there is a monetary policy which will guarantee us, assure us, of 4½-percent growth in real output in 1971?

Mr. Burns: I know of no such monetary policy. But I am also not quarreling with Mr. Shultz.

Chairman Proxmire: Well, if you are not quarreling with Mr. Shultz on that score, let me see if I can get you into a quarrel with him on something else.

Predictions of most economists, as you know, are that the gross national product will be about a trillion 45 billion dollars during this year. And a great deal hinges on the administration's proposal that it will not be at that level, but at a trillion 65 billion dollars. If it is that high the deficit will be less, unemployment will be less, and the economy will be growing at a good rate.

Wednesday we had the Department of Commerce appear and their top experts told us that in their judgment, the administration is wrong—they said the Council of Economic Advisers and the Office of Management and Budget are wrong; the Commerce model indicates that they expect the economy to be about a trillion 45 billion dollars.

Now, you have some of the ablest economists in the Government on your staff. I think it is well that we know what the Federal Reserve Board thinks is likely to be the result of our fiscal policies in 1971 in GNP.

Mr. Burns: Senator, when you speak of this or that economist disagreeing with another in this or that area, you are speaking of a situation that has existed in Government for many years and will exist as long as you and I do. And when one economist speaks of another economist as being wrong about the future, let us all remember that good historians are often uncertain about what happened in the past.

Now, to come more directly to your question, Senator, I think the administration's projection may be viewed either as a target or as an outright prediction. Viewed as a target, I think it is admirable.

Chairman Proxmire: So do I.

Mr. Burns: Viewed as a prediction, I consider it optimistic.

Now, you would like to know what the able economists in the Federal Reserve System think. They think the administration's projection, viewed as an outright prediction, is very optimistic. And perhaps I have said enough in answer to your question. . . .

Representative Widnall: Thank you, Mr. Chairman.

Mr. Burns, you certainly made a very fine statement and I think, in many ways, a good appraisal of the actual economy at the present time. I think one of the extremely important things you said, at the tag end of your statement, concerns the considered judgment of the Federal Reserve

Board that under present conditions, monetary and fiscal policies need to be supplemented with an incomes policy—"that is to say, with measures that aim to improve the workings of our labor and product markets so that upward pressures on costs and prices will be reduced."

You discuss then some of the steps the President has taken on an ad hoc basis to deal with the specific industry problems. Do you see the need for a more comprehensive plan or approach to the incomes policy question and what sort of program do you see?

Mr. Burns: Well, I would welcome a more comprehensive approach; yes. I would welcome it very much.

I have no offhand views on this subject. I want to see movement, I want to see progress, and I am willing to grant that the other fellow may have better ideas than I have in this area.

To give you my views, I feel disturbed that we have had great excesses in the construction industry. What is happening in that industry is spreading to other industries, and special measures with regard to that industry are therefore necessary.

Second, I am inclined to think that it would be helpful to our country at a time such as this to establish a wage and price review board which would deal with industry problems generally. That review board would not have enforcement powers, but it could initiate inquiries into specific wage adjustments or into specific price adjustments. It could hold hearings on such developments at the request of the President or the Council of Economic Advisers.

I would expect that after several months such a wage and price review board would evolve, through a process akin to case law, guidelines for prices and wages. I think it is difficult to set forth guidelines that would be workable without some actual experience. . . .

Representative Moorhead: . . . Mr. Burns, I was very much interested in your statement about an incomes policy. . . . I notice that you recommend the creation of a Wage and Price Board but with no mandatory powers. Do you think that it would be advisable to give, let us say, to the President reserve powers so that he would have the shotgun in the corner in case the parties before the Board ignored their recommendations?

Mr. Burns: I am a conservative economist, Congressman, a little too old to change. The thought of mandatory controls except in time of war or great national emergency just frightens me. I have come to believe, and I have taught thousands of students to believe—I hope I taught them to believe—that the free market system is this country's greatest economic asset. Therefore, I look with great misgivings on any proposal for mandatory controls.

But I am also a realist, and I think we may be approaching an emergency in our country. I must confess to you that there are times when in the dead hours of night, I find myself even thinking about a price and wage freeze. But when I rise and have a cup of coffee, I still don't want it.

Representative Moorhead: My mind goes back to before the automobile strike when the President, properly authorized by the Congress, could have called in the parties and said, I don't like wage and price controls; I am philosophically opposed to them. But if you make too unreasonable a settlement on the wage side and expect an unreasonable, therefore, price increase, I would feel forced to use it. I think the existence of the power might even prevent its use.

Mr. Burns: Well, let me just make two observations.

First, before we go to any mandatory controls, we certainly ought to try milder measures—measures that are more in harmony with our national traditions and that promises some success. True, a Wage and Price Review Board may turn out to be ineffective. But I would try it, along with some other measures that the President and the Congress may take.

Second, if the Congress feels differently, then the Congress should consider legislating to impose price controls directly.

Let's put it a little differently: You are giving too much power to the President under this legislation. You are giving the President virtually dictatorial power. Do you really want to give any man that much power? That worries me. I can see some advantages, and you have pointed them out. I have considered them, and I do not dismiss them lightly.

But let me say this: If you do give this power to the President . . . I hope you will do so only for a very brief period, because you will be giving dictatorial powers to the President, and you ought to do that with the greatest of caution. . . .

George P. Shultz: The Federal Budget and the Nation's Economy

---

. . . The budget is a massive document involving a tremendous amount of money. As we go through the process of budget review, we question everything and review all the agency requests, not being so impressed

---

From "The 1971 Economic Report of the President," Hearings before Joint Economic Committee, 92nd Congress, 1st Session, Part I, February 1971. Government Printing Office, 1971. Mr. Shultz is Director of the Federal Office of Management and Budget.

with this or more impressed with that. To an extent, that puts us into a negative frame of mind. That is, a frame of mind that questions what is put forward.

Nonetheless, we want to look upon this document as a positive document. The large sum of money that is expected to be spent, $229 billion, is a sum of money with which we hope to accomplish things for the American people, and we want to look at it in that regard.

The budget contains a large number of important initiatives that the President has spelled out in his State of the Union message and, of course, detailed here to a greater extent in the budget document itself. The revenue-sharing proposal and the reorganization proposal come to mind first. The President will be sending up a health message very soon. The environmental message came up yesterday. Incidentally, there is a great deal of material in the budget on that subject.

You made reference to the full employment budget concept. The President has very explicitly had this in mind; it provided the basic guide for the 1972 budget.

The full employment concept is a helpful one from the standpoint of looking at the impact of the budget on the economy. In a deeper sense, however, it should be regarded not so much as a short-term fiscal policy guideline but a long-term guideline. The basic idea of the concept is to relate budget outlays to the revenues that the tax system can generate when the economy is at full employment and to guide decisions about outlays by that market.

The full employment budget concept does not mean that we would spend all of that all the time, but experience indicates when outlays exceed full employment revenues—and the excess tends to cascade over a period of years—we get into very serious economic trouble. Then we have to wrench the economy back to get it on to a different path. We had to do that between fiscal 1968 and fiscal 1969; as a result, there was a very large fiscal swing in the budget of almost $30 million from one year to the next.

It is important to avoid that kind of a wrench to the economy.

I might note that there was a bipartisan effort involving the passage of the surtax by the Congress.

So using as a guide the full employment revenue, it is possible to make a plan for Government expenditures that is more orderly and that is sustainable over a period of years. At the same time, when the economy is operating at less than full employment actual outlays tend to exceed receipts. Under those circumstances, the Government budget is helping to stimulate the economy and, the actual deficit that arises is not something to be deplored but to be accepted as a means of helping the economy move forward.

The use of the full employment budget concept—a new idea but an important idea—has been helpful to us in the budget process.

Mr. Chairman, as I said, we are here to respond to your questions and we look forward to exploring the budget, the budget in relationship to the economy, and other questions that you may raise. We will do the best job we can in answering your questions.

Thank you.

Chairman Proxmire: Thank you very much, Mr. Shultz.

One measure of the straits of our economy at the present time is that you predict or expect, have as your goal, unemployment which will be approaching 5 percent as the year goes on. Five percent and inflation which will be four and a half percent during the year.

Now, both of these are shockingly high on the basis of recent history, over the past 20 years, and yet at the same time, the irony is that everybody says these are very optimistic, and it is unlikely you can do even that well.

In view of the fact that the administration has been in office, this is its third year, what is your explanation of the grim state of the economy and what many people seem to feel is the grim outlook for the economy?

Mr. Shultz: I think that the outlook for the economy is not grim but rather it is quite good. If we hold to a reasonable and steady course, we will be able to get the economy into the zone of full employment, and where we will have the rate of inflation will be declining and moving toward a more acceptable rate.

The basic explanation for the difficulties that we are having with inflation lies in the extraordinary excesses that were built into the 1966, 1967, and 1968 fiscal year budgets, accompanied as they were by a very rapid increase in the money supply. The increase in money supply continued even after President Johnson tried to bring some sense to the situation in the latter half of 1968, and it left us with a residue of inflation that is very hard to whip. The current indicators say that the back of the inflation problem has been broken, even though there is no doubt that the inflation problem is still very much with us.

I share your sense of puzzlement at the criticisms of the administration's outlook. It is important to achieve a gross national product of at least $1,065 billion—and I would hope that we can do better—if we are to have success in bringing unemployment down. The prospects are that the rate of inflation will continue to decline while we have that kind of expansion. Obviously you can't have an expansion that blows the lid off and expect to continue to make progress against inflation.

Chairman Proxmire: I want to get into both of these in turn, both the employment outlook and effects in unemployment, and also on inflation. I just wonder in view of your response how long the administration is going to justify and how long the Republicans are going to campaign against Lyndon Johnson's inflationary actions of 1966 and 1967. It reminds me of the fact we Democrats have been campaigning with some success for 40 years against Herbert Hoover. I wonder if you expect to campaign 40 years against Lyndon Johnson.

Senator Percy: No. Thirty, 35 years. [Laughter.]

Chairman Proxmire: . . . Let me point to the details of that budget of yours. It seems to me that unless you have some kind of magic up your sleeve it is very hard to see how you are going to get to this 4½ percent zone of unemployment. Although it is extraordinarily high on the basis of recent standards. Let's examine the budget piece by piece.

In the first place, defense spending is going back up but that is in dollar terms only. In real terms it is certainly not going to stimulate the economy. Quite the reverse. Commerce and transportation is declining, no stimulation there. Income security, largest civilian item in the budget by far, the programs that really get money into the hands of consumers. Social security and veterans' pensions, et cetera, that is increasing less than half as much in fiscal 1972 as in fiscal 1971. Education and manpower up just half as much in 1972 as in 1971. Less than half in percentage terms. Health up just a little more than half as much in 1972 as in 1971. Again less than half in percentage terms. Veterans' benefits, up just a little more than half as much in 1972 as 1971, again less than half in percentage terms. Community development and housing, a smaller increase in 1972 than in 1971. As badly as we need housing, up only 17 percent in 1972.

In short, the whole civilian budget is increasing by $5 billion less in 1972 than it did in 1971. That is including revenue sharing and everything else except defense.

Now, I don't say that you are not right in holding down some of this spending. I would agree especially in the defense area, but unless we are going to reduce taxes or take some other kind of action, I can't see that there is a fiscal stimulus of the kind you described that would move us in the direction of substantial lowering of unemployment. Where is it?

Mr. Shultz: Well, when we are talking about the economy as a whole, we want to look to the budget as a whole. The fallacy of trying to pick apart particular things as suggested by your comments about housing is that in doing so we tend to lose sight of the major forces that drive the economy. Housing starts have gone up very sharply during the past year, and, for the most part, people didn't quite anticipate the strength of that rise. It has been a reflection of many things, including household formations. It is partially a reaction to the quite sharp decline in interest rates. To some extent, the strong recovery of housing is a budget matter; to some extent it isn't. In any event, the strong recovery is something that is going on. . . .

Chairman Proxmire: My question, Mr. Shultz, was what stimulus we are going to get out of this budget? You immediately referred to housing, pointed out housing has been rising more rapidly than many people expected. It is a sort of thing most people didn't anticipate. Senator Percy and I are on the Housing Subcommittee. We are unhappy about the relatively low levels against our goals which are 2.6 million housing starts per year.

I can see some stimulus here. I don't think it flows from the budget and I doubt very much if it is enough to provide the kind of employment increase that is needed.

Mr. Shultz: Well, I would say that concentrating exclusively on the budget as the sole and only tool of economic policy is not correct and that we should also look at monetary policy. That is an extremely important ingredient. Beyond that, when we are thinking of these broad aggregates that we are talking about, it is much better to consider the economy as a whole. The process, whether in the form of very fancy econometric models or less elaborate techniques, of looking at the economy piece by piece and trying to add it up has consistently over the years led people to underestimate the strengths of the economy.

I think that is a pretty well demonstrated proposition. . . .

Chairman Proxmire: Well, my time is up but let me just say that both you and Mr. McCracken primarily defended the administration's forecast by pointing historically how poor the forecasts of other people have been in the past. There hasn't been the kind of detailed specific justification, affirmative justification, of why the administration's analysis is right. I don't see how you can provide an analysis unless you break it down by ingredients and say what is going to happen to personal investments, what is going to happen to personal income, what is going to happen to Government purchases, et cetera. You can vaguely generalize, I suppose, but I just don't see how this is going to be convincing.

Mr. Shultz: No; there is another method and that has a more empirical basis. It goes at the problem in a different way. We have used this different method and in some respects have elaborated it to quite an extensive degree. We will be glad to discuss that with you and show you some of the bases for our own estimates.

Chairman Proxmire: As I say, my time is up. . . .

Mr. Shultz: Well, let me address the public service employment question, since it is one that people have been interested in, and it has been receiving continued attention.

First, I would state that the Nixon administration pioneered a public service employment program which got started a little more than a year ago. It has been working quite well. It is an effort to put into place a public service counterpart of the private job opportunities in the business sector program. That is, you would contract with units of Federal, State, and local governments to employ a disadvantaged worker, particularly on a public service job, train that person and get that person into the regular employment.

The program has been going along well; it is a constructive and helpful program. Beyond that, as the manpower bill was being worked on last year by the Congress, the idea of federally subsidized temporary public service jobs that would be viewed essentially as a training device was welcomed by the administration. We worked with the Members of the House of Representatives who are trying hard to make that a reality.

The bill that finally came to the President proposed essentially a return to personal public works and subsidization of personal government jobs, not necessarily jobs that needed to be done but jobs that were created in order to employ somebody.

Our feeling has been that the kind of jobs that we want in a healthy economy are jobs that are there because somebody wants that service, whether it is a public service or a private service. We think that the public service area is an area in which job development can take place and where support of the kind I have mentioned is appropriate. More than that, we think the way to have healthy employment opportunities is to have a healthy economy, and a healthy economy will absorb people and give jobs that have permanence to them and that have the attribute that they are there because the community wants to have the job done. I think that this is the kind of job that people want. . . .

Senator Percy: I wonder if you could comment, Mr. Shultz, on what will happen to inflation and unemployment levels if we do not achieve the 9 percent projected growth rate in fiscal 1972? If we see that we are not achieving that level as we go into that year, what steps might the Federal Government take to stimulate the economy more than would otherwise be the case?

Mr. Shultz: We estimate that if the economy moves at the prospected 9 percent rate in calendar year 1971, the rate of inflation will continue to fall and unemployment will fall. Those are counterparts, so to speak, of the $1,065 billion estimate.

Now, if the economy operates at a lesser pace, then we would expect to see the rate of inflation decline even more and, obviously, the rate of unemployment would be higher. So that as you think about economic policy, trying to see what the Government can do that will help the economy be a healthy economy, you always have to think about the problems of both inflation and employment or plant utilization, to see how much thrust there is together. You never can lose sight of either one. The objectives that we have set, and the expectations that we have, are compatible with the balance moving on both of these fronts.

Our view is that with the budget that has been put into place—one that doesn't have a full employment deficit—and with strong support from monetary policy, we will be able to achieve a lessening of the rate of inflation and a fall in unemployment.

I know that a great deal has been said about policies toward wages and prices and I welcomed your comment on it. The administration's position has been from the outset that it is extremely important to examine the way in which individual wage and price markets are working, and try to make them operate as competitively as possible so that all the discipline of the marketplace can be exercised.

There have been quite a number of examples of action of that kind and we will continue to take actions of that kind. . . .

Senator Percy: I support the full employment budget concept. I think it is a brilliant concept. It is hard for some Republicans to swallow, I suppose, but I think it does give us a guide by which we should project our budget surplus or deficit.

Could you comment, however, on the Committee on Economic Development's call for a $6 to $9 billion full employment surplus as against the $0.1 billion surplus in the actual budget? How do you reconcile these differences in viewpoint?

Mr. Shultz: Well, the idea of operating with a large full employment surplus in a year when we would like to see the economy expand did not strike the President as very sensible economic policy. There may be times when you would want to have a substantial full employment surplus, in effect, the Government doing the saving on behalf of the community. But in this day, with very high personal savings and with the economy operating at a rate less than we would like, the President's view was we should bring the budget at full employment about into balance.

His decisions, which were not simply spending decisions—the tax impact decision that you mentioned was part of it—were designed to do just that. In this sense, the budget goes right up to the limit of what the President feels it can do to sustain a strong expansion in the economy.

Senator Percy: Thank you very much, Mr. Shultz.

Chairman Proxmire: Congressman Reuss.

Representative Reuss: Mr. Shultz, suppose that Congress behaves angelically with regard to the President's economic program, does everything that is asked of it, and suppose all the other blocks fall into place except that as you go ahead with this program in the months to come, it develops that actually you are not progressing at the 9 percent rate and aren't on your way to the $1,065 billion GNP which you confidently predict.

If that should happen, what would be your recommendation at that time as to monetary policy? Or to put it another way, this would indicate, would it not, that the Fed has not been creating enough new money to validate the projections.

Mr. Shultz: Well, our analysis of the situation, and our way of looking at the economy, shows that monetary policy is a very important active ingredient in determining the direction of the economy. And we would look to monetary policy to be expansive and to be a strong support of attaining the kind of objective that we have set forth, which—

Representative Reuss: But suppose, though, that at this projected time, say 4 months from now, 6 months from now, the Fed has been creating new money narrowly defined as the 7 percent a year which is ordinarily considered to be expansive but still even though everybody else has been cooperating the thing isn't working and you aren't on your way toward the $1,065 billion GNP upon which hang all the hopes as to reducing unemployment, inflation, and so on.

Would that situation indicate to you that 7 percent new money has not been enough and that the Fed should be more expansive?

Mr. Shultz: Well, I would certainly be surprised if that rate of monetary growth were sustained—

Representative Reuss: We would both be surprised.

Mr. Shultz (continuing): Up and down—

Representative Reuss: But suppose that is what happened?

Mr. Shultz: We would have to go back and look at the textbooks again because I think the evidence is very clear in economic history that when you combine the kind of big budget swing that occurred between fiscal 1968 and fiscal 1969 with the extremely tight money policy that followed in the latter half of 1969 and 1970, that the input gets an output. I think that we have been feeling the effects of those policy devices, particularly the very, very tight money policy in 1969 and early 1970.

Now, I think by the same token you can turn that around. Budget policy has been more expansive beginning in the wintertime of last year, and monetary policy has also shifted. All our economic history teaches us that when you get this kind of a switch, particularly if one were to have a certain monetary policy that you suggest, that we would have a strongly expanding economy.

Representative Reuss: But if we should turn out to be wrong, if we do everything in the budget that you and the President have recommended, but we aren't growing sufficiently to meet our target in this case, monetary policy would have to be the culprit, would it not, and whatever rate of monetary increment had been the order of the day for the Fed would in the event it should turn out to be wrong and should be increased.

I suppose I am trying to put words in your mouth but not maliciously because this seems to me—

Representative Brown: Or successfully.

Representative Reuss (continuing): That is what you have been saying.

Mr. Shultz: I suppose that people all have their own ideas about who is the culprit for what, and we have our analysis of the economy operating. We do put a lot of weight on monetary policy. At least, it looks to us from our analysis that monetary policy is exceedingly important, and all of our experience suggests that what you are suggesting as a monetary policy will bring a very strong expansion. I would like the record to show that the 7-percent figure was your suggestion, not my suggestion.

Representative Reuss: Yes.

Mr. Shultz: I don't want to have that word in my mouth.

Representative Reuss: It so shows.

Turning to another field, it is still your view, is it not, that it would be a mistake for the administration to impose a temporary price-wage freeze in order to get a handle on inflation?

Mr. Shultz: My analysis of the wage and price situation is that the problem, to the extent that there is a problem, is widely dispersed. Particularly if we look at the wages, the picture varies a great deal across the economy. There are many sectors of the economy where it looks to me as though the wage changes that are being put into place are quite moderate and, given the rate of inflation that accompanies them, are barely keeping workers even in terms of their real income.

It never has appeared to me that you can solve the inflation problem by forcing workers to take reductions in real income. I just don't think the situation works that way or that this is tolerable.

Now, by the same token, I think there are areas where the wage bargaining picture seems to have gotten out of control and badly so. Perhaps the most important and obvious one is the construction industry, where rates of increase have soared way beyond what is happening in most other industries. . . .

Representative Reuss: In addition to opposing price-wage compulsory controls, do you still continue to oppose the evolution of wage-price guideposts?

Mr. Shultz: My analysis of that approach, whether it is an enunciated guidepost that is enforced to some extent by the Council of Economic Advisers and the strong right arm of the President or by the Justice Department or by somebody that has some clout over individual companies, is that it really hasn't been very successful in dealing with the problem of inflation broadly speaking. To the extent that it has been successful, it has been exclusively concentrated on large visible firms. I don't know of instances where that approach has really had much impact on the wage picture. As I have heard the people who talk the most about this kind of thing, they complain the most about construction wage settlements. I agree with the analysis that those are real problems, and I think that whatever is proposed has to meet the test of whether or not it is going to do anything about those wage settlements. That is what we are concentrating on. . . .

9 Environmental Quality

Surely no issue in 1972 other than peace will receive wider attention than environmental quality. Every legislator and every presidential candidate will have a position on this issue. In less than a decade we have witnessed a growing public concern about the environmental consequences of a rising population and an expanding technology. Few communities have been spared the effects of air and water pollution and the misuse and abuse of the land. In some respects it would be easy to dismiss environmental quality as a political issue. It is a popular cause, and no one defends the right to pollute; the issue doesn't divide the nation. The Republicans and Democrats stand united against pollution and for environmental quality. They stand united because the issue has not yet been stated in political terms. We are only vaguely aware of the full governmental, social, economic, and technological consequences of the need to blend environmental quality into an economy that is geared to the consumer.

Environmental quality is likely to remain outside of mainstream politics until such time as it becomes grounded in some commonly accepted political principle. The civil rights movement floundered for years until racial equality received fairly common acceptance as an American political principle, even though it was a principle in search of practice. It is likely that the ecology movement will have to run a similar evolutionary course, a course that runs from horror stories and moralizing through accepted principles and concerted action. It will not be easy to modify the historic freedoms associated with our laissez-faire economy. True, we have a long-standing commitment to resource conservation and public health, and more recently a small commitment to the preservation of natural beauty. But a "Keep America Beautiful" outlook is a far cry from a programmatic commitment for the governmental preservation of the quality of the environment.

In the meantime we need, as Max Ways has suggested, to learn to think environmentally. Each of the essays selected for this chapter is a step in that direction. We begin the chapter with John Fischer's statement of his apostasy—his loss of faith in growth, technology, and private property and his call for radical political action to change the whole structure of government and the economy. Mr. Fischer, an editor of *Harper's,* reflects the new pessimism of the ecology movement, a pessimism which rejects confidence in the creative and predictive power of science. This new pessimism that has surrounded at least part of the ecology movement not only rejects science but with strongly romantic overtones has called for a return to the simple virtues of nature. Both Max Ways and René J. Dubos reject such an approach. Dubos, a biologist, contends that we have not yet seriously applied scientific thinking to the creation of a desirable human life; his plea is not for less science, but for a new science subservient to the fundamental needs of man.

In a similar view Max Ways, an editor of *Fortune,* acknowledges that modern technology is the root cause of our blight and congestion but warns against any technological retreat. Indeed, as Ways suggests, a technological retreat would force Grandpa to return to living in the abandoned hencoop, Mother to return to a washboard, and the children to a one-room schoolhouse. It can't and won't be done.

There is one theme, however, that is common to Fischer, Dubos, and Ways—a call for new methods to unify our fragmented economy and fragmented government. Each of the authors recognizes that the quality of the environment will never be equal to the needs of man until we plan and implement appropriate agencies to integrate our social, economic, and political institutions. We will continue, Mr. Fischer's view notwithstanding, to be a society of high technology. The choice is whether it will be a society with or without adequate institutions of coordination.

John Fischer: How I Got Radicalized

To my astonishment, the political convictions that I had cherished for most of my life have suddenly deserted me. Like my children, these were convictions I loved dearly and had nurtured at considerable expense. When last seen they were—like all of us—somewhat battered by the events of the last decade, but they looked durable enough to last out my time. So I was

---

disconcerted when I found that somehow, during the past winter, they sort of melted away, without my consent and while I was looking somewhere else.

Their place has been usurped by a new set of convictions so radical that they alarm me. If the opposite kind of thing had happened, I would have felt a little melancholy but not surprised, since people traditionally grow more conservative as they get older. But to discover that one has suddenly turned into a militant subversive is downright embarrassing; at times I wonder whether it signals the onset of second childhood.

Except that I seem to be a lot more radical than the children. Those SDS youngsters who go around breaking windows and clubbing policemen now merely depress me with their frivolous irrelevance. So do most other varieties of New Leftists, such as the Women's Liberation movement; if some dire accident should, God forbid, throw one of those ladies into my clutches, she can be sure of instant liberation. I am equally out of tune with those old fogies, the Communists. The differences between capitalism and Communism no longer seem to me worth fighting about, or even arguing, since they are both wrong and beside the point. Or so it seems to me, since the New Vision hit me on my own small road to Damascus.

Let me make it plain that none of this was my doing. I feel as Charles Darwin must have felt during the last leg of his voyage on the *Beagle*. When he embarked he had been a conventional (if slightly lackadaisical) Christian, who took the literal truth of Genesis for granted. He had been raised in that faith, as I was raised a Brass Collar Democrat, and had no thought of forsaking it. Only gradually, while he examined fossil shellfish high in the Andes and measured the growth of coral deposits and the bills of Galapagos finches, did he begin to doubt that the earth and all its inhabitants had been created in six days of October, 4004 B.C., according to the pious calculations of Archbishop James Ussher. By the time he got back to England, he found himself a reluctant evolutionist, soon to be damned as a heretic and underminer of the Established Church. This was not his fault. It was the fault of those damned finches.

Recently I too have been looking at finches, so to speak, although mine are mostly statistical and not nearly as pretty as Darwin's. His gave him a hint about the way the earth's creatures came into being; mine, to my terror, seem to hint at the way they may go out. While I am by no means an uncritical admirer of the human race, I have become rather fond of it, and would hate to see it disappear. Finding ways to save it—if we are not too late already—now strikes me as the political issue which takes precedence over all others.

One of the events which led to my conversion was my unexpected appointment to a committee set up by Governor John Dempsey of Connecticut to work out an environmental policy for our state. Now I had been

fretting for quite a while about what is happening to our environment—
who hasn't?—but until the work of the committee forced me into systematic study, I had not realized that my political convictions were in
danger. Then after looking at certain hairy facts for a few months, I found
myself convinced that the Democratic party, and most of our institutions
of government, and even the American Way of Life are no damned good.
In their present forms, at least, they will have to go. Either that, or everybody goes—and sooner than we think.

To begin with, look at the American Way of Life. Its essence is a belief in growth. Every Chamber of Commerce is bent on making its Podunk
grow into the Biggest Little City in the country. Wall Street is dedicated to
its search for growth stocks, so that Xerox has become the American ideal
—superseding George Washington, who expressed *his* faith in growth by
speculating in land. Each year Detroit prays for a bigger car market. Businessmen spend their lives in pursuit of an annual increase in sales, assets,
and net profits. All housewives—except for a few slatterns without ambition—yearn for bigger houses, bigger cars, and bigger salary checks. The
one national goal that everybody agrees on is an ever-growing Gross National Product. Our modern priesthood—the economists who reassure us
that our mystic impulses are moral and holy—recently announced that the
GNP would reach a trillion dollars early in this decade. I don't really understand what a trillion is, but when I read the news I rejoiced, along with
everybody else. Surely that means that we were in sight of ending poverty,
for the first time in human history, so that nobody would ever again need
to go hungry or live in a slum.

Now I know better. In these past months I have come to understand
that a zooming Gross National Product leads not to salvation, but to sui-
cide. So does a continuing growth in population, highway mileage, kilo-
watts, plane travel, steel tonnage, or anything else you care to name.

The most important lesson of my life—learned shamefully late—was
that nonstop growth just isn't possible, for Americans or anybody else. For
we live in what I've learned to recognize as a tight ecological system: a
smallish planet with a strictly limited supply of everything, including air,
water, and places to dump sewage. There is no conceivable way in which
it can be made bigger. If Homo sapiens insists on constant growth, within
this system's inelastic walls, something has to pop, or smother. Already the
United States is an overpopulated country: not so hopelessly overcrowded
as Japan or India, of course, but well beyond the limits which would make
a good life attainable for everybody. Stewart Udall, former Secretary of
Interior and now a practicing ecologist, has estimated that the optimum
population for America would be about 100 million, or half of our present
numbers. And unless we do something, drastic and fast, we can expect
another 100 million within the next thirty years.

So our prime national goal, I am now convinced, should be to reach Zero Growth Rate as soon as possible. Zero growth in people, in GNP, and in our consumption of everything. That is the only hope of attaining a stable ecology: that is, of halting the deterioration of the environment on which our lives depend.

This of course is a profoundly subversive notion. It runs squarely against the grain of both capitalism and the American dream. It is equally subversive of Communism, since the Communists are just as hooked on the idea of perpetual growth as any American businessman. Indeed, when Khrushchev was top man in the Kremlin, he proclaimed that 1970 would be the year in which the Russians would surpass the United States in output of goods. They didn't make it: a fact for which their future generations may be grateful, because their environment is just as fragile as ours, and as easily damaged by headlong expansion. If you think the Hudson River and Lake Erie are unique examples of pollution, take a look at the Volga and Lake Baikal.

No political party, here or abroad, has yet even considered adopting Zero Growth Rate as the chief plank in its platform. Neither has any politician dared to speak out loud about what "protection of the environment" really means—although practically all of them seem to have realized, all of a sudden, that it is becoming an issue they can't ignore. So far, most of them have tried to handle it with gingerly platitudes, while keeping their eyes tightly closed to the implications of what they say. In his January State of the Union message, for instance, President Nixon made the customary noises about pollution; but he never even mentioned the population explosion, and he specifically denied that there is any "fundamental contradiction between economic growth and the quality of life." He sounded about as convincing as a doctor telling a cancer patient not to worry about the growth of his tumor.

The Democrats are no better. I have not heard any of them demanding a halt to all immigration, or a steeply progressive income tax on each child beyond two, or an annual bounty to every woman between the ages of fifteen and forty-five who gets through the year without becoming pregnant. Neither Ted Sorensen nor any of the other Kennedy henchmen has yet suggested that a politician with a big family is a spacehog and a hypocrite, unworthy of public trust. No Democrat, to my knowledge, has ever endorsed the views of Dr. René Dubos of Rockefeller University, one of the truly wise men of our time. In an editorial in the November 14, 1969, issue of *Science* he predicted that in order to survive, "mankind will have to develop what might be called a steady state . . . a nearly closed system" in which most materials from tin cans to sewage would be "recycled instead of discarded." His conclusion—that a viable future depends on the creation of "social and economic systems different from the ones in which we live today"—apparently is too radical for any politician I know.

Consequently I feel a little lonesome in my newfound political convictions. The only organization which seems to share them is a tiny one, founded only a few months ago: Zero Population Growth, Inc., with headquarters at 367 State Street, Los Altos, California 94022. Yet I have a hunch that I may not be lonesome for long. Among college students a concern with ecology has become, almost overnight, nearly as popular as sideburns. On many campuses it seems to be succeeding civil rights and Vietnam as The Movement. For example, when the University of Oregon announced last January a new course, "Can Man Survive?", it drew six thousand students, the biggest class in the university's history. They had to meet in the basketball court because no classroom would hold them.

Who knows? Maybe we agitators for Zero may yet turn out to be the wave of the future.

At the same time I was losing my faith in the virtues of growth, I began to doubt two other articles of the American credo.

One of them is the belief that technology can fix anything. Like most of us, I had always taken it for granted that any problem could be solved if we just applied enough science, money, and good old American know-how. Is the world's population outrunning its food supply? Well, then, let's put the laboratories to work inventing high-yield strains of rice and wheat, better fertilizers, ways to harvest seaweed, hydroponic methods for growing food without soil. If the air is becoming unbreathable, surely the technologists can find ways to clean it up. If our transportation system is a national disgrace, all we have to do is call in the miracle men who built a shuttle service to the moon; certainly they should be able to figure out some way to get a train from New York to New Haven on time.

I was in East Haddam, Connecticut, looking at an atomic power plant, when I began to suspect that technology might not be the answer after all. While I can't go along with the young Luddites who have decided that science is evil and that all inventions since the wheel ought to be destroyed, I am persuaded that technology is a servant of only limited usefulness, and highly unreliable. When it does solve a problem, it often creates two new ones—and their side effects are usually hard to foresee.

One of the things that brought me to East Haddam was curiosity about the automobile. Since the gasoline engine is the main polluter of the air, maybe it should be replaced with some kind of electric motor? That of course would require an immense increase in our production of electric power, in order to recharge ten million batteries every night. Where would it come from? Virtually all waterpower sites already are in use. More coal- and oil-fired power stations don't sound like a good idea, since they too pour smoke into the atmosphere—and coal mining already has ruined countless streams and hundreds of thousands of acres of irreplaceable land. Atomic power, then?

At first glance, the East Haddam plant, which is fairly typical of the new technology, looked encouraging. It is not as painful an eyesore as coal-burning stations, and not a wisp of smoke was in sight. When I began to ask questions, however, the company's public-relations man admitted that there are a few little problems. For one thing, the plant's innards are cooled with water pumped out of the Connecticut River. When it flows back in, this water raises the river's temperature by about twenty degrees, for a considerable distance. Apparently this has not yet done any serious damage to the shad, the only fish kept under careful surveillance; but its effect on other fish and algae, fish eggs, microorganisms, and the general ecology of the river is substantial though still unmeasured.

It would be possible, though expensive, for the company to build cooling towers, where the water would trickle over a series of baffles before returning to the river. In the process it would lose its heat to the atmosphere. But this, in turn, threatens climatic changes, such as banks of artificial fog rolling eastward over Long Island Sound, and serious wastage of water through evaporation from a river system where water already is in precarious supply. Moreover, neither this process nor any other now known would eliminate the slight, but not negligible, radiation which every atomic plant throws off, nor the remote but still omnipresent chance of a nuclear accident which could take thousands of lives. The building of an additional twenty plants along the banks of the Connecticut—which some estimates call for, in order to meet future demand for electricity—would be a clear invitation to an ecological disaster.

In the end I began to suspect that there is no harmless way to meet the demands for power of a rising population, with rising living standards—much less for a new herd of millions of electric cars. Every additional kilowatt levies some tax upon the environment, in one form or another. The Fourth Law of Thermodynamics seems to be: "There is no free lunch."

Every time you look at one of the marvels of modern technology, you find a by-product—unintended, unpredictable, and often lethal. Since World War II American agriculture has performed miracles in increasing production. One result was that we were able for years to send a shipload of free wheat every day to India, saving millions from starvation. The by-products were: (1) a steady rise in India's population; (2) the poisoning of our streams and lakes with insecticides and chemical fertilizers; (3) the forced migration of some ten million people from the countryside to city slums, as agriculture became so efficient it no longer needed their labor.

Again, the jet plane is an unquestionable convenience, capable of whisking a New Yorker, say, to either the French Riviera or Southern California in a tenth of the time he could travel by ship or car, and at lower cost. But when he reaches his destination, the passenger finds the beaches coated with oil (intended to fuel planes, if it hadn't spilled) and the air thick with smog (thanks in good part to the jets, each of which spews out as much hydrocarbon as ten thousand automobiles).

Moreover, technology works best on things nobody really needs, such as collecting moon rocks or building supersonic transport planes. Whenever we try to apply it to something serious, it usually falls on its face.

An obvious case in point is the railroads. We already have the technology to build fast, comfortable passenger trains. Such trains are, in fact, already in operation in Japan, Italy, and a few other countries. Experimental samples—the Metroliners and Turbotrains—also are running with spectacular success between Washington and Boston. If we had enough of them to handle commuter and middle-distance traffic throughout the country, we could stop building the highways and airports which disfigure our countryside, reduce the number of automobiles contaminating the air, and solve many problems of urban congestion. But so far we have not been able to apply the relatively simple technology needed to accomplish these aims, because some tough political decisions have to be made before we can unleash the scientists and engineers. We would have to divert to the railroads many of the billions in subsidy which we now lavish on highways and air routes. We would have to get rid of our present railway management—in general, the most incompetent in American industry—and retire the doddering old codgers of the Railway Brotherhoods who make such a mess out of running our trains. This might mean public ownership of a good many rail lines. It certainly would mean all-out war with the unions, the auto and aviation industries, and the highway lobby. It would mean ruthless application of the No Growth principle to roads, cars, and planes, while we make sensible use instead of something we already have: some 20,000 miles of railways.

All this requires political action, of the most radical kind. Until our Great Slob Society is willing to take it, technology is helpless.

My final apostasy from the American Creed was loss of faith in private property. I am now persuaded that there no longer is such a thing as truly private property, at least in land. That was a luxury we could afford only when the continent was sparsely settled. Today the use a man makes of his land cannot be left to his private decision alone, since eventually it is bound to affect everybody else. This conclusion I reached in anguish, since I own a tiny patch of land and value its privacy above anything money can buy.

What radicalized me on this score was the Department of Agriculture and Dr. Ian McHarg. From those dull volumes of statistics which the Department publishes from time to time, I discovered that usable land is fast becoming a scarce resource—and that we are wasting it with an almost criminal lack of foresight. Every year, more than a million acres of farm and forest land is being eaten up by highways, airports, reservoirs, and real-estate developments. The best, too, in most cases, since the rich, flat bottom lands are the most tempting to developers.

Since America is, for the moment, producing a surplus of many crops, this destruction of farmland has not yet caused much public alarm. But some day, not too far off, the rising curve of population and the falling curve of food-growing land inevitably are going to intersect. That is the day when we may begin to understand what hunger means.

Long before that, however, we may be gasping for breath. For green plants are our only source of oxygen. They also are the great purifiers of the atmosphere, since in the process of photosynthesis they absorb carbon dioxide—an assignment which gets harder every day, as our chimneys and exhaust pipes spew out ever-bigger tonnage of carbon gases. This is a function not only of trees and grass, but also of the tiny microorganisms in the sea. Indeed, its phytoplankton produces some 70 percent of all the oxygen on which life depends. These are delicate little creatures, easily killed by the sewage, chemicals, and oil wastes which already are contaminating every ocean in the world. Nobody knows when the scale will tip: when there are no longer enough green growing things to preserve the finely balanced mixture of gases in the atmosphere, by absorbing carbon dioxide and generating oxygen. All we know is that man is pressing down hard on the lethal end of the scale.

The Survivable Society, if we are able to construct it, will no longer permit a farmer to convert his meadow into a parking lot any time he likes. He will have to understand that his quick profit may, quite literally, take the bread out of his grandchildren's mouths, and the oxygen from their lungs. For the same reasons, housing developments will not be located where they suit the whim of a real-estate speculator or even the convenience of the residents. They will have to go on those few carefully chosen sites where they will do the least damage to the landscape, and to the life-giving greenery which it supports.

This is one of the lessons taught by Ian McHarg in his extraordinary book, *Design with Nature,* recently published by Natural History Press. Alas, its price, $19.95, will keep it from reaching the people who need it most. It ought to be excerpted into a pocket-size volume—entitled, perhaps, "The Thoughts of McHarg"—and distributed free in every school and supermarket.

The current excitement about the environment will not come to much, I am afraid, unless it radicalizes millions of Americans. The conservative ideas put forth by President Nixon—spending a few billion for sewage-treatment plants and abatement of air pollution—will not even begin to create the Survivable Society. That can be brought about only by radical political action—radical enough to change the whole structure of government, the economy, and our national goals.

How the Survivable State will work is something I cannot guess; its design is a job for the coming generation of political scientists. The radical vision can, however, give us a glimpse of what it might look like. It will measure every new law, every dollar of investment by a cardinal yardstick: Will this help us accomplish a zero rate of growth and a stabilized environment? It will be skeptical of technology, including those inventions which purport to help clean up our earthly mess. Accordingly it will have an Anti-Patent Office, which will forbid the use of any technological discovery until the Office figures out fairly precisely what its side effects might be. (If they can't be foreseen, then the invention goes into deep freeze.) The use of land, water, and air will not be left to private decision, since their preservation will be recognized as a public trust. The landlord whose incinerator smokes will be pilloried; the tanker skipper who flushes his oil tanks at sea will be hanged at the nearest yardarm for the capital crime of oxygen destruction. On the other hand, the gardener will stand at the top of the social hierarchy, and the citizen who razes a supermarket and plants its acreage in trees will be proclaimed a Hero of the Republic. I won't live to see the day, of course; but I hope somebody will.

**Max Ways: How To Think about
the Environment**

Who Killed the Illinois Rivers?

. . . Although environmental issues do have a grave moral content, there's little sense in the tendency to present the case in the dominant art form of a TV horse opera. This isn't, really, a confrontation between "the

---

From "How To Think about the Environment," by Max Ways, *Fortune*, February, 1970. Copyright © 1970 by Time, Inc. Condensed. Reprinted by permission. Mr. Ways is a member of Fortune's Board of Editors. This article has appeared in a book, *The Environment: A National Mission for the Seventies*, published by Harper & Row, Publishers.

polluters" and the good guys in the white hats. Nevertheless, casting for the villainous roles proceeds briskly. "Greed" is to blame. "Man, the dirtiest animal," is to blame, especially because his numbers are increasing. "Technology" is to blame—and this charge, as we shall see, contains much truth, though far less than the whole truth. "Capitalism" is to blame. "The poor," who throw garbage in the streets, are to blame. "Democracy," which seems unable to find remedies, is to blame. And, of course, "the establishment," everyone's goat of atonement, is to blame.

In general, the nomination of villains follows the familiar pattern of dumping the ashes of contrition on somebody else's head. A Columbia law-school senior this year was reported to have boasted that he told recruiters for law firms he "would not defend a client who was a polluter— and most of the clients who pollute are the big ones," a remark indicating that even law-school seniors may have something to learn.

For all men are polluters—and all living Americans are big polluters. The greedy and the ungreedy alike befoul the air with automobile exhaust fumes, the humble 1960 jalopy contributing somewhat more poison than the arrogant 1970 Cadillac. So long as our laws and habits of land use foster chaos, the homes of saints will aggress as rudely upon nature as the haunts of sinners. Who killed the rivers of Illinois by extinguishing perhaps forever their ability to cleanse and renew themselves? The effluents of big industries did a substantial part of the damage. Sewage from towns did part. But most of the damage to the rivers of Illinois came from farms onto which decent and well-meaning "little" men, in the pursuit of the legitimate aim of increasing crop yields, poured nitrogen fertilizers. The result bears the mellifluous name of "eutrophication": algae, slimy green gunk, rampantly feed upon the fertilizer drained into the rivers; the decay of dead algae consumes so much of the available oxygen as to destroy the bacterial action that once cleansed the rivers of organic wastes.

At the root of our environmental troubles we will not find a cause so simple as the greed of a few men. The wastes that besmirch our land are produced in the course of fulfilling widespread human wants that are in the main reasonable and defensible. Nor will we find capitalism at the root of the trouble. The Soviet Union, organized around central planning, has constructed some of the most terrifyingly hideous cityscapes on earth, while raping the countryside with strip mines, industrial pollutants, and all the other atrocities that in the U.S. are ascribed to selfish proprietary interests. Aware, as well they might be, of American environmental mistakes in handling the mass use of the automobile, Russians keep saying they will do it better; but today, as automobiles become more numerous in the U.S.S.R., it is hard to find in city or highway planning, in automobile design, or in any other tangible area signs that they are in fact better prepared for the automobile onslaught than the U.S. was in 1920.

The Japanese, though their basic culture lays great stress on harmony between man and nature, are not handling their environmental relations significantly better than the Americans or the Russians. Japan's economy, combining private enterprise with government central planning, seems able to do anything—except cherish the material beauty and order that the people value so highly.

If we wish to think seriously about the environment, we have to give up indulgence in barefoot moralism and the devil theory of what's wrong. We have to identify a root cause that explains the environmental failures of systems as different as the American, the Russian, and the Japanese. Obviously, all three are high-powered industrialized, technologized societies, and our quest for a root cause can start by tentatively picking technology as the villain.

For Every Man, 500 "Slaves"

Despite billions of words on the subject, we still underestimate the magnitude of technological advance and its implications. Thirty years ago in Fortune's tenth anniversary issue, R. Buckminster Fuller found an apt way of expressing what had occurred. He calculated the total energy generated in the U.S. as equal to the muscular energy that would be generated if every American had 153 slaves working for him. Today a similar calculation would indicate about 500 "slaves" for every American man, woman, and child.

These slaves enable us to increase our own mobility hundreds of times and to toss around incredible masses of materials, altering not only their location and external shapes but their very molecules. Excluding construction, earth moving, and many other operations, the U.S. economy, according to one estimate, uses 2,500,000,000 tons of material a year. That's nearly thirteen tons per person.

These figures explain a lot of environmental woes that are otherwise mysterious. Although our cities are not more densely populated, they produce more maddening and wasteful congestion than any cities of the past. Our crowding is not basically a matter of too many human beings to the square mile but of the enormous retinue of energy and material that accompanies each of us. Like King Lear with his hundred riotous knights and squires, we strain the hospitality of our dwelling space, and from our situation, as from Lear's, much grief may follow.

Two hundred million of us are bustling about the U.S., every one sheathed in a mass-and-energy nimbus very much bigger, noisier, dirtier, smellier, clumsier, and deadlier than he is. The paper, plastics, scrap, ash, soot, dust, sludge, slag, fumes, and weird compounds thrown off by the mass-and-energy nimbus exceed by many magnitudes our own bodily wastes. If ten billion mere people, sans technological nimbus, inhabited the U.S., they could not create more congestion, blight, and confusion. The three million high-technology U.S. farmers put more adverse pressure on their land and rivers than the hundred and fifty million low-productivity peasant families of China put upon their land and rivers.

The Rats Who Rule the Elephants

How should a city be designed and its circulatory system arranged to accommodate a people that employs energy and mass at present American levels? The past offers only wisps of inspiration, but no usable models. Consistently we have failed to face the sheer physical challenge of the contemporary city, assuming that old urban forms would be adequate if we amended them a little to meet one crisis after another.

Along with all kinds of congestion, our cities produce a paradoxical effect of isolation and desolation. Not rationally shaped for the needs of this society, the cities may be shaping us toward irrationality. Frequently mentioned in environmentalist circles these days is a research project carried out by John Calhoun at Bethesda, Maryland. He placed Norway rats in a closed area ample for the original population. As they multiplied, the crowded animals, though well fed, developed most distressing psychoses, which, out of a decent respect for the privacy of rats, will not be here detailed. Many who have heard of this project see a close parallel with our cities.

But the analogy is not quite true to the situation of contemporary urban man. It would be better to find a strain of rats each one of which had the services of a half-house-broken elephant to do its work, run its errands, and cater to its wants. In an ill-organized space these lordly rats, even if they did not multiply, might go crazier quicker than did their cousins in Bethesda.

People who center their anxiety on "the population explosion" see the challenge much too narrowly. In the U.S. and other advanced countries, population has been increasing less rapidly by far than the explosive acceleration of the total energy and total mass deployed. If the population declined and technology continued to breed, without any improvement in the arrangements for its prudent use, a small fraction of the present U.S. population could complete the destruction of the physical environment while jostling one another for room.

A Retreat to Poverty?

We come, then, to the question of whether a headlong retreat from technology would be the right strategy. This option needs to be honestly appraised, not toyed with as it is every day by nostalgic romanticists wiggling their toes in secondhand memories of Thoreau's Walden Pond.

The casualties of a withdrawal from technology would be heavier than many suppose. Everybody, of course, has his own examples of unnecessary technologies, unnecessary products, unnecessary activities. But because we are, thank God, diverse in our wants, the lists do not agree. The man who has since childhood said to hell with spinach has a ready-made response to the news that a high incidence of "blue babies" recorded in Germany has been attributed to heavy use of nitrogen fertilizer on the spinach crop. But other consumers will have good reasons for wishing spinach yields to increase. We will not improve our environmental situation by recommending a technological retreat on the basis of what each of us considers the superfluous items in the households of his neighbors.

To be effective in protecting the environment a technological retreat would extend over a wide front and go back a long, long way. A century ago we had already slaughtered the bison, felled the eastern forests, and degraded the colonial cities. Retreat to the 1870 level of technology, while not giving long-range protection to the environment, would place the median American standard of living far below the 1970 poverty line. Among the consequences of such a retreat would be the closing of 75 percent of the present colleges and most of the high schools. We would give up not only automobiles and airplanes but also mass education and social services. Grandpa would return to living in the abandoned hencoop.

Since we are not going to choose such a retreat from technology as a deliberate social policy, sheer practicality forces us to seek another way out. In that quest we have to ask seriously why the U.S. and all the other advanced countries have failed so dismally in handling the unwanted effects of technology.

Modern technology did not spring out of the void. It did not well up simultaneously in all the world's peoples. It appears first in European culture, and, although it is now disseminated over the whole globe, its main generative fonts remain to this day Western.

The Western origin and leadership in technology, the main agent of environmental destruction, inevitably raises uncomfortable questions about Western culture itself. The Judeo-Christian religious formation is not essentially "anti-nature," as some angry men now aver. But in contrast to Oriental religions, it does sharply separate its idea of God from its idea of nature and does look upon man as having a special relationship with the Creator and a unique place within creation.

What the Garbage Specialists Overlook

Western culture has never denied that a society stressing the individuality of its members needs the restraint and to some degree the positive leadership of government. But the character of government has also been affected by the trend toward differentiation. The Lord's anointed, with unspecified and even "absolute" power, has been split up into sharply segregated bureaucratic functions.

These, too, generate undesirable side effects. A highway department's mission is defined by statute and by specific appropriations. As it goes about its assigned task of building the most road for the least measured cost, it rips up neighborhoods and landscapes, creating enormous social disutilities that never get into the department's benefit-cost calculations. A sanitation department, told to dispose of garbage, may tow it offshore and dump it. When the refuse washes back upon the beaches and into the estuaries, the problem belongs to some other department. Or the specialists in solid-waste disposal may burn trash and garbage in places and in ways that transfer the pollution to the air.

Fragmentation of modern government occurs even in "totalitarian" countries. Administration of the Soviet economy is divided among fifty-odd ministries for the sake of efficiency. If a paper mill is needed, the men told off for that responsibility look around, like any capitalist, for plentiful timber, plentiful water, and cheap electric power. One paper mill was placed on the shore of beautiful Lake Baikal because the protection of this unique body of water lay outside the field of assigned vision of the men in charge of paper production. They were not being "greedy" or even "stupid" in the ordinary meaning of those words. They were wearing the blinkers of concentration, using the great Western device of fixing attention on the job at hand, of dealing intelligently with one segment of reality at a time.

A Problem of Balance

Though the principle of segregated attention proves gloriously successful—in research, in work, and in government—it can collide disastrously with the principle of unity. For each man is a unit though his skills and wants may be various. A society is a unit as well as a multitude. Nature, most marvelously connected throughout all its diversities, is a unit. Violation of these unities invites penalties and poses formidable tasks of reintegration.

Here we come to the root cause of our abuse of the environment: *in modern society the principle of fragmentation, outrunning the principle of unity, is producing a higher and higher degree of disorder and disutility.*

How can balance be restored? Since it is profoundly unrealistic to believe that we will or should retreat from such bastions of diversity as science, technology, and human individuality, then we have to seek improved methods of coordinating our fragmented thought and action.

During recent centuries, institutions of coordination, though lagging behind diversity, have not stood still. In economic affairs the market performs, albeit imperfectly, a stupendous job of mediating disparate wants, skills, resources. Government, amidst its bureaucratic fragments, has not completely lost the notion that it is supposed to serve such unitary purposes as "the general welfare." Specialized knowledge has a medium of transfer in the great modern webs of information, particularly the universities where all the sciences meet even if they do not fluently communicate.

How might such integrative agencies as market, government, and university be used, separately or in combination, so as to minimize the damage that fragmented action now does to the environment? This is the question on which the chance of actual reform, as distinguished from alarm and breast-beating, depends.

Subsidizing Destruction

In two areas, air and water pollution, a moment's reflection should convince anybody that the market, as now set up, is rigged against the environment. A hundred and fifty years ago it was almost unimaginable that clean water, much less clean air, could become scarce in the U.S. economy. Rightly, these resources were then considered common property and used without charge. The price of everything else the economy uses—land, minerals, food, labor, time—becomes dearer. But clean air and water, though now precious, are still left out of the pricing system, still free of charge.

Because the market has failed to keep pace with changing economic reality, the pricing system, expressing relative demand and supply, works against the conservation of clean air and water. A manufacturer is under great pressure to offset rising labor and material costs by developing new techniques. He has been under no comparable pressure with respect to clean air and water. Not surprisingly, techniques for conserving these resources have developed very slowly. The effect of omitting free resources from the pricing system is to make the economy as a whole pay a huge subsidy to those activities that put above average pressure on free resources. In short, we are now providing a huge, unintentional market incentive to pollution.

The most direct and logical way of getting clean air and water into the market system is by a federal tax graduated in respect to the quantity and undesirability of the pollutants. Such a tax, escalating over the first five or ten years so as not to destroy industries whose cost structures are based on the present system, would stimulate the development of antipollution techniques.

Taxes on the abuse of water and air would not replace the present trend toward stricter antipollution measures enforced by police power. Radioactive wastes, for instance, can be dangerous in very small quantities because they concentrate as they move up the food chain. The strictest control of such wastes is required—and may prove expensive. Nuclear power will be better able to absorb such costs if its competitor, fossil fuel, is forced to pay for the clean air and water it displaces. By such combination of government police power and taxing power we can turn the market toward protection of the environment—or at least achieve its "neutrality."

Correcting the market is much more difficult in that growing class of cases where the bad environmental side effects do not occur until the product is in the hands of the consumer or even until after he has disposed of it. It is by no means clear that automobiles, for instance, now carry taxes equivalent to the true social costs incurred by their use and disposal. If we become serious about the preservation or restoration of public transport in American cities the first step would be to make sure that public policy is not subsidizing the automobile.

Still more difficult to deal with is the product that is innocent until it interferes with some technique of protecting the environment. Many plastics give trouble in this indirect way. The polyvinyl chloride bottle causes no problems unless it is burned in a trash incinerator that is equipped with a scrubber designed to catch soot and fly ash. The burning PVC causes hydrochloric acid to form in the scrubber, destroying its metal casing. Some companies that hoped to sell more scrubbers for smaller incinerators have given up because they cannot guarantee their devices against the increasing incidence of PVC in trash. A small tax based on the nuisance side effect of certain plastics would either drive them off the market or encourage a new technology that abated the nuisance. As technology advances into more and more esoteric compounds, each carefully designed for a particular use, protection of the environment will require public policies that force innovators to pay more attention to the side effects of their products.

Evolution from Bureaucracy

The beginning of a shift from fragmented to integrative government action can be illustrated by a brief look at the history of a field where concern for the physical environment and concern for the social environment overlap. Generations of indignation about "the slums" came to a head in the Thirties. Crime, ignorance, disease, unemployment and, of course, poor housing were all among the reasons for anxiety. Governmental antislum action concentrated on one element, housing. Here was a material object that we surely knew how to produce in quantity. Without much study it was assumed that new public housing would somehow lever upward all the other adverse conditions of the slums.

So a large, competent, and militant bureaucracy was assembled on the narrow front of public housing. Over the years it went from triumph to triumph, if you measured by the size of the appropriation and the number of units built. People began to notice, however, that this program was not delivering, in human terms, what it had promised. The poor displaced by slum clearance were in many cases worse off than before. The new projects, more grim and sterile than the old slums, did not produce falling crime rates, better health, and improved school performance. Typically, the housing bureaucrats and their supporters brushed off these observations as inspired by reactionary politics and, inevitably, private greed.

A day came when the inadequacies of the narrow approach could no longer be ignored. More general terms, like "urban renewal," began to replace "slum clearance" and "public housing." In 1966 evolution of the governmental approach took a big step forward in the Model Cities program, which envisions a coordinated attack on such disparate fronts as medical care, educational enrichment, improved police work—and housing. Moreover, the Model Cities program calls for a decision-making structure in which people who live in the neighborhoods involved will have an important voice in determining what is done.

Because it runs against the familiar grain of fragmentation and bureaucratic control by the specialized experts, the Model Cities program breeds problems and conflicts. More accurately, it makes explicit and open those problems and conflicts that the old public-housing approach, eyes fixed straight ahead, would have ignored. "The community," now assumed to have its own values about its living arrangements, has been given an integrative role; it is forced to think in terms of priorities and of the relationship between, say, health and education. As a decision-maker, the community sometimes asks questions that would not have occurred to experts working within discrete programs. The broad approach puts pressure on the social and environmental sciences to coordinate their specialized knowledge and to undertake investigations of what needs, in a practical sense, to be discovered.

Plan for the Valleys

There will be many cases where a high measure of integrative action can be achieved with government playing only a secondary, though necessary, role. One of the most fascinating innovations in protection of the environment is on trial just northwest of Baltimore, in the area formed by the Green Spring and Worthington valleys.

These 45,000 acres are inhabited by well-to-do and rich landowners who breed horses and cattle in one of the loveliest landscapes to be found in the U.S. The appearance of the valleys had changed little in this century, but the handwriting was on the hillsides. New highways had made the area more accessible to Baltimore. New real-estate developments pressed in from three sides. There was a wide and deep consensus among the area's 5,000 families that they would like to keep it the way it was. Despite their wealth, they doubted that they would be able to do this. Some landowner would sell to a developer. Reading this as the beginning of the end, another and another would sell. They would do so not out of greed, but because the system as it actually functioned seemed to give them no other real choice. Soon the valley floor would be covered. People who had paid premium prices to live "in the beautiful Green Spring Valley" would discover that they were living in a replica of ten thousand other undistinguished suburbs.

The valley landowners, banding together, sought advice from Dr. David A. Wallace, who had planned Charles Center in midtown Baltimore. To make an ecological study he called in Ian L. McHarg, a landscape architect out of the University of Pennsylvania. Together they worked out a "Plan for the Valleys," described as a chapter in McHarg's book, *Design with Nature*. The plan's most striking characteristic is its contrast to the purely negative approach of most conservationists. It accepted change for the area not only as inevitable but as socially desirable. Wallace and McHarg, estimating that unplanned development would generate $33,500,000 in profits, sought to devise a way of orderly development that would add as much.

The unique aesthetic asset of the area was the pastoral scene on the valley floors. There, housing subdivisions would be prohibited. Development could occur in rather dense clusters on some of the area's plateaus, now sparsely inhabited. Within thirty years, population of the area might rise from 17,000 to 110,000 or more. By 1980 more than $40 million would be added to total value.

The big jump, of course, would be in the price of development land on the plateaus. The plan calls for some of this profit to be piped down to the valley-floor owners whose abstention from sales to developers would cause the price rise on the plateaus.

Whether this plan will work remains to be seen. But it is the kind of effort that should provoke study all over the U.S. The essential elements of the plan are (1) the wishes of the private owners; (2) their recognition that the housing needs of other people require great change in the area; (3) the combination of ecological and socio-economic planning principles; and (4) support of the plan by government.

"Plan for the Valleys" runs counter to many ingrained ideas of "absolute" private-property rights and untrammeled market action. The main purpose of institutions based on these ideas is to widen freedom of choice. As our technological power rises it becomes more and more obvious that the use and value of one man's land depend on what his neighbor does with his land. If this new reality is not reflected in our laws and other social institutions then actual freedom of choice diminishes. The wholesome "fragmentation" represented by private landownership will defeat itself in the absence of balancing institutions that can coordinate social action in respect, say, to the preservation of a beautiful environment, a unity that gives value to the ownership of its parts.

Can We Afford It All?

Environmental damage is so widespread and is continuing so rapidly that there is a serious question as to whether we can afford reform—a question that is not necessarily answered by the glib truth that we cannot afford to go on as we are. . . .

If certain twentieth-century trends such as population growth and, especially, the enlargement of the per capita mass-and-energy nimbus are simply extrapolated into the future, it's obvious that at some point we will destroy ourselves by consuming the earth. But these rates may not soar on forever. After ten years of falling U.S. birthrates, it has become possible to believe that the U.S. population may stabilize between the years 2000 and 2020 at not much above its present level, as a few demographers have predicted.

Limits of growth are also in sight for the more important rate of mass-and-energy used. The heavy environmental pressures come from agriculture and manufacturing (including mining). We are already producing more food than we consume and more than we would need to feed all the hungry in the U.S. The total value of manufactured goods will probably continue to rise for several decades, although substantial reductions in this demand could result from better environmental policies. Many things (e.g., the second family car, the second home) that we now buy are made "necessary" by wasteful environmental arrangements. The U.S. will probably reach saturation in manufactured goods in any event at some point in the next fifty years, if only because the time to use all the things we buy is becoming scarce.

Meanwhile, this economy will be very hard pressed to keep up with its increasing needs on the "services" front. A society that is both highly specialized and rapidly changing requires, as ours has already demonstrated, an elaborate "nerve system," employing millions, to maintain its cohesion and determine its direction. Among the elements of the "nerve system" are education, communications, law, finance, etc., which burn little fuel and consume small tonnages of materials.

We Won't Snuggle Back

The probability that gross pressure on the environment is due to stabilize does not of itself constitute a ground for optimism. It merely indicates that our prospect is not hopeless, and that by a huge and intelligent effort we might reverse the present devastation.

Whether that effort will be made depends primarily on how we think about the challenge. We did not get into this mess through such vices as gluttony, but rather through our virtues, our unbalanced and uncoordinated strengths. If we do not succeed in bringing under control our newfound powers, the failure will be attributable to the father of all vices, inattention to the consequences of our actions.

Modern man, Western or Westernized, is not going to snuggle back into the bosom of nature, perceiving all reality as a blurred continuum. That possibility of innocence we lost long ago in—of all places—a garden. We have understood differentiation, specialization, individuation; we have known the glories of action concentrated upon a specific purpose. Our path toward unity lies *through* diversity and specialization, not in recoil from them. A high-technology society without adequate institutions of coordination will produce either chaos or tyranny or both. Freedom will become meaningless because individual men will cease to believe that what they want has any relevance to what they get. But a high-technology society that can innovate adequate structures of decision will expand the freedom of individual choice far beyond any dream of the low-technology centuries.

The chief product of the future society is destined to be not food, not things, but the quality of the society itself. High on the list of what we mean by quality stands the question of how we deal with the material world, related as that is to how we deal with one another. That we have the wealth and the power to achieve a better environment is sure. That we will have the wisdom and charity to do so remains—and must always remain—uncertain.

René J. Dubos: The Human Landscape

In your letter inviting me to present this lecture you suggested, Mr. Secretary, that I discuss the impact of man on his environment and its likely effects on the future of the world community. The importance of this topic for our times was poignantly expressed by Ambassador Adlai E. Stevenson in his last speech before the United Nations Economic and Social Council just a few days before his death. These were the words:

> We travel together, passengers on a little spaceship, dependent on its vulnerable reserves of air and soil; all committed for our safety to its security and peace; preserved from annihilation only by the care, the work, and, I will say, the love we give our fragile craft.

At the turn of the 17th century, John Donne realized that no man is an island and that the bell tolls for us all. Picturesque as these images are, they were too parochial for so contemporary a man as Stevenson. He changed the parable to spaceship because he realized that we are all dependent not only on our neighbors but also on all other men and on the conditions prevailing over the whole earth.

The expression "spaceship earth" is no mere catchphrase. Now that all habitable parts of the globe are occupied, the careful husbandry of its resources is a *sine qua non* of survival for the human species, more important than economic growth or political power. We are indeed like travelers bound to the earth's crust, drawing breath from its shallow envelope

From the 1968 Department of State Science Lecture, "The Human Landscape," by René J. Dubos, *Department of State Bulletin*, Vol. LX, No. 1546, February 10, 1969, pp. 128–136. Condensed.

of air, using and reusing its limited supply of water. Yet we collectively behave as if we were not aware of the problems inherent in the limitations of the spaceship earth.

It would be easy, far too easy, to conclude from the present trend of events that mankind is on a course of self-destruction. I shall not discuss this possibility but shall instead focus my remarks on the certainty that the values and amenities identified with humanness are rapidly deteriorating.

Some of the supplies on which man depends are rapidly being depleted; even water will soon become scarce, not only in arid countries but also in the Temperate Zone. Most environments are being so grossly polluted that they may not long remain suitable for human existence. Smogs of various composition produced in urban and industrial areas are now hovering over the countryside and are beginning to spread over ocean masses. Sewage and chemical effluents are spoiling rivers, lakes, and coastlines and slowly but surely contaminating even the most carefully protected urban water supplies. Tin cans, plastic containers, discarded machines of all sorts, oil and other indegradable garbage, are accumulating all over the landscape, and in many cases ruining the land. Excessive sensory stimuli, and especially the mind-bewildering noise so ubiquitous as to be unavoidable, threaten to destroy the human quality of urban agglomerations.

The ancient words "soil," "air," "water," "freedom" are loaded with emotional content because they are associated with biological and mental needs that are woven in the fabric of man's nature. These needs are as vital today as they were in the distant past. Scientists and economists may learn a great deal about the intricacies of natural processes and of cost accounting. But scientific knowledge of environmental management will contribute little to health and happiness if it does not take into account the human values symbolized by phrases such as "the good earth," "a brilliant sky," "sparkling waters," "a place of one's own." Furthermore, the increase in population densities and in social complexity inevitably spells social regimentation, loss of privacy, and other interferences with individual freedom, which may eventually prove incompatible with the traditional ways of civilized life.

Man can, of course, invent devices and techniques to minimize the effects of environmental pollutants, but he cannot protect himself against everything all the time. He is so adaptable that he can learn to tolerate many shortages and environmental insults, but medical and social experience shows that such tolerances eventually have to be paid in the form of decreases in the quality of life.

We might take comfort from the fact that during its long biological history, mankind has become adapted to many different kinds of environment and has been able to survive under very difficult conditions. However, this adaptive process required thousands and thousands of years, whereas profound environmental changes now occur in the course of a few years—far too rapidly to allow for biological adaptation.

The fact that modern man is now moving into nonterrestrial environments might also be interpreted as evidence that he has escaped from the bondage of his evolutionary past and is becoming independent of his ancient biological attributes. But this is an erroneous interpretation. The human body and brain have not changed significantly during the past 100,000 years, and there is no ground for the belief that they will change appreciably in the foreseeable future. The biological needs of modern man as well as his biological capabilities and limitations are essentially the same as those of the paleolithic hunter and the neolithic farmer. Civilization provides man with techniques that greatly enlarge the scope of his activities, but it does not change his fundamental nature.

Wherever he goes and whatever he does, in tropical deserts or arctic wastes, in outer space or ocean depths, man must maintain around himself a microenvironment similar to the one under which he evolved. He can survive outlandish areas only by functioning within enclosures that almost duplicate a Mediterranean atmosphere, as if he remained linked to the surface of the earth by an umbilical cord. He may engage in casual flirtations with nonterrestrial worlds, but he is wedded to the earth, his sole source of sustenance.

The strict dependence of the human organism on the narrow range of terrestrial conditions imposes inescapable constraints on civilized life. In practice, social and technological innovations are viable and humanly successful only to the extent that they are compatible with the unchangeable aspects of man's nature. Man can retain his biological and mental health only if his civilizations maintain a healthy environment.

As used in the preceding paragraph, the phrase "healthy environment" implies much more than the maintenance of ecological equilibrium, the conservation of natural resources, and the control of the forces that threaten biological and mental health. Man does not only survive and function in his environment; he is *shaped* by it, biologically, mentally, and socially. To be really "healthy" the environment must therefore provide conditions that favor the development of desirable human characteristics.

The very process of living involves a constant feedback between man and his environment with the result that both are constantly being modified in the course of this interplay. Individual persons, and their social groups, acquire their distinctive characteristics as a consequence of the responses they make to the total environment. The exciting richness of the human landscape results not only from the genetic diversity of mankind but also and perhaps even more from the shaping influence that surroundings and ways of life exert on biological and social man.

The New Pessimism

Until a few decades ago, scientists and technologists took it for granted that all aspects of their work enriched human life and made it healthier and happier. Most enlightened persons also realized that scientific research generates wealth and power, as well as better understanding of man's nature and of the cosmos.

Confidence in the creative and predictive power of science is so great that several groups of scholars have now made it an academic profession to forecast the technological and medical advances that can be expected for the year 2000. Naturally enough, they predict spectacular breakthroughs in the production of nuclear energy, the development of electronic gadgets, the chemical synthesis of materials better than the natural ones, the discovery of drugs and surgical techniques that will keep men healthy or save them from death. From permanent lunar installations to robot human slaves and to programed dreams, many are the scientific miracles that can be anticipated for the year 2000. Individual scientists would differ as to what theoretical possibilities will be converted into reality during the forthcoming decades. But all of them would agree that scientific research is capable of providing very soon powerful new techniques for manipulating external nature and man's nature.

In view of the miraculous achievements of modern science and of the promise of many more to come, one might expect the general public to believe that life in the near future will be safe, abundant, comfortable, and exhilarating. Yet there prevails in modern societies—in particular among educated groups—a feeling of uneasiness and even hostility toward science and its technological applications.

Most persons still trust that scientific research can increase the factual knowledge of man's nature and of the cosmos. Few are those who now believe, however, that such knowledge necessarily improves health and happiness. In fact, so many environmental values are being threatened by technological and social forces that the word "environment" has acquired almost a pejorative meaning which reflects public concern for the quality of man's relationship to the rest of creation. . . . For most laymen and not a few scientists, the word "environment" evokes not fitness but nightmares.

This atmosphere of anxiety, which has been called "the new pessimism" by Mr. James Reston in a *New York Times* editorial, has several different manifestations.

One is the feeling that science has weakened or destroyed many of the traditional values by which men function, yet has failed to provide a new ethical system. Science, the saying goes, gives man everything to live with but nothing to live for.

Experience has shown, furthermore, that the advantages derived from scientific discoveries and technological achievements usually have to be paid for in the form of new dangers and new threats to human welfare. The fact that nuclear science promises endless sources of energy but also makes it possible to build ever more destructive weapons symbolizes the two faces of the scientific enterprise. All too often, there exists a painful discrepancy between what man aims for and what he gets. He sprays pesticides to get rid of insects and weeds but thereby kills birds, fishes, and flowering trees. He drives long distances to find unspoiled nature but poisons the air and gets killed on the way. He builds machines to escape from physical work but becomes their slave and experiences boredom. Every week the pages of magazines bear witness to the public's somber anticipation that the legend of the sorcerer's apprentice may soon be converted from a literary symbol into a terrifying reality.

The tactical triumphs and human failures of technological civilization call to mind the remark made to Hannibal by one of his officers at the end of the Second Punic War: "You know how to win victories, Hannibal, but you do not know how to use them." No one doubts the power of science, yet a characteristic aspect of the new pessimism is the feeling that the most distressing social problems generated by scientific technology are not amenable to scientific solutions. Many are those who believe, indeed, that an environmental catastrophe is inevitable.

Fortunately, the word "catastrophe" can have two very different meanings, both applicable to the relationship between scientific technology and the future of the world community. In common usage, the word "catastrophe" denotes a disastrous event. In its etymological Greek sense, however, it means a change of course, an overturn not necessarily resulting in disaster. The disasters that threaten mankind are too obvious to need elaboration. But we can avoid these disasters if we keep in mind the etymological meaning of the word "catastrophe" and try to alter the present course of scientific technology.

In my judgment, scientists will contribute to the solution of the problems they create as soon as the scientific enterprise addresses itself in earnest to the present preoccupations of mankind. From this point of view, the technological breakthroughs predicted for the year 2000 are trivial and, indeed, irrelevant. They have no bearing on such problems as the raping of nature, environmental pollution, urban crowding, the feeling of alienation, racial and national conflicts, and other threats to decent life. The man of flesh and bone will not be much impressed by the fact that a few of his contemporaries can explore the moon, program their dreams, or use robots as slaves, if the planet earth has become unfit for his everyday life. He will not long continue to be interested in space acrobatics if he has to watch them with his feet deep in garbage and his eyes half-blinded by smog.

Despite our boasts, we do not truly *live* in an age of science. What we have done is to develop techniques for exploiting the external world, usually without regard to real human needs, and for correcting a few disorders of the body and of the mind, often without much concern for the achievement of happiness. In many cases, we know next to nothing of the consequences—especially the indirect and long-range consequences— that eventually result from the manipulations of the external world and of man's nature in which we engage so thoughtlessly.

Science and the technologies derived from it obviously exert profound effects on all human enterprises in the modern world. But we have not yet seriously applied scientific thinking to the creation of a desirable human life in the here and now, let alone in the future.

Man inevitably changes nature, and inevitably also he is changed by the environmental forces that he manipulates and to which he exposes himself. Human societies have always manipulated nature—clearing forests, plowing prairies, developing irrigation or drainage systems, then converting farmland into roads, dwellings, or industrial plants. The word "environment" now includes all the technological forces that modern man sets in motion and that in turn shape his biological and mental characteristics. Sir Winston Churchill expressed this profound biological law in a picturesque sentence: "We shape our buildings, and afterwards our buildings shape us."

I shall illustrate with a few examples how the scientific enterprise can provide the kind of information that will help in maintaining the earth in a state suitable for human life and in creating environments favorable for the more complete expression of human potentialities.

a. Physicists have shown that nuclear technologies could provide mankind with an endless source of energy. On the other hand, any perceptive person knows that energy improperly used contributes to the degradation of the environment. The so-called "conquest" of nature by the use of any form of energy is potentially dangerous if it is not carried out within the imperatives of certain ecological laws. Tagore's "wooing of the earth" means the achievement of a state in which man, other living things, and the physical environment can all survive and prosper.

The wise use of nuclear technologies requires that we develop the kind of ecological sciences that will enable us to foresee the consequences of environmental manipulations, measured not so much in the terms of economics as in present and future human values. From this point of view, the creation and maintenance of sound ecological systems is more important than the "conquest" of nature.

b. Chemists and engineers will unquestionably produce more and more new materials and processes that will change many aspects of human life. It is commonly assumed that man can and must adapt to these changes. But in fact human adaptability is not limitless.

We know little of the thresholds and ranges of human adaptability. It is certain in any case that the ready acceptance of social and technological changes does not mean that these are desirable. Past experience has shown for example that ionizing radiations and environmental pollution (of air, food, and water) have deleterious effects that manifest themselves very slowly; they behave like the pestilence that stealeth in the darkness. Similarly, social and technological innovations that appear to be readily tolerated may eventually ruin the quality of human life. The real limits of adaptability are not determined by what can be tolerated for a certain period of time, but by future consequences. These consequences are essential factors to be considered in deciding what technological and social innovations are safe and desirable.

c. Medical scientists will certainly develop new techniques and new drugs for the treatment of the degenerative and chronic diseases that are now plaguing mankind. But such treatments will be increasingly expensive and, more importantly, will require highly specialized personnel. They cannot solve the massive health problems of the general public.

There is good reason to believe that most of the degenerative conditions that are becoming increasingly prevalent in the modern world need not have occurred in the first place. Greater knowledge of the environmental and social factors that cause disease would go much further toward improving human health than the discovery of drugs, surgical procedures, and other esoteric methods of treatment. Prevention is much less expensive than cure and always more effective.

d. Parochial man could theoretically be replaced by global man because technical procedures enable him to read, hear, and see anything that goes on in the world. But in practice communications technology is only a small part of the communication.

We need more knowledge concerning the receptiveness of sense organs and of the brain to the information that technology can provide. We need to learn also how to make information become really *formative,* instead of being merely informative. Only those influences that are formative contribute to human development.

Pointing to some of the present inadequacies of science does not imply either a defeatist or an anti-intellectual attitude. It directs attention rather to the need for engaging scientific inquiry into new channels. The solution to our social and environmental problems is not in less science but in a kind of science which is subservient to the fundamental needs of man.

The Fitness of the Environment

Our societies are slowly realizing that many social and technological practices are threatening human and environmental health; rather grudgingly, they are developing palliative measures to control some of the most obvious dangers. This piecemeal social engineering will be helpful in many cases, but it will not solve the ecological crisis and its attendant threats to the quality of life. Technological fixes amount to little more than putting a finger in the dike, whereas what is needed is a comprehensive philosophy of man in his environment. L. J. Henderson's concept of the "fitness of the environment," provides a framework for such a philosophy.

Fitness implies that man has achieved some kind of adaptation to his environment. Many populations in the past have achieved a tolerable state of adaptation to their surroundings and ways of life, even when these were very primitive according to our own standards. In any case, however, adaptive fitness lasts only as long as conditions are stable. Changes that upset the equilibrium between man and environment are likely to disturb physical and mental health and thereby to generate unhappiness.

More interestingly, fitness also implies that all aspects of human development reflect the adaptive responses made by the organism to environmental stimuli. In the long run, most forms of adaptation involve evolutionary alterations of the genetic endowment. But in addition, the biological and mental characteristics of each individual person are shaped by his responses to the environmental forces that impinge on him in the course of his development. Genes do not determine the traits by which we know a person; what they do is only to govern his biological responses to environmental influences. As a result each person is shaped by his environment as much as by his genetic endowment.

The environmental influences that are experienced very early during the formative phases of development (prenatal and early post-natal) have the most profound and lasting effects. From early nutrition to education, from technological forces to esthetic and ethical attitudes, countless are the early influences that make an irreversible imprint on the human body and mind. Most of the biological and mental characteristics that are assumed to be distinctive of the various ethnic groups—anywhere in the world—turn out to be the consequences of early environmental influences (biological and social) rather than of genetic constitution.

Human beings actualize only a small part of the potentialities they inherit in their genetic code, because these potentialities become reality only to the extent that circumstances favor phenotypic expression. In practice, mental development is greatly facilitated if the person—especially the child—is exposed at a critical time to the proper range of stimuli and acquires a wide awareness of the cosmos. Science and technology can play a crucial role in the shaping of mental attributes by making it possible to create environments more diversified and thereby more favorable for the expression of a wider range of human potentialities.

The Collective Search for Knowledge

Programs of social betterment should be based on the ability to predict the effects that social and technological manipulations will exert on the human organism and on ecological systems, both the immediate and the long-range effects. Unfortunately, interest in scientific forecasting has been concerned almost exclusively with the technological and social developments themselves, rather than with their effects on human life and on ecological systems.

Many scientific problems of relevance to human life in the urban and technological world cry out for investigation. Three examples will be mentioned here merely as illustrations:

a. Everyone agrees that it is desirable to control environmental pollution. But what are the pollutants of air, water, or food that are really significant? Sulfur dioxide, carbon monoxide, and the nitrogen oxides generated by automobile exhausts are the air pollutants most widely discussed. But the colloidal particles released from automobile tires and from the asbestos lining of brakes grossly contaminate the air of our cities and may well be more dangerous than some of the gases against which control efforts are now directed.

The acute effects of environmental pollution can be readily recognized, but what about the cumulative, delayed, and indirect effects? Does the young organism respond as does the adult? Does he develop forms of tolerance or hypersusceptibility that affect his subsequent responses to the same or other pollutants?

Priorities with regard to the control of environmental pollution cannot be established rationally until such knowledge is available.

b. Everyone agrees that all cities of the world must be renovated or even rebuilt. Technologies are available for almost any kind of scheme imagined by city planners, architects, and sociologists. But hardly anything is known concerning the effects that the urban environments so created will have on human well-being and especially on the physical and mental development of children.

We know how to create sanitary environments that permit the body to become large and vigorous. But what about the effect of the environmental factors on the mind? All too often housing developments are designed as if they were to be used as disposable cubicles for dispensable people.

c. Everyone agrees that all citizens should be given the same educational opportunities. But what are the critical ages for receptivity to various kinds of stimuli and for the development of mental potentialities?

We must develop a science concerned with the effects that the environmental influences created by massive urbanization and by ubiquitous technology exert on physical, physiological, and mental characteristics.

We must learn how the effects of early deprivation or overstimulation can be prevented and corrected.

The Diversity of Civilizations

Certain general principles are valid for all environmental problems, because they are based on unchangeable and universal aspects of ecological systems, and especially of man's nature.

The biological and mental constitution of *Homo sapiens* has changed only in minor details since the late Stone Age; and despite progresses in theoretical genetics, there is no chance that it can be significantly or safely modified in the foreseeable future. This genetic stability defines the limits within which human life can be safely altered by social or technological innovations. Beyond these limits, any change is likely to have disastrous effects.

On the other hand, mankind has a large reserve of potentialities that have not yet been expressed. By enlarging the range of experiences and increasing the numbers of options, science and technology can facilitate the actualization of these latent potentialities and thus bring to light much unsuspected richness in man's nature and in ecological systems.

As more persons find it possible to express their innate endowments because they can select from a variety of conditions, society becomes richer and civilizations continue to unfold. In contrast, if the surroundings and ways of life are highly stereotyped—whether in prosperity or in poverty—the only components of man's nature that can flourish are those adapted to the narrow range of prevailing conditions. Mankind becomes actualized to the extent that we shun uniformity of surroundings and absolute conformity in behavior. Creating diversified environments may result in some loss of efficiency, but diversity is vastly more important than efficiency because it makes possible the germination of the seeds dormant in the human species. In the light of these facts, the continued existence of independent nations may be desirable even though it generates political problems, because the cultivation of national characteristics probably contributes to the cultural richness of mankind.

Diversity, however, does not imply complete permissiveness. Individual man must accept some form of discipline because he can survive and, indeed, exist only when integrated in a social structure. For related ecological and social reasons, no group, large or small, can be entirely independent of the other groups within the confines of the spaceship earth. Total rejection of discipline is unbiologic because it would inevitably result in the disintegration of individual lives, of the social order, and of ecological systems.

In the final analysis, the interplay between man and his environment must therefore be considered from three different points of view:

a. The frontiers of social and technological changes are determined not by availability of power and technical prowess but by unchangeable aspects of man's nature and of ecological systems.

b. The total environment must be sufficiently diversified to assure that each person can express as completely as possible his innate potentialities in accordance with his selected goals.

c. The expressions of individuality can be allowed only to the extent that they are compatible with the requirements of the social group and of the world community.

The universality of mankind, the uniqueness of each person, and the need for social integration are three determinants of human life that must be reconciled in order to achieve individual freedom, social health, and the diversity of civilizations.

10

Foreign Commitments

As the war in Vietnam began to wind down in 1970 and 1971 and we began to assess this costly adventure, it became increasingly apparent that the price of Vietnam was not to be measured solely in terms of wasted human and economic resources. The Vietnam war and the accompanying protest movement have caused not only a crisis in the public's confidence in our foreign policy in Southeast Asia but, perhaps more seriously, the long years of war have contributed to a rising isolationist sentiment in the United States. The long-term implications of the war may well be even more costly than the short-term balance sheet indicates.

In the years following World War II there was a strong internationalist sentiment in the United States, at least among certain major leadership groups. The military presence of the Soviet Union in Eastern Europe and the fall of Nationalist China gave a sense of urgency to American foreign policy. Containment of communism became the keystone to our foreign and military policy, and bipartisanship was the watchword. It is doubtful, however, if any President or Secretary of State in the 1940s, 1950s, or early 1960s ever thought he had an easy task in persuading the public in general and the Congress in particular, to fully support their foreign policy programs. Each year the President, his associates, and certain key members of Congress had to launch a campaign to persuade the public and Congress that America as a major world power had responsibilities and security interests abroad. There was always a fear that after the euphoria of the 1945 victory had subsided America would slip back into isolationism, to a "They hired the money, didn't they?" Calvin Coolidge view of international relations.

In the 25 years following World War II, Congress did pass legislation authorizing the Marshall Plan, the Point Four Program, the Mutual Security Agency, the Alliance for Progress, and appropriated billions of dollars for foreign economic aid and military assistance. But no one can read the congressional foreign policy hearings and debates during those years and not conclude that Congress was frequently an unwilling partner in American foreign policy. This is not to imply that Congress is fundamentally isolationist. Certainly the Senate demonstrated a strong internationalist position throughout most of the 1950s and 1960s. Nonetheless, there have been strong critics of both foreign economic aid and foreign military assistance. In general, Senate liberals began to move against military assistance programs in the middle 1960s. On the other hand, many Senate conservatives had long opposed foreign economic aid programs. By the late 1960s there were at least a dozen senators who were voting consistently against both foreign military and foreign economic aid programs—Gruening of Alaska, Morse of Oregon, Ervin of North Carolina, Fulbright of Arkansas, Ellender of Louisiana, Jordan of Idaho, Bible of Nevada, Williams of Delaware, Cotton of New Hampshire, McClellan of Arkansas, and Proxmire of Wisconsin.

The war in Vietnam, in combination with growing but unresolved domestic problems and a dip in the economy, allowed a latent isolationism to surface again in the early 1970s. Isolationism is not likely in the immediate future to get the grip on America that it had in the 1920s; it has been unfashionable too long to become a popular banner. Still, one senses an air of neoisolationism in the public and congressional debates over military and foreign aid commitments. The comments by Senator Stuart Symington (Democrat, Missouri) are reasonably close to what some might characterize as a neoisolationship position.

Clearly the neoisolationists have not received much aid and comfort from the foreign policy statements of President Nixon. His "New Strategy for Peace," while it recognizes a changing scene in international politics, does not appear to signal any fundamental retreat in foreign affairs, although it did vaguely suggest that the new China policy was being considered. Contrary to Senator Symington's approach, President Nixon focuses on the interests that shape our commitments, whereas Senator Symington's observations lead one to conclude that he is principally concerned about the burden of our commitments. The swing in Senator Symington's position, a former Secretary of the Air Force, is illustrative of the growing concern in Congress about the scope of our security commitments abroad, particularly secret security commitments. We have included here a portion of a recent Senate committee report that was highly critical of foreign policy agreements that have not been subjected to "the broad daylight of public discussion."

Paul C. Warnke, former Assistant Secretary for Defense, was asked by the House Committee on Foreign Affairs to testify in response to President

Nixon's foreign policy address. The thrust of his comments was that Mr. Nixon had not gone far enough in delimiting the narrower range of national security interests America has today than it thought it had a decade ago. Furthermore, he warned that no American foreign policy can remain viable without broad-based public support. The clear implication of his statement is that while the United States has important security interests abroad, these interests are largely centered in our relationships with the Soviet Union and to a lesser extent our relationships with the People's Republic of China; these relationships should not be jeopardized by commitments and adventures that fundamentally undermine our strength.

The next article by Richard J. Barnet, codirector of the Institute for Policy Studies, presents an entirely different perspective on American foreign policy. Mr. Barnet suggests that our national security policy has been based on a misconception of the nature of security in the post–World War II era. He argues that our ultimate national security depends on our willingness to accept three propositions:

1. That poor countries will experiment with revolutionary methods for changing their political, social, and economic conditions;
2. That disorder and instability are a part of the modern international scene;
3. That we are not the problem-solver, but an integral part of the problem; that is, our disproportionate share of power and resources and attempts to maintain them increasingly isolates us from the poorer nations.

In effect, Mr. Barnet suggests that the United States' security depends on a willingness to fundamentally alter our domestic life, including our military policy and perhaps even our domestic economic policies. The difficulty with Mr. Barnet's analysis is that while he disavows the United States as a "problem solver," he strongly hints that America's vast resources should be, at least in part, freed to solve the problems of the poor in Asia, Africa, and Latin America.

The final selection is from the congressional testimony of Hans J. Morgenthau, Professor of International Relations, University of Chicago. It provides an interesting contrast to the article by Barnet. Morgenthau contends that we have confused the political purposes of our foreign economic policy by packaging the policy in the guise of foreign aid for economic development and foreign military assistance. He suggests that the chances for success in economic development programs in underdeveloped countries are quite limited and are dependent on a realistic preassessment of the political and cultural conditions in the recipient country. The political and cultural conditions in such countries frequently do not favor economic development; in consequence, successful programs may require that the donor nation actively promote drastic social change—with all the attendant instability—in the recipient nation as a precondition for success. Yet if the goal of this aspect of American foreign policy is international stability, then Morgenthau suggests the programs may well be counterproductive. In any event, if Morgenthau's assumptions about preconditions are valid, then we face the dilemma that if we are to bridge successfully the economic gulf separating affluent Americans from the poor of Asia, Africa, and Latin America, we must do what Mr. Barnet considers to be improper—become the intervening problem-solver in the affairs of other nations. On the other hand, if we do not insist on the necessary preconditions, then foreign aid is likely to be used by the recipient nations to maintain the status quo. Assuming that the United States would be willing to divest itself of a considerable portion of its resources and power and that the divested resources could bridge the gulf—and these are tenuous assumptions—we would still face the practical programmatic problem of transferring the resources by methods that would not cast the United States in the role of "problem-solver of the world." That would be no mean task in terms of resource allocation and diplomacy.

Richard M. Nixon: A New Strategy for Peace

When I took office, the most immediate problem facing our nation was the war in Vietnam. No question has more occupied our thoughts and energies during this past year.

Yet the fundamental task confronting us was more profound. We could see that the whole pattern of international politics was changing. Our challenge was to understand that change, to define America's goals for the next period, and to set in motion policies to achieve them. For all Americans must understand that because of its strength, its history and its concern for human dignity, this nation occupies a special place in the world. Peace and progress are impossible without a major American role. . . .

From "U.S. Foreign Policy for the 1970's: A New Strategy for Peace," by Richard M. Nixon, *The Department of State Bulletin,* Vol. LXII, March 9, 1970.

A New Era

The postwar period in international relations has ended.

Then, we were the only great power whose society and economy had escaped World War II's massive destruction. Today, the ravages of that war have been overcome. Western Europe and Japan have recovered their economic strength, their political vitality, and their national self-confidence. Once the recipients of American aid, they have now begun to share their growing resources with the developing world. Once almost totally dependent on American military power, our European allies now play a greater role in our common policies, commensurate with their growing strength.

Then, new nations were being born, often in turmoil and uncertainty. Today, these nations have a new spirit and a growing strength of independence. Once, many feared that they would become simply a battleground of cold-war rivalry and fertile ground for Communist penetration. But this fear misjudged their pride in their national identities and their determination to preserve their newly won sovereignty.

Then, we were confronted by a monolithic Communist world. Today, the nature of that world has changed—the power of individual Communist nations has grown, but international Communist unity has been shattered. Once a unified bloc, its solidarity has been broken by the powerful forces of nationalism. The Soviet Union and Communist China, once bound by an alliance of friendship, had become bitter adversaries by the mid-1960's. The only times the Soviet Union has used the Red Army since World War II have been against its own allies—in East Germany in 1953, in Hungary in 1956, and in Czechoslovakia in 1968. The Marxist dream of international Communist unity has disintegrated.

Then, the United States had a monopoly or overwhelming superiority of nuclear weapons. Today, a revolution in the technology of war has altered the nature of the military balance of power. New types of weapons present new dangers. Communist China has acquired thermonuclear weapons. Both the Soviet Union and the United States have acquired the ability to inflict unacceptable damage on the other, no matter which strikes first. There can be no gain and certainly no victory for the power that provokes a thermonuclear exchange. Thus, both sides have recognized a vital mutual interest in halting the dangerous momentum of the nuclear arms race.

Then, the slogans formed in the past century were the ideological accessories of the intellectual debate. Today, the "isms" have lost their vitality—indeed the restlessness of youth on both sides of the dividing line testifies to the need for a new idealism and deeper purposes.

This is the challenge and the opportunity before America as it enters the 1970's.

The Framework for a Durable Peace

In the first postwar decades, American energies were absorbed in coping with a cycle of recurrent crises, whose fundamental origins lay in the destruction of World War II and the tensions attending the emergence of scores of new nations. Our opportunity today—and challenge—is to get at the causes of crises, to take a longer view, and to help build the international relationships that will provide the framework of a durable peace.

I have often reflected on the meaning of "peace," and have reached one certain conclusion: Peace must be far more than the absence of war. Peace must provide a durable structure of international relationships which inhibits or removes the causes of war. Building a lasting peace requires a foreign policy guided by three basic principles:

—Peace requires *partnership*. Its obligations, like its benefits, must be shared. This concept of partnership guides our relations with all friendly nations.

—Peace requires *strength*. So long as there are those who would threaten our vital interests and those of our allies with military force, we must be strong. American weakness could tempt would-be aggressors to make dangerous miscalculations. At the same time, our own strength is important only in relation to the strength of others. We—like others—must place high priority on enhancing our security through cooperative arms control.

—Peace requires a *willingness to negotiate*. All nations—and we are no exception—have important national interests to protect. But the most fundamental interest of all nations lies in building the structure of peace. In partnership with our allies, secure in our own strength, we will seek those areas in which we can agree among ourselves and with others to accommodate conflicts and overcome rivalries. We are working toward the day when *all* nations will have a stake in peace, and will therefore be partners in its maintenance.

Within such a structure, international disputes can be settled and clashes contained. The insecurity of nations, out of which so much conflict arises, will be eased, and the habits of moderation and compromise will be nurtured. Most important, a durable peace will give full opportunity to the powerful forces driving toward economic change and social justice.

This vision of a peace built on partnership, strength and willingness to negotiate is the unifying theme of this report. In the sections that follow, the first steps we have taken during this past year—the policies we have devised and the programs we have initiated to realize this vision—are placed in the context of these three principles.

1. Peace through Partnership—
The Nixon Doctrine

As I said in my address of November 3, "We Americans are a do-it-yourself people—an impatient people. Instead of teaching someone else to do a job, we like to do it ourselves. This trait has been carried over into our foreign policy."

The postwar era of American foreign policy began in this vein in 1947 with the proclamation of the Truman Doctrine and the Marshall Plan, offering American economic and military assistance to countries threatened by aggression. Our policy held that democracy and prosperity, buttressed by American military strength and organized in a worldwide network of American-led alliances, would insure stability and peace. In the formative years of the postwar period, this great effort of international political and economic reconstruction was a triumph of American leadership and imagination, especially in Europe.

For two decades after the end of the Second World War, our foreign policy was guided by such a vision and inspired by its success. The vision was based on the fact that the United States was the richest and most stable country, without whose initiative and resources little security or progress was possible.

This impulse carried us through into the 1960's. The United States conceived programs and ran them. We devised strategies, and proposed them to our allies. We discerned dangers and acted directly to combat them.

The world has dramatically changed since the days of the Marshall Plan. We deal now with a world of stronger allies, a community of independent developing nations, and a Communist world still hostile but now divided.

Others now have the ability and responsibility to deal with local disputes which once might have required our intervention. Our contribution and success will depend not on the frequency of our involvement in the affairs of others, but on the stamina of our policies. This is the approach which will best encourage other nations to do their part, and will most genuinely enlist the support of the American people.

This is the message of the doctrine I announced at Guam—the "Nixon Doctrine." Its central thesis is that the United States will participate in the defense and development of allies and friends, but that America cannot—and will not—conceive *all* the plans, design *all* the programs, execute *all* the decisions and undertake *all* the defense of the free nations of the world. We will help where it makes a real difference and is considered in our interest.

America cannot live in isolation if it expects to live in peace. We have no intention of withdrawing from the world. The only issue before us is how we can be most effective in meeting our responsibilities, protecting our interests, and thereby building peace.

A more responsible participation by our foreign friends in their own defense and progress means a more effective common effort toward the goals we all seek. Peace in the world will continue to require us to maintain our commitments—and we will. . . . In my State of the Union Address, I affirmed that "to insist that other nations play a role is not a retreat from responsibility; it is a sharing of responsibility." This is not a way for America to withdraw from its indispensable role in the world. It is a way—the only way—we can carry out our responsibilities.

It is misleading, moreover, to pose the fundamental question so largely in terms of commitments. Our objective, in the first instance, is to support our *interests* over the long run with a sound foreign policy. The more that policy is based on a realistic assessment of our and others' interests, the more effective our role in the world can be. We are not involved in the world because we have commitments; we have commitments because we are involved. Our interests must shape our commitments, rather than the other way around.

We will view new commitments in the light of a careful assessment of our own national interests and those of other countries, of the specific threats to those interests, and of our capacity to counter those threats at an acceptable risk and cost.

We have been guided by these concepts during the past year in our dealings with free nations throughout the world.

—In Europe, our policies embody precisely the three principles of a durable peace: partnership, continued strength to defend our common interests when challenged, and willingness to negotiate differences with adversaries.

—Here in the Western Hemisphere we seek to strengthen our special relationship with our sister republics through a new program of action for progress in which all voices are heard and none predominates.

—In Asia, where the Nixon Doctrine was enunciated, partnership will have special meaning for our policies—as evidenced by our strengthened ties with Japan. Our cooperation with Asian nations will be enhanced as they cooperate with one another and develop regional institutions.

—In Vietnam, we seek a just settlement which all parties to the conflict, and all Americans, can support. We are working closely with the South Vietnamese to strengthen their ability to defend themselves. As South Vietnam grows stronger, the other side will, we hope, soon realize that it becomes ever more in their interest to negotiate a just peace.

—In the Middle East, we shall continue to work with others to establish a possible framework within which the parties to the Arab-Israeli conflict can negotiate the complicated and difficult questions at issue. Others must join us in recognizing that a settlement will require sacrifices and restraints by all concerned.

—Africa, with its historic ties to so many of our own citizens, must always retain a significant place in our partnership with the new nations. Africans will play the major role in fulfilling their just aspirations—an end to racialism, the building of new nations, freedom from outside interference, and cooperative economic development. But we will add our efforts to theirs to help realize Africa's great potential.

—In an ever more interdependent world economy, American foreign policy will emphasize the freer flow of capital and goods between nations. We are proud to have participated in the successful cooperative effort which created Special Drawing Rights, a form of international money which will help insure the stability of the monetary structure on which the continued expansion of trade depends.

—The great effort of economic development must engage the cooperation of all nations. We are carefully studying the specific goals of our economic assistance programs and how most effectively to reach them.

—Unprecedented scientific and technological advances as well as explosions in population, communications, and knowledge require new forms of international cooperation. The United Nations, the symbol of international partnership, will receive our continued strong support as it marks its 25th Anniversary.

2. America's Strength

The second element of a durable peace must be America's strength. Peace, we have learned, cannot be gained by good will alone.

In determining the strength of our defenses, we must make precise and crucial judgments. We should spend no more than is necessary. But there is an irreducible minimum of essential military security: for if we are less strong than necessary, and if the worst happens, there will be no domestic society to look after. The magnitude of such a catastrophe, and the reality of the opposing military power that could threaten it, present a risk which requires of any President the most searching and careful attention to the state of our defenses.

The changes in the world since 1945 have altered the context and requirements of our defense policy. In this area, perhaps more than in any other, the need to re-examine our approaches is urgent and constant.

The last 25 years have seen a revolution in the nature of military power. In fact, there has been a series of transformations—from the atomic to the thermonuclear weapon, from the strategic bomber to the intercontinental ballistic missile, from the surface missile to the hardened silo and the missile-carrying submarine, from the single to the multiple warhead, and from air defense to missile defense. We are now entering an era in which the sophistication and destructiveness of weapons present more formidable and complex issues affecting our strategic posture.

The last 25 years have also seen an important change in the relative balance of strategic power. From 1945 to 1949, we were the only nation in the world possessing an arsenal of atomic weapons. From 1950 to 1966, we possessed an overwhelming superiority in strategic weapons. From 1967 to 1969, we retained a significant superiority. Today, the Soviet Union possesses a powerful and sophisticated strategic force approaching our own. We must consider, too, that Communist China will deploy its own intercontinental missiles during the coming decade, introducing new and complicating factors for our strategic planning and diplomacy.

In the light of these fateful changes, the Administration undertook a comprehensive and far-reaching reconsideration of the premises and procedures for designing our forces. We sought—and I believe we have achieved—a rational and coherent formulation of our defense strategy and requirements for the 1970's.

The importance of comprehensive planning of policy and objective scrutiny of programs is clear:

> —Because of the lead-time in building new strategic systems, the decisions we make today substantially determine our military posture—and thus our security—five years from now. This places a premium on foresight and planning.

> —Because the allocation of national resources between defense programs and other national programs is itself an issue of policy, it must be considered on a systematic basis at the early stages of the national security planning process.

> —Because we are a leader of the Atlantic Alliance, our doctrine and forces are crucial to the policy and planning of NATO. The mutual confidence that holds the allies together depends on understanding, agreement, and coordination among the 15 sovereign nations of the Treaty.

> —Because our security depends not only on our own strategic strength, but also on cooperative efforts to provide greater security for everyone through arms control, planning weapons systems and planning for arms control negotiations must be closely integrated.

For these reasons, this Administration has established procedures for the intensive scrutiny of defense issues in the light of overall national priorities. We have re-examined our strategic forces; we have reassessed our general purpose forces; and we have engaged in the most painstaking preparation ever undertaken by the United States Government for arms control negotiations.

3. Willingness To Negotiate— An Era of Negotiation

Partnership and strength are two of the pillars of the structure of a durable peace. Negotiation is the third. For our commitment to peace is most convincingly demonstrated in our willingness to negotiate our points of difference in a fair and businesslike manner with the Communist countries.

We are under no illusions. We know that there are enduring ideological differences. We are aware of the difficulty in moderating tensions that arise from the clash of national interests. These differences will not be dissipated by changes of atmosphere or dissolved in cordial personal relations between statesmen. They involve strong convictions and contrary philosophies, necessities of national security, and the deep-seated differences of perspectives formed by geography and history.

The United States, like any other nation, has interests of its own, and will defend those interests. But any nation today must define its interests with special concern for the interests of others. If some nations define their security in a manner that means insecurity for other nations, then peace is threatened and the security of all is diminished. This obligation is particularly great for the nuclear superpowers on whose decisions the survival of mankind may well depend.

The United States is confident that tensions can be eased and the danger of war reduced by patient and precise efforts to reconcile conflicting interests on concrete issues. Coexistence demands more than a spirit of good will. It requires the definition of positive goals which can be sought and achieved cooperatively. It requires real progress toward resolution of specific differences. This is our objective.

As the Secretary of State said on December 6:

> We will continue to probe every available opening that offers a prospect for better East-West relations, for the resolution of problems large or small, for greater security for all.
> In this the United States will continue to play an active role in concert with our allies.

This is the spirit in which the United States ratified the Non-Proliferation Treaty and entered into negotiation with the Soviet Union on control of the military use of the seabeds, on the framework of a settlement in the Middle East, and on limitation of strategic arms. This is the basis on which we and our Atlantic allies have offered to negotiate on concrete issues affecting the security and future of Europe, and on which the United States took steps last year to improve our relations with nations of Eastern Europe. This is also the spirit in which we have resumed formal talks in Warsaw with Communist China. No nation need be our permanent enemy.

America's Purpose

These policies were conceived as a result of change, and we know they will be tested by the change that lies ahead. The world of 1970 was not predicted a decade ago, and we can be certain that the world of 1980 will render many current views obsolete.

The source of America's historic greatness has been our ability to see what had to be done, and then to do it. I believe America now has the chance to move the world closer to a durable peace. And I know that Americans working with each other and with other nations can make our vision real.

Stuart Symington: United States Commitments Abroad

Number of and Secrecy Concerning Tactical Nuclear Weapons Abroad

Senator Symington: Why does the United States have so many tactical nuclear weapons deployed abroad? Inasmuch as everybody abroad knows that they're there and I personally have gone to many of the places and found out that the people in the towns know it as well as the people in the military services of the other country. The only people who don't know are the people of the United States. First, why do we have to have them there, based on the new strategic and tactical aspects; and secondly, why should they be kept so secret?

Dr. Kaysen: I am not sure I can answer the second question. There has been a mystique about nuclear weapons, nuclear energy.

From "United States Security Agreements and Commitments Abroad," Hearing before Committee on Foreign Relations, United States Senate, 91st Congress, 2nd Session, November 24, 1970. Edited. Government Printing Office, 1971.

Senator Symington: Excuse me, there has been testimony by the Secretary of Defense, in open hearings, that we have 7,000 nuclear weapons in Europe; and that was sometime back.

Why Don't U.S. Allies Contribute More to Mutual Defense?

Senator Symington: It is clear that national security involves a viable economy plus confidence of the people in the wisdom of their government as well as physical strength in the form of weaponry. With that premise, why do you think it is, despite the increasing economic difficulties over here which are primarily due to the money we put out abroad around $100 million a day, counting Europe and all around the world? Why do you think it is that our allies whom we have helped over the years don't contribute more to their mutual defense, in percentage of their gross national product?

Dr. Kaysen: I think there are fundamentally two reasons: One reason is that in the last decade, 7 years or so, our European allies have had a rather different perception of the imminence and nature of the threats to them than at least our official public posture in these matters goes. The second reason is that as they see us doing more, their incentive for doing more is perhaps a little dulled. It is unnecessary for anybody to instruct a Member of the Senate about the political pains of raising taxes, and no popularly elected legislature enjoys raising taxes or increasing budgets if they can avoid it. And to the extent that we have said, "Everybody ought to do more, we ought to do more, you ought to do more," they have been rather content to accept the first part of that proposition.

Lack of Support for United States Concerning Vietnam

Senator Symington: The same kind of thinking runs through the minds of many people with respect to the support we have had from others in Vietnam. Would you have any additional thoughts with respect to the support, or lack of support, we have had in this Vietnam venture?

Dr. Kaysen: I am not sure what you are referring to. If you are talking about our allies in Europe, it is my impression that almost all of them think it is a very unwise activity and that they wouldn't want to be involved in it. The French have been not the least bit shy about letting us know their opinion about it, and while other European countries haven't been officially vocal, I don't think their views are really very different.

If you are speaking about those countries allied with us in Southeast Asia—

Senator Symington: I was also thinking of Australia, New Zealand, Japan, the Philippines, et cetera. If it is important for us to continue defending whatever it is we are trying to defend that far away from our own homes, it should be more important to them. They are much closer. Why is it we get practically no help from anybody except the South Koreans and a little from the Australians, and we have a good deal more Americans in South Korea than there are South Koreans in Vietnam. In any case, why is it we have to carry all this load practically by ourselves?

Dr. Kaysen: I think there are two reasons: One, that in any relationship of the sort that we have, a very big, rich and powerful country with these much smaller, much poorer, much less powerful countries, there is a certain bargaining asymmetry. It is just hard for us to avoid the situation in which we are doing "more than our share." In other words, I think it is hard to find an agreement on what fair shares are, and to these people who are living at very, very low levels, don't have the economic capacity that we have—

Senator Symington: Would you include the Australians and the Japanese?

Dr. Kaysen: No, I don't include the Australians and the Japanese, but even the Australians and the Japanese have per capita incomes considerably lower than ours, Senator. It is hard to get an agreement on what fair shares are. In those countries and indeed, I think, in the countries nearby, there are deep divisions about the wisdom of the policy. . . .

Domestic Effects of U.S. Foreign Spending and Trade Agreements

Senator Symington: Before turning you over to Chairman Fulbright, I believe he and Senator Case agree with you more on this trade business than I do. There are things about it that worry me. First, when we take over the problem of defending these countries as well as financing them, we make it possible for them to have constantly better standards of living, and at the same time, not high taxes as we have. Take the standard of living of Germany today as against 10 or 15 years ago. The same thing is true of Italy and also of Japan. They have a great advantage because we not only defend them, but also finance them. Today we are trying to borrow back at high interest rates on a short-term basis the money we lent Europe at low-interest rates on long-term. We are also creating heavy unemployment by letting these products increasingly come in here. When people want to work and can't get work, it is rough. Somebody said a recession is when your friend loses a job, and a depression when you lose your own. There is a lot of unemployment all over the United States and it worries me.

I agree with you about the Marshall plan, but don't think we should get into any habit of continuing it. We had that fine development shortly after World War II. A lot has happened since.

I became deeply involved in agricultural trading sometime back, incident to the Kennedy round, and found that, after we made tariff agreements with a lot of these countries, they turned to nontariff barriers, which made us look silly and lost us trade and jobs, in other words, export subsidies and import quotas. The late, great General De Gaulle was one of the leaders in this particular operation when it came to American agriculture.

So I am for freer trade, but hope we don't get to a point in this country where we lose awareness about the importance of maintaining work for our citizens who want to work and can't find jobs. This is especially true if we are going to continue to try to finance and defend the world, because unemployment reduces our tax base. . . .

Is Current Defense Budget in Excess?

Mr. Paul: Dr. Kaysen, referring to the table in your statement, I would like the record to be clear as to your opinion concerning the savings that could be made in the defense budget. Do I understand from your recommending moving toward line one that perhaps the current budget is in excess by as much as $14 billion?

Dr. Kaysen: That is what the arithmetic says. . . . The figures here suggest that we could save on the order of $10 billion a year in the general purpose forces. Part of this would be by having a smaller number of men under arms; part of it would be cutting down forward deployments in Asia. Some of that would be reducing the size of the forward fleet operation, so we would be reducing base operations. It would include cutting forces, for instance, in Korea, cutting Air Force in Japan, just to give some specific examples of what it would mean. It would also involve some reductions in Europe.

Risk of Western European Political Collapse from U.S. Force Reductions

Mr. Paul: Now, you suggested a minute ago that some of the savings could come out of Europe. The subcommittee has been told that the greatest risk perhaps from substantial reductions in Europe is a political collapse on the part of the Western European countries. You mentioned in your statement that even the Germans "do not act—in terms of military budgets and force levels—as if they gave high priority to the Soviet military threat." In light of that comment, I wondered what you thought of the view expressed to the subcommittee that there would be a political collapse if the United States reduced its forces substantially in Europe.

Dr. Kaysen: Well, let me make a very flat statement. I can't agree with that. There won't be a political collapse. On the other hand, I think it is fair to say that there is a very difficult negotiating problem, that this is something which does have to be done by agreement. It cannot be done, you know, bingo, surprise, and, therefore, I think there is a negotiating problem. We have to do this in a concerted way, and in a way which we explain to our allies what we are doing, how we are doing it, why we are doing it, and what we think, and listen to what they think.

Necessity for Further Troop Reduction Negotiations Questioned

Senator Symington: If counsel will yield, we have been negotiating it for 25 years. I was in the Executive Branch when it started out. The original specifications were for 87 divisions; and for all the years we have fulfilled everything we said we would do, but no other country has ever come up with what they said they would do, even though it is their own homeland, not ours.

The person who felt first, to the best of my knowledge, that it should be possible to heavily reduce our forces abroad was the man who probably knew the most about it, President Eisenhower.

We have been negotiating for many years. In 1966 we brought up troop reduction in the Democratic Policy Committee. They immediately sent over our Ambassador to Germany, who made a lot of statements about how strong we were over there. Now, especially since the French have pulled out and do not cooperate with the whole SHAPE concept, to me it is not tripwire or shield; it would be a parade. After the first few days we would have to reinforce across the Atlantic Ocean our conventional forces; therefore you are really thrown back on the nuclear picture if you are going to have a true defense.

Servan-Schreiber said that the whole SHAPE idea over there now has gotten sort of silly. I don't see why we have to continue. We have been there now for over a quarter of a century. Why can't we simply state from here on, "You take care of more of your interests and we will take care of ours." Schreiber said there were only two basic obligations in his opinion—

one the nuclear umbrella over Europe, the other West Berlin. I asked "Aren't they comparable," and he said, "In effect, they are the same." So why do we have to go on letting these countries drain us of our assets for a pretty theoretical operation from the standpoint of true defense, but a very practical operation from the standpoint of balance of payments and further trouble with our economy?

Dr. Kaysen: Senator Symington, I don't think we differ very much. I am simply saying that we first have to make a determination. Then, second, we have to communicate that determination to our allies in a politically acceptable way. I do not think it would be desirable for the U.S. Government to say, "We determined that the forces are going to be reduced to so and so and the President is going to hold a press conference and announce this," and then let the Europeans figure out what they are going to do. . . .

Senator Symington: We made a decision to change it once and told the Germans we were going to reduce. They protested vehemently and agreed to buy a lot of equipment from us, military equipment. They then came to us later and said, "We don't want to continue to buy the military equipment, but we will buy your bonds." Senator Mansfield thereupon made a speech and said: "The bonds pay good interest, so now we are going to pay them to defend them." This thinking runs through my mind when one looks at the state of deterioration in our own economy.

Possibility of U.S. Force Reductions
Leading to West German Buildup

Senator Case: My . . . question relates to whether a substantial reduction of our forces in Europe would lead to a West German buildup, with all the concerns that Germany's neighbors have about that?

Dr. Kaysen: I think this, which has been a real question, is considerably diminished.

I think the German-Polish Treaty and German-Soviet Treaty—though they will wait for ratification until we get more clarity in Berlin—are making easier the relations of Germany to its allies. The Allies no longer have the feeling that they will be pressed into supporting German claims that they don't want to support, and I think that is very important for the possibility of a more stable situation and a lower level of troops.

Senator Case: Thank you.

Senator Symington: Following the Senator from New Jersey's pertinent observations, I was on the National Security Council when we originally went into this matter, and remember the considerations brought up in justification for putting people of ours in Europe. Today we have a half million Americans, counting dependents living over there, at the same time that Chancellor Willy Brandt and Mr. Kosygin are signing agreements of amity and friendship. So it does seem things have changed. Nevertheless, we have not taken one step to reduce, in any major fashion, the military commitments we originally made in 1950.

Paul C. Warnke: Our Real National Security Interests

Thank you very much, Mr. Chairman. I am delighted to have the opportunity to appear before the committee and to discuss what I regard as a very useful document; namely, President Nixon's message on the U.S. foreign policy.

I regard it as useful in a couple of respects—both from the standpoint of its content and also from the standpoint of the precedent which it represents.

It seems to me that we are in an era at the present time in which the American public is demanding greater participation in the formulation of foreign policy.

Now, of course, the present acute indication of this is that just 3 months after the issuance of President Nixon's new strategy for peace we find the Nation divided by the strategy of a wider war in Indochina.

I think many of our citizens are beginning to question whether our national security requires that we remain militarily involved in Indochina.

I think many others are asking whether there are many other instances in which our foreign policy may require the commitment of American troops.

There is beginning to be considerable question as to whether we are perhaps too ready in today's world to rely on military force to achieve foreign policy objectives.

So that the underlying issue is whether in fact we have yet developed a foreign policy for the 1970's which will satisfy two key criteria. The first is, of course, whether it is consistent with our international interests.

From "United States Foreign Policy for the 1970's," Hearings before House of Representatives Committee on Foreign Affairs, 91st Congress, 2nd Session, May 27, 1970. Government Printing Office, 1970.

The second, and I think a novel criterion, is whether it has the ability to attract the wide-based popular support without which no foreign policy for the 1970's can be truly successful.

The two objectives, in my opinion, are related, but they are not identical.

Our international interests and our international commitments are not absolutes. They don't and they can't outweigh the need for domestic tranquility and unity in the attempt to solve our international problems.

For the 1970's a foreign policy that does not have broad-based popular support may in fact diminish rather than increase our national security.

In past years, there has been a feeling on the part of the American public that foreign policy necessarily is a field for experts only. In fact, I have been troubled by the growing assumption that even the Congress of the United States might have a relatively little role in the development and the execution of the foreign affairs of the United States.

Some have seemed to feel that Congress had a right to advise but in the final analysis had almost a constitutional duty to consent.

I believe that largely as a result of our involvement in Vietnam this attitude has begun to change. The almost plenary authority of the President in the field of foreign relations is receiving serious review, in particular as it involves the power to commit our Armed Forces. . . .

What I would like to do then in my statement, sir, is to discuss briefly the question of our developing perception of our real national security interests and how this perception relates to the general principles set forth in the President's foreign policy statement. . . .

As I have suggested, there is today a demand for broader participation in the formulation of American foreign policy. The demand stems from two sources. The first is the major dissatisfaction with our continued involvement in Vietnam and an inarticulate feeling that there must be something wrong with a foreign policy that got us in but doesn't seem to be able to get us out.

The second source of this demand for participation is that now, and I believe for the first time in our history, there is genuine competition for resources between our national defense expenditures and our domestic demands.

At one time the unchallenged assumption was that we could afford for defense any amount that might be necessary to insure that we have the best and the most in the way of military hardware.

We were ready and I believe too eager to use our resources to prepare against even quite remote external threats of aggression.

We lacked, I believe, a feeling of urgency when it came to some of our internal social needs. In many instances we did not even have the structure that would enable us to meet these domestic needs.

Under these circumstances a billion dollars spent on defense did not mean that a billion dollars or even half a billion dollars had been diverted from some domestic demand.

There was very real question whether the people would push for and whether the Congress would appropriate the funds for some international purpose in the event that funds were freed from the Defense budget.

Under those circumstances the choice usually was between a higher Defense budget or lower taxes.

Moreover, in the 1950's and throughout most of the decade of the 1960's, we viewed the Soviet Union and international communism as the overriding threat to our national security.

Conditioned by the cold war, the thinking majority of the American public believed that we had to take steps to contain communism anywhere because of the possibility that we might be faced with communism everywhere and find ourselves an isolated bastion of freedom in a hostile world.

In such a world we knew we could not survive as the kind of free society that we have been and which we are determined to remain.

The real question for the 1970's is whether that world has changed. I think it has. I think in today's world, fortunately, the Communists are even more divided than we are.

The President's foreign policy message notes the significant changes that have occurred in the pattern of international politics and the disintegration of the Communist monolith, but I find in its defense of the current Vietnam policy and program some continuation of the old cold war view of the threat to the United States.

For example, President Nixon suggested in his speech of November 3, 1969, that our disengagement in Vietnam would be regarded as an indication of weakness that would lead to renewed Soviet pressure in the Middle East and Western Europe and even ultimately to violence in the Western Hemisphere.

From this viewpoint, Vietnam would have to be regarded as one skirmish in a continuing confrontation between the free world and the Communist world. And if, indeed, we were faced with that sort of unified imminent international Communist threat, then I suspect we would have to remain involved militarily in Indochina, whatever the cost and whatever the duration.

But there are many who question today whether this view of the world in the 1970's is correct. At a recent conference convened by some Members of the Congress, Dr. Jeremy Stone said that, as he saw it, only one country today is surrounded by hostile Communist states. That is the Soviet Union.

The President's message notes the real and serious differences between the two Communist giants, China and Russia, and the fact that the Red

Army has been used since World War II only against Soviet allies in Eastern Europe.

So that in today's world there are some who believe and believe deeply that the major threats to our national security derive more from internal inequities than from external expression.

The growing prevalence of this view is largely responsible for the current demand for participation in the development and execution of American foreign policy.

With the mounting dissent, in particular about Vietnam, has come the charge that this apparent division can encourage our enemies and threaten our objectives.

I would have to say that there is obviously some substance to that fear. But more important I believe is the question of whether the policy and the objectives are sound when they are at odds with the views of a sizable segment of a free society.

I would not suggest that President Nixon or any other President can govern by referendum but at the same time I do not believe that President Nixon or any other President can run a democratic country without paying considerable attention to the responsible voices of all segments of that society.

I obviously am no expert in the assignment of national priorities as between defense expenditures and the competing domestic needs and my experience has led me to believe that no one can safely pose as an expert in the field of foreign policy.

All opinions on that subject should be regarded as highly suspect. There are, however, I believe, a few principles that we can accept. The first of these is that today there is only one country in the world that possesses the power to threaten us militarily. Only the Soviet Union has the nuclear capability which could even absorb an American first strike and still inflict upon us unacceptable damage.

Only the Soviet Union has the conventional military forces that could threaten either us or areas of vital strategic interest to the United States.

China obviously possesses the potential at some point of acquiring both the nuclear armament and the conventional capability to pose that sort of threat. But this capability and this sort of nuclear stockpile is well in the future and I question whether we can prepare for it usefully today with the kind of technology that could be obsolete before any possible need for it would exist.

If I am correct in my analysis of the threat, then the ultimate aim of our foreign policy for the 1970's should be to avoid the kind of confrontation with the Soviet Union that could lead to the ultimate crisis for us and for the world.

There is much in the President's foreign policy message with which I certainly would agree. I am unable to find, however, from its necessarily general statements, whether we are in fact moving toward the kind of foreign policy which would be best adapted to prevent that sort of confrontation and to avoid that sort of crisis. . . .

The message asserts that we will keep our treaty commitments but I think the question that we have to consider is just what is the content of those commitments and how are they to be interpreted?

Are they absolute and self-executing or are they subject to interpretation in terms of our current self-interest?

As a second point in the message's exposition of the Nixon doctrine, it states that we will provide a shield if a nuclear power threatens the freedom of a nation allied with us or of a nation whose survival we consider vital to our security and the security of the region as a whole.

I am troubled about the failure of the message to explain what we would consider as threats to such freedoms and also the possible implication that we might respond with nuclear weapons to even conventional aggression if that aggression is practiced by a nuclear power.

The third element in the doctrine as set forth in the message is that in the case of other types of aggression, by which I would assume the message means aggression by nonnuclear powers, we shall furnish military and economic assistance but the country threatened will have the prime responsibility of providing manpower for its defense.

I am not clear whether or not this envisions American intervention in local disputes in which neither the Soviet Union nor Communist China is involved. If so, that would trouble me. If so, it would mean that the Nixon doctrine does not in fact signal a lower profile and a predisposition against American military involvement.

If this third point means that we would continue to contemplate the use of American troops in local disputes involving neither of the great Communist powers, then it would be fully consistent with an American role as peacekeeper for the entire world and it would be more consistent with a cut-rate cold war strategy than with a new strategy for peace.

I think we have to consider during the 1970's whether America's vital security interests in fact depend upon the nature of the political institutions in most or even many of the countries of the world.

We have, of course, had the experience which would lead us to conclude that our own national security would be jeopardized if the people and the potential of Western Europe were to fall under the domination of a hostile power. That was the reason for the Marshall plan. That was the reason for the efforts that we have made to build up and strengthen NATO, and it has proven successful.

I believe that the Soviet Union today recognizes that this is our view of our security interests and I would certainly hope that we would be sure that they continue to recognize this fact.

Similarly, any sort of combination of a hostile nature between the vast population of China and the vast capability of Japan would constitute a real threat to our national security interests.

But I think that we should not fall into the trap of viewing Southeast Asia as being somehow parallel to Western Europe and we should not view the capability of China today as being in any respect parallel to that of the Soviet Union.

Accordingly, I doubt that we need to worry much about any policy which would involve close-in containment of China and I doubt that we need worry too much about the extension of Chinese influence in Asia.

From this standpoint I remain convinced that whatever finally happens in Vietnam will do nothing to help China solve its massive problems and that it will constitute no threat to a thriving Japan.

Under these circumstances, it is my opinion that we can view with equanimity the political compromise in Southeast Asia that would be the inevitable concomitant of substantial American military disengagement.

For the 1970's, we have to find an American role which is consistent with world realities and with our domestic needs. This role should not, in my opinion, be that of a roving unilateral peacekeeper either in Asia or anywhere else. That sort of peacekeeping role, if it is to be acceptable to those whom we would try to pacify and to be tolerable to the people of the United States, would have to be conducted on a multilateral international basis.

From the unilateral standpoint, our security demands, and I believe it will continue to demand, that we maintain the capacity to deter the Soviet Union from the use of its military force against our interests. In fact, any Soviet use of its great military power must be for us a source of major concern.

I think this is true even when, as in Czechoslovakia or earlier in Hungary, Soviet military force is used to maintain its total control over Eastern Europe.

We are certainly rightly concerned about the Soviet pilots in Egypt and the apparent Russian willingness to play a direct role in the violence of the Middle East.

But I think similarly we should reflect on the possibility that the Soviet Union can be alarmed and perhaps encouraged in its use of its military force by an apparent willingness on our part to go to war in East Asia to advance or protect Western influence.

The President's report refers to this as the era of negotiation. If there is to be genuine movement from confrontation to negotiation, I believe we have also to consider the importance of an atmosphere of calm and confidence. In the past few weeks, I have been troubled by some statements which appear to be to the effect that the Presidential power to deploy American military force must remain untrammeled in order to preserve the principle of unpredictability. By this thinking, as I understand it, and I am not sure I do, what will keep the Communists in line is their inability to guess when and where we may resort to military force.

I find this concept not only unpersuasive but frightening. In a bipolar world where we and the Russians have offsetting military strength the prime characteristics of a sane foreign policy would seem to be consistency and caution.

As the President's message notes, "peace requires confidence." It also asserts, and I agree, that we should seek to maintain our security at the lowest possible level of uncertainty.

The foreign policy message also states that:

> Our commitment to peace is most convincingly demonstrated in our willingness to negotiate our points of difference in a fair and businesslike manner with the Communist countries.

We would all agree with that, I believe, and I think we should also recognize that neither for us nor for the Soviets would it be fair or businesslike or even intelligent to try to scare the other side into concessions. Effective agreements between ourselves and the Russians, in my opinion, can be reached only if subsequent behavior can be predicted with reasonable reliability.

Any efforts to bargain between the two of us by threats will bring about no bargain but will bring about only more threats.

Productive negotiation with the Soviet Union could certainly yield today a degree of security that we can never attain by military means.

The major areas are the limitation of strategic arms, the damping down of the fire in the Middle East and the lessening of tensions through mutual reduction of the opposing military forces in Europe.

I do not think in any of these areas scare tactics by either side can do anything but destroy the chances of reaching agreement. . . .

If we are able to reach an effective agreement we can avoid the enormous costs of continuing the nuclear arms race and the enormous risks which are involved in more, and even more awesome, technological developments.

We must recognize that neither side will negotiate from weakness and that only the fact of rough nuclear equality has put the Soviet Union in a position where they are willing to negotiate at all.

But if each side tries to better its position in order to negotiate from greater strength, then the arms talks, rather than ending up with a limitation on the nuclear arms race, could lead to its escalation.

Our own response to Soviet threats has always been more weapons and more defense expenditures—certainly not more concessions.

I believe we must expect the Soviet response to be the same.

Similarly, I do not think we advance the hopes for peace in the Middle East by widening the scope of the conflict in Indochina. We are in a position where neither we nor the Soviet Union can bend the other to its will. Accordingly, force must be expected to beget force and impetuosity to breed impetuosity.

The confidence of our allies, particularly those in NATO and Western Europe, depends upon their faith in our consistency of purpose and the predictability of our response.

If we resort precipitately to military escalation in Indochina or any place else, I doubt that they will be heartened by the feeling that we are keeping the Russians off balance.

I feel that they might be led instead to question the dependability of our NATO guarantees.

The absence of a modern and moderate foreign policy could do much to justify such fears on the part of our NATO allies.

The American public will not, I believe, continue to support the use of American force in causes of dubious importance to our national security. They will be increasingly hard to persuade that American survival or the avoidance of world war III may somehow depend on the fate of any weak and unresponsive government that happens to be anti-Communist.

A policy that continues to find threats everywhere will shake belief in the reality of genuine threats anywhere. The need for the 1970's and beyond is a foreign policy that the thinking public can understand and respect based on a perception of our security interests which the Soviet Union will understand and must respect.

Such a policy and only such a policy can command broad-based support. With that support will come a restoration and strengthening of effective American influence in international affairs.

Even more, it will free a major share of our resources and talents to deal with the real threats to the quality of life in the 1970's and to enable us to prevent the erosion of the trust in one another that is essential if we are genuinely to assure the blessings of liberty to ourselves and to our children.

Thank you very much, Mr. Chairman.

**Senate Committee on Foreign
Relations: Foreign Policy
and Executive Secrecy**

Secrecy from the Public

The Executive Branch consistently over-classified information relating to foreign policy that should be a matter of public record.

This is partly the result of bureaucratic timidity, especially at middle and lower levels, where the prevailing approach is to look for some reason either to cover up or withhold facts.

At least as important, this tendency to over-classification is but part of the process of "creeping commitments," frequently done at the request of a foreign government because the latter desires to keep a particular agreement or program secret from its own people.

More often than not, these governments are found in countries which have neither a free press, nor a responsible political opposition.

Examples: The Government of Thailand did not want it known that the United States was using air bases in that country. The Government of Laos did not want it known that the United States was fighting in major fashion in that country. Even in the Philippines where there is a free press and a highly articulate political opposition, the Government of the Philippines did not want it known that the United States was paying heavy allowances to the Philippine non-combat contingent that went to Vietnam.

Yet in each of these instances—and others could be cited—one secret agreement or activity led to another, until the involvement of the United States was raised to a level of magnitude far greater than that originally intended.

All of this occurred, not only without the knowledge of the American people, but even without the full knowledge of their representatives on the proper Committees of the Congress.

Whether or not each of these expensive and at times clearly unneces-

From "Security Agreements and Commitments Abroad," Report of the Committee on Foreign Relations, United States Senate, 91st Congress, 2nd Session. Government Printing Office, 1970.

sary adventures would have run its course if the Congress and/or the people had been informed, there would have been greater subsequent national unity, often a vital prerequisite to any truly successful outcome.

The dissembling to which the Congress and the American people have been subjected, however, cannot be attributed entirely to foreign governments. In the beginning, the Executive Branch of the United States, as much as the Governments of the Philippines and Thailand desired to keep secret the arrangements under which Filipino and Thai troops were sent to Vietnam. This secrecy made it appear that United States policy in Vietnam had far greater support from other countries than was the case.

This was pure deception, and it is one of the worst offenses a supposedly free and democratic government can commit against its own people, because it tends to destroy that trust which is an indispensable element of self-government.

Classification often permits an ambiguity about various commitments to be purposely developed by the Executive Branch.

The practice often is to:

Maximize commitment in secret discussions with foreign governments; then minimize the risk of commitment in statements made to the American public.

Maximize in public the importance of our friendly relationship and cooperation with a foreign government; then minimize, and often classify, that government's obstructiveness, failures and non-cooperation.

These actions make policy change and review both unlikely and politically difficult.

Americans pride themselves on having an open society. Nevertheless it is becoming an increasingly closed government. Yet neither the Congress nor the people can make intelligent judgments without questions which may literally involve our survival unless they have free access to all pertinent information which would not aid a possible enemy.

There is no merit to the argument that certain activities must be kept secret because a foreign government demanded they would be kept secret. Such a policy involves the Government of the United States in a web of intrigue which is alien to American traditions.

None of this is to say that there is no room for confidential discussions between governmental representatives. When agreements result from these discussions, however, particularly agreements which lead to large expenditures or even the commitment of Americans to combat, those agreements should be subjected to what Woodrow Wilson called "the broad daylight of public discussion."

Developments incident to our relationship with Laos provide basic examples of the problems incident to classification.

Without knowledge of the range of United States commitments and activities in and over Laos, neither the American people nor the Congress could understand, and thus either approve or disapprove, our policies toward that country.

Everyone recognizes that national security imposes limits on the disclosure of information. Knowledge of much intelligence information deserves to be held, even within the government, by a relatively small number of people. But the multimillion dollar support of a 30,000 man army can in no way be considered an intelligence operation; and to try to keep it classified is to deny information to those who also have responsibility and authority for our defense structure and its functioning. . . .

A wide assortment of reasons for this type of classification have been given to the Subcommittee, to individual Senators, to newsmen on the scene, even to high officials of our government. The result of such effort to classify over here information that is available to the public overseas has contributed to a growing discontent among the American people as to the credibility of their own government.

In the area of foreign policy, classification is readily applied to bar public knowledge of failures of our allies to come through with their share of military assistance programs.

The disclosure of such information could arouse the ire of the foreign governments involved; but that possibility must be weighed against the responsibility of the Executive Branch to give the American taxpayer proper knowledge of how his money is being spent, and make him aware of the possibility of more direct military involvement in various foreign countries.

The American people have the right to know the details of past failures of our military assistance program in the Philippines which, the Subcommittee has found, were caused by the domestic Philippine political situation.

Secrecy from Congress

In at least one instance, security classification has been used to prevent legitimate inquiry by the proper committees of the Senate into matters which the Executive Branch did not want to discuss.

In one striking instance, the Executive Branch, by means of the use of classification, sought to prevent any discussion in closed session by the Foreign Relations Committee, apparently because of concern over the context in which the information in question would be discussed.

At issue was the placement of United States tactical nuclear weapons in foreign countries. The Committee's interest and concern was directed toward the foreign policy aspects stemming from the placement of nuclear weapons in a foreign country.

The Subcommittee sought information with respect to the understandings made with the host governments having to do with the introduction of United States nuclear weapons, the manner in which they would be used, the manner in which they were to be protected, and the manner in which they could be removed from those countries.

Inevitably, any such discussion led to the military reasons behind the introduction of such weapons, also knowledge about those weapons on the part of citizens of the host country.

There can be no question that the placement of nuclear weapons in a foreign country automatically creates—in itself constitutes—a new relationship between that country and the United States.

The Executive Branch agencies cooperated fully in providing such information during trips by the Subcommittee staff to the Mediterranean area in the spring of 1969 and to the Far East in the summer of 1969. During those trips the staff had full discussion about those nuclear weapons and visited sites in several countries where these weapons were stored.

It was with great surprise, therefore, that the Subcommittee found, when it began its hearings, that at the direction of the Executive Branch there was to be no discussion of nuclear weapons overseas. Only after many months did the Executive Branch justify its negative position on the grounds that initially such information was only to be transmitted from the Executive Branch to the Legislative Branch through the Joint Atomic Energy Committee.

Subsequently, the Executive Branch withdrew from that position and granted a single-day worldwide briefing to the full Foreign Relations Committee on the subject of tactical nuclear weapons abroad. The Executive Branch stipulated, however, that there be only one transcript; and that this one transcript be held by the State Department, and only made available to the Foreign Relations Committee upon specific request.

The argument for this position on the part of the Administration was based on the high classification attributed to this information, and on the allegation that the Foreign Relations Committee security facilities were not satisfactory for the storage of such information.

Review of earlier Subcommittee records shows that in the spring of 1969, shortly after the Subcommittee was formed, the question of nuclear weapons abroad was raised tangentially in a discussion with the Chairman of the Joint Chiefs of Staff. At that time, responding to a question, General Wheeler volunteered the names of countries in which nuclear weapons were stored in a specific area of the world. No effort was made to hold back any such information. The context in which the question was asked, however, was a military one, not political. That transcript was classified "Secret" and is in the files of the Subcommittee.

A supplementary question was asked at that same hearing, the answer to which required both the Departments of State and Defense to provide information on the type and location of nuclear weapons in a specific foreign country. Not only was this information provided to the Subcommittee, but it was included in a document the overall classification of which was "Secret"—not "Top Secret." Note that the information contained facts relating to the types of nuclear weapons that were located in a named foreign country.

The only conclusion that can be drawn with logic from this sequence of actions is that the Executive Branch decided to upgrade the classification of this type of information because it did not wish the Foreign Relations Committee to have information incident to this vital aspect of foreign policy.

Recommendations

The Congress should now face up to the grave implications contained in this development of classification as a means and method of keeping the people and the Congress itself in the dark with respect to important aspects of our foreign policy and the implementation of that policy through military action. The proper Committees of the Senate should seek to set basic standards as to the character of information which Congress will accept on a classified basis from the Executive Branch. They should seek to work out a common understanding about the classification of material.

In addition, since the basis for security classification today is a combination of the Espionage Act and various Presidential directives, an inquiry should be undertaken in order to determine if this basic legislation should be revised and whether new standards should be applied to the Executive Branch with respect to the current practice of security classification.

**Richard J. Barnet: The Illusion
of Security**

The crisis of national security now faced by the United States stems, in my view, from a fundamental misconception of the nature of the problem. For twenty-five years we have been building a Maginot Line against the threats of the 1930's while the threats of the 1970's are rapidly overwhelming us along with the rest of mankind.

United States national security policy is designed to deal with three classic threats. The first is a nuclear attack on the United States. In a world where nuclear weapons exist no one can say that such an attack could not happen. The question is whether American planners have (a) put that threat into proper perspective and (b) whether the strategy they have developed to deal with it has decreased or increased the threat. It seems likely that for much of the cold war period the United States has been running an arms race with itself. It was always *possible* that the Soviet Union would launch a nuclear attack on the United States; but everything we know about the nature of nuclear weapons, budgetary constraints, political pressures in the Soviet Union, and Communist ideology suggests that it was *highly unlikely*. The United States has had an enormous superiority in numbers of nuclear weapons, a fact that has neither made the people of the United States feel more secure, nor provided the "strength" to intimidate Communists to negotiate on our terms. Indeed, as one might have expected, the Soviets have seemed to be more willing to negotiate as they have approached nuclear parity with the United States. At the same time, the U.S. attempt to maintain superiority has encouraged the Soviet Union and China to develop their own nuclear capabilities and has given them greater power of life and death over the people and territory of the United States. In an arms race, neither side will permit the other to continue amassing an ever-widening lead.

The United States has believed that it could promote security by preserving the "option" to use nuclear weapons not only to retaliate for a nuclear attack, but also to protect "vital interests" of a lesser sort, pri-

"The Illusion of Security," by Richard J. Barnet, *Foreign Policy,* Number 3, Summer 1971. Copyright © 1971 by National Affairs, Inc. Reprinted by permission. Mr. Barnet is codirector of the Institute for Policy Studies.

marily in Western Europe. The unwillingness to renounce the first use of nuclear weapons has thus led to less security, not more. We have communicated to all countries the fact that the greatest power in the world must rely on nuclear weapons to promote its foreign policy interests. Weaker countries, such as France, have taken this cue and have concluded that no country can be "sovereign" unless it, too, commands a powerful nuclear arsenal.

During the Cuban missile crisis President Kennedy said that the chances were at least one in three that nuclear weapons would be used by the United States and that if they had been used, at least 150 million people would have been killed. In a later speech he said that as many as five hundred million would be killed in the opening hours of a nuclear conflict. Yet it was prestige, not military security, that was at stake in the Soviet-American confrontation of 1962. From a U.S. security standpoint, the resolution of the Cuba crisis was a disaster. Washington gave up everything it would have had to give in a negotiated settlement (Jupiter missiles in Turkey and Italy, and a pledge not to invade Cuba). And the 1962 humiliation of the Soviet Union led directly to a major rearmament program which has now made Moscow a far more formidable adversary than it was nine years ago.

There is no objective, including the survival of the United States as a political entity, that merits destroying millions or jeopardizing the future of man. The pretense that it is legitimate to threaten nuclear war for political ends creates an international climate of fear in which Americans will continue to have less security, not more.

Guardians at the Gate

National security planners have been reluctant to renounce the "option" to destroy millions of human beings in a nuclear "first strike" because of a mistaken analysis of the second threat to national security. This is the problem of aggression, its causes and its cure. The official theory has been presented many times in Presidential speeches: we must assure peace by preparing for war and by making governments believe that we will do exactly what we say we will do to protect our positions of strength in the world, including our alliances. Thus we fight in small wars now to prevent fighting in larger wars later.

These ideas are not mere rhetoric. They are deeply held beliefs of a generation of National Security Managers for whom the decisive learning experience was the Second World War. Staggered by the apocalyptic events of the war, the demonic Hitlerian vision of a world order, the death camps,

the fire bombings, the saturation raids, and the nuclear attacks, this generation has believed with the first Secretary of Defense, James Forrestal, that
"the cornerstone in any plan which undertakes to rid us of the curse of
war must be the armed might of the United States." Despite the standard
denial that the United States is not the "policeman of the world," which
has been inserted in Presidential statements and State Department press
releases since opposition developed to the Vietnam war, this is precisely
the official image we have had of ourselves. "History and our own achievements have thrust upon us the principal responsibility for the protection
of freedom on earth," President Johnson declared at a Lincoln Day dinner
in 1965. Earlier, President Kennedy called our nation "the watchman on
the wall of world freedom." Both expressed their generation's judgment
of America's security role. "We did not choose to be the guardians at the
gate," Johnson declared, but "history" has "thrust" that "responsibility"
upon us. Imperial nations always have a view of their own unique destiny.

In the early postwar period American planners had a self-conscious
notion that they were playing out for their generation the particular imperial roles that England and France had played in the last—filling "power
vacuums" and picking up "responsibilities" for keeping order. Unless the
forces of international "stability," so the argument went, were always
ready, and, most important, *willing* to use whatever force was necessary,
aggressor nations would take over their weaker neighbors one by one. Unless nations with an impulse to upset the *status quo* were opposed at the
outset, they would expand as far as their power permitted—even to the
point of world domination. In this view of the world which has dominated
American thinking on world affairs for a generation, there is an infinite
supply of potential aggressors. Any "have-not" nation that can field an
army will do. General Thomas Power of the Strategic Air Command, for
example, warned in the mid-sixties of a possible "African Hitler" whom
we might have to confront once we had disposed of the Communist threat.

Because the principal threats to peace and security were foreign "aggressors" bent on world conquest, it was necessary for the United States
as the world's most powerful country to attempt to organize an alliance
of threatened nations to try to contain those threats. Postwar planners
looked on their own time as a direct continuation of the pre-1945 period.
The United States was spearheading a crusade against totalitarianism and
militarism in behalf of a "free world" deemed to represent the forces of
good, if only because of the evil of the Communist adversaries. Stalin was
the postwar Hitler, the leader of an infinitely expansionist power who
could be stopped only by the very show of strength England and France
failed to make against Hitler. When President Truman enunciated the far-
reaching doctrine that bears his name with its commitment to "support
free peoples who are resisting attempted subjugation by armed minorities

or by outside pressures," he defended this momentous change of policy as a protection of the investment already made in World War II.

Myths of the Managers

A visitor from another planet in the early postwar days would have had a hard time reconciling the official American analogy, "Stalin is the Hitler of today," with the facts as they emerged. Indeed, the naive visitor might well have concluded that the problem of military aggression in the postwar period had its source in the United States. Soviet armies stopped at the point of their farthest advance in World War II and withdrew from adjacent areas such as Czechoslovakia only to return when political domination threatened to fail. The United States retained the major bases it had acquired in World War II and acquired more. Within a few years the Soviet Union was surrounded by air and later missile bases from which devastating nuclear attacks could be launched—all at a time when the Soviet Union lacked a similar capacity to attack the United States. It has been the United States and not the Soviet Union that has stationed its military forces on every continent and spread nuclear weapons in the tens of thousands on the continents of Asia and Europe and on the high seas. It is the United States and not the Soviet Union that has intervened with its military and para-military forces almost every year since 1945 on the territory of other countries either to prevent local insurgent forces from taking power or displacing them from power.

Despite Stalin's monumental crimes against his own people, a kind of permanent internal war, Dean Acheson, along with most of the National Security Managers of his generation, now admits that the early postwar fears of a Soviet military invasion of Western Europe may have been exaggerated. The problem of European security was whether the West European countries would move toward domestic Communism, not whether the Soviets would attack them. As in Vietnam almost twenty years later, the National Security Managers used military measures in an effort to give psychological support to allies facing domestic economic and political crises. In Europe the policy worked—but at the cost of perpetuating the myth of outside military aggression on which it was premised. A generation later, there is still no historical evidence that Stalin or his successors ever contemplated an invasion of West Germany, or that they were deterred, as Winston Churchill claimed in a speech at M.I.T. in 1950, only because of the American possession of the atomic bomb. Indeed, the Soviet Union in Stalin's day, as many historians now conclude, was following a highly cautious course, more conservative in most respects than that in the present "era of negotiations." Today's Soviet leaders play a more active and dangerous role in world affairs, for example in Cuba and the Middle East, than Stalin ever dared to do. Indeed, it is ironical that the strategy chosen by the U.S. to deal with the limited Soviet challenge to American supremacy may well have helped to create a Soviet Union with global interests and commitments.

Although there were very few objective reasons for believing that Stalin, with his country ruined, was about to embark on a campaign of Hitler-like aggression, U.S. National Security Managers did indeed feel insecure. It is important to try to understand the source of that insecurity, which still persists. The United States will not change its role in the world as long as the official belief continues that the United States can be safe in the world only by running as much of it as possible.

Despite its unparalleled monopoly of power it was not surprising that the United States felt insecure at the close of the Second World War. The managers of the Number One Nation always feel the insecurity that comes with winning and having to defend the crown. Moreover, the floodgates of technological and political change were opened by the war and America's leaders felt the anxiety of being swept by unfamiliar currents, particularly when, because of the atomic bomb, the stakes were supremely high. It was natural that the managers of the new American empire should construct an analysis that justified their power and sanctified its use.

Thus the political analysis of security threats took on the character of military contingency planning. Many of the contingencies on which policies have been constructed have been highly implausible. During the whole postwar period there have been very few cases of World War II type "aggression," i.e. invasion of one state by another for the purpose of occupying it or dominating it. It must be said that a high percentage of the invasions of the last generation have been carried out by the United States in its self-appointed role as "guardian at the gates." The closest analogy to Hitler-type aggression from the Communist side was the invasion of South Korea by North Korea and the Soviet invasion of Czechoslovakia, neither of which was or looked like the first slice of a "salami" program of world conquest, or so U.S. intelligence agencies concluded at the time. Other examples of old-fashioned "aggression" include the 1962 incursions of Communist China into India, the 1965 India-Pakistan war, and the 1967 Israeli invasions of Egypt and Syria which the United States did not oppose with military power. Although the United States has sought to enlist many other countries in a network of alliances aimed at containing one or another "aggressive" or "expansionist" power, the nations whose security is much more directly threatened by such powers have tended to drag their feet. This is especially true in Southeast Asia where Thailand and the Philippines, supposedly among the next "dominoes" to fall, refuse to give more than token cooperation in the Vietnam war and exact major political and economic concessions for their participation. If they accepted the American analysis of the security threat, they would act as if their own security was gravely threatened.

There are two principal reasons why the problem of war and violence in the postwar world does not resemble the prewar problem of aggression. First, the development of technology has made the acquisition of strategic real estate for powerful nations much less important. Big powers like the United States and the Soviet Union can now hit any part of the globe with missiles launched from their own territory. The United States can dispatch powerful military forces by air transport anywhere within a matter of days, and the Soviet Union is developing its capacity to do likewise. Thus the pressure to achieve security by invading other countries is less than it used to be. The arms race has reduced the tactical incentive of both major powers to resort to territorial aggression.

Second, despite technology, the extension of formal physical and juridical control by a great power over other countries has become much more difficult because of the development of the techniques of partisan and guerrilla warfare, the ideology of self-determination and nationalism, and the resulting politicization of formerly colonized populations. The history of the last decade makes it clear that the entry of new countries into the Communist bloc involves heavy costs as well as benefits for the Soviet Union. Indeed, the extension of Soviet power into Cuba appears to have complicated life for Moscow. It has been a financial burden for the Soviet Union, has posed risk of conflict with the United States, and has involved conflict with the Cubans themselves. The same might be said of the Middle East. It has become more and more difficult to manage empires or to derive the prestige traditionally associated with empires. That is one reason why the United States does not officially admit to being an empire and prefers to conduct so many of its activities abroad by covert means.

The Counterrevolutionary Impulse

The third major security threat which, in my view, has been misperceived in the official U.S. world-view is the problem that John Foster Dulles used to refer to as "indirect aggression." Most of the violence and instability in the postwar world has arisen not from confrontation between national states but from revolutions and internal insurgencies. Between 1958 and 1966, according to Robert McNamara, there were over 149 serious internal insurgencies.

The counterrevolutionary impulse has been a cornerstone of American policy since the end of the Second World War. On an average of once every eighteen months the United States has sent its military or para-military forces into other countries either to crush a local revolution or to arrange a coup against a government which failed to acquire the State Department seal of approval.

Why has this been thought necessary to make the world safe for the United States? There have been essentially two theories about the connection between indigenous revolutionary change and American security. In the early days of the cold war it was assumed that any Communist revolutionary was a Kremlin agent. Ho Chi Minh's independence movement, Ambassador William C. Bullitt explained in 1947, was designed to "add another finger to the hand that Stalin is closing around China." According to Dean Rusk, in a speech made twenty years ago, Mao's regime was "a colonial Russian government."

It is now generally accepted that Communism is no longer "monolithic." Of course it never was in the Rusk–Bullitt sense. Far from being planned and initiated by the Soviet Union, the revolutionary movements in China, Indo-China, Greece, Cuba, and elsewhere were often at the outset opposed and discouraged by the Kremlin as embarrassments to the diplomatic relationships the Soviet Union was pursuing as a Great Power. The Soviet Union has barely disguised its reluctance at being sucked into the Vietnam war to oppose American intervention, although, as in the Cuban case, it has given aid to counter American military attacks. For years after the Geneva settlement of 1954 the Soviet Union acquiesced in the maintenance of a U.S. protected anti-Communist South Vietnam, which was contrary to the spirit of the settlement. The Soviets proposed the admission of North and South Vietnam as separate members of the United Nations as late as 1959.

As long as the myth of "indirect aggression"—the transformation of local revolutions into Soviet invasions by Trojan Horse—was credible, a counter revolutionary policy could be defended as traditional balance of power politics. Every revolution was part of a pattern of world conquest emanating from a rival center of power. Thus the situation was sufficiently like Hitler's expansionism to justify a similar military response.

The Soviet Union sought to dominate every nation into which its troops marched in the Second World War and to establish subservient "revolutionary" governments. But every revolutionary government that has come to power without the Red Army has turned out to be ambivalent, cool, or even hostile to the Soviet Union—Yugoslavia, Albania, North Vietnam, China, and Cuba. In each case the relationship is complex, but in none of them can it be said that the existence of the Communist regime necessarily makes the Soviet Union stronger or more threatening to the physical safety of the United States.

There is another connection between revolutionary change in other countries and American national security which is not military, but psychological. The United States has consciously sought to expand its system so that other countries will not only buy our products but accept our values. We have wanted to be accepted as the world's definition of the good society. To a considerable extent this has happened. Only a few revolutionary societies have held out a vision of the future different from the American model—what Walt Rostow called "the high mass consumption society." Even the Soviet Union has adopted as its goal the American model of the highly industrialized consumer society. Its brand of socialism is a means for "overtaking and surpassing the United States" on the way to the same Utopia.

"We're Number One?"

For almost fifty years, however, America has been experiencing a continuing national identity crisis. In the thirties, amidst depression, seemingly permanent unemployment, and great social unrest, there was a serious loss of faith in the American system as it then existed. The pretensions of the foreign "isms"—state capitalism, Communism, fascism, and others —that they, rather than "free enterprise America," represented the wave of the future caused shudders of doubt in the United States. Victory in the Second World War brought new confidence. Yet there was enough awareness that the war had transcended but had not solved the domestic crises of the thirties to make both managers and the public uneasy about the future at the very moment of America's supreme power. Thus the rhetorical claims of Communist ideologues that they were the new "wave of the future" struck a terror out of all proportion to the real strength of what the State Department called "international Communism."

Much of what the United States does in the name of national security is designed to allay the inner fears of America's leaders that the United States may be slipping from the pinnacle of power. They spend hundreds of billions of dollars and tens of thousands of lives to preserve their "credibility" for toughness so that no one would dare to think of the nation which they manage as a "pitiful, helpless giant." The principal argument in the government for persisting in Vietnam despite the obvious catastrophic political, economic, military, and social consequences has been based on reputation and prestige. It may have been an error to have made a commitment in Vietnam, but to back down would put the nation in a bad light. Reputation, as Thomas Schelling has said, is one of the few things worth fighting for. "We are the Number One Nation," Lyndon

Johnson told a National Foreign Policy Conference at the State Department less than a year before he left office, "and we are going to stay the Number One Nation."

Like many empires before us we have used reputation abroad as the criterion of national success and as a diversion from intractable domestic problems. As long as our criteria of "development" and "progress"—such as the ratio of cars to bicycles on the main street of the capital—were accepted by other nations, this amounted to a kind of validation for the American system at home. American scientific achievements, American books, American magazines, American educational materials, American business techniques appeared to be changing the face of the world, making it look like an extension of America and hence giving the illusion that the globe was becoming a friendlier and more manageable place.

It is as illusory, however, to measure national security by the willingness of elites in other nations to imitate the United States as it is to do so by counting nuclear warheads. Whether American methods work elsewhere will not help solve the pressing security problem of a society unable to deal with its own internal violence. Indeed, there is now strong evidence that the export of American consumption values and American technology creates long-term security problems for the United States by encouraging economies of waste in the Third World which add to world pollution and resource allocation problems. It is in our own selfish interest, if we care about prolonging the life support systems of the planet, that the irrational and destructive patterns of development and consumption of resources that have evolved in the United States not be repeated elsewhere.

Facing the Realities

The United States cannot achieve national security until we begin to accept certain realities of our age. The first is that poor countries will, and many probably must, experiment with revolution to solve political and economic problems fast enough to permit survival for their people. Whether a country in Asia, Africa, or Latin America chooses another political and economic system, whether it looks to another country as its model, does not threaten our national security unless we define such events (over which we have no effective control in any event) as "defeats."

Second, the United States must be prepared to live with a high degree of disorder and instability, which are characteristics of a world experiencing rapid political and technological change. To set as a national security goal the enforcement of "stability" in a world in convulsion, a world in which radical change is as inevitable as it is necessary, is as practical as

King Canute's attempt to command the tides. Real stability can come only with the building of a legitimate international order which offers genuine hope for people, whatever their history and wherever they are located. That sort of stability requires change and not always the sort that can be easily controlled.

Third, it is in the real security interest of the United States to ease rather than complicate the life of people with whom we coexist on the planet, whatever the political ideology of their governments. It does not increase American national security, for example, for Castro to suffer economic reverses, whatever the U.S. may have done to help bring them about. The point would be equally true if Castro were a right wing military dictator. When governments oppress their own citizens, stepping up outside military pressure hardly creates a more liberal atmosphere.

There is no existing political solution to the major problems of human development that can be called "the wave of the future." The problems transcend all existing ideologies. It is in the interest of the people of the United States as a whole, although not in the short-term interest of those who fear change because it threatens privilege, to encourage a variety of experiments around the globe to find ways to solve the worldwide crisis of political order. Until Americans can begin to identify with the people of other countries as members of the same species with the same basic problems, we will continue to treat other countries as abstractions to be manipulated for our own psychological and political needs and will continue to build our power on their suffering. The attempt to isolate, contain, or overthrow revolutionary governments makes them more likely to resort to terror against their own people and to adopt a militant nationalism to protect themselves from American attack. No nation, including the United States, can enforce virtue, moderation, or justice in another country. Making war on Germany did not save the Jews. Indeed, the mass exterminations did not begin until the war was on. All a nation can do is to help create an international political environment that will encourage other governments to permit freedom and a decent life for their own citizens.

A national security policy for the United States which can minimize the resort to violence and promote an international system for the resolution of the basic human problems of justice and order must see the United States not as the problem-solver of the world but as an integral part of the problem. America's extraordinarily disproportionate share of resources and power, which we have celebrated as proof of a messianic destiny, is itself a long term threat to our own national security. The United States will become increasingly isolated from the rest of humanity if we continue to set as a national security goal the preservation of present power and economic relationships in the world rather than the rapid evolution towards world community. The *status quo,* which we call "stable," will come to be seen by more and more other peoples as intolerable. Vietnam shows that despite the massive employment of military power the United States cannot always maintain positions of domination that it has acquired around the world. Perhaps in the short term the strategy that succeeded in Greece and the Dominican Republic and failed in Vietnam may succeed elsewhere. But it is clear that we need new criteria for defining "success." A military dictatorship that supports the United States in the United Nations and welcomes its military mission but uses American aid to hold down its population and to forestall institutional change contributes to the sum of repression, misuse of resources, and misery in the world. It should not be counted an American success.

Survival Isn't Guaranteed

American security is inextricably linked with the problem of global security. For this reason much of the debate in the United States about "neo-isolationism" seems Orwellian. Those who favor continuation of the policy of military intervention around the world whenever the United States decides it is in America's interest to "project its power" advertise themselves as "internationalists." Those who wish to renounce the right to threaten nuclear war on behalf of American vital interests, to stop seeking American security by killing or assisting in the killing of Asians, Africans, and Latin Americans, are stigmatized as "isolationists."

The issue is not whether the United States should or can withdraw from the world but the character of American involvement. The development of technology and communication has multiplied international and transnational contacts of all kinds. Americans cannot and will not resign from the world. But they can renounce the myths on which their contact with the world has been so largely based: that the United States government can manage social and political change around the world; that it can police a stable system of order; that it can solve problems in other countries it has yet to solve for its own people; that there is no real conflict of interest between the people of the United States, with their high standard of living, and people in Asia, Africa, or Latin America, who make less than $100 a year; that the United States government, unlike all other governments, is capable of true philanthropy.

The United States cannot develop a national security policy that will improve the prospects for global survival until we seriously examine the extent to which a new foreign policy requires domestic changes. How much, for example, can we change America's present destructive definition of national security without dismantling the bureaucratic structures which promote a militarist definition of the national interest? Can we still have a military establishment anything like the present one without continuing to have an interventionist policy? I am virtually certain that the answer is no. Can we have relations with Third World countries that will close instead of further widen the gap between rich and poor countries without making major changes in the patterns of consumption in the United States and basic structural changes in the economy? On this question I am less clear. Both Marxists and the National Association of Manufacturers appear convinced that the standard of living cannot be maintained in the U.S. except through the continuation of imperialist policies. It is crucial to the building of a real national security policy to determine whether they are right or wrong. If they are right, then it is a prime security task to change consumption patterns in the United States. The alternative would be global class war.

No national security problem can ultimately be solved except within the context of planetary security. The overshadowing risk to mankind is the destruction of the earth through nuclear war or the collapse of life support systems as a consequence of pollution and maldistribution of resources. The policy of seeking national security through permanent war preparation and intermittent wars directly contributes to the crisis of planetary survival in a variety of specific ways. Military establishments pre-empt resources. They produce waste. They generate an atmosphere of conflict and competition in which the minimal measures of cooperation necessary to insure planetary survival become impossible.

There is nothing to suggest that achieving security in the final third of the twentieth century will be easy, or even that the survival of civilization is guaranteed. No one has yet developed a global security system that works.

But we do know what does not work.

Hans J. Morgenthau: The Realities of Foreign Aid

. . . The burden of my argument is twofold. First, one must distinguish sharply between foreign aid for political purposes and foreign aid for economic development. Second, foreign aid for economic development has

From "Foreign Economic Policy For The 1970s," Hearings before Joint Economic Committee, Part III, 91st Congress, 2nd Session, May 14, 1970. Government Printing Office, 1970.

a chance to be successful only within relatively narrow limits which are raised by cultural and political conditions impervious to direct outside influence.

Foreign Aid for Political Purposes

Foreign aid for political purposes is about as old as foreign policy itself. Bribes proffered by one government to another for political advantage were, until the beginning of the nineteenth century, an integral part of the armory of diplomacy. It was proper and common for a government to pay the foreign minister or ambassador of another country a pension. Nor was it regarded less proper or less usual for a government to compensate foreign statesmen for their cooperation in the conclusion of treaties. The Prussian Ambassador in Paris summed up well the main rule of this game when he reported to his government in 1802: "Experience has taught everybody who is here on diplomatic business that one ought never to give anything before the deal is definitely closed, but it has only proved that the allurement of gain will often work wonders."

Much of what goes by the name of foreign aid today is in the nature of bribes. The transfer of money and services from one government to another performs here the function of a price paid for political services rendered or to be rendered by the recipient. These bribes differ from the traditional ones in two respects: They are justified primarily in terms of foreign aid for economic development, and money and services are transferred through elaborate machinery fashioned for genuine economic aid. In consequence, these bribes are a less effective means for the purpose of purchasing political favors than were the traditional ones.

The compulsion to substitute for the traditional businesslike transmission of bribes the pretense and elaborate machinery of foreign aid for economic results from a climate of opinion which accepts as universally valid the proposition that the highly developed industrial nations have an obligation to transfer money and services to underdeveloped nations to foster economic development. Thus, aside from humanitarian and military foreign aid, the only kind of transfer of money and services that seems to be legitimate is the one made for the purpose of economic development. Economic development has become an ideology by which the transfer of money and services from one government to another is rationalized and justified.

However, the present climate of opinion assumes not only that affluent industrial nations have an obligation to extend foreign aid for economic development to nations of the third world. It also assumes as a universally valid proposition that economic development can actually be promoted through such transfer of money and services. Thus economic development as an ideology requires machinery that makes plausible the assumption of the efficacy of the transfer of money and services for the purpose of economic growth. The government of Nation A, trying to buy political advantage from the government of Nation B for, say, the price of $20 million, not only must pretend, but also must act out in elaborate fashion the pretense, that what it is actually doing is giving aid for economic development to the government of Nation B.

The practice of giving bribes as though they were contributions to economic development necessarily creates expectations, in the donor and the recipient, which are bound to be disappointed. Old-fashioned bribery is a straightforward transaction: Services are to be rendered at a price, and both sides know what to expect. Bribery disguised as foreign aid for economic development makes of donor and recipient actors in a play which in the end they can no longer distinguish from reality. In consequence, both expect results in economic development which, in the nature of things, could not have been forthcoming. Thus both are bound to be disappointed, the donor blaming the recipient for his inefficiency and the recipient accusing the donor of stinginess.

Foreign aid for military purposes is a traditional means for nations to buttress their alliances. Rome used to receive tribute from its allies for the military protection it provided. The seventeenth and eighteenth centuries were the classic period of military subsidies, by which especially Great Britain endeavored to increase the military strength of her continental allies. This traditional military aid can be understood as a division of labor between two allies who pool their resources, one supplying money, material, and training, the other providing primarily manpower.

In contrast to traditional practice, military aid is today extended not only to allies but also to certain uncommitted nations. The purpose here is not so much military as political, for political advantage is sought in exchange for military aid. This kind of aid obligates the recipient to the donor. The latter expects the former to abstain from a political course that might put in jeopardy the continuation of military aid, which is thus really in the nature of a bribe.

What appears as military aid may also be actually in the nature of prestige aid, to be discussed below. The provision of jet fighters and other modern weapons for certain underdeveloped nations can obviously perform no genuine military function. It increases the prestige of the recipient nation both at home and abroad. Being in the possession of some of the more spectacular instruments of modern warfare, a nation can at least enjoy the illusion that it has become a modern military power.

As bribery appears today in the guise of aid for economic development, so does aid for economic development appear in the guise of military assistance. In the session of 1967, Congress, for instance, appropriated $600 million for economic aid to strategic areas, and it is likely that in the total appropriations for military aid in excess of $1 billion other items of economic aid were hidden. This mode of operation results from the reluctance of Congress to vote large amounts for economic aid in contrast to its readiness to vote for military purposes. Yet the purposes of aid for economic development are likely to suffer when they are disguised as military assistance, as we saw the purposes of bribery suffer when disguised as aid for economic development. The military context within such aid is bound to operate, even though its direct administration may be in the hands of the civilian authorities, is likely to deflect such aid from its genuine purposes. More particularly, it strengthens the ever-present tendency to subordinate the requirements of aid for economic development to military considerations.

Prestige aid has in common with modern bribes that its true purpose, too, is concealed by the ostensible purpose of economic development. The unprofitable or idle steel mill, the highway without traffic and leading nowhere, the airline operating with foreign personnel and at a loss but under the flag of the recipient country—they ostensibly serve the purposes of economic development and under different circumstances could do so. Actually, however, they perform no positive economic function. They owe their existence to the penchant, prevalent in many underdeveloped nations, for what might be called "conspicuous industrialization," an industrialization that produces symbols of, and monuments to, industrial advancement rather than satisfying the objective economic needs of the country.

For many of the underdeveloped nations the steel mill, the highway, the airline, the modern weapons perform a function that is not primarily economic or military but psychological and political. They are sought as symbols and monuments of modernity and power. Nehru is reported to have said, when he showed Chou En-lai a new dam: "It is in these temples that I worship."

The advantage for the donor of prestige aid is threefold. He may receive specific political advantages in return for the provision of aid, very much after the model of the advantage received in return for a bribe. The spectacular character of prestige aid establishes a patent relationship between the generosity of the giver and the increased prestige of the recipient: the donor's prestige is enhanced, as it were, by the increase of the recipient's prestige. Finally, prestige aid comes relatively cheap. A limited commitment of resources in the form of a spectacular but economically useless symbol of, or monument to, modernity may bring disproportionate political dividends.

It is in the nature of prestige aid that it is justified by the prospective recipient in terms of genuine economic development. The prospective donor, unaware of the distinction, is likely to fall into one of two errors. By mistaking prestige aid for economic development, he will either waste human and material resources in support of the latter, while the purpose of prestige aid could have been achieved much more simply and cheaply. Or else he will reject out of hand a request for prestige aid because it cannot be justified in terms of economic development, and may thereby forego political advantages he could have gained from the provision of the aid requested.

Foreign Aid for Economic Development

These different types of foreign aid require the same kind of political judgment as do the other, more obvious methods of foreign policy, such as diplomatic inducements or military pressure. When we try to develop a sensible foreign-aid policy for economic development, we must take into account two other factors: The cultural and political conditions in the recipient country.

Since Western economic development, from the first Industrial Revolution onward, has been the result of the formation of capital and the accumulation of technical knowledge, we have tended to assume that these two factors would by themselves provide the impetus for the economic development of the underdeveloped nations of Asia, Africa, and Latin America. This tendency has been powerfully supported by the spectacular success of the Marshall Plan, conceived and executed as a strictly economic measure for the provision of capital and technological know-how. Yet it is not always recognized that this success was made possible only by the fact that, in contrast to the underdeveloped nations of Asia, Africa, and Latin America, the recipients of Marshall aid were among the leading industrial nations of the world, whose economic systems were only temporarily in disarray.

By contrast, many of the underdeveloped nations suffer from cultural and political disabilities which stand in the way of economic development and which cannot be removed by foreign aid. A civilization, for instance, which depreciates success in this world because it stands in the way of success in the other world, which is the only success that counts, puts a cultural obstacle in the path of industrial development which foreign aid by itself cannot overcome. Saving—that is, the accumulation of capital or goods for future use—has become so integral a part of our economic thought and action that it is hard for us to realize that there are hundreds of millions of people in the underdeveloped areas of the world who are oblivious to this mode of operation, indispensable to economic development. We have come to consider the productive enterprise as a continuum in which the individual owner or manager has a personal stake. Yet in many underdeveloped areas the productive enterprise is regarded primarily as an object for financial exploitation, to be discarded when it has performed its function of bringing the temporary owner a large financial return in the shortest possible time. Foreign aid poured into such a precapitalistic and even prerational mold is not likely to transform the mold, but rather it will be forced by it into channels serving the interests of a precapitalistic or prerational society.

The economic interests that stand in the way of foreign aid being used for economic development are typically tied in with the distribution of political power in underdeveloped societies. The ruling groups in these societies derive their political power in good measure from the economic status quo. The ownership and control of arable land, in particular, is in many of the underdeveloped societies the foundation of political power. Land reform and industrialization are therefore an attack upon the political status quo. In the measure that they are successful, they are bound to affect drastically the distribution of economic and political power. According to the *New York Times* of March 11, 1970, the head of the Indian Affairs Department of Salta Province in Argentina was dismissed because "I stepped on the toes of too many landholders and others who benefit from Indian poverty." Even illiteracy, which we tend to attribute to poverty, is frequently a weapon in defense of the status quo. It is perpetuated on purpose, for illiterates are more likely to be quiescent than people who are able to absorb ideas by reading and disseminate them by writing.

Yet the beneficiaries of both the economic and political status quo are the typical recipients of foreign aid given for the purpose of changing the status quo! Their use of foreign aid for this purpose requires a readiness for self-sacrifice and a sense of social responsibility that few ruling groups have shown throughout history. Foreign aid proffered under such circumstances is likely to fail in its purpose of economic development and, as a bribe to the ruling group, rather will strengthen the economic and political status quo. It is likely to accentuate unsolved social and political problems rather than bring them closer to solution. A team of efficiency experts and public accountants might well have improved the operations of the Al Capone gang: yet, by doing so, it would have aggravated the social and political evils that the operations of that gang brought forth.

Given this likely resistance of the ruling group to economic development, foreign aid requires drastic political change as a precondition for its success. Foreign aid must go hand in hand with political change, either voluntarily induced from within or brought about through pressure from without. The latter alternative faces the donor nation with a dual dilemma. On the one hand, to give foreign aid for economic development without stipulating conditions that maximize the chances for success maximizes the chances for failure. On the other hand, to give aid "with strings" arouses xenophobic suspicions and nationalistic resentments, to be exploited both by the defenders of the status quo and by the promoters of revolution.

The promotion of drastic social change on the part of the donor nation creates the precondition for economic development, but it also conjures up the specter of uncontrollable revolution. In many of the underdeveloped nations, peace and order are maintained only through the ruthless use of the monopoly of violence by the ruling group. Determined and skillful foreign intervention may not find it hard to weaken the power of the ruling group or to remove it from power altogether. While it may be able to control events up to this point—that is, to instigate drastic reform and revolution—it may well be unable to control the course of the revolution itself.

Successful foreign aid for economic development may have similar unsettling political results. Economic development, especially by way of industrialization, is likely to disrupt the social fabric of the underdeveloped nation. By creating an urban industrial proletariat, it loosens and destroys the social nexus of family, village, and tribe, in which the individual had found himself secure. And it will not be able, at least not right away, to provide a substitute for this lost social world. The vacuum thus created will be filled by social unrest and political agitation. Furthermore, it is not the downtrodden masses living in a static world of unrelieved misery who are the likely protagonists of revolution, but rather those groups that have begun to rise in the social and economic scale but not enough to satisfy their aroused expectations. Thus, economic development is bound to disturb not only the economic status quo but, through it, the political status quo as well. If the change is drastic enough, the social and political effects of economic development may well amount to a prerevolutionary or revolutionary situation. And while the United States may have started the revolutionary process, it has no control over the auspices under which it will be ended.

Thus we arrive at the disconcerting conclusion that successful foreign aid for economic development can be counterproductive if the donor nation's goal is the recipient's social and political stability. In some cases at least, the failure of American aid for economic development may have been a blessing in disguise in that it did not disturb a status quo whose continuing stability was our main interest.

Foreign aid for economic development, then, has a very much smaller range of potentially successful operation than is generally believed, and its success depends in good measure not so much upon its soundness in strictly economic terms as upon intellectual, moral, and political preconditions, which are not susceptible to economic manipulation, if they are susceptible to manipulation from the outside at all. Furthermore, the political results of successful foreign aid for economic development may be either unpredictable or counterproductive in terms of the goals of the donor nation. In any event, they are in large measure uncontrollable. Foreign aid proffered and accepted for purposes of economic development may turn out to be something different from what it was intended to be, if it is not oriented toward the political conditions within which it must operate. Most likely, it will turn out to be a bribe or prestige aid, or else a total waste. To do too much may here be as great a risk as to do too little, and "masterly inactivity" may sometimes be the better part of wisdom.